Workshop on Computational Approaches to Subjectivity and Sentiment Analysis 2011

(WASSA 2011)

Held at ACL HLT 2011

Portland, Oregon, USA
24 June 2011

ISBN: 978-1-61839-246-6

Printed from e-media with permission by:

Curran Associates, Inc.
57 Morehouse Lane
Red Hook, NY 12571

Some format issues inherent in the e-media version may also appear in this print version.

Printed by Curran Associates, Inc. (2011)

Association for Computational Linguistics
209 N. Eighth Street
Stroudsburg, Pennsylvania 18360

Phone: 1-570-476-8006
Fax: 1-570-476-0860

acl@aclweb.org

Additional copies of this publication are available from:

Curran Associates, Inc.
57 Morehouse Lane
Red Hook, NY 12571 USA
Phone: 845-758-0400
Fax: 845-758-2634
Email: curran@proceedings.com
Web: www.proceedings.com

Foreword

Recent years have marked the beginning and expansion of the Social Web, in which people freely express and respond to opinion on a whole variety of topics. While the growing volume of subjective information available allows for better and more informed decisions of the users, the quantity of data to be analyzed imposed the development of specialized Natural Language Processing (NLP) systems that automatically detect subjectivity and sentiment in text and subsequently extract, classify and summarize the opinions available on different topics. Although the subjectivity and sentiment analysis research fields have been highly dynamic in the past years, dealing with subjectivity and sentiment in text has proven to be a complex, interdisciplinary problem that remains far from being solved. Its challenges include the need to address the issue from different perspectives and at different levels, depending on the characteristics of the textual genre, the language(s) treated and the final application for which the analysis is done.

Inspired by the objectives we aimed at in the first edition of the Workshop on Computational Approaches to Subjectivity Analysis (WASSA 2010) and the final outcome, the purpose of the second edition of the Workshop on Computational Approaches to Subjectivity and Sentiment Analysis (WASSA 2.011) was to create a framework for presenting and discussing the challenges related to subjectivity and sentiment analysis in NLP, from an interdisciplinary theoretical and practical perspective.

WASSA 2.011 was organized in conjunction to the 49th Annual Meeting of the Association for Computational Linguistics: Human Language Technologies, on June 24, 2011, in Portland, Oregon, U.S.A. We received a total of 51 submissions, from a wide range of countries, of which 9 were accepted as full papers (17%) and another 15 as short papers (29%). Each paper has been reviewed by 2 members of the Program Committee. The accepted papers were all highly assessed by the reviewing committee, the best paper receiving an average punctuation of 4.5 out of 5.

The main topics of the accepted papers are the creation, annotation and evaluation of resources for subjectivity and sentiment analysis in a monolingual, cross-lingual and multilingual setting, subjectivity and sentiment analysis in different text types and at different levels of granularity. Additionally, WASSA 2.011 authors have contemplated interdisciplinary analyses, concerning the gender-specificity analysis in subjective texts, the relation between sentiment and subjectivity analysis with social network mining, opinion question answering and emotion detection.

The invited talks reflected the interdisciplinary nature of the research in affect-related phenomena as well. Prof. Jonathan Gratch, from the University of Southern California presented a talk on “Emotion theories, models and their relevance to sentiment analysis”, from a more general Artificial Intelligence perspective. Prof. Claire Cardie gave a talk on the challenges related to the implementation of sentiment analysis systems in real-world applications.

Given the demonstrated and increasingly growing interest in the topics addressed, we hope that WASSA will continue to be organized in the next years and become an established forum for researchers to discuss and debate the best practices in subjectivity and sentiment analysis.

We would like to thank the ACL-HLT 2011 Organizers for the help and support at the different stages of the workshop organization process. We are also especially grateful to the Program Committee members and the external reviewers for the time and effort spent assessing the papers. We would like to extend our thanks to our invited speakers – Prof. Jonathan Gratch and Prof. Claire Cardie, for accepting to deliver the keynote talks.

Secondly, we would like to express our gratitude for the official endorsement we received from SIGANN (ACL Special Interest Group for Annotation) and SIGNLL (ACL Special Interest Group on Natural Language Learning).

Further on, we would like to thank the Editors of the Decision Support Systems Journal, published by Elsevier, for accepting to organize a Special Issue of this journal containing the extended versions of the WASSA 2.011 full papers.

We would like to express our gratitude to the team at the Department of Software and Computing Systems at the University of Alicante - Javier Fernández, who created the WASSA logo and to Miguel Ángel Varo and Miguel Ángel Baeza - for the technical support they provided.

Last, but not least, we are grateful for the financial support given by Academic Institute for Research in Computer Science of the University of Alicante (Instituto Universitario para la Investigación en Informática, Universidad de Alicante), the Spanish Ministry of Science and Education of the Spanish Government (Ministerio de Ciencia e Innovación - Gobierno de España) through the TIN2009-13391-C04-01 grant, and to the Education Council of the Valencian Community (Conselleria d'Educació - Generalitat Valenciana), through the PROMETEO/2009/119 and ACOMP/2010/286 grants.

Alexandra Balahur, Ester Boldrini, Andrés Montoyo, Patricio Martínez-Barco
WASSA 2.011 Chairs

Organizers:

Alexandra Balahur - University of Alicante, Spain
Ester Boldrini - University of Alicante, Spain
Andrés Montoyo - University of Alicante, Spain
Patricio Martínez-Barco - University of Alicante, Spain

Program Committee:

Eneko Agirre - University of the Basque Country, Spain
Nicoletta Calzolari - CNR Pisa, Italy
Erik Cambria - University of Stirling, U.K.
José Carlos Cortizo - European University Madrid, Spain
Jesús M. Hermida - University of Alicante, Spain
Veronique Hoste - University of Ghent, Belgium
Mijail Kabadjov - EC-Joint Research Centre, Italy
Zornitsa Kozareva - Information Sciences Institute, U.S.A.
Rada Mihalcea - University of North Texas, U.S.A.
Rafael Muñoz - University of Alicante, Spain
Günter Neumann - DFKI, Germany
Constantin Orasan - University of Wolverhampton, U.K.
Manuel Palomar - University of Alicante, Spain
Viktor Pekar - University of Wolverhampton, U.K.
Paolo Rosso - Polytechnic University of Valencia, Spain
Josef Steinberger - EC-Joint Research Centre, Italy
Ralf Steinberger - EC-Joint Research Centre, Italy
Veselyn Stoyanov - Cornell University, U.S.A.
Carlo Strapparava - FBK, Italy
Maite Taboada - Simon Fraser University, Canada
Hristo Tanev - EC- Joint Research Centre, Italy
Mike Thelwall - University of Wolverhampton, U.K.
José Antonio Troyano - University of Seville, Spain
Dan Tufis - RACAI, Romania
Alfonso Ureña - University of Jaén, Spain
Taras Zagibalov - Brandwatch, U.K.

Additional Reviewers:

Elena Lloret - University of Alicante, Spain
María-Teresa Martín Valdivia - University of Jaén, Spain
Saif Mohammad - National Research Council, Canada

Invited Speakers:

Claire Cardie - Cornell University, U.S.A. - Appinions, U.S.A.
Jonathan Gratch - University of Southern California, U.S.A.

Table of Contents

Workshop Program

Friday June 24, 2011

(8:45) Opening Remarks

(9:00) Invited talk (I): Prof. Jonathan Gratch

(9:40) Invited talk (II): Prof. Claire Cardie

(10:15) Best Paper Award

Cats Rule and Dogs Drool!: Classifying Stance in Online Debate
Pranav Anand, Marilyn Walker, Rob Abbott, Jean E. Fox Tree, Robeson Bowmani and Michael Minor

(10:40) Break

(11:00) Session 1: Resources for Sentiment Analysis

A verb lexicon model for deep sentiment analysis and opinion mining applications
Isa Maks and Piek Vossen

Experiments with a Differential Semantics Annotation for WordNet 3.0
Dan Tufis and Dan Stefanescu

Creating Sentiment Dictionaries via Triangulation
Josef Steinberger, Polina Lenkova, Mohamed Ebrahim, Maud Ehrman, Ali Hurriyetoglu, Mijail Kabadjov, Ralf Steinberger, Hristo Tanev, Vanni Zavarella and Silvia Vazquez

Generating Semantic Orientation Lexicon using Large Data and Thesaurus
Amit Goyal and Hal Daume

Friday June 24, 2011 (continued)

(12:30) Lunch Break

(13:30) Session 2: Resources and Applications of Sentiment Analysis

(15:30) Break

(16:00) Session 3: Sentiment Classification

Friday June 24, 2011 (continued)

(17:30) Poster Session

Cats Rule and Dogs Drool!: Classifying Stance in Online Debate

Pranav Anand, Marilyn Walker, Rob Abbott, Jean E. Fox Tree,
Robeson Bowmani, and Michael Minor
University of California Santa Cruz

Abstract

A growing body of work has highlighted the challenges of identifying the stance a speaker holds towards a particular topic, a task that involves identifying a holistic subjective disposition. We examine stance classification on a corpus of 4873 posts across 14 topics on ConvinceMe.net, ranging from the playful to the ideological. We show that ideological debates feature a greater share of rebuttal posts, and that rebuttal posts are significantly harder to classify for stance, for both humans and trained classifiers. We also demonstrate that the number of subjective expressions varies across debates, a fact correlated with the performance of systems sensitive to sentiment-bearing terms. We present results for identifing rebuttals with 63% accuracy, and for identifying stance on a per topic basis that range from 54% to 69%, as compared to unigram baselines that vary between 49% and 60%. Our results suggest that methods that take into account the dialogic context of such posts might be fruitful.

1 Introduction

Recent work has highlighted the challenges of identifying the STANCE that a speaker holds towards a particular political, social or technical topic. Classifying stance involves identifying a holistic subjective disposition, beyond the word or sentence (Lin et al., 2006; Malouf and Mullen, 2008; Greene and Resnik, 2009; Somasundaran and Wiebe, 2009; Somasundaran and Wiebe, 2010). Our work is inspired by the large variety of such conversations now freely available online, and our observation that the contextual affordances of different debate and discussion websites vary a great deal. One important contextual variable, discussed at length below, is the percentage of posts that are **rebuttals** to previous posts, which varies in our data from 34% to 80%. The ability to explicitly rebut a previous post gives these debates both monologic and dialogic properties (Biber, 1991; Crystal, 2001; Fox Tree, 2010); Compare Figure 1 to Figure 2. We believe that discussions containing many rebuttal links require a different type of analysis than other types of debates or discussions.

Dialogic Capital Punishment
Studies have shown that using the death penalty saves 4 to 13 lives per execution. That alone makes killing murderers worthwhile.
What studies? I have never seen ANY evidence that capital punishment acts as a deterrant to crime. I have not seen any evidence that it is "just" either.
When Texas and Florida were executing people one after the other in the late 90's, the murder rates in both states plunged, like Rosie O'donnel off a diet.. .
That's your evidence? What happened to those studies? In the late 90s a LOT of things were different than the periods preceding and following the one you mention. We have no way to determine what of those contributed to a lower murder rate, if indeed there was one. You have to prove a cause and effect relationship and you have failed.

Figure 1: Capital Punishment discussions with posts linked via rebuttal links.

This paper utilizes 1113 two-sided debates (4873 posts) from Convinceme.net for 14 different debate topics. See Table 1. On Convinceme, a person starts a debate by posting a topic or a question and providing sides such as *for* vs. *against*. Debate participants can then post arguments for one side or the other, essentially self-labelling their post for stance. These debates may be heated and emotional, discussing weighty issues such as euthanasia and capital punishment, such as the example in Figure 1. But they also appear to be a form of entertainment via playful

Proceedings of the 2nd Workshop on Computational Approaches to Subjectivity and Sentiment Analysis, ACL-HLT 2011, pages 1–9,
24 June, 2011, Portland, Oregon, USA ©2011 Association for Computational Linguistics

debate. Popular topics on Convinceme.net over the past 4 years include discussions of the merits of Cats vs. Dogs, or Pirates vs. Ninjas (almost 1000 posts). See Figure 3.

Monologic Capital Punishment
I value human life so much that if someone takes one than his should be taken. Also if someone is thinking about taking a life they are less likely to do so knowing that they might lose theirs
Death Penalty is only a costlier version of a lifetime prison sentence, bearing the exception that it offers euthanasia to criminals longing for an easy escape, as opposed to a real punishment.
There is no proof that the death penalty acts as a deterrent, plus due to the finalty of the sentence it would be impossible to amend a mistaken conviction which happens with regualirty especially now due to DNA and improved forensic science. Actually most hardened criminals are more afraid to live-then die. I'd like to see life sentences without parole in lieu of capital punishment with hard labor and no amenities for hard core repeat offenders, the hell with PC and prisoner's rights-they lose priveledges for their behaviour.

Figure 2: Posts on the topic Capital punishment without explicit link structure. The discussion topic was "Death Penalty", and the argument was framed as yes we should keep it vs. no we should not.

Our long term goal is to understand the discourse and dialogic structure of such conversations. This could be useful for: (1) creating automatic summaries of each position on an issue (Sparck-Jones, 1999); (2) gaining a deeper understanding of what makes an argument persuasive (Marwell and Schmitt, 1967); and (3) identifying the linguistic reflexes of perlocutionary acts such as persuasion and disagreement (Walker, 1996; Greene and Resnik, 2009; Somasundaran and Wiebe, 2010; Marcu, 2000). As a first step, in this paper we aim to automatically identify rebuttals, and identify the speaker's stance towards a particular topic.

Dialogic Cats vs. Dogs
Since we're talking much of $hit, then Dogs rule! Cat poo is extremely foul to one's nostrils you'll regret ever handling a cat. Stick with dogs, they're better for your security, and poo's not too bad. Hah!
Dog owners seem infatuated with handling sh*t. Cat owners don't seem to share this infatuation.
Not if they're dog owners who live in the country. If your dog sh*ts in a field you aren't going to walk out and pick it up. Cat owners HAVE to handle sh*t, they MUST clean out a litter box...so suck on that!

Figure 3: Cats vs. Dogs discussions with posts linked by rebuttal links.

The most similar work to our own is that of Somasundaran & Wiebe (2009, 2010) who also focus on automatically determining the stance of a debate participant with respect to a particular issue. Their data does not provide explicit indicators of dialogue structure such as are provided by the rebuttal links in Convinceme. Thus, this work treats each post as a monologic text to be classified in terms of stance, for a particular topic. They show that discourse relations such as concessions and the identification of argumentation triggers improves performance over sentiment features alone (Somasundaran and Wiebe, 2009; Somasundaran and Wiebe, 2010). This work, along with others, indicates that for such tasks it is difficult to beat a unigram baseline (Pang and Lee, 2008).

Other similar related work analyzes Usenet forum quote/response structures (Wang and Rosé, 2010). We believe quote/response pairs have a similar discourse structure to the rebuttal post pairs in Convinceme, but perhaps with the linguistic reflexes of stance expressed even more locally. However agreement vs. disagreement is not labelled across quote/response pairs and Wang & Rose (2010) do not attempt to distinguish these different discourse relations. Rather they show that they can use a variant of LSA to identify a parent post, given a response post, with approximately 70% accuracy. A recent paper by (Abbott et al., 2011) examines agreement and disagreement in quote/response pairs in idealogical and nonidealogical online forum discussions, and shows that you can distinguish the agreement relation with 68% accuracy. Their results indicate that contextual features do improve performance for identifying the agreement relation between quotes and responses.

Other work has utilized the social network structure of online forums, either with or without textual features of particular posts (Malouf and Mullen, 2008; Mishne and Glance, 2006; Murakami and Raymond, 2010; Agrawal et al., 2003). However this work does not examine the way that the dialogic structure varies by topic, as we do, and the threading structure of their debates does not distinguish between agreement and disagreement responses. (Mishne and Glance, 2006) show that most replies to blog posts are disagreements, while Agarwal's work assumed that adjacent posts always disagree, and did not use any of the information in the text. Murakami & Raymond (2010) show that simple rules for identifying disagreement, defined on the textual content of the post, can improve over Agarwal's results and (Malouf and Mullen, 2008) show that a combination of textual and social network features provides the best performance. We leave the incorporation of social network information for stance classification to future work.

Section 3 discusses our corpus in more detail, and presents the results of a human debate-side classification task conducted on Mechanical Turk. Section 3 describes two different machine learning experiments: one for identifying rebuttals and the other for automatically determining stance. Section 4 presents our results. We show that we can identify rebuttals with 63% accuracy, and that using sentiment, subjectivity and dialogic features, we can achieve debate-side classification accuracies, on a per topic basis, that range from 54% to 69%, as compared to unigram baselines that vary between 49% and 60%.

2 Corpus Description and Analysis

Table 1 provides an overview of our corpus. Our corpus consists of 1113 two-sided debates (4873 posts) from Convinceme.net for 12 topics ranging from playful debates such as Cats vs. Dogs to more heated political topics such as Capital Punishment. In Table 1, the topics above the line are either technical or playful, while the topics below the line are ideological. In total the corpus consists of 2,722,340 words; the topic labeled debates which we use in our experiments contain 507,827 words.

Convinceme provides three possible sources of dialogic structure: (1) the SIDE that a post is placed on indicates the poster's stance with respect to the original debate topic, and thus can be considered as a response to that post; (2) REBUTTAL LINKS between posts which are explicitly indicated by the poster using the affordances of the site; and (3) the TEMPORAL CONTEXT of the debate, i.e. the state of the debate at a particular point in time, which a debate participant orients to in framing their post.

Topics vary a great deal in terms of their dialogic structure and linguistic expression. In Table 1, the columns providing counts for different variables are selected to illustrate ways in which topics differ in the form and style of the argument and in its subjective content. One important variable is the percentage of the topic posts that are linked into a rebuttal dialogic structure (**Rebuttals**). Some of these differences can be observed by comparing the dialogic and monologic posts for the Capital Punishment topic in Figures 1 and 2 to those for the Cats vs. Dogs topic in Figures 3 and 4. Ideological

Monologic Cats vs. Dogs
First of all, cats are about a thousand times easier to care for. You don't have to walk them or bathe them because they're smart enough to figure out all that stuff on their own. Plus, they have the common courtesy to do their business in the litter box, instead of all over your house and yard. Just one of the many reasons cats rule and dogs, quite literally drool!
Say, you had a bad day at work, or a bad breakup, you just wanna go home and cry. A cat would just look at you like "oh ok, you're home" and then walk away. A dog? Let's see, the dog would most likely wiggle its tail, with tongue sticking out and head tilted - the "you're home! i missed you so much, let's go snuggle in front of the TV and eat ice-cream" look. What more do I need to say?

Figure 4: Posts on the topic Cats vs. Dogs without explicit rebuttal links.

topics display more author investment; people feel more strongly about these issues. This is shown by the fact that there are more rebuttals per topic and more posts per author (**P/A**) in the topics below the line in Table 1. It follows that these topics have a much higher degree of context-dependence in each post, since posts respond directly to the parent post. Rebuttals exhibit more markers of dialogic interaction: greater pronominalization (especially *you* as well as propositional anaphora such as *that* and *it*), ellipsis, and dialogic cue words; Figure 5 shows the difference in counts of 'you' between rebuttals and non-rebuttals (Rebuttals $\bar{x} = 9.6$ and Non-Rebuttals $\bar{x} = 8.5$, $t(27) = 24.94$, $p < .001$). Another indication of author investment is the percentage of authors with more than one post (**A > 1P**). Post Length (**PL**), on the other hand, is not significantly correlated with degree of investment in the topic.

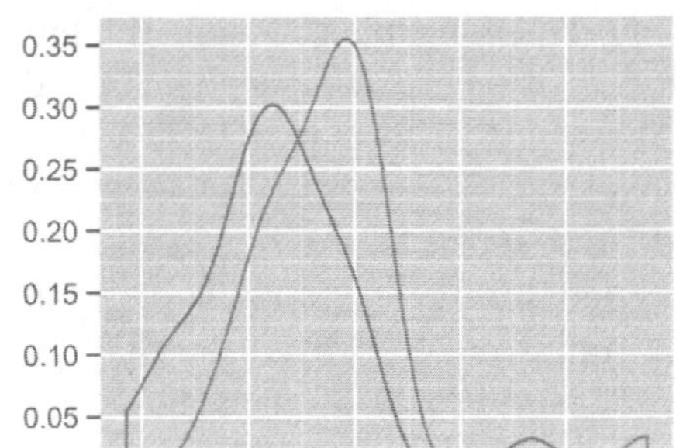

Figure 5: Kernel density estimates for 'you' counts across rebuttals (green) and non-rebuttals (red).

Other factors we examined were words per sen-

Topic	Post and Threading Variables					Normalized LIWC Variables				
	Posts	Rebuttals	P/A	A > 1p	PL	Pro	WPS	6LTR	PosE	NegE
Cats v. Dogs	148	40%	1.68	26%	242	3.30	-1.95	-2. 43	1.70	.30
Firefox vs. IE	218	40%	1.28	16%	167	-0.11	-0.84	0.53	1.23	-0.81
Mac vs. PC	126	47%	1.85	24%	347	0.52	0.28	-0.85	-0.11	-1.05
Superman/Batman	140	34%	1.41	21%	302	-0.57	-1.78	-0.43	1.21	.99
2nd Amendment	134	59%	2.09	45%	385	-1.38	1.74	0.58	-1.04	0.38
Abortion	594	70%	2.82	43%	339	0.63	-0.27	-0.41	-0.95	0.68
Climate Change	202	69%	2.97	40%	353	-0.74	1.23	0.57	-1.25	-0.63
Communism vs. Capitalism	212	70%	3.03	47%	348	-0.76	-0.15	1.09	0.39	-0.55
Death Penalty	324	62%	2.44	45%	389	-0.15	-0.40	0.49	-1.13	2.90
Evolution	798	76%	3.91	55%	430	-0.80	-1.03	1.34	-0.57	-0.94
Exist God	844	77%	4.24	52%	336	0.43	-0.10	0.34	-0.24	-0.32
Gay Marriage	505	65%	2.12	29%	401	-0.13	.86	.85	-0.42	-0.01
Healthcare	110	80%	3.24	56%	280	0.28	1.54	.99	0.14	-0.42
Marijuana Legalization	214	52%	1.55	26%	423	0.14	0.37	0.53	-0.86	0.50

Table 1: Characteristics of Different Topics. Topics below the line are considered "ideological". Normalized LIWC variable z-scores are significant when more than 1.94 standard deviations away from the mean (two-tailed).
KEY: Number of posts on the topic (**Posts**). Percent of Posts linked by Rebuttal links (**Rebuttals**). Posts per author (**P/A**). Authors with more than one post (**A > 1P**). Post Length in Characters (**PL**). **Pro** = percent of the words as pronominals. **WPS** = Words per sentence. **6LTR** = percent of words that are longer than 6 letters. **PosE** positive emotion words. **NegE** negative emotion words.

tence (**WPS**), the length of words used (**6LTR**) which typically indicates scientific or low frequency words, the use of pronominal forms (**Pro**), and the use of positive and negative emotion words (**PosE**,**NegE**) (Pennebaker et al., 2001). For example, Table 1 shows that discussions about Cats vs. Dogs consist of short simple words in short sentences with relatively high usage of positive emotion words and pronouns, whereas 2nd amendment debates use relatively longer sentences, and death penalty debates (unsurprisingly) use a lot of negative emotion words.

Human Topline. The best performance for siding ideological debates in previous work is approximately 64% accuracy over all topics, for a collection of 2nd Amendment, Abortion, Evolution, and Gay Rights debate posts (Somasundaran and Wiebe, 2010). Their best performance is 70% for the 2nd amendment topic. The website that these posts were collected from apparently did not support dialogic threading, and thus there are no explicitly linked rebuttals in this data set. Given the dialogic nature of our data, as indicated by the high percentage of rebuttals in the ideological debates, we first aim to determine how difficult it is for humans to side an individual post from a debate *without context*. To our knowledge, none of the previous work on debate side classification has attempted to establish a human topline.

We set up a Mechanical Turk task by randomly selected a subset of our data excluding the first post on each side of a debate and debates with fewer than 6 posts on either side. Each of our 12 topics consists of more than one debate: each debate was mapped by hand to the topic and topic-siding (as in (Somasundaran and Wiebe, 2010)). We selected equal numbers of posts for each topic for each side, and created 132 tasks (Mechanical Turk HITs). Each HIT consisted of choosing the correct side for 10 posts divided evenly, and selected randomly without replacement, from two debates. For each debate we presented a title, side labels, and the initial post on each side. For each post we presented the first 155 characters with a SEE MORE button which expanded the post to its full length. Each HIT was judged by 9 annotators using Mechanical Turk with each annotator restricted to at most 30 HITS (300 judgments). Since many topics were US specific and we wanted annotators with a good grasp of English, we required Turkers to have a US IP address.

Figure 6 plots the number of annotators over all topics who selected the "true siding" as the side that the post was on. We defined "true siding" for this purpose as the side that the original poster placed their post. Figure 6 illustrates that humans often placed the post on the wrong side. The majority of posters agreed with the true siding 78.26% of the time. The Fleiss' kappa statistic was 0.2656.

Importantly and interestingly, annotator accuracy varied across topics in line with rebuttal percentage. Annotators correctly labeled 94 of 100 posts for Cats vs. Dogs but only managed 66 of 100 for the Cli-

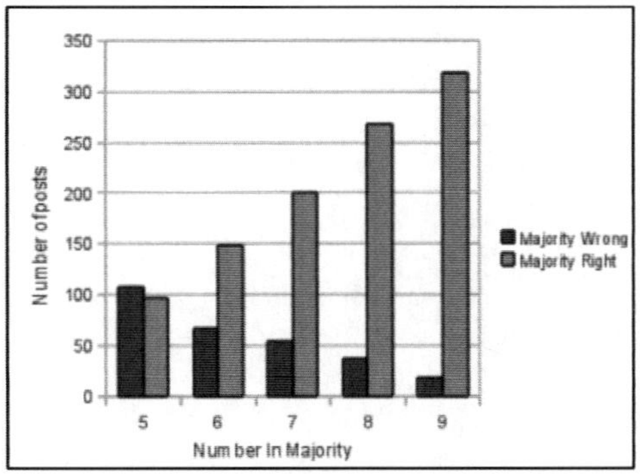

Figure 6: Accuracies of Human Mechanical Turk judges at selecting the True Siding of a post without context.

mate Change topic. This suggests that posts may be difficult to side without context, which is what one might expect given their dialogic nature. Rebuttals were clearly harder to side: annotators correctly sided non-rebuttals 87% of the time, but only managed 73% accuracy for rebuttals. Since all of the less serious topics consisted of $\leq$50% rebuttals while all of the more serious ideological debates had >50% rebuttals, 76% of ideological posts were sided correctly, while 85% of non-ideological posts were correctly sided. See Table 2.

Class	Correct	Total	Accuracy
Rebuttal	606	827	0.73
Non-Rebuttal	427	493	0.87

Table 2: Human Agreement on Rebuttal Classification

Looking at the data by hand revealed that when nearly all annotators agreed with each other but disagreed with the self-labeled side, the user posted on the wrong side (either due to user error, or because the user was rebutting an argument the parent post raised, not the actual conclusion).

The difficult-to-classify posts (where only 4-6 annotators were correct) were more complex. Our analysis suggests that in 28% of these cases, the annotators were simply wrong, perhaps only skimming a post when the stance indicator was buried deep inside it. Our decision to show only the first 155 characters of each post by default (with a SHOW MORE button) may have contributed to this error. An additional 39% were short comments or ad hominem responses, that showed disagreement, but no indication of side and 17% were ambiguous out of context. A remaining 10% were meta-debate comments, either about whether there were only two sides, or whether the argument was meaningful. Given the differences in siding difficulty depending on rebuttal status, in Section 4 we present results for both rebuttal and stance classification.

3 Features and Learning Methods

Our experiments were conducted with the Weka toolkit. All results are from 10 fold cross-validation on a balanced test set. In the hand examination of annotators siding performance, 101 posts were determined to have incorrect self-labeling for side. We eliminated these posts and their descendants from the experiments detailed below. This resulted in a dataset of 4772 posts. We used two classifiers with different properties: NaiveBayes and JRip. JRip is a rule based classifier which produces a compact model suitable for human consumption and quick application. Table 3 provides a summary of the features we extract for each post. We describe and motivate these feature sets below.

Set	Description/Examples
Post Info	IsRebuttal, Poster
Unigrams	Word frequencies
Bigrams	Word pair frequencies
Cue Words	Initial unigram, bigram, and trigram
Repeated Punctuation	Collapsed into one of the following: ??, !!, ?!
LIWC	LIWC measures and frequencies
Dependencies	Dependencies derived from the Stanford Parser.
Generalized Dependencies	Dependency features generalized with respect to POS of the head word and opinion polarity of both words.
Opinion Dependencies	Subset of Generalized Dependencies with opinion words from MPQA.
Context Features	Matching Features used for the post from the parent post.

Table 3: Feature Sets, Descriptions, and Examples

Counts, Unigrams, Bigrams. Previous work suggests that the unigram baseline can be difficult to beat for certain types of debates (Somasundaran and Wiebe, 2010). Thus we derived both unigrams and bigrams as features. We also include basic counts such as post length.

Cue Words. We represent each posts **initial** unigram, bigram and trigram sequences to capture the useage of cue words to mark responses of particular type, such as *oh really*, *so*, and *well*; these features were based on both previous work and our examination of the corpus (Fox Tree and Schrock, 1999; Fox Tree and Schrock, 2002; Groen et al., 2010).

Repeated Punctuation. Our informal analyses suggested that repeated sequential use of particular types of punctuation such as **!!** and **??** did not mean the same thing as simple counts or frequencies of punctuation across a whole post. Thus we developed distinct features for a subset of these repetitions.

LIWC. We also derived features using the Linguistics Inquiry Word Count tool (LIWC-2001) (Pennebaker et al., 2001). LIWC provides meta-level conceptual categories for words to use in word counts. Some LIWC features that we expect to be important are words per sentence (WPS), pronominal forms (Pro), and positive and negative emotion words (PosE) and (NegE). See Table 1.

Syntactic Dependency. Previous research in this area suggests the utility of dependency structure to determine the TARGET of an opinion word (Joshi and Penstein-Rosé, 2009; Somasundaran and Wiebe, 2009; Somasundaran and Wiebe, 2010). The dependency parse for a given sentence is a set of triples, composed of a grammatical relation and the pair of words for which the grammatical relation holds (rel_i, w_j, w_k), where rel_i is the dependency relation among words w_j and w_k. The word w_j is the HEAD of the dependency relation. We use the Stanford parser to parse the utterances in the posts and extract dependency features (De Marneffe et al., 2006; Klein and Manning, 2003).

Generalized Dependency. To create generalized dependencies, we "back off" the head word in each of the above features to its part-of-speech tag (Joshi and Penstein-Rosé, 2009). Joshi & Rose's results suggested that this approach would work better than either fully lexicalized or fully generalized dependency features. We call these POS generalized dependencies in the results below.

Opinion Dependencies. Somasundaran & Wiebe (2009) introduced features that identify the TARGET of opinion words. Inspired by this approach, we used the MPQA dictionary of opinion words to select the subset of dependency and generalized dependency features in which those opinion words appear. For these features we replace the opinion words with their positive or negative polarity equivalents (Lin et al., 2006).

Context Features. Given the difficulty annotators had in reliably siding rebuttals as well as their prevalence in the corpus, we hypothesize that features representing the parent post could be helpful for classification. Here, we use a naive representation of context, where for all the feature types in Table 3, we construct both **parent** features and **post** features. For top-level parentless posts, the **parent** features were null.

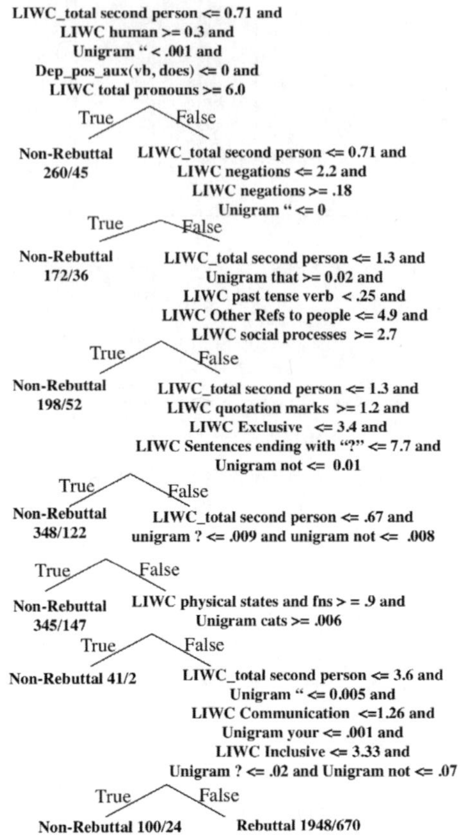

Figure 7: Model for distinguishing rebuttals vs. nonrebuttals across all topics.

4 Results

The primary aim of our experiments was to determine the potential contribution, to debate side classification performance, of contextual dialogue features, such as linguistic reflexes indicating a poster's orientation to a previous post or information from a parent post. Because we believed that identification of whether a post is a rebuttal or not might be helpful in the long term for debate-side classification, we also establish a baseline for rebuttal classification.

4.1 Rebuttal Classification Results

The differences in human performance for siding depended on rebuttal status. Our experiments on rebuttal classification using the rule-based JRip classifer on a 10-fold cross-validation of our dataset produced 63% accuracy. Figure 7 illustrates a sample model learned for distinguishing rebuttals from non-rebuttals across all topics. The Figure shows that, although we used the full complement of lexical and syntactic features detailed above, the learned rules were almost entirely based on LIWC and unigram lexical features, such as 2nd person pronouns (7/8 rules), quotation marks (4/8 rules), question marks (3/8), and negation (4/8), all of which correlated with rebuttals. Other features that are used at several places in the tree are LIWC Social Processes, LIWC references to people, and LIWC Inclusive and Exclusive. One tree node reflects the particular concern with bodily functions that characterizes the Cats vs. Dogs debate as illustrated in Figure 3.

4.2 Automatic Debate-Side Classification Results

We first compared accuracies using Naive Bayes to JRip for all topics for all feature sets. A paired t-test showed that Naive Bayes over all topics and feature sets was consistently better than JRip ($p < .0001$). Thus the rest of our analysis and the results in Table 4 focus on the Naive Bayes results.

Table 4 presents results for automatic debate side classification using different feature sets and the Naive Bayes learner which performs best over all topics. In addition to classifying using only post-internal features, we ran a parallel set of experiments adding contextual features representing the parent post, as described in Section 3. The results in Table 4 are divided under the headers *Without Context* and *With Context* depending on whether features from the parent post were used if it existed (e.g. in the case of rebuttals).

We conducted paired t-tests over all topics simultaneously to examine the utility of different feature sets. We compared unigrams to LIWC, opinion generalized dependencies, POS generalized dependencies, and all features. We also compared experiments using context features to experiments using no contextual features. In general, our results indicate that if the data are aggregated over **all topics**, that indeed it is very difficult to beat the unigram baseline. Across all topics there are generally no significant differences between experiments conducted with unigrams and other features. The mean accuracies across all topics for unigrams vs. LIWC features was 54.35% for unigrams vs. 52.83% for LIWC. The mean accuracies for unigram vs POS generalized dependencies was 54.35% vs. 52.64%, and for unigrams vs. all features was Unigram 54.35% vs 54.62%. The opinion generalized dependencies features actually performed significantly worse than unigrams with an accuracy of 49% vs. 54.35% ($p < .0001$).

It is interesting to note that in general the unigram accuracies are significantly below what Somasundaran and Wiebe achieve (who report overall unigram of 62.5%). This suggests a difference between the debate posts in their corpus and the Convinceme data we used which may be related to the proportion of rebuttals.

The overal lack of impact for either the POS generalized dependency features (**GDepP**) or the Opinion generalized dependency features (**GDep0**) is surprising given that they improve accuracy for other similar tasks (Joshi and Penstein-Rosé, 2009; Somasundaran and Wiebe, 2010). While our method of extracting the **GDepP** features is identical to (Joshi and Penstein-Rosé, 2009), our method for extracting **GDepO** is an approximation of the method of (Somasundaran and Wiebe, 2010), that does not rely on selecting particular patterns indicating the topics of arguing by using a development set.

The LIWC feature set, which is based on a lexical hierarchy that includes social features, negative and positive emotion, and psychological processes, is the only feature set that appears to have the potential to systematically show improvement over a good range of topics. We believe that further analysis is needed; we do not want to handpick topics for which particular feature sets perform well.

Our results also showed that context did not seem to help uniformly over all topics. The mean performance over all topics for contextual features using the combination of all features and the Naive Bayes learner was 53.0% for context and 54.62% for no context ($p = .15\%$, not significant). Interesting, the use of contextual features provided surprisingly greater performance for particular topics. For example for 2nd Amendment, unigrams with context yield a performance of 69.23% as opposed to the best performing without context features using LIWC of 64.10%. The best performance of (Somasundaran and Wiebe, 2010) is also 70% for the 2nd amendment topic. For the Healthcare topic, LIWC with context features corresponds to an accuracy of 60.64% as opposed to GDepP without context performance of 54.26%. For Communism vs. Capitism, LIWC with context features gives an accuracy of 56.55% as opposed to accuracies actually

		Without Context					With Context				
	Turk	**Uni**	**LIWC**	**GdepO**	**GdepP**	**All**	**Uni**	**LIWC**	**GdepO**	**GdepP**	**All**
Cats v. Dogs	94	59.23	55.38	56.15	61.54	**62.31**	50.77	56.15	55.38	60.77	50.00
Firefox vs. IE	74	51.25	**53.75**	43.75	48.75	50.00	51.25	**53.75**	52.50	52.50	51.25
Mac vs. PC	76	53.33	**56.67**	55.00	50.83	**56.67**	53.33	55.83	**56.67**	49.17	54.17
Superman Batman	89	54.84	45.97	42.74	45.97	54.03	50.00	**57.26**	43.55	50.81	53.23
2nd Amendment	69	56.41	64.10	51.28	58.97	57.69	**69.23**	61.54	44.87	52.56	67.95
Abortion	75	50.97	51.56	50.58	52.14	51.17	51.36	**53.70**	51.75	**53.70**	50.78
Climate Change	66	53.65	**58.33**	38.02	46.35	50.52	48.96	56.25	38.02	38.54	48.96
Comm vs. Capitalism	68	48.81	47.02	46.43	47.02	48.81	45.83	**56.55**	47.02	51.19	48.81
Death Penalty	79	51.80	53.96	46.76	49.28	52.52	51.80	56.12	56.12	**57.55**	53.24
Evolution	72	**57.24**	48.36	54.93	56.41	**57.24**	54.11	46.22	50.82	52.14	52.96
Existence of God	73	52.71	51.14	49.72	52.42	51.99	52.28	52.28	50.14	**53.42**	51.42
Gay Marriage	88	**60.28**	56.11	56.11	58.61	59.44	56.94	52.22	54.44	53.61	54.72
Healthcare	86	52.13	51.06	51.06	54.26	52.13	45.74	**60.64**	59.57	57.45	53.19
MJ Legalization	81	57.55	46.23	43.40	53.77	**59.43**	52.83	46.23	49.06	49.06	50.94

Table 4: Accuracies achieved using different feature sets and 10-fold cross validation as compared to the human topline from MTurk. Best accuracies are shown in **bold** for each topic in each row. **KEY:** Human topline results (**Turk**). Unigram features (**Uni**). Linguistics Inquiry Word Count features (**LIWC**). Generalized dependency features containing MPQA terms (**GdepO**) & POS tags (**GdepP**). NaiveBayes was used, no attribute selection was applied.

below the majority class baseline for all of the features without context.

Should we conclude anything from the fact that 6 of the topics are idealogical, out of the 7 topics where contextual features provide the best performance? We believe that the significantly greater percentage of rebuttals for these topics should give a greater weight to contextual features, so it would be useful to examine stance classification performance on the subset of the posts that are rebuttals. We believe that context is important; our conclusion is that our current contextual features are naive – they are not capturing the relationship between a post and a parent post. Sequential models or at least better contextual features are needed.

The fact that we should be able to do much better is indicated clearly by the human topline, shown in the column labelled **Turk** in Table 4. Even without context, and with the difficulties siding rebuttals, the human annotators achieve accuracies ranging from 66% to 94%.

5 Discussion

This paper examines two problems in online-debates: rebuttal classification and debate-side or stance classification. Our results show that we can identify rebuttals with 63% accuracy, and that using lexical and contextual features such as those from LIWC, we can achieve debate-side classification accuracies on a per topic basis that range from 54% to 69%, as compared to a unigram baselines that vary between 49% and 60%. These are the first results that we are aware of that establish a human topline for debate side classification. These are also the first results that we know of for identifying rebuttals in such debates.

Our results for stance classification are mixed. While we show that for many topics we can beat a unigram baseline given more intelligent features, we do not beat the unigram baseline when we combine our data across all topics. In addition, we are not able to show across all topics that our contextual features make a difference, though clearly use of context should make a difference in understanding these debates, and for particular topics, classification results using context are far better than the best feature set without any contextual features. In future work, we hope to develop more intelligent features for representing context and improve on these results. We also plan to make our corpus available to other researchers in the hopes that it will stimulate further work analyzing the dialogic structure of such debates.

Acknowledgments

This work was funded by Grant NPS-BAA-03 to UCSC and Intelligence Advanced Research Projects Activity (IARPA) through the Army Research Laboratory to UCSC by subcontract from the University of Maryland. We'd like to thank Craig Martell and Joseph King for helpful discussions over the course of this project, and the anonymous reviewers for useful feedback. We would also like to thank Jason Aumiller for his contributions to the database.

References

Rob Abbott, Marilyn Walker, Jean E. Fox Tree, Pranav Anand, Robeson Bowmani, and Joseph King. 2011. How can you say such things?!?: Recognizing Disagreement in Informal Political Argument. In *Proceedings of the ACL Workshop on Language and Social Media.*

R. Agrawal, S. Rajagopalan, R. Srikant, and Y. Xu. 2003. Mining newsgroups using networks arising from social behavior. In *Proceedings of the 12th international conference on World Wide Web*, pages 529–535. ACM.

D. Biber. 1991. *Variation across speech and writing.* Cambridge Univ Pr.

David Crystal. 2001. *Language and the Internet.* Cambridge University Press.

M.C. De Marneffe, B. MacCartney, and C.D. Manning. 2006. Generating typed dependency parses from phrase structure parses. In *Proceedings of LREC*, volume 6, pages 449–454. Citeseer.

J.E. Fox Tree and J.C. Schrock. 1999. Discourse Markers in Spontaneous Speech: Oh What a Difference an Oh Makes. *Journal of Memory and Language*, 40(2):280–295.

J.E. Fox Tree and J.C. Schrock. 2002. Basic meanings of you know and I mean. *Journal of Pragmatics*, 34(6):727–747.

J. E. Fox Tree. 2010. Discourse markers across speakers and settings. *Language and Linguistics Compass*, 3(1):113.

S. Greene and P. Resnik. 2009. More than words: Syntactic packaging and implicit sentiment. In *Proceedings of Human Language Technologies: The 2009 Annual Conference of the North American Chapter of the Association for Computational Linguistics*, pages 503–511. Association for Computational Linguistics.

M. Groen, J. Noyes, and F. Verstraten. 2010. The Effect of Substituting Discourse Markers on Their Role in Dialogue. *Discourse Processes: A Multidisciplinary Journal*, 47(5):33.

M. Joshi and C. Penstein-Rosé. 2009. Generalizing dependency features for opinion mining. In *Proceedings of the ACL-IJCNLP 2009 Conference Short Papers*, pages 313–316. Association for Computational Linguistics.

D. Klein and C.D. Manning. 2003. Accurate unlexicalized parsing. In *Proceedings of the 41st Annual Meeting on Association for Computational Linguistics-Volume 1*, pages 423–430. Association for Computational Linguistics.

W.H. Lin, T. Wilson, J. Wiebe, and A. Hauptmann. 2006. Which side are you on?: identifying perspectives at the document and sentence levels. In *Proceedings of the Tenth Conference on Computational Natural Language Learning*, pages 109–116. Association for Computational Linguistics.

R. Malouf and T. Mullen. 2008. Taking sides: User classification for informal online political discourse. *Internet Research*, 18(2):177–190.

Daniel Marcu. 2000. Perlocutions: The Achilles' heel of Speech Act Theory. *Journal of Pragmatics*, 32(12):1719–1741.

G. Marwell and D. Schmitt. 1967. Dimensions of compliance-gaining behavior: An empirical analysis. *sociomety*, 30:350–364.

G. Mishne and N. Glance. 2006. Leave a reply: An analysis of weblog comments. In *Third annual workshop on the Weblogging ecosystem.* Citeseer.

A. Murakami and R. Raymond. 2010. Support or Oppose? Classifying Positions in Online Debates from Reply Activities and Opinion Expressions. In *Proceedings of the 23rd International Conference on Computational Linguistics: Posters*, pages 869–875. Association for Computational Linguistics.

B. Pang and L. Lee. 2008. Opinion mining and sentiment analysis. *Foundations and Trends in Information Retrieval*, 2(1-2):1–135.

J. W. Pennebaker, L. E. Francis, and R. J. Booth, 2001. *LIWC: Linguistic Inquiry and Word Count.*

S. Somasundaran and J. Wiebe. 2009. Recognizing stances in online debates. In *Proceedings of the Joint Conference of the 47th Annual Meeting of the ACL and the 4th International Joint Conference on Natural Language Processing of the AFNLP: Volume 1-Volume 1*, pages 226–234. Association for Computational Linguistics.

S. Somasundaran and J. Wiebe. 2010. Recognizing stances in ideological on-line debates. In *Proceedings of the NAACL HLT 2010 Workshop on Computational Approaches to Analysis and Generation of Emotion in Text*, pages 116–124. Association for Computational Linguistics.

Karen Sparck-Jones. 1999. Automatic summarizing; factors and directions. In Inderjeet Mani and Mark Maybury, editors, *Advances in Automatic Text Summarization.* MIT Press.

Marilyn A. Walker. 1996. Inferring acceptance and rejection in dialogue by default rules of inference. *Language and Speech*, 39-2:265–304.

Y.C. Wang and C.P. Rosé. 2010. Making conversational structure explicit: identification of initiation-response pairs within online discussions. In *Human Language Technologies: The 2010 Annual Conference of the North American Chapter of the Association for Computational Linguistics*, pages 673–676. Association for Computational Linguistics.

A verb lexicon model for deep sentiment analysis and opinion mining applications

Isa Maks
VU University, Faculty of Arts
De Boelelaan 1105, 1081 HV Amsterdam,
The Netherlands
e.maks@let.vu.nl

Piek Vossen
VU University, Faculty of Arts
De Boelelaan 1105, 1081 HV Amsterdam,
The Netherlands
p.vossen@let.vu.nl

Abstract

This paper presents a lexicon model for subjectivity description of Dutch verbs that offers a framework for the development of sentiment analysis and opinion mining applications based on a deep syntactic-semantic approach. The model aims to describe the detailed subjectivity relations that exist between the participants of the verbs, expressing multiple attitudes for each verb sense. Validation is provided by an annotation study that shows that these subtle subjectivity relations are reliably identifiable by human annotators.

1 Introduction

This paper presents a lexicon model for the description of verbs to be used in applications like sentiment analysis and opinion mining. Verbs are considered as the core of the sentence as they name events or states with participants expressed by the other elements in the sentence. We consider the detailed and subtle subjectivity relations that exist between the different participants as part of the meaning of a verb that can be modelled in a lexicon.

Consider the following example:

Ex. (1) ... Damilola's killers were boasting about his murder...

This sentence expresses a positive sentiment of the killers towards the fact they murdered Damilola and it expresses the negative attitude on behalf of the speaker/writer who has negative opinion of the the murderers of Damilola. Both attitudes are part of the semantic profile of the verb and should be modelled in a subjectivity lexicon.

As opinion mining and sentiment analysis applications tend to utilize more and more the composition of sentences (Moilanen (2007), Choi and Cardie (2008), Jia et al. (2009)) and to use the value and properties of the verbs expressed by its dependency trees, there is a need for specialized lexicons where this information can be found. For the analysis of more complex opinionated text like news, political documents, and (online) debates the identification of the attitude holder and topic are of crucial importance. Applications that exploit the relations between the verb meaning and its arguments can better determine sentiment at sentence-level and trace emotions and opninions to their holders.

Our model seeks to combine the insights from a rather complex model like Framenet (Ruppenhofer et al. (2010)) with operational models like Sentiwordnet where simple polarity values (positive, negative, neutral) are applied to the entire lexicon. Subjectivity relations that exist between the different participants are labeled with information concerning both the identity of the attitude holder and the orientation (positive vs. negative) of the attitude. The model accounts for the fact that verbs may express multiple attitudes. It includes a categorisation into semantic categories relevant to opinion mining and sentiment analysis and provides means for the identification of the attitude holder and the polarity of the attitude and for the description of the emotions and sentiments of the different

Proceedings of the 2nd Workshop on Computational Approaches to Subjectivity and Sentiment Analysis, ACL-HLT 2011, pages 10–18,
24 June, 2011, Portland, Oregon, USA ©2011 Association for Computational Linguistics

participants involved in the event. Attention is paid to the role of the speaker/writer of the event whose perspective is expressed and whose views on what is happening are conveyed in the text.

As we wish to provide a model for a lexicon that is operational and can be exploited by tools for deeper sentiment analysis and rich opinion mining, the model is validated by an annotation study of 580 verb lexical units (cf. section 4).

2 Related Work

Polarity and subjectivity lexicons are valuable resources for sentiment analysis and opinion mining. For English, a couple of smaller and larger lexicons are available.

Widely used in sentiment analysis are automatically derived or manually built polarity lexicons. These lexicons are lists of words (for example, Hatzivassiloglou and McKeown (1997), Kamps et al. (2004), Kim and Hovy (2004) or word senses (for example, Esuli and Sebastiani (2006), Wiebe and Mihalcea (2006), Su and Markert, (2008)) annotated for negative or positive polarity. As they attribute single polarity values (positive, negative, neutral) to words they are not able to account for more complex cases like *boast* (cf. example 1) which carry both negative and positive polarity dependening on who is the attitude holder.

Strapparava and Valitutti (2004) developed Wordnet-Affect, an affective extension of Wordnet. It describes 'direct' affective words, i.e. words which denote emotions. Synsets are classified into categories like emotion, cognitive state, trait, behaviour, attitude and feeling. The resource is further developed (Valittutti and Strapparava, 2010) by adding the descriptions of 'indirect' affective words according to a specific appraisal model of emotions (OCC). An indirect affective word indirectly refers to emotion categories and can refer to different possible emotions according to the subjects (actor, actee and observer) semantically connected to it. For example, the word *victory*, if localized in the past, can be used for expressing pride (related to the actor or "winner"), and disappointment (related to the actee or "loser"). If *victory* is a future event the expressed emotion is hope. Their model is similar to ours, as we both relate attitude to the participants of the event. However, their model focuses on a rich description of different aspects and implications of emotions for each participant whereas we infer a single positive or negative attitude. Their model seems to focus on the cognitive aspects of emotion whereas we aim to also model the linguistic aspects by including specifically the attitude of the Speaker/Writer in our model. Moreover, our description is not at the level of the synset but at lexical unit level which enables us to differentiate gradations of the strength of emotions within the synsets. This enables us to relate the attitudes directly to the syntactic-semantic patterns of the lexical unit.

Also Framenet (Ruppenhofer et al. (2010)) is used as a resource in opinion mining and sentiment analysis (Kim and Hovy (2006)). Framenet (FN) is an online lexical resource for English that contains more than 11,600 lexical units. The aim is to classify words into categories (frames) which give for each lexical unit the range of semantic and syntactic combinatory possibilities. The semantic roles range from general ones like Agent, Patient and Theme to specific ones such as Speaker, Message and Addressee for Verbs of Communication. FN includes frames such as Communication, Judgment, Opinion, Emotion_Directed and semantic roles such as Judge, Experiencer, Communicator which are highly relevant for opinion mining and sentiment analysis. However, subjectivity is not systematically and not (yet) exhaustively encoded in Framenet. For example, the verb *gobble (eat hurriedly and noisily)* belongs to the frame Ingestion (consumption of food, drink or smoke) and neither the frame nor the frame elements account for the negative connotation of *gobble.* Yet, we think that a resource like FN with rich and corpus based valency patterns is an ideal base/ starting point for subjectivity description.

None of these theories, models or resources is specifically tailored for the subjectivity description of verbs. Studies which focus on verbs for sentiment analysis, usually refer to smaller subclasssess like, for example, emotion verbs (Mathieu, 2005, Mathieu and Fellbaum, 2010) or quotation verbs (Chen 2005, 2007).

3 Model

The proposed model is built as an extension of an already existing lexical database for Dutch, i.e.

Cornetto (Vossen et al. 2008). Cornetto combines two resources with different semantic organisations: the Dutch Wordnet (DWN) which has, like the Princeton Wordnet, a synset organization and the Dutch Reference Lexicon (RBN) which is organised in form-meaning composites or lexical units. The description of the lexical units includes definitions, usage constraints, selectional restrictions, syntactic behaviors, illustrative contexts, etc. DWN and RBN are linked to each other as each synonym in a synset is linked to a corresponding lexical unit. The subjectivity information is modelled as an extra layer related to the lexical units of Reference Lexicon thus providing a basis for the description of the verbs at word sense level.

3.1 Semantic Classes

For the identification of relevant semantic classes we adopt – and broaden – the definition of subjective language by Wiebe et al. (2006). Subjective expressions are defined as words and phrases that are used to express *private states* like opinions, emotions, evaluations, speculations.
Three main types are distinguished:

Type I:
Direct reference to private states (e.g. his alarm grew, he was boiling with anger). We include in this category emotion verbs (like *feel*, *love* and *hate*) and cognitive verbs (like *defend, dare,realize etc.)* ;

Type II:
Reference to speech or writing events that express private states (e.g. he condemns the president, they attack the speaker). According to our schema, this category includes all speech and writing events and the annotation schema points out if they are neutral (*say, ask)* or bear polarity (*condemn, praise);*

Type III:
Expressive subjective elements are expressions that indirectly express private states (e.g. superb, that doctor is a quack). According to our annotation schema this category is not a separate one , but verbs senses which fall in this category are always also member of one of the other categories. For example, *boast* (cf. ex. 1) is both a Type II (i.e. speech act verb) verb and a Type III verb as it indirectly expresses the negative attitude of the speaker/writer towards the speech event. By considering this category as combinational, it enables to make a clear distinction between Speaker/Writer subjectivity and participant subjectivity.

Moreover, we add a fourth category which includes verbs which implicitly refer to private states. If we consider the following examples:

Ex. (2) the teacher used to beat the students
Ex. (3) C.A is arrested for public intoxication by the police

Neither *beat* nor *arrest* are included in one of the three mentioned categories as neither of them explicitly expresses a private state. However, in many contexts these verbs implicitly and indirectly refer to the private state of one of the participants. In ex. (2) the teacher and the students will have bad feelings towards each other and also in ex. (3) C.A. will have negative feelings about the situation. To be able to describe also these aspects of subjectivity we define the following additional category:

Type IV:
Indirect reference to a private state that is the source or the consequence of an event (action, state or process). The event is explicitly mentioned.

Verb senses which are categorized as Type I, II or III are considered as subjective; verb senses categorized as Type IV are only subjective if one of the annotation categories (see below for more details) has a non-zero value; otherwise they are considered as objective.
We assigned well-known semantic categories to each of the above mentioned Types (I, II and IV). Table 1 presents the resulting categories with examples for each category. The first column lists the potential subjectivity classes that can apply.

Type	Name	Description	Examples
I (+III)	EXPERIENCER	Verbs that denote emotions. Included are both experiencer subject and experiencer object verbs.	hate, love, enjoy, enter-tain, frighten, upset, fru-strate
I(+III)	ATTITUDE	A cognitive action performed by one of the participants, in general the structural subject of the verb. The category is rele-vant as these cognitive actions may imply attitudes between participants.	defend, think, dare, ig-nore, avoid, feign, pre-tend, patronize, devote, dedicate
II(+III)	JUDGMENT	A judgment (mostly positive or negative) that someone may have towards something or somebody. The verbs directly refer to the thinking or speech act of judgment.	praise, admire, rebuke, criticize, scold, reproach, value, rate, estimate
II(+III)	COMM-S	A speech act that denotes the transfer of a spoken or written message from the perspective of the sender or speaker (S) of the message. The sender or speaker is the structural subject of the verb.	speak, say, write, grum-ble, stammer, talk, email, cable, chitchat, nag, in-form
II(+III)	COMM-R	A speech act that denotes the transfer of a spoken or written message from the perspective of the receiver(R) of the mes-sage. The receiver is the structural subject of the verb	read, hear, observe, record, watch, compre-hend
IV(+III)	ACTION	A physical action performed by one of the participants, in general the structural subject of the verb. The category is rele-vant as in some cases participants express an attitude by per-forming this action.	run, ride, disappear, hit, strike, stagger, stumble
IV(+III)	PROCESS_STATE	This is a broad and underspecified category of state and process verbs (non-action verbs) and may be considered as a rest cate-gory as it includes all verbs which are not included in other categories.	grow, disturb, drizzle, mizzle

Table 1 Semantic Categories

3.2 Attitude and roles

In our model, verb subjectivity is defined in terms of verb arguments carrying attitude towards each other, i.e. as experiencers holding attitudes towards targets or communicators expressing a judgment about an evaluee. The various participants or attitude holders which are involved in the events expressed by the verbs all may have different attitudes towards the event and/or towards each other. We developed an annotation schema (see Table 2 below) which enables us to relate the attitude holders, the orientation of the attitude (positive, negative or neutral) and the syntactic valencies of the verb to each other.

To be able to attribute the attitudes to the relevant participants we identify for each form-meaning unit the semantic-syntactic distribution of the arguments, the associated Semantic Roles and some coarse grained selection restrictions.

We make a distinction between participants which are part of the described situation, the so-called event internal participants, and participants that are outside the described situation, the external participants.

- Event internal attitude holders

The event internal attitude holders are participants which are lexicalized by the structural subject (A1), direct object (A2 or A3) or indirect/prepositional object (A2 or A3). A2 and A3 both can be syntactically realized as an NP, a PP, that-clause or infinitive clause. Each participant is associated with coarse-grained selection restrictions: SMB (somebody +human), SMT (something -human) or SMB/SMT (somebody/something + – human).

Attitude (positive, negative and neutral) is attributed to the relations between participants A1 vs. A2 (A1A2) and A1 vs. A3 (A1A3) and/or the relation between the participants (A1, A2 and A3) and the event itself (A1EV, A2EV and A3EV, respectively) as illustrated by the following examples.

verdedigen (defend: argue or speak in defense of)		
A1A2: positive		
A1A3: negative		
SMB (A1)	SMB/SMT (A2)	tegen SMB/SMT (A3)
He(A1) defends his decision(A2) against critique(A3)		

verliezen (lose: miss from one's possessions)	
A1EV: negative	
SMB(A1)	SMB/SMT(A2)
He (A1) loses his sunglasses (A2) like crazy	

- Event external attitude holders

Event external attitude holders are participants who are not part of the event itself but who are outside observers. We distinguish two kind of perspectives, i.e. that of the Speaker or Writer (SW) and a more general perspective (ALL) shared by a vast majority of people.

- Speaker /Writer (SW)

The Speaker/Writer (SW) expresses his attitude towards the described state of affairs by choosing words with overt affective connotation (cf. ex. 4) or by conveying his subjective interpretation of what happens (cf. ex. 5).

Ex. 4: He gobbles down three hamburgers a day

In (ex. 4) the SW not only describes the eating behavior of the 'he' but he also expresses his negative attitude towards this behavior by choosing the negative connotation word *gobble.*

(Ex. 5) B. S. misleads district A voters

In (ex. 5), the SW expresses his negative attitude towards the behavior of the subject of the sentence, by conceptualizing it in a negative way.

- ALL

Some concepts are considered as negative by a vast majority of people and therefore express a more general attitude shared by most people. For example, *to drown*, will be considered negative by everybody, i.e. observers, participants to the event and listener to the speech event. These concepts are labeled with a positive or negative attitude label for ALL. The annotation model is illustrated in table 2.

FORM	SUMMARY	SEMTYPE	COMPLEMENTATION	A1A2	A1A3	A1EV	A2EV	A3EV	SW	ALL
vreten (devour, gobble)	eat immoderately and hurriedly	ACTION	SMT (A2)	2	0	0	0	0	-4	0
afpakken (take away)	take without the owner's consent	ACTION	SMT(A2) van SMB (A3)	0	0	0	0	-3	0	0
verliezen (lose)	lose: fail to keep or to maintain	PROCESS	SMT (A2)	0	0	-3	0	0	0	0
dwingen (force)	urge a person to an action	ATTITUDE	SMB (A2) tot SMT (A3)	-3	2	0	0	0	0	0
opscheppen (boast)	to speak with exaggeration and excessive pride	COMM-S	over SMB/SMT (A2)	3	0	0	0	0	-4	0
helpen (help)	give help or assis-tance ; be of service	ACTION	SMB(A2) met SMT (A3)	2	1	0	0	0	0	0
bekritiseren(criticize)	express criticism of	COMM-S	SMB (A2)	-3	0	0	0	0	0	0
zwartmaken (slander)	charge falsely or with malicious intent	COMM-S	SMB (A2)	-3	0	0	0	0	-4	0
verwaarlozen (neglect)	fail to attend to	ATTITUDE	SMB (A2)	-3	0	0	0	0	-4	0
afleggen (lay out)	prepare a dead body	ACTION	SMB (A2)	0	0	0	0	0	0	-1

Explanation:

A1A2	A1 has a positive (+) or negative(-) attitude towards A2
A1A3	A1 has a positive (+) or negative(-) attitude towards A3
A1EV	A1 has a positive or negative attitude towards the event
A2EV	A2 has a positive or negative attitude towards the event
A3EV	A3 has a positive or negative attitude towards the event
SW	SW has a positive or negative attitude towards event or towards the structural subject of the event
ALL	there is a general positive or negative attitude towards the event

Table 2: Annotation Schema

4 Intercoder Agreement Study

To explore our hypothesis that different attitudes associated with the different attitude holders can be modelled in an operational lexicon and to explore how far we can stretch the description of subtle subjectivity relations, we performed an inter-annotator agreement study to assess the reliability of the annotation schema.

We are aware of the fact that it is a rather complex annotation schema and that high agreement rates are not likely to be achieved. The main goal of the annotation task is to determine what extent this kind of subjectivity information can be reliably identified, which parts of the annotation schema are more difficult than others and perhaps need to be redefined. This information is especially valuable when – in future- lexical acquisition tasks will be carried out to acquire automatically parts of the information specified by the annotation schema. .

Annotation is performed by 2 linguists (i.e. both authors of this paper). We did a first annotation task for training and discussed the problems before the gold standard annotation task was carried out. The annotation is based upon the full description of the lexical units including glosses and illustrative examples.

4.1 Agreement results

All attitude holder categories were annotated as combined categories and will be evaluated together and as separate categories.

- Semantic category polarity

Overall percent agreement for all 7 attitude holder categories is 66% with a Cohen kappa (κ) of 0.62 (cf. table 3, first row). Table 3 shows that not all semantic classes are of equal difficulty.

	Number of items	Kappa Agreement	Percent Agreement
All	581	0.62	0.66
Comm-s	57	0.75	0.77
Comm-r	16	0.55	0.81
Attitude	74	0.55	0.60
Action	304	0.60	0.66
StateProcess	83	0.47	0.55
Judgment	25	0.82	0.84
Experiencer	23	0.74	0.83

Table 3: Agreement for semantic categories

- Attitude Holder Polarity

Table 4 shows that agreement rates for each separate attitude holder differ. Although some categories are not reliable identifiable (cf. A1EV, A2EV, A3EV, ALL), the larger categories with many sentiment-laden items (cf. the third column which gives the coverage in percentage with regard to positive or negative annotations) are the ones with high agreement rates.

	Kappa	Percent agreement	PosOrNeg
A1-A2	0.73	0.89	25%
A1-A3	0.73	0.98	2%
A1EV	0.41	0.93	6%
A2EV	0.56	0.94	7%
A3EV	0.54	0.98	2%
SW	0.76	0.91	23%
ALL	0.37	0.87	10%

Table 4: Agreement rates for attitude holder categories

- Attitude Holder Polarity

Table 5 gives agreement figures for the most important attitude holder categories (A1A2 and SW) with respect to the different semantic categories. Low scores are found especially in categories (like State_Process) less relevant for Sentiment Analysis and opinion mining.

	A1A2(κ)	SW(κ)
Comm-s	0.83	0.93
Comm-r	1.00	1.00
Experiencer	0.82	0.84
Action	0.61	0.78
Judgment	0.92	0.63
State-process	0.33	0.64
Attitude	0.72	0.68

Table 5: Kappa agreement for SW and A1A2

- Single Polarity

One single polarity value for each item is derived by collapsing all attitude holder polarity values into one single value. If an item is tagged with different polarity values we apply them in the following order: SW, A1A2, A1A3, A1EV, A2EV, A3EV, ALL. As can be seen from table 6, observed agreement is 84% and kappa=0.75. Separate polarity computation (positive, negative and neutral) – with one polarity value of interest and the other values combined into one non-relevant category - shows that all polarity values are reliable identifiable.

	Kappa	Percent Agreement
Single polarity	0.75	0.84
Positive	0.70	0.91
Negative	0.82	0.92
Neutral	0.72	0.86

Table 6: agreement rates for polarity categories

4.2 Disagreement Analysis

Overall agreement is 66% (K=0.62) which is a reasonable score, in particular for such a complicated annotation schema. Moreover, scores are high for semantic categories such as Communication (0.75), Judgment (0.80), Experiencer (0.74) which are relevant for subjectivity analysis.

Table 4 shows that low performance is largely due to the attitude holder categories A1EV, A2EV, A3EV and ALL which have scores ranging from 0.37 to 0.56 whereas the categories A1A2, A1A3 and SW are reliably identifiable. As the last 3 categories are the largest ones with respect to sentiment bearing items, overall scores do not degrade much.

The low scores of A1EV, A2EV, A3EV and ALL are probably due to the fact that they are easily confused with each other. For example, *jagen (hunt), vallen (fall), klemmen (stick, jam)* and *flauwvallen (faint)* all have negative polarity but the annotators do not agree about who is the attitude holder: ALL (i.e. ALL have a negative attitude towards hunting, falling, being jammed, and fainting) or A1/2-RES (i.e. the person who falls, is jammed, is fainted or is hunted is the one who has the negative attitude). Confusion is found also between A2EV and A1A2. For example, with respect to *misleiden (mislead)*, annotators agree about a negative attitude from A1 vs. A2 , but one annotator marks additionally a negative attitude on behalf of A2 (A2EV: negative) whereas the other does not.

Especially the category ALL seems not to be defined well as many items are marked positive or negative by one annotator and neutral by the other. Examples of disagreements of this kind are *ploegen (plough), ontwateren (drain), omvertrekken (pull over)* and *achternalopen (follow, pursue)*. Both annotators regard these items as objective expressions but they do not agree about whether some general positive or negative feelings are associated to them or not.

Disagreement occurs also where collocational information may lead one annotator to see subjectivity in a sense and the other not. For example, *houden (keep - conform one's action or practice to)* associated with collocations like *to keep appointments* and *to keep one's promises* is considered positive (A1A2) by one annotator and neutral by the other. This seems to apply to all frequent light verbs with little semantic content like *make, do* and *take.*

With respect to the category SW disagreements do not arise from confusions with other categories but from judgments which differ between neutral vs. non-neutral. Consider for example, *tevredenstellen (mollify)* as in *I mollified her (A2) by cleaning my room.* Both annotators agree about the positive attitude between A1 and A2, but they disagree (SW:positive vs. SW:neutral) about whether the SW conveys a positive attitude towards 'I' by describing her behavior or not. Other examples of this type are *ignoreren (ignore), zich verzoenen (make up), redden (deal with),* and *dwingen (force).*

Overall agreement for one polarity is rather high with $\kappa = 0.75$. (cf. table 6). The scores are comparible to agreement rates of other studies where verbs are marked for single polarity. For example, inter-annotator agreement between 2 annotators who annotated 265 verb senses of the Micro-WNop corpus (Cerini et al. (2007)) is 0.75 (κ) as well. It shows that a complicated and layered annotation does not hamper overall agreement and may also produce lexicons which are appropriate to use within applications that use single polarity only.

Summarizing, we conclude that overall agreement is good, especially with regard to most semantic categories relevant for subjectivity analysis and with respect to the most important attitude holder categories, SW and A1A2. When defining an operational model the small and low scoring categories, i.e. A1/A2/A3EV and ALL, will be collapsed into one underspecified attitude holder category.

5 Conclusions

In this paper we presented a lexicon model for the description of verbs to be used in applications like deeper sentiment analysis and opinion mining, describing the detailed and subtle subjectivity relations that exist between the different participants of a verb. The relations can be labeled with subjectivity information concerning the identity of the attitude holder, the orientation (positive vs. negative) of the attitude and its target. Special attention is paid to the role of the speaker/writer of the event whose perspective is expressed and whose views on what is happening are conveyed in the text.

We measured the reliability of the annotation. The results show that when using all 7 attitude holder categories, 3 categories, SW, A1A2 and A1A3 are reliable and the other 4 are not. As these not reliable categories are also small, we think that the annotation schema is sufficiently validated.

An additional outcome to our study is that we created a gold standard of 580 verb senses. In the future we will use this gold standard to test methods for the automatic detection of subjectivity and polarity properties of word senses in order to build a rich subjectivity lexicon for Dutch verbs.

6 Acknowledgments

This research has been carried out within the project From Text To Political Positions (http: //www2.let.vu.nl/oz/cltl/t2pp/). It is funded by the VUA Interfaculty Research Institute CAMeRA.

7 References

Andreevskaia, A. and S. Bergler (2006) Mining WordNet for Fuzzy Sentiment:Sentiment Tag Extraction fromWordNet Glosses. In: EACL-2006, Trento, Italy.

Chen, L. (2005) Transitivity in Media Texts: negative verbal process sub-functions and narrator bias. In International Review of Applied Linguistics in Teaching, (IRAL-vol. 43) Mouton De Gruyter, The Hague, The Netherlands.

Cerini, S., Compagnoni, V., Demontis, A., Formentelli, M., and Gandini, G. (2007). Language resources and linguistic theory: Typology, second language acquisition, English linguistics (Forthcoming), chapter Micro-WNOp: A gold standard for the evaluation of automatically compiled lexical resources for opinion mining. Milano, Italy.

Choi Y. and C. Cardie (2008). Learning with Composi tional Semantics as Structural Inference for subsen tential Sentiment Analysis. Proceedings of Recent Advances in Natural Language Processing (RANLP), Hawaii.

Esuli, Andrea and Fabrizio Sebastiani. (2006). SentiWordNet: A Publicly Available Lexical Resource for Opinion Mining. In: Proceedings of LREC-2006, Genova, Italy.

Hatzivassiloglou, V., McKeown, K.B. (1997) Predicting the semantic orientation of adjectives. In Proceedings of ACL-97, Madrid, Spain.

Jia, L., Yu, C.T., Meng, W. (2009) The effect of negation on sentiment analysis and retrieval effectiveness. In CIKM-2009, China.

Kamps, J., R. J. Mokken, M. Marx, and M. de Rijke (2004). Using WordNet to measure semantic orientation of adjectives. In Proceedings LREC-2004, Paris.

Kim, S. and E. Hovy (2004) Determining the sentiment of opinions. In Proceedings of COLING, Geneva, Swtizerland.

Kim, S. and E. Hovy (2006) Extracting Opinions Expressed in Online News Media Text with Opinion Holders and Topics. In: Proceedings of the Workshop on Sentiment and Subjectivity in Text (SST-06). Sydney, Australia.

Maks, I.and P. Vossen (2010) Modeling Attitude, Polarity and Subjectivity in Wordnet. In Proceedings of Fifth Global Wordnet Conference, Mumbai, India.

Mathieu, Y. Y. (2005). A Computational Semantic Lexicon of French Verbs of Emotion. In: Computing Attitude and Affect in Text: Theory and Applications J. Shanahan, Yan Qu, J.Wiebe (Eds.). Springer, Dordrecht, The Netherlands.

Mathieu,Y.Y. and C. Felbaum (2010). Verbs of emotion in French and English. In: Proceedings of GWC-2010, Mumbai, India.

Moilanen K. and S. Pulman. (2007). Sentiment Composition. In Proceedings of Recent Advances in Natural Language Processing (RANLP), Bulgaria.

Ruppenhofer, J. , M. Ellsworth, M. Petruck, C. Johnson, and J. Scheffzcyk (2010) Framenet II: Theory and Practice (e-book) http://framenet.icsi. berkeley.edu/ book/book.pdf.

C. Strapparava and A. Valitutti (2004). WordNet-Affect: an affective extension of WordNet. In Proceedings LREC 2004, Lisbon, Portugal

Su, F.and K. Markert (2008). Eliciting Subjectivity and Polarity Judgements on Word Senses. In Proceedings of Coling-2008, Manchester, UK.

Valitutti, A. and C. Strapparava (2010). Interfacing Wordnet-Affect withj OCC model of emotions. In Proceedings of EMOTION-2010, Valletta, Malta.

Wiebe, Janyce and Rada Micalcea.(2006) . Word Sense and Subjectivity. In Proceedings of ACL'06, Sydney, Australia.

Experiments with a Differential Semantics Annotation for WordNet 3.0

Dan Tufiş
Research Institute for Artificial Intelligence
Romanian Academy
Calea "13 Septembrie", no.13
Bucharest 5, 050711, Romania
tufis@racai.ro

Dan Ştefănescu
Research Institute for Artificial Intelligence
Romanian Academy
Calea "13 Septembrie", no.13
Bucharest 5, 050711, Romania
danstef@racai.ro

Abstract

This article reports on the methodology and the development of a complementary information source for the meaning of the synsets of Princeton WordNet 3.0. This encoded information was built following the principles of the Osgoodian differential semantics theory and consists of numerical values which represent the scaling of the connotative meanings along the multiple dimensions defined by pairs of antonyms (factors). Depending on the selected factors, various facets of connotative meanings come under scrutiny and different types of textual subjective analysis may be conducted (opinion mining, sentiment analysis).

1 Introduction

According to "Semantic Differential" theory (Osgood et al., 1957), the connotative meaning of most adjectives can be, both qualitatively and quantitatively, differentiated along a scale, the ends of which are antonymic adjectives. Such a pair of antonymic adjectives is called a factor. The intensive experiments Osgood and his colleagues made with their students[1] outlined that most of the variance in the text judgment was explained by only three major factors: the evaluative factor (e.g., good-bad), the potency factor (e.g., strong-weak), and the activity factor (e.g., active-passive).

Kamps and Marx (2002) implemented a WordNet-based method in the spirit of the theory of semantic differentials and proposed a method to assess the"*attitude*" of arbitrary texts. In their approach, a text unit is regarded as a bag of words and the overall scoring of the sentence is obtained by combining the scores for the individual words of the text. Depending on the selected factor, various facets of subjective meanings come under scrutiny.

The inspiring work of Kamps and Marx still has several limitations. The majority of researchers working on subjectivity agree that the subjectivity load of a given word is dependent on the senses of the respective word (Andreevskaia and Bergler, 2006), (Bentivogli et al., 2004), (Mihalcea et al., 2007), (Valiutti et al., 2004) and many others.; yet, in Kamps and Marx's model (KMM, henceforth), because they work with words and not word-senses, the sense distinctions are lost, making it impossible to assign different scores to different senses of the word in case. Going up from the level of word to the level of sentence, paragraph or entire text, the bag of words approach can easily be fooled in the presence of valence shifters (Polanyi and Zaenen, 2006). In order to cope with this problem, the text under investigation needs a minimal level of sentence processing, required for the identification of the structures that could get under the scope of a valence shifter (Tufiş, 2008). For dealing with irony or sarcasm, processing requirements go beyond sentence level, and discourse structure of the text might be necessary.

On the other hand, although the adjectives make up the obvious class of subjectivity words, the other open class categories have significant potential for expressing subjective meanings.

[1] The students were asked to rate the meaning of words, phrases, or texts on different scales defined in terms of pairs of bipolar adjectives such as *good-bad*, *active-passive*, *strong-weak*, *optimistic-pessimistic*, *beautiful-ugly*, etc.)

Proceedings of the 2nd Workshop on Computational Approaches to Subjectivity and Sentiment Analysis, ACL-HLT 2011, pages 19–27,
24 June, 2011, Portland, Oregon, USA ©2011 Association for Computational Linguistics

In our models, unlike KMM, the building block is the word sense, thus making possible to assign different connotation values to different senses of a word. This was possible by using an additional source of information besides the WordNet itself, namely the SUMO/MILO ontology. Moreover, we considered all the word classes contained in WordNet, not only adjectives.

From this point of view, our work, although through a different approach, shares objectives with other wordnet-based methods such as SentiWordNet (Esuli and Sebastiani, 2006) (Baccianella et al., 2010) and WordNet Affect (Valiuttti et al. 2004).

2 Base Definitions

Let us begin with some definitions, slightly modified, from KMM. We will progressively introduce new definitions to serve our extended approach.

Definition 1: Two words w_α and w_β are *related* if there exists a sequence of words (w_α w_1 $w_2 \ldots w_i \ldots$ w_β) so that each pair of adjacent words in the sequence belong to the same synset. If the length of such a sequence is n+1 one says that w_α and w_β are *n-related.*

Two words may not be related at all or may be related by many different sequences, of various lengths. In the latter case, one would be interested in their minimal path-length.

Definition 2: Let MPL(w_i, w_j) be the partial function:

$$MPL(w_i, w_j) = \begin{cases} n & \text{the smallest n when } w_i \text{ and } w_j \text{ are n-related} \\ \textit{undefined} & \text{otherwise} \end{cases}$$

Kamps and Marx (2002) showed that MPL is a distance measure that can be used as a metric for the semantic relatedness of two words. Observing the properties of the MPL partial function, one can quantify the relatedness of an arbitrary word w_i to one or the other word of a bipolar pair. To this end, KMM introduced another partial function as in Definition 3.

Definition 3: Let TRI (w_i, w_α, w_β), with $w_\alpha \neq w_\beta$ be:

$$TRI(w_i, w_\alpha, w_\beta) = \begin{cases} \dfrac{MPL(w_i, w_\alpha) - MPL(w_i, w_\beta)}{MPL(w_\alpha, w_\beta)} & \text{if MPLs defined} \\ \textit{undefined} & \text{otherwise} \end{cases}$$

When defined, **TRI(w_i, w_α, w_β)** is a real number in the interval [-1, 1]. The words w_α and w_β are the antonymic words of a factor, while w_i is the word of interest for which TRI is computed. If one takes the negative values returned by the partial function **TRI (w_i, w_α, w_β)** as an indication of w_i being more similar to w_α than to w_β and the positive values as an indication of w_i being more similar to w_β than to w_α, then a zero value could be interpreted as w_i being neutrally related with respect to w_α and w_β. This is different from being unrelated.

Definition 4: If α-β is a factor used for the computation of relatedness of w_i to α and β, the proper function $\mathbf{TRI}^*_{\alpha\text{-}\beta}(w_i)$ returns a value outside the interval [-1, 1] when w_i is unrelated to the α-β factor:

$$TRI^*_{\alpha-\beta}(w_i) = \begin{cases} TRI(w_i, \alpha, \beta) & \text{iff } TRI(w_i, \alpha, \beta) \text{ defined} \\ 2 & \text{otherwise} \end{cases}$$

Given a factor α-β, for each word w_i in WordNet that *can be reached on a path* from α to β, the function $\mathbf{TRI}^*_{\alpha\text{-}\beta}(w_i)$ computes a score number, which is a proportional to the distances from w_i to α and to β. The set of these words defines the coverage of the factor – COV(α, β).

Our experiments show that the coverage of the vast majority of the factors, corresponding to the same POS category, is the same. From now on, we will use LUC (Literal Unrestricted[2] Coverage) to designate this common coverage. The table below gives coverage figures for each of the POS categories in Princeton WordNet 3.0 (PWN 3.0).

Class	Factors	LUC
Adjectives	199	4,402 (20.43%)
Nouns	106	11,964 (10,05%)
Verbs	223	6,534 (56,66%)
Adverbs	*199*	*1,291 (28,81%)*

Table 1: LUC Statistics According to the POS of the Literals in PWN 3.0

The PWN structuring does not allow us to compute TRI* scores for adverbs using this approach, but, more than half of the total number of adverbs (63.11%) are derived from adjectives. For those adverbs, we transferred the score values from their correspondent adjectives in the LUC set and we used the adjectival factors.

[2] In the following we will gradually introduce several restrictions, thus justifying the acronym used here.

The results reported for adjectives by Kamps and Marx[3] are consistent with our findings. The difference in numbers might be explained by the fact that the two compared experiments used different versions of the Princeton WordNet.

3 Introducing Word-Sense Distinctions

KMM defines a factor as a pair of words with antonymic senses. We generalize the notion of a factor to a pair of synsets. In the following, we will use the colon notation to specify the sense number of a literal that licenses the synonymy relation within a synset. Synonymy is a lexical relation that holds not between a pair of words but between specific senses of those words. That is, the notation {literal$_1$:n$_1$ literal$_2$:n$_2$ … literal$_k$:n$_k$} will mean that the meaning given by the sense number n$_1$ of the literal$_1$, the meaning given by sense number n$_2$ of the literal$_2$ and so on are all pair-wise synonymous. The term *literal* is used to denote the dictionary entry form of a word (lemma).

The antonymy is also a lexical relation that holds between specific senses of a pair of words. The synonyms of the antonymic senses, taken pairwise, definitely express a semantic opposition. Take for instance the antonymic pair <rise:1 fall:2>. These two words belong to the synsets {rise:1, lift:4, arise:5, move up:2, go up:1, come up:6, uprise:6} and {descend:1, fall:2, go down:1, come down:1}. The pair <rise:1 fall:2> is explicitly encoded as antonymic. However, there is a conceptual opposition between the synsets to which the two word senses belong, that is between any pair of the Cartesian product: {rise:1, lift:4, arise:5, move up:2, go up:1, come up:6, uprise:6}⊗{descend:1, fall:2, go down:1, come down:1}. This conceptual opposition is even more obvious in this example, as the pairs <go up:1 go down:1> and <come up:1 come down:1> are also explicitly marked as antonymic.

Definition 5: An **S-factor** is a pair of synsets (S_α, S_β) for which there exist $w_i^\alpha : s_i^\alpha \in S_\alpha$ and $w_j^\beta : s_j^\beta \in S_\beta$ so that $w_i^\alpha : s_i^\alpha$ and $w_j^\beta : s_j^\beta$ are antonyms and $MPL\left(w_i^\alpha, w_j^\beta\right)$ is defined. S_α and S_β have opposite meanings, and we consider that $MPL(S_\alpha, S_\beta) = MPL\left(w_i^\alpha, w_i^\beta\right)$.

The previous example shows that the semantic opposition of two synsets may be reinforced by multiple antonymic pairs. Because of how MPL is defined, choosing different antonymic pairs might produce different values for $MPL(S_\alpha, S_\beta)$. That is why, wherever is the case, we need to specify the antonymic pair which defines the S-factor.

Based on the definition of the coverage of a factor $< w_i^\alpha , w_i^\beta >$, one may naturally introduce the notion of coverage of a S-factor - <S_α,S_β>: the set of synsets containing the words in COV$< w_i^\alpha , w_i^\beta >$. The coverage of an S-factor <S_α,S_β> will be onward denoted by SCOV<S_α, S_β>.

Since the word-relatedness and MPL definitions ignore the word senses, it might happen that the meaning of some synsets in the coverage of an S-factor have little (if anything) in common with the semantic field defined by the respective S-factor. More often than not, these outliers must be filtered out and, to this end, we further introduce the notions of *semantic type of a synset, typed S-factor,* and *scoped synset with respect to a typed S-factor,* which represent major deviations from KMM.

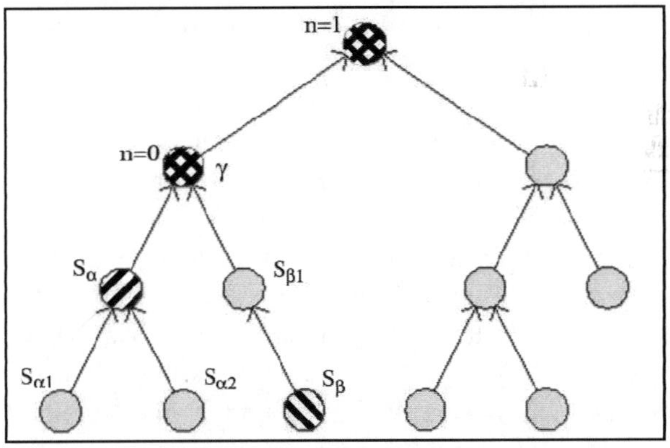

Figure 1. Different levels of coverage (marked with cross hatching) for the S-factor <S_α-S_β>

Before that, we need to introduce the mapping between the WordNet synsets and the SUMO/ MILO concepts. The Suggested Upper Merged Ontology (SUMO), Mid-Level Ontology (MILO) and its domain ontologies form the largest formal public[4] ontology in existence today, containing roughly 20,000 terms and 70,000 axioms (when

[3] They found 5410 adjectives that were in the coverage of the factors they investigated (WordNet 1.7). For PWN 2.0, the total number of covered adjectives is 5307.

[4] http://www.ontologyportal.org/

SUMO, MILO, and domain ontologies are combined). One of the major attractions of this ontology (Niles and Pease, 2003) is that it has been mapped to the WordNet lexicon. Using this mapping, synsets are labeled with a SUMO/MILO concept which we will refer to as the synset's *semantic type*. The hierarchical structure of SUMO/MILO induces a partial ordering of the S-factors.

Definition 6: An S-factor $<S_{\alpha}, S_{\beta}>$ is said to be a *typed S-factor* if the types of the synsets S_{α} and S_{β} are identical or they have a common ancestor. If this ancestor is the lowest common ancestor, it is called the *0-semantic type* of the S-factor. The direct parent of the *n-semantic type* of an S-factor is the *n+1-semantic type* of the S-factor (Fig. 1).

A typed S-factor is represented by indexing the S-factor with its type as in the examples below:

<{unfairness:2...}, { fairness:1...}>$_{\text{NormativeAttribute}}$

<{discomfort:1...}, {comfort:1...}>$_{\text{StateOfMind}}$

<{distrust:2...}, {trust:3...}>$_{\text{TraitAttribute}}$

<{decrease:2... }, {increase:3...}>$_{\text{QuantityChange}}$

In the following, if not otherwise specified, by S-factors we mean typed S-factors. Unless there is ambiguity, the type of an S-factor will be omitted.

Definition 7: A synset S_i with the type L is *n-scoped* relative to a typed S-factor $<S_{\alpha}, S_{\beta}>$ if L is a node in a sub-tree of the SUMO/MILO hierarchy having as root the n-semantic type of the S-factor $<S_{\alpha}, S_{\beta}>$. We say that **n** defines the **level of the scope coverage of the S-factor** $<S_{\alpha}, S_{\beta}>$ and that every synset in this coverage is **n-scoped**.

We use the notation $SCOV_n<S_{\alpha}, S_{\beta}>$ for the scope coverage of level n of an S-factor $<S_{\alpha}, S_{\beta}>$. If the root of the tree has the semantic type γ, we will use also use the notation $SCOV_n<S_{\alpha}, S_{\beta}>_{\gamma}$ or simply $SCOV<S_{\alpha}, S_{\beta}>_{\gamma}$. In other words, $SCOV<S_{\alpha}, S_{\beta}>_{\gamma}$ is the set of synsets the semantic types of which are subsumed by γ. For the example in Fig. 1, only the synsets $S_{\alpha 1}$, $S_{\alpha 2}$ and $S_{\beta 1}$ are in the $SCOV_0<S_{\alpha}, S_{\beta}>$. All depicted synsets are in $SCOV_1<S_{\alpha}, S_{\beta}>$.

It is easy to see that when the value of the scope coverage level is increased so as to reach the top of the ontology, $SCOV_n<S_{\alpha}, S_{\beta}>_{\gamma}$ will be equal to the set of synsets containing the literals in *LUC* (see Table 1). Let us call this set *SUC* (Synset Unrestricted Coverage).

Class	S-Factors	SUC
Adjectives	264	4,240 (23.35%)
Nouns	118	11,704 (14.25%)
Verbs	246	8,640 (62.75%)
Adverbs	*264*	*1,284 (35.45%)*

Table 2: SUC Statistics According to the POS of the Synsets in PWN 3.0

From the differential semantics point of view, the S-factor $<S_{\alpha}, S_{\beta}>$ quantitatively characterizes each synset in $SCOV_n<S_{\alpha}, S_{\beta}>$ by a TRI^*-like score (Definition 4). The synsets in $SCOV_0<S_{\alpha}, S_{\beta}>$ are best discriminated, meaning that their scores for the $<S_{\alpha}, S_{\beta}>$ factor are the highest. For the synsets in $SCOV_n<S_{\alpha}, S_{\beta}>$ but not in $SCOV_{n-1}<S_{\alpha}, S_{\beta}>$, the scores are smaller and we say that the characterization of these synsets in terms of the $<S_{\alpha}, S_{\beta}>$ factor is weaker. Our model captures this through a slight modification of the TRI function in Definition 3, where w_{α} and w_{β} are the antonyms belonging to S_{α} and S_{β} respectively, and w_i is a literal of a synset S_j in $SCOV_n<S_{\alpha}, S_{\beta}>$ but not in $SCOV_{n-1}<S_{\alpha}, S_{\beta}>$:

Definition 8: The *differential score for a literal* w_i occurring in a synset S_j in $SCOV_n<S_{\alpha}, S_{\beta}>$ but not in $SCOV_{n-1}<S_{\alpha}, S_{\beta}>$ is computed by the function TRI^+:

$$TRI^+(w_i, S_{\alpha}, S_{\beta}) = \frac{MPL(w_i, w_{\alpha}) - MPL(w_i, w_{\beta})}{MPL(w_{\alpha}, w_{\beta}) + n}$$

Since we imposed the requirement that S_j be in $SCOV_n<S_{\alpha}, S_{\beta}>$, $TRI^+(w_i, S_{\alpha}, S_{\beta})$ is defined for all literals in S_j, thus for any $w_i \in S_j$ the value of $TRI^+(w_i, S_{\alpha}, S_{\beta})$ is in the [-1,1] interval. The scores computed for the synsets in $SCOV_n<S_{\alpha}, S_{\beta}>$ remained unchanged in $SCOV_{n+k}<S_{\alpha}, S_{\beta}>$ for any $k \geqslant 0$. The above modification of the TRI function insures that the score of a synset gets closer to zero (neutrality) with the increase of *n*.

It is worth mentioning that using different antonymic literal pairs from the same opposed synsets does not have any impact on the sign of TRI^+ scores, but their absolute values may differ.

If one associates a semantic field with γ, the type of an S-factor $<S_{\alpha}, S_{\beta}>$, then all the synsets in $SCOV_n<S_{\alpha}, S_{\beta}>_{\gamma}$ are supposed to belong to the semantic field associated with γ. This observation should clarify why different senses of a given word may belong to different semantic coverages and thus, may have different scores for the S-factor in case.

Definition 9: The differential score of a synset S_i in $SCOV_n<S_\alpha, S_\beta>$ with respect to the S-factor $<S_\alpha, S_\beta>$ is given by the function TRIS (S_i, S_α, S_β), defined as the average of the TRI^+ values associated with the *m* literals in the synset S_i.

$$TRIS(S_i, S_\alpha, S_\beta) = \frac{\sum_{j=1}^{m} TRI^+(w_j, S_\alpha, S_\beta)}{m}$$

4 Computing the S-Factors and the Differential Scores for Synsets

In accordance with the equations in the previous definitions, we associated each synset S_k of WordNet 3.0 with an ordered vector $<F_1, F_2 \ldots F_n>$ where F_i is a pair *(score; level)* with *score* and *level* representing the value of the ith S-factor and, respectively, the minimal S-factor coverage level in which S_k was found.

For instance, let us assume that the first S-factor in the description of the adjectival synsets is: $<${*nice:3*}, {*nasty:2* …}$>_{\text{SubjectiveAssesmentAttribute}}$ then for the synset {*fussy:1, crabby:1, grumpy:1, cross:2, grouchy:1, crabbed:1, bad-tempered:1, ill-tempered:1*}$_{\text{SubjectiveAssesmentAttribute}}$ the vector $<F_1, \ldots>$ is <(0,66;0) ...> while for the synset {unplayful:1 serious:5 sober:4}$_{\text{SubjectiveAssesmentAttribute}}$ the vector $<F_1, \ldots>$ is <(-0,166 ; 0) ...>.

The values signify that the synset {*fussy:1, crabby:1, grumpy:1, cross:2…*}$_{\text{SubjectiveAssesment Attribute}}$ is 0-scoped with respect to the S-factor <{*nice:3*}, {*nasty*:2 …}> and its connotative meaning is significantly closer to the meaning of nasty:2 (0,66). Similarly, the synset {unplayful:1 serious:5 sober:4} is 0-scoped with respect to the considered S-factor and its connotative meaning is closer to the meaning of nice:3 (-0,166)

Our experiments showed that in order to ensure the same sets of synsets for all factors of a given part-of-speech we had to set the level of the semantic coverages to 7 (corresponding to the SUC). For each of the typed S-factors $<S_\alpha, S_\beta>$ and for each synset S_i in their respective semantic coverage $SCOV<S_\alpha, S_\beta>_\gamma$ we computed the $\text{TRIS}(S_i, S_\alpha, S_\beta)$ score. Each synset from the coverage of each POS category was associated with a vector of scores, as described above. Since the number of S-factors depends on the POS category the lengths of each of the four type vectors is different. The cell values in a synset vector have uneven values, showing that factors have different discriminative power for a given meaning. Because we considered SUC, all S-factors are relevant and the cells in any synset vector are filled with pairs *(score; level*).

For the noun part of the PW3.0 we identified 118 typed S-factors, all of them covering the same set of 11,898 noun literals (9.99%) with their senses clustered into 11,704 synsets (14.25%).

For the verb part of the PWN 3.0, we identified 246 typed S-factors, all of them covering the same set of 6,524 verb literals (56.57%) with their senses clustered into 8,640 synsets (62.75%).

For the adjective part of the PWN 3.0, we identified 264 typed S-factors, all of them covering the same set of 4,383 literals (20.35%) with their senses clustered into 4,240 synsets (23.35%)[5]. As previously mentioned, the same factors were used for the adverbs derived from adjectives. In this way, a total of 1,287 adverbs (28.72%) clustered into 1,284 synsets (35.45%) were successfully annotated (see Table 2).

Apparently, the cardinals of the factor sets in Table 2 should be identical with those in Table 1. The differences are due to the fact that a pair of opposed synsets may contain more than a single pair of antonymic senses each of them specifying a distinct S-factor.

In case the user restricted the coverages to lower levels, the original maximal semantic coverages are split into different subsets for which several S-factors become irrelevant. The cell values corresponding to these factors are filled in with a conventional value outside the interval [-1, 1].

Thus, we have the following annotation cases:

A synset of a certain POS is not in the corresponding SUC. This case signifies that the synset cannot be characterized in terms of the differential semantics methodology and we conventionally say that such a synset is "objective" (insensitive to any S-factor). Since this situation would require a factor vector with each cell having the same value (outside the [-1, 1] interval) and as

[5] In PWN 2.0 the number of covered literals (and synsets) is with almost 20% higher (Tufiş and Ştefănescu, 2010). This difference is explained by the fact that 1081 adjectives (5%), mostly participial, from PWN 2.0 are not any more listed as adjectives in PWN 3.0.

such a vector would be completely uninformative, we decided to leave the "objective" synsets un-annotated. As one can deduce from Table 2, the majority of the synsets in PWN3.0 are in this category (89,556 synsets, i.e. 77.58%).

Any synset of a certain POS in the corresponding SUC will have an associated factor vector. There are 25,868 such synsets. The ith cell of such a vector will correspond to the ith S-factor $<S_{\alpha}, S_{\beta}>$. We may have the following sub-cases:

(a) All cell scores are in the [-1,1] interval, and in this case all S-factors are relevant, that is, from any word in the synset one could construct a path to both words prompting an S-factor, irrespective of the S-factor itself. A negative score in the ith cell of the S-factor vector signifies that the current synset is more semantically related to S_{α} than to S_{β}, while a positive score in the ith cell of the factor vector signifies that the synset is more semantically related to S_{β} than to S_{α}. A zero score in the ith cell of the factor vector signifies that the synset is neutral with respect to the $<S_{\alpha}, S_{\beta}>$ S-factor.

(b) Several cell scores are not in the interval [-1, 1], say $FV[i_1]=FV[i_2] \ldots =FV[i_k]=2$. This signifies that the S-factors corresponding to those cells ($<S_{\alpha1},S_{\beta1}>,<S_{\alpha2},S_{\beta2}>,\ldots,<S_{\alpha3},S_{\beta3}>$) are irrelevant for the respective synset and that the current synset is not included in the scope of the above-mentioned S-factors, owing to the selected scope level of the coverage[6]. We say that, at the given scope level, the synset became "objective" with respect to the S-factors $FV[i_1]$, $FV[i_2] \ldots FV[i_k]$.

There are various ways to select, for a given POS coverage, those S-factors which are most informative or more interesting from a specific point of view. The simplest criterion is based on the coverage level: for a specified coverage level, select only those S-factors the coverage of which contains the analyzed synsets. In general, the most restrictive condition is choosing the 0-level coverage. This condition is equivalent to saying that the S-factors and the analyzed synsets should be in the same semantic class as defined by the SUMO/MILO labeling. For instance, assume that the synset under investigation is {good:1} with the definition "*having desirable or positive qualities especially those suitable for a thing specified*" and the semantic type *SubjectiveAssessmentAttribute.* Imposing the restriction that the semantic type of the selected factors should be the same with the semantic type of good:1, some relevant factors for estimating the various connotations of "*good*" from different perspectives are given below. In the shown factors, the words in bold face are those the meaning of which is closer to "good".

good 01123148-a (SubjectiveAssessmentAttribute)

----

effective ineffective#00834198-a_00835609-a
(SubjectiveAssessmentAttribute) -0,78
reasonable unreasonable#01943406-a_01944660-a
(SubjectiveAssessmentAttribute) -0,71
rich lean#02026785-a_02027003-a
(SubjectiveAssessmentAttribute) -0,63
ample meager#00105746-a_00106456-a
(SubjectiveAssessmentAttribute) -0,5
safe dangerous#02057829-a_02058794-a
(SubjectiveAssessmentAttribute) -0,33
brave cowardly#00262792-a_00264776-a
(SubjectiveAssessmentAttribute) -0,14
distant close#00450606-a_00451510-a
(SubjectiveAssessmentAttribute) 0,64
busy idle#00292937-a_00294175-a
(SubjectiveAssessmentAttribute) 0,63
cursed blessed#00669478-a_00670741-a
(SubjectiveAssessmentAttribute) 0,5
old new#01638438-a_01640850-a
(SubjectiveAssessmentAttribute) 0,45
formal informal#01041916-a_01044240-a
(SubjectiveAssessmentAttribute) 0,38

These factors' values should be clearer in the context of adequate examples:

A *good* tool is an **effective** tool;
A *good* excuse is a **reasonable** excuse;
A *good* vein of copper is a **reach** vein of copper;
A *good* resource is an **ample** resource;
A *good* position is a **safe** position;
A *good* attitude is a **close** attitude;
A *good* soldier is a **brave** soldier
A *good* time is an **idle** time;
A *good* life is a **blessed** life;
A *good* car is a **new** car;
A *good* party is an **informal** party.

From the definitions in the previous sections, one can easily see that the sign of a S-factor score depends on the order in which the semantically opposite pairs are considered. If one wishes to have a consistent interpretation of the factor scores (e.g. negative scores are "bad" and positive scores are "good") the synset ordering in the S-factors is

[6] Remember that for the highest level (7) that corresponds to SUC, all factors are relevant. When the user selects coverages of lower levels some factors might become irrelevant for various synsets.

significant. We used a default ordering of antonyms in all factors, yet a text analyst could modify this ordering. For each POS, we selected a representative factor for which the synset order, from a subjective point of view, was very intuitive. For instance, for the adjective factors we selected the factor <good:1, bad:1>, for noun factors we selected the factor <order:5, disorder:2>, and for verb factors we selected the factor <succeed:1, fail:2>, the first word sense in each of the representative factors having a clear positive connotation. Then for each POS factor $<S_\alpha, S_\beta>$ we computed the distance of its constituents to the synsets of the representative factor of the same POS. The one that was closer to the "positive" side of the reference factor was also considered "positive" and the order of the synsets was established accordingly. This empirical approach proved to be successful for most of the factors, except for a couple of them, which were manually ordered.

We developed an application that allows text analysts to choose the S-factors they would like to work with. The interface allows the user to both select/deselect factors and to switch the order of the poles in any given factor. Once the user decided on the relevant S-factors, the synsets are marked up according to the selected S-factors. This version of the WordNet can be saved and used as needed in the planned application.

5 Extending the LUCs and SUCs

Although the maximum semantic coverage of the S-factors for the adjectives contains more than 28% of the PWN3.0 adjectival synsets, many adjectives with connotative potential are not in this coverage. This happens because the definition of the *relatedness* (Definition 1) implicitly assumes the existence of synonyms for one or more senses of a given word. Therefore from mono-semantic words in mono-literal synsets a path towards other synsets cannot be constructed anymore. Because of this, there are isolated "bubbles" of *related* synsets that are not connected with synsets in maximum semantic coverage. In order to assign values to at least a part of these synsets, we experimented with various strategies out of which the one described herein was considered the easiest to implement and, to some extent motivated, from a conceptual point of view. The approach is similar for all the synsets which are not in the SUCs, but the algorithms for extending these coverages slightly differ depending on the part of speech under consideration.

Class	**E-LUCs**	**E-SUCs**
Adjectives	7,124 (33.07%)	6,216 (34.23%)
Nouns	27,614 (23.19%)	22,897 (27.88%)
Verbs	8,910 (77.26%)	10,798 (78.43%)
Adverbs	*1,838 (41.01%)*	*1,787 (49.35%)*

Table 3: Extended LUCs and SUCs

The basic idea is to transfer the vectors of the synsets in SUC to those in the complementary set $\overline{SUC}$, provided they have "similar meanings". We say that $S_i^{POS} \in SUC_{POS}$ and $S_j^{POS} \in \overline{SUC}_{POS}$ have "similar meanings" if $SUMO/MILO(S_i^{POS}) = SUMO/MILO(S_j^{POS})$ and S_i^{POS} and S_j^{POS} are directly linked by a semantic WordNet relation of a certain type. For adjectival synsets we consider the relations *similar_to* and *also_see*, for verbal synsets we consider the relations *hyponym* and *also_see*, and for the nominal synsets we take into account only the *hyponymy*. Consequently, the S-factors coverage increased as shown in Table 3.

6 A Preliminary Comparison with SentiWordnet 3.0

SentiWordNet 3.0 (Baccianella, et al. 2010) is the only public resource we are aware of, which considers sense distinctions and covers all synsets in Princeton WordNet 3.0. Although in SentiWordNet (henceforth SWN3.0) only the Subjective-Objective dichotomy is marked-up, with a further distinction between Positive-Subjectivity and Negative-Subjectivity, using it for the comparison with our annotations is meaningful and relevant for both approaches. First, the connotative meanings are subjective meanings. Then, while the SWN3.0 mark-up is based on ML techniques and various heuristics exploiting the structure of PWN3.0 and some other external resources, the differential semantics approach, as implemented here, is a deterministic one, considering only the content and structural information in PWN3.0 + SUMO/MILO. Identifying contradictions in the two annotations might reveal limitations in the ML techniques and heuristics used by SWN3.0 on one hand, and, on the other hand, flaws in our method, possible incompleteness or inconsistencies in PWN3.0+ SUMO/MILO. It has to be noted that the possible incompleteness or inconsistencies in PWN3.0 would also affect the accuracy of the SWN3.0 values.

Synset	SWN	DSA	Definition
dangerous, grave grievous, serious, severe …	-0,63	0,42	causing fear or anxiety by threatening great harm
live	0,5	-0,5	exerting force or containing energy
bastardly, mean	-0,5	0,5	of no value or worth
dangerous, unsafe	-0,75	0,5	involving or causing danger or risk; liable to hurt or harm
delirious, excited, unrestrained, mad, frantic	0,5	-0,5	marked by uncontrolled excitement or emotion
haunted	0,5	-0,43	showing emotional affliction or disquiet
impeccable	-0,63	0,8	not capable of sin
evil, vicious	0,5	-0,75	having the nature of vice
delectable, sexually attractive	*0,63*	*-0,5*	capable of arousing desire
ordinary	*-0,5*	*0,75*	not exceptional in any way especially in quality or ability or size or degree
serious	*-0,75*	*0,75*	requiring effort or concentration; complex and not easy to answer or solve
excusable	*0,63*	*-0,4*	capable of being overlooked

Table 4: Examples of divergent scores among the SWN3.0 and DSA

For the partial comparison we selected the adjectives in SWN3.0 with Positive-Subjectivity or Negative-Subjectivity greater than or equal to 0.5. From our differential semantic (DSA) annotation we extracted all the adjectives which along the good-bad differential dimension had an absolute value greater than 0.4. Those adjectives closer to good were considered to be Subjective-Positive while the others were considered to be Subjective-Negative. The threshold value was empirically selected, by observing that beyond the 0.4 and –0.4 values the factorial annotation was closer to our intuition concerning the connotative load of the analyzed words. We computed the intersection of the two adjectival synsets extracted this way and retained only the synsets contradictorily annotated. We found only 150 differences, which by itself is a small difference, showing that, at least with respect to the good-bad factor, SWN3.0 and DSA annotations are to a large extent consistent.

We manually checked-out the 150 synsets marked-up with contradictory scores and the authors and 6 MSc students negotiated the scores towards reaching the consensus. For 142 of these synsets the consensus was easily reached with 76 considered to be correct in the DSA annotation and 65 correct in the SWN3.0 annotation. Table 4 shows some examples of synsets, the scores of which were correctly judged (in bold) either by SWN3.0 or DSA as well as some examples of non-consensual annotations (in underlined italics).

7 Conclusions

Differential semantics annotation addresses the connotative meanings of the lexical stock, the denotative meanings of which are recorded in WordNet 3.0. We revised and improved our previous method (Tufiş and Ştefănescu, 2010). It generalizes the SWN3.0 subjectivity mark-up, according to a user-based multi-criteria differential semantics model.

The partial comparison with SWN3.0 revealed specific limitations of our approach. The major one is due to the definitions of n-relatedness and the TRI relation. The problem resides in indiscriminate treatment of literals which have senses with different polarities with respect to a factor. If one of these senses is significantly closer to one of the poles of the factor, that sense might impose the sign for the rest of the senses. This risk is amplified when literals with high degrees of polysemy and/or high degrees of synonymy are reached on the way from the synset of interest to the synsets defining the S-factor (higher the polysemy/synonymy, higher the number of paths to the constituents of the S-factor). Most of the erroneous scores we noticed were explained by this drawback. We say that the words affected by this limitation of the current algorithm have a significant *connotation shift* potential (Tufiş, 2009), (Ştefănescu, 2010). As such words could generate undesired implicatures, they should be avoided in formal texts and replaced by synonyms with less connotation shift potential.

We also observed some inconsistencies regarding the association of SUMO/MILO (and the additional domain ontologies) concepts to PWN 3.0 synsets. The semantic types of two opposable synsets (in the same semantic field) should be closely related, if not the same. However, for some S-factors, such as <agreement:3, disagreement:1> this does not happen. The semantic type of the synset {agreement:3…} is "Cooperation", while the semantic type of {disagreement:1…} is "SubjectiveAssessmentAttribute". "Cooperation" is a "Process" (subsumed by "Physical") but, "SubjectiveAssessmentAttribute" is an "Attribute" (subsumed by "Abstract"). There are 9 such cases for nouns, 30 for verbs and 16 for adjectives.

The current multi-factored annotation vectors for nominal, verbal, and adjectival synsets for PWN3.0, as well as an application to manage these annotations, can be freely downloaded from http://www.racai.ro/differentialsemantics/.

Acknowledgments

This research has been supported by the grant no. ID_1443, awarded by the Romanian Ministry for Education, Research, Youth and Sport. We thank also to SentiWordNet authors for making it public.

References

Andreevskaia Alina and Sabine Bergler. 2006. Mining WordNet for a fuzzy sentiment: Sentiment tag extraction from WordNet glosses. In Proceedings of the 11th Conference of the European Chapter of the Association for Computational Linguistics (EACL-2006), Trento, Italy, pages 209–216.

Stefano Baccianella, Andrea Esuli, and Fabrizio Sebastiani. 2010. SENTIWORDNET 3.0: An Enhanced Lexical Resource for Sentiment Analysis and Opinion Mining, in Proceedings of LREC2010, Malta, pp.2200-2204.

Luisa Bentivogli, Pamela Forner, Bernardo Magnini, and Emanuele Pianta. 2004. Revising WordNet domains hierarchy: Semantics, coverage, and balancing. In Proceedings of COLING 2004 Workshop on "Multilingual Linguistic Resources", Geneva, Switzerland, pages 101–108.

Andrea Esuli, and Fabrizio Sebastiani. 2006. SENTIWORDNET: A publicly available lexical resource for opinion mining. In Proceedings of the 5th Conference on Language Resources and Evaluation LREC-06, Genoa, Italy, pages 417–422. See also: http://sentiwordnet.isti.cnr.it/

Christiane Fellbaum. 1998. WordNet: An Electronic Lexical Database. Academic Press, Cambridge, MA.

Jaap Kamps and Maarten Marx. 2002. Words with attitude. In Proceedings of the 1st International WordNet Conference, Mysore, India, pages 332–341.

Rada Mihalcea, Carmen Banea, and Janice Wiebe. 2007. Learning multilingual subjective language via cross-lingual projections. In Proceedings of the 45th Annual Meeting of the Association of Computational Linguistics, Prague, Czech Republic, pages 976–983.

Ian Niles and Adam Pease. 2003. Linking Lexicons and Ontologies: Mapping WordNet to the Suggested Upper Merged Ontology. In Proceedings of the 2003 International Conference on Information and Knowledge Engineering (IKE 03), Las Vegas, pages 23–26.

Charles E. Osgood, George Suci and Percy Tannenbaum. 1957. The measurement of meaning, University of Illinois Press, Urbana IL.

Bo Pang and Lillian Lee, 2008. Opinion mining and sentiment analysis. Foundations and Trends in Information Retrieval, 2(1–2): 1–135.

Livia Polanyi, and Annie Zaenen. 2006. Contextual valence shifters. In J. G. Shanahan, Y. Qu and J. Wiebe, editors, Computing Attitude and Affect in Text: Theory and Applications, The Information Retrieval Series, Vol. 20, Springer Verlag, Dordrecht, Netherlands, pages 1-10.

Dan Ştefănescu. 2010. Intelligent Information Mining from Multilingual Corpora (in Romanian). PhD Thesis, Romanian Academy, Bucharest.

Dan Tufiş. 2008. Mind your words! You might convey what you wouldn't like to. Int. J. of Computers, Communications & Control, III, pages 139–143.

Dan Tufiş. 2009. Playing with word meanings,.In Lotfi A. Zadeh, Dan Tufiş, Florin Gh. Filip and Ioan Dziţac, (editors) From Natural Language to Soft Computing: New Paradigms in Artificial Intelligence. Publishing House of the Romanian Academy, Bucharest, pages 211–223.

Dan Tufiş, Dan Ştefănescu. 2010. A Differential Semantics Approach to the Annotation of the Synsets in WordNet. In Proceedings of LREC 2010, Malta, pages 3173-3180

Alessandro Valitutti, Carlo Strapparava, and Oliviero Stock. 2004. Developing affective lexical resources, Psychology Journal, 2(1), pages 61–83.

Creating Sentiment Dictionaries via Triangulation

Josef Steinberger,
Polina Lenkova, Mohamed Ebrahim,
Maud Ehrmann, Ali Hurriyetoglu,
Mijail Kabadjov, Ralf Steinberger,
Hristo Tanev and **Vanni Zavarella**
EC Joint Research Centre
21027, Ispra (VA), Italy
Name.Surname@jrc.ec.europa.eu

Silvia Vázquez
Universitat Pompeu Fabra
Roc Boronat, 138
08018 Barcelona
silvia.vazquez@upf.edu

Abstract

The paper presents a semi-automatic approach to creating sentiment dictionaries in many languages. We first produced high-level gold-standard sentiment dictionaries for two languages and then translated them automatically into third languages. Those words that can be found in both target language word lists are likely to be useful because their word senses are likely to be similar to that of the two source languages. These dictionaries can be further corrected, extended and improved. In this paper, we present results that verify our triangulation hypothesis, by evaluating triangulated lists and comparing them to non-triangulated machine-translated word lists.

1 Introduction

When developing software applications for sentiment analysis or opinion mining, there are basically two main options: (1) writing rules that assign sentiment values to text or text parts (e.g. names, products, product features), typically making use of dictionaries consisting of sentiment words and their positive or negative values, and (2) inferring rules (and sentiment dictionaries), e.g. using machine learning techniques, from previously annotated documents such as product reviews annotated with an overall judgment of the product. While movie or product reviews for many languages can frequently be found online, sentiment-annotated data for other fields are not usually available, or they are almost exclusively available for English. Sentiment dictionaries are also mostly available for English only or, if they exist for other languages, they are not comparable, in the sense that they have been developed for different purposes, have different sizes, are based on different definitions of what sentiment or opinion means.

In this paper, we are addressing the resource bottleneck for sentiment dictionaries, by developing highly multilingual and comparable sentiment dictionaries having similar sizes and based on a common specification. The aim is to develop such dictionaries, consisting of typically one or two thousand words, for tens of languages, although in this paper we only present results for eight languages (English, Spanish, Arabic, Czech, French, German, Italian and Russian). The task raises the obvious question how the human effort of producing this resource can be minimized. Simple translation, be it using standard dictionaries or using machine translation, is not very efficient as most words have two, five or ten different possible translations, depending on context, part-of-speech, etc.

The approach we therefore chose is that of triangulation. We first produced high-level gold-standard sentiment dictionaries for two languages (English and Spanish) and then translated them automatically into third languages, e.g. French. Those words that can be found in both target language word lists (En Fr and Es Fr) are likely to be useful because their word senses are likely to be similar to that of the two source languages. These word lists can then be used as they are or better they can be corrected, extended and improved. In this paper, we present evaluation results verifying our triangulation hypothesis, by evaluating triangulated lists and comparing them

Proceedings of the 2nd Workshop on Computational Approaches to Subjectivity and Sentiment Analysis, ACL-HLT 2011, pages 28–36,
24 June, 2011, Portland, Oregon, USA ©2011 Association for Computational Linguistics

to non-triangulated machine-translated word lists.

Two further issues need to be addressed. The first one concerns morphological inflection. Automatic translation will yield one word form (often, but not always the base form), which is not sufficient when working with highly inflected languages: A single English adjective typically has four Spanish or Italian word forms (two each for gender and for number) and many Russian word forms (due to gender, number and case distinctions). The target language word lists thus need to be expanded to cover all these morphological variants with minimal effort and considering the number of different languages involved without using software, such as morphological analysers or generators. The second issue has to do with the subjectivity involved in the human annotation and evaluation effort. First of all, it is important that the task is well-defined (this is a challenge by itself) and, secondly, the inter-annotator agreement for pairs of human evaluators working on different languages has to be checked in order to get an idea of the natural variation involved in such a highly subjective task.

Our main field of interest is news opinion mining. We would like to answer the question how certain entities (persons, organisations, event names, programmes) are discussed in different media over time, comparing different media sources, media in different countries, and media written in different languages. One possible end product would be a graph showing how the popularity of a certain entity has changed over time across different languages and countries. News differs significantly from those text types that are typically analysed in opinion mining work, i.e. product or movie reviews: While a product review is about a product (e.g. a printer) and its features (e.g. speed, price or printing quality), the news is about any possible subject (news content), which can by itself be perceived to be positive or negative. Entities mentioned in the news can have many different roles in the events described. If the method does not specifically separate positive or negative news content from positive or negative opinion about that entity, the sentiment analysis results will be strongly influenced by the news context. For instance, the automatically identified sentiment towards a politician would most likely to be low if the politician is mentioned in the context of negative news content such as bombings or disasters. In our approach, we therefore aim to distinguish news content from sentiment values, and this distinction has an impact on the sentiment dictionaries: unlike in other approaches, words like death, killing, award or winner are purposefully not included in the sentiment dictionaries as they typically represent news content.

The rest of the paper is structured as follows: the next section (2) describes related work, especially in the context of creating sentiment resources. Section 3 gives an overview of our approach to dictionary creation, ranging from the automatic learning of the sentiment vocabulary, the triangulation process, the expansion of the dictionaries in size and regarding morphological inflections. Section 4 presents a number of results regarding dictionary creation using simple translation versus triangulation, morphological expansion and inter-annotator agreement. Section 5 summarises, concludes and points to future work.

2 Related Work

Most of the work in obtaining subjectivity lexicons was done for English. However, there were some authors who developed methods for the mapping of subjectivity lexicons to other languages. Kim and Hovy (2006) use a machine translation system and subsequently use a subjectivity analysis system that was developed for English. Mihalcea et al. (2007) propose a method to learn multilingual subjective language via cross-language projections. They use the Opinion Finder lexicon (Wilson et al., 2005) and two bilingual English-Romanian dictionaries to translate the words in the lexicon. Since word ambiguity can appear (Opinion Finder does not mark word senses), they filter as correct translations only the most frequent words. The problem of translating multi-word expressions is solved by translating word-by-word and filtering those translations that occur at least three times on the Web. Another approach in obtaining subjectivity lexicons for other languages than English was explored in Banea et al. (2008b). To this aim, the authors perform three different experiments, with good results. In the first one, they automatically translate the annotations of the MPQA corpus and thus obtain subjectivity annotated sentences in Romanian. In the second approach, they use the automatically translated entries in the Opinion Finder lexicon to annotate a set of sentences in Romanian. In the last experiment, they reverse the direction of translation and verify the assumption that subjective language can be translated and thus new subjectivity lexicons can be obtained for languages with no such resources. Finally, another approach to building lexicons for languages with scarce resources is presented in Banea et al. (2008a). In this research, the authors apply bootstrapping to build a subjectivity lexicon for Romanian, starting with a set of seed subjective entries, using electronic bilingual dictionaries and a training set of words. They start with a set of 60 words pertaining to the categories of noun, verb, adjective and adverb obtained by translating words in the Opinion Finder lexicon. Translations are filtered using a measure of similarity to the original words, based on Latent Semantic Analysis (Landauer and Dumais, 1997) scores. Wan (2008) uses co-training to classify un-annotated Chinese reviews using a corpus of annotated English reviews. He first translates the English reviews into Chinese and subsequently back to English. He then performs co-training using all generated corpora. Banea et al. (2010) translate the MPQA corpus into five other languages (some with a similar ethimology, others with a very different structure). Subsequently, they expand the feature space used in a Naive Bayes classifier using the same data translated to 2 or 3 other languages. Their conclusion is that expanding the feature space with data from other languages performs almost as well as training a classifier for just one language on a large set of training data.

3 Approach Overview

Our approach to dictionary creation starts with semi-automatic way of colleting subjective terms in English and Spanish. These pivot language dictionaries are then projected to other languages. The 3rd language dictionaries are formed by the overlap of the translations (triangulation). The lists are then manually filtered and expanded, either by other relevant terms or by their morphological variants, to gain a wider coverage.

3.1 Gathering Subjective Terms

We started with analysing the available English dictionaries of subjective terms: General Inquirer (Stone et al., 1966), WordNet Affect (Strapparava and Valitutti, 2004), SentiWordNet (Esuli and Sebastiani, 2006), MicroWNOp (Cerini et al., 2007). Additionally, we used the resource of opinion words with associated polarity from Balahur et al. (2009), which we denote as JRC Tonality Dictionary. The positive effect of distinguishing two levels of intensity was shown in (Balahur et al., 2010). We followed the idea and each of the emloyed resources was mapped to four categories: positive, negative, highly positive and highly negative. We also got inspired by the results reported in that paper and we selected as the base dictionaries the combination of MicroWNOp and JRC Tonality Dictionary which gave the best results. Terms in those two dictionaries were manually filtered and the other dictionaries were used as lists of candidates (their highly frequent terms were judged and the relevant ones were included in the final English dictionary). Keeping in mind the application of the dictionaries we removed at this step terms that are more likely to describe bad or good news content, rather than a sentiment towards an entity. In addition, we manually collected English diminishers (e.g. *less* or *approximately*), intensifiers (e.g. *very* or *indeed*) and invertors (e.g. *not* or *barely*). The English terms were translated to Spanish and the same filtering was performed. We extended all English and Spanish lists with the missing morphological variants of the terms.

3.2 Automatic Learning of Subjective Terms

We decided to expand our subjective term lists by using automatic term extraction, inspired by (Riloff and Wiebe, 2003). We look at the problem of acquisition of subjective terms as learning of semantic classes. Since we wanted to do this for two different languages, namely English and Spanish, the multilingual term extraction algorithm Ontopopulis (Tanev et al., 2010) was a natural choice.

Ontopopulis performs weakly supervised learning of semantic dictionaries using distributional similarity. The algorithm takes on its input a small set of seed terms for each semantic class, which is to be learnt, and an unannotated text corpus. For example, if we want to learn the semantic class *land_vehicles*, we can use the seed set - *bus*, *truck*, and *car*. Then it searches for the terms in the corpus and finds linear context patterns, which tend to co-occur immediately before or after these terms. Some of the highest-scored patterns, which Ontopopulis learned about *land_vehicles* were *driver of the X*, *X was parked*, *collided with another X*, etc. Finally, the algorithm searches for these context patterns in the corpus and finds other terms which tend to fill the slot of the patterns (designated by X). Considering the *land_vehicles* example, new terms which the system learned were *van*, *lorry*, *taxi*, etc. Ontopopulis is similar to the NOMEN algorithm (Lin et al., 2003). However, Ontopopulis has the advantage to be language-independent, since it does not use any form of language-specific processing, nor does it use any language-specific resources, apart from a stop word list.

In order to learn new subjective terms for each of the languages, we passed the collected subjective terms as an input to Ontopopulis. For English, we divided the seed set in two classes: class A – verbs and class B – nouns and adjectives. It was necessary because each of these classes has a different syntactic behaviour. It made sense to do the same for Spanish, but we did not have enough Spanish speakers available to undertake this task, therefore we put together all the subjective Spanish words - verbs, adjectives and nouns in one class. We ran Ontopopulis for each of the three classes - the class of subjective Spanish words and the English classes A and B. The top scored 200 new learnt terms were taken for each class and manually reviewed.

3.3 Triangulation and Expansion

After polishing the pivot language dictionaries we projected them to other languages. The dictionaries were translated by Google translator because of its broad coverage of languages. The overlapping terms between English and Spanish translations formed the basis for further manual efforts. In some cases there were overlapping terms in English and Spanish translations but they differed in intensity. There was the same term translated from an English positive term and from a Spanish very positive term. In these cases the term was assigned to the positive category. However, more problematic cases arose when the same 3rd language term was assigned to more than one category. There were also cases with different polarity. We had to review them manually. However, there were still lots of relevant terms in the translated lists which were not translated from the other language. These *complement* terms are a good basis for extending the coverage of the dictionaries, however, they need to be reviewed manually. Even if we tried to include in the pivot lists all morphological variants, in the triangulation output there were only a few variants, mainly in the case of highly inflected languages. To deal with morphology we introduced wild cards at the end of the term stem (* stands for whatever ending and _ for whatever character). This step had to be performed carefully because some noise could be introduced. See the Results section for examples. Although this step was performed by a human, we checked the most frequent terms afterwards to avoid irrelavant frequent terms.

4 Results

4.1 Pivot dictionaries

We gathered and filtered English sentiment terms from the available corpora (see Section 3.1). The dictionaries were then translated to Spanish (by Google translator) and filtered afterwards. By applying automatic term extraction, we enriched the sets of terms by 54 for English and 85 for Spanish, after evaluating the top 200 candidates suggested by the Ontopolulis tool for each language. The results are encouraging, despite the relevance of the terms (27% for English and 42.5% for Spanish where some missing morphological variants were discovered) does not seem to be very high, considering the fact that we excluded the terms already contained in the pivot lists. If we took them into account, the precision would be much better. The initial step resulted in obtaining high quality pivot sentiment dictionaries for English and Spanish. Their statistics are in table 1. We gathered more English terms than Spanish (2.4k compared to 1.7k). The reason for that is that some translations from English to Spanish have been filtered. Another observation is that there is approximately the same number of negative terms as positive ones, however, much more highly negative than highly positive terms. Although the

Language	English	Spanish
HN	554	466
N	782	550
P	772	503
HP	171	119
INT	78	62
DIM	31	27
INV	15	10
TOTAL	2.403	1.737

Table 1: The size of the pilot dictionaries. HN=highly negative terms, N=negative, P=positive, HP=highly positive, INV=invertors, DIM=diminishers, INV=invertors.

frequency analysis we carried out later showed that even if there are fewer highly positive terms, they are more frequent than the highly negative ones, which results in almost uniform distribution.

4.2 Triangulation and Expansion

After running triangulation to other languages the resulted terms were judged for relevance. Native speakers could suggest to change term's category (e.g. negative to highly negative) or to remove it. There were several reasons why the terms could have been marked as 'non-sentiment'. For instance, the term could tend to describe rather negative news content than negative sentiment towards an entity (e.g. *dead*, *quake*). In other cases the terms were too ambiguous in a particular language. Examples from English are: *like* or *right*.

Table 2 shows the quality of the triangulated dictionaries. In all cases except for Italian we had only one annotator assessing the quality. We can see that the terms were correct in around 90% cases, however, it was a little bit worse in the case of Russian in which the annotator suggested to change category very often.

Terms translated from English but not from Spanish are less reliable but, if reviewed manually, the dictionaries can be expanded significantly. Table 3 gives the statistics concerning these judgments. We can see that their correctness is much lower than in the case of the triangulated terms - the best in Italian (54.4%) and the worst in Czech (30.7%). Of course, the translation performance affects the results here. However, this step extended the dictionaries by approximately 50%.

When considering terms out of context, the most common translation error occurs when the original word has several meanings. For instance, the English word *nobility* refers to the social class of nobles, as well as to the quality of being morally good. In the news context we find this word mostly in the second meaning. However, in the Russian triangulated list we have found *dvoryanstvo* , which refers to a social class in Russian. Likewise, we need to keep in mind that a translation of a monosemantic word might result polysemantic in the target language, thereby leading to confusion. For example, the Italian translation of the English word *champion campione* is more frequently used in Italian news context in a different meaning - *sample*, therefore we must delete it from our sentiment words list for Italian. Another difficulty we might encounter especially when dealing with inflectional languages is the fact that a translation of a certain word might be homographic with another word form in the target language. Consider the English negative word *bandit* and its Italian translation *bandito*, which is more frequently used as a form of the verb *bandire* (*to announce*) in the news context. Also each annotator had different point of view on classifying the borderline cases (e.g. *support*, *agreement* or *difficult*).

Two main reasons are offered to explain the low performance in Arabic. On the one hand, it seems that some Google translation errors will be repeated in different languages if the translated words have the same etymological root. For example both words – the English *fresh* and the Spanish *fresca* – are translated to the Arabic as جديد meaning *new*. The Other reason is a more subtle one and is related to the fact that Arabic words are not vocalized and to the way an annotator perceive the meaning of a given word in isolation. To illustrate this point, consider the Arabic word المناسبة, which could be used as an adjective, meaning *appropriate*, or as a noun, meaning *The occasion*. It appears that the annotator would intuitively perceive the word in isolation as a noun and not as an adjective, which leads to disregarding the evaluative aspects of a given word.

We tried to include in the pivot dictionaries all morphological variants of the terms. However, in highly inflected languages there are much more variants than those translated from English or Spanish.

We manually introduced wild cards to capture the variants. We had to be attentive when compiling wild cards for languages with a rich inflectional system, as we might easily get undesirable words in the output. To illustrate this, consider the third person plural of the Italian negative word *perdere* (*to lose*) *perdono*, which is also homographic with the word meaning *forgiveness* in English. Naturally, it could happen that the wildcard captures a non-sentiment term or even a term with a different polarity. For instance, the pattern *care%* would capture either *care*, *careful*, *carefully*, but also *career* or *careless*. That is way we perform the last manual checking after matching the lists expanded by wildcards against a large number of texts. The annotators were unable to check all the variants, but only the most frequent terms, which resulted in reviewing 70-80% of the term mentions. This step has been performed for only English, Czech and Russian so far. Table 5 gives the statistics. By introducing the wildcards, the number of distinct terms grew up significantly - 12x for Czech, 15x for Russian and 4x for English. One reason why it went up also for English is that we captured compounds like: *well-arranged*, *well-balanced*, *well-behaved*, *well-chosen* by a single pattern. Another reason is that a single pattern can capture different POSs: *beaut%* can capture *beauty*, *beautiful*, *beautifully* or *beautify*. Not all of those words were present in the pivot dictionaries. For dangerous cases like *care%* above we had to rather list all possible variants than using a wildcard. This is also the reason why the number of patterns is not much lower than the number of initial terms. Even if this task was done manually, some noise was added into the dictionaries (92-94% of checked terms were correct). For example, highly positive pattern *hero%* was introduced by an annotator for capturing *hero*, *heroes*, *heroic*, *heroical* or *heroism*. If not checked afterwards *heroin* would score highly positively in the sentiment system. Another example is taken from Russian: word meaning *to steal ukra%* - might generate *Ukraine* as one most frequent negative word in Russian.

4.3 How subjective is the annotation?

Sentiment annotation is a very subjective task. In addition, annotators had to judge single terms without any context: they had to think about all the senses of the term. Only if the main sense was subjective they agreed to leave it in the dictionary. Another subjectivity level was given by concentrating on distinguishing news content and news sentiment. Defining the line between negative and highly negative terms, and similarly with positive, is also subjective. In the case of Italian we compared judgments of two annotators. The figures of inter-annotator agreement of annotating the triangulated terms are in table 6 and the complement terms in table 7. Based on the percent agreement the annotators agree a little bit less on the triangulated terms (76.6%) compared to the complement terms (82.6%). However, if we look at Kappa figures, the difference is clear. Many terms translated only from English were clearly wrong which led to a higher agreement between the annotators (0.318 compared to 0.614). When looking at the difference between positive and negative terms, we can see that there was higher agreement on the negative triangulated terms then on the positive ones.

Metric	Percent Agreement	Kappa
HN	0.909	0.465
N	0.796	0.368
P	0.714	0.281
HP	0.846	0
N+HN	0.829	0.396
P+HP	0.728	0.280
ALL	0.766	0.318

Table 6: Inter-annotator agreement on checking the triangulated list. In the case of HP all terms were annotated as correct by one of the annotators resulting in Kappa=0.

Metric	Percent Agreement	Kappa
HN	0.804	0.523
N	0.765	0.545
P	0.686	0.405
HP	0.855	0.669
N+HN	0.784	0.553
P+HP	0.783	0.559
ALL	0.826	0.614

Table 7: Inter-annotator agreement on checking the candidates. In ALL diminishers, intensifiers and invertors are included as well.

Language	Triangulated	Correct	Removed	Changed category
Arabic	926	606 (65.5%)	316 (34.1%)	4 (0.4%)
Czech	908	809 (89.1%)	68 (7.5%)	31 (3.4%)
French	1.085	956 (88.1%)	120 (11.1%)	9 (0.8%)
German	1.053	982 (93.3%)	50 (4.7%)	21 (2.0%)
Italian	1.032	918 (89.0%)	36 (3.5%)	78 (7.5%)
Russian	966	816 (84.5%)	49 (5.1%)	101 (10.4%)

Table 2: The size and quality of the triangulated dictionaries. Triangulated=No. of terms coming directly from triangulation, Correct=terms annotated as correct, Removed=terms not relevant to sentiment analysis, Change category=terms in wrong category (e.g., positive from triangulation, but annotator changed the category to highly positive).

Language	Terms	Correct	Removed	Changed category
Czech	1.092	335 (30.7%)	675 (61.8%)	82 (7.5%)
French	1.226	617 (50.3%)	568 (46.3%)	41 (3.4%)
German	1.182	548 (46.4%)	610 (51.6%)	24 (2.0%)
Italian	1.069	582 (54.4%)	388 (36.3%)	99 (9.3%)
Russian	1.126	572 (50.8%)	457 (40.6%)	97 (8.6%)

Table 3: The size and quality of the candidate terms (translated from English but not from Spanish). Terms=No. of terms translated from English but not from Spanish, Correct=terms annotated as correct, Removed=terms not relevant to sentiment analysis, Change category=terms in wrong category (e.g., positive in the original list, but annotator changed the category to highly positive).

Language	Terms	Correct	Removed	Changed category
Czech	2.000	1.144 (57.2%)	743 (37.2%)	113 (5.6%)
French	2.311	1.573 (68.1%)	688 (29.8%)	50 (2.1%)
German	2.235	1.530 (68.5%)	660 (29.5%)	45 (2.0%)
Italian	2.101	1.500 (71.4%)	424 (20.2%)	177 (8.4%)
Russian	2.092	1.388 (66.3%)	506 (24.2%)	198 (9.5%)

Table 4: The size and quality of the translated terms from English. Terms=No. of (distinct) terms translated from English, Correct=terms annotated as correct, Removed=terms not relevant to sentiment analysis, Change category=terms in wrong category (e.g., positive in the original list, but annotator changed the category to highly positive).

Language	Initial terms	Patterns	Matched terms		
			Count	Correct	Checked
Czech	1.257	1.063	15.604	93.0%	74.4%
English	2.403	2.081	10.558	93.8%	81.1%
Russian	1.586	1.347	33.183	92.2%	71.0%

Table 5: Statistics of introducing wild cards and its evaluation. Initial terms=checked triangulated terms extended by relevant translated terms from English, Patterns=number of patterns after introducing wildcards, Matched terms=terms matched in the large corpus - their count and correctness + checked=how many mentions were checked (based on the fact that the most frequent terms were annotated).

4.4 Triangulation vs. Translation

Table 4 present the results of simple translation from English (summed up numbers from tables 2 and 3). We can directly compare it to table 2 where only results of triangulated terms are reported. The performance of triangulation is significantly better than the performance of translation in all languages. The highest difference was in Czech (89.1% and 57.2%) and the lowest was in Italian (89.0% and 71.4%).

As a task-based evaluation we used the triangulated/translated dictionaries in the system analysing news sentiment expressed towards entities. The system analyses a fixed word window around entity mentions. Subjective terms are summed up and the resulting polarity is attached to the entity. Highly negative terms score twice more than negative, diminishers lower and intensifiers lift up the score. Invertors invert the polarity but for instance inverted highly positive terms score as only negative preventing, for instance, *not great* to score as *worst*. The system searches for the invertor only two words around the subjective term.

We ran the system on 300 German sentences taken from news gathered by the Europe Media Monitor (EMM)[1]. In all these cases the system attached a polarity to an entity mention. We ran it with three different dictionaries - translated terms from English, raw triangulated terms (without the manual checking) and the checked triangulated terms. This pilot experiment revealed the difference in performance on this task. When translated terms were used there were only 41.6% contexts with correct polarity assigned by the system, with raw triangulated terms 56.5%, and with checked triangulated terms 63.4%. However, the number does not contain neutral cases that would increase the overall performance. There are lots of reasons why it goes wrong here: the entity may not be the target of the subjective term (we do not use parser because of dealing with many languages and large amounts of news texts), the system can miss or apply wrongly an invertor, the subjective term is used in different sense, and irony is hard to detect.

[1] http://emm.newsbrief.eu/overview.html

4.5 State of progress

We finished all the steps for English, Czech and Russian. French, German, Italian and Spanish dictionaries miss only the introduction of wild cards. In Arabic we have checked only the triangulated terms. For other 7 languages (Bulgarian, Dutch, Hungarian, Polish, Portuguese, Slovak and Turkish) we have only projected the terms by triangulation. However, we have capabilities to finish all the steps also for Bulgarian, Dutch, Slovak and Turkish. We haven't investigated using more than two pivot languages for triangulation. It would probably results in more accurate but shortened dictionaires.

5 Conclusions

We presented our semi-automatic approach and current state of work of producing multilingual sentiment dictionaries suitable of assessing the sentiment in news expressed towards an entity. The triangulation approach works significantly better than simple translation but additional manual effort can improve it a lot in both recall and precision. We believe that we can predict the sentiment expressed towards an entity in a given time period based on large amounts of data we gather in many languages even if the per-case performance of the sentiment system as on a moderate level. Now we are working on improving the dictionaries in all the discussed languages. We also run experiments to evaluate the system on various languages.

Acknowledgments

We thank Alexandra Balahur for her collaboration and useful comments. This research was partly supported by a IULA-Universitat Pompeu Fabra grant.

References

Alexandra Balahur, Ralf Steinberger, Erik van der Goot, and Bruno Pouliquen. 2009. Opinion mining from newspaper quotations. In *Proceedings of the Workshop on Intelligent Analysis and Processing of Web News Content at the IEEE / WIC / ACM International Conferences on Web Intelligence and Intelligent Agent Technology (WI-IAT)*.

A. Balahur, R. Steinberger, M. Kabadjov, V. Zavarella, E. van der Goot, M. Halkia, B. Pouliquen, and J. Belyaeva. 2010. Sentiment analysis in the news. In *Proceedings of LREC'10*.

C. Banea, R. Mihalcea, and J. Wiebe. 2008a. A bootstrapping method for building subjectivity lexicons for languages with scarce resources. In *Proceedings of LREC*.

C. Banea, R. Mihalcea, J. Wiebe, and S. Hassan. 2008b. Multilingual subjectivity analysis using machine translation. In *Proceedings of EMNLP*.

C. Banea, R. Mihalcea, and J. Wiebe. 2010. Multilingual subjectivity: Are more languages better? In *Proceedings of COLING*.

S. Cerini, V. Compagnoni, A. Demontis, M. Formentelli, and G. Gandini. 2007. Micro-WNOp: A gold standard for the evaluation of automatically compiled lexical resources for opinion mining. In Andrea Sansò, editor, *Language resources and linguistic theory: Typology, second language acquisition, English linguistics*. Franco Angeli, Milano, IT.

A. Esuli and F. Sebastiani. 2006. SentiWordNet: A publicly available resource for opinion mining. In *Proceeding of the 6th International Conference on Language Resources and Evaluation*, Italy, May.

S.-M. Kim and E. Hovy. 2006. Extracting opinions, opinion holders, and topics expressed in online news media text. In *Proceedings of the ACL Workshop on Sentiment and Subjectivity in Text*.

T. Landauer and S. Dumais. 1997. A solution to plato's problem: The latent semantic analysis theory of the acquisition, induction, and representation of knowledge. *Psychological Review*, 104:211–240.

W. Lin, R. Yangarber, and R. Grishman. 2003. Bootstrapped learning of semantic classes from positive and negative examples. In *Proceedings of the ICML-2003 Workshop on The Continuum from Labeled to Unlabeled Data, Washington DC*.

R. Mihalcea, C. Banea, and J. Wiebe. 2007. Learning multilingual subjective language via cross-lingual projections. In *Proceedings of ACL*.

E. Riloff and J. Wiebe. 2003. Learning extraction patterns for subjective expressions. In *Proceeding of the Conference on Empirical Methods in Natural Language Processing*.

P.J. Stone, D.C. Dumphy, M.S. Smith, and D.M. Ogilvie. 1966. The general inquirer: a computer approach to content analysis. *M.I.T. studies in comparative politics, M.I.T. Press, Cambridge, MA*.

C. Strapparava and A. Valitutti. 2004. WordNet-Affect: an affective extension of wordnet. In *Proceeding of the 4th International Conference on Language Resources and Evaluation*, pages 1083–1086, Lisbon, Portugal, May.

H. Tanev, V. Zavarella, J. Linge, M. Kabadjov, J. Piskorski, M. Atkinson, and R.Steinberger. 2010. Exploiting machine learning techniques to build an event extraction system for portuguese and spanish. *Linguamatica: Revista para o Processamento Automatico das Linguas Ibericas*.

X. Wan. 2008. Co-training for cross-lingual sentiment classification. In *Proceedings of the Joint Conference of the 47th Annual Meeting of the Association for Computational Linguistics and 4th International Joint Conference on Natural Language Processing of the Asian Federation of Natural Language Processing*.

T. Wilson, J. Wiebe, and P. Hoffman. 2005. Recognizing contextual polarity in phrase-level sentiment analysis. In *Proceedings of HLT-EMNLP*.

Generating Semantic Orientation Lexicon using Large Data and Thesaurus

Amit Goyal and Hal Daumé III
Dept. of Computer Science
University of Maryland
College Park, MD 20742
{amit,hal}@umiacs.umd.edu

Abstract

We propose a novel method to construct semantic orientation lexicons using large data and a thesaurus. To deal with large data, we use Count-Min sketch to store the approximate counts of all word pairs in a bounded space of 8GB. We use a thesaurus (like Roget) to constrain near-synonymous words to have the same polarity. This framework can easily scale to any language with a thesaurus and a unzipped corpus size $\geq$ 50 GB (12 billion tokens). We evaluate these lexicons intrinsically and extrinsically, and they perform comparable when compared to other existing lexicons.

1 Introduction

In recent years, the field of natural language processing (NLP) has seen tremendous growth and interest in the computational analysis of emotions, sentiments, and opinions. This work has focused on many application areas, such as sentiment analysis of consumer reviews e.g., (Pang et al., 2002; Nasukawa and Yi, 2003), product reputation analysis e.g., (Morinaga et al., 2002; Nasukawa and Yi, 2003), tracking sentiments toward events e.g., (Das and Chen, 2001; Tong, 2001), and automatically producing plot unit representations e.g., (Goyal et al., 2010b). An important resource in accomplishing the above tasks is a list of words with semantic orientation (SO): positive or negative. The goal of this work is to automatically create such a list of words using large data and a thesaurus structure.

For this purpose, we store exact counts of all the words in a hash table and use Count-Min (CM) sketch (Cormode and Muthukrishnan, 2004; Goyal et al., 2010) to store the approximate counts of all word pairs for a large corpus in a bounded space of 8GB. (Storing the counts of all word pairs is computationally expensive and memory intensive on large data (Agirre et al., 2009; Pantel et al., 2009)). Storage space saving in CM sketch is achieved by *approximating* the frequency of word pairs in the corpus without explicitly storing the word pairs themselves. Both updating (adding a new word pair or increasing the frequency of existing word pair) and querying (finding the frequency of a given word pair) are constant time operations making it an efficient online storage data structure for large data.

Once we have these counts, we find semantic orientation (SO) (Turney and Littman, 2003) of a word using its association strength with positive (e.g. good, and nice) and negative (e.g., bad and nasty) seeds. Next, we make use of a thesaurus (like Roget) structure in which near-synonymous words appear in a single group. We compute the SO of the whole group by computing SO of each individual word in the group and assign that SO to all the words in the group. The hypothesis is that near synonym words should have similar polarity. However, similar words in a group can still have different connotations. For example, one group has "slender", "slim", "wiry" and "lanky". One can argue that, first two words have positive connotation and last two have negative. To remove these ambiguous words errors from the lexicon, we discard those words which have conflicting SO compared to their group SO. The idea behind using thesaurus structure is motivated from the idea of using number of positive and negative seed words (Mohammad et al., 2009) in thesaurus group to determine the polarity of words in the group.

In our experiments, we show the effectiveness of the lexicons created using large data and freely avail-

Proceedings of the 2nd Workshop on Computational Approaches to Subjectivity and Sentiment Analysis, ACL-HLT 2011, pages 37–43,
24 June, 2011, Portland, Oregon, USA ©2011 Association for Computational Linguistics

able thesaurus both intrinsically and extrinsically.

2 Background

2.1 Related Work

The literature on sentiment lexicon induction can be broadly classified into three categories: (1) Corpora based, (2) using thesaurus structure, and (3) combination of (1) and (2). Pang and Lee (2008) provide an excellent survey on the literature of sentiment analysis. We briefly discuss some of the works which have motivated our research for this work. A web-derived lexicon (Velikovich et al., 2010) was constructed for all words and phrases using graph propagation algorithm which propagates polarity from seed words to all other words. The graph was constructed using distributional similarity between the words. The goal of their work was to create a high coverage lexicon. In a similar direction (Rao and Ravichandran, 2009), word-net was used to construct the graph for label propagation. Our work is most closely related to Mohammad et al. (2009) which exploits thesaurus structure to determine the polarity of words in the thesaurus group.

2.2 Semantic Orientation

We use (Turney and Littman, 2003) framework to infer the Semantic Orientation (SO) of a word. We take the seven positive words (good, nice, excellent, positive, fortunate, correct, and superior) and the seven negative words (bad, nasty, poor, negative, unfortunate, wrong, and inferior) used in (Turney and Littman, 2003) work. The SO of a given word is calculated based on the strength of its association with the seven positive words, and the strength of its association with the seven negative words using pointwise mutual information (PMI). We compute the SO of a word "w" as follows:

$$SO(w) = \sum_{p \in Pwords} PMI(p, w) - \sum_{n \in Nwords} PMI(n, w)$$

where, Pwords and Nwords denote the seven positive and seven negative prototype words respectively. If this score is negative, the word is predicted as negative. Otherwise, it is predicted as positive.

2.3 CM sketch

The Count-Min sketch (Cormode and Muthukrishnan, 2004) with user chosen parameters (ϵ,δ) is represented by a two-dimensional array with width w and depth d. Parameters ϵ and δ control the amount of tolerable error in the returned count (ϵ) and the probability with which the returned count is not within this acceptable error (δ) respectively. These parameters determine the width and depth of the two-dimensional array. We set $w{=}\frac{2}{\epsilon}$, and $d{=}\log(\frac{1}{\delta})$. The depth d denotes the number of pairwise-independent hash functions and there exists an one-to-one mapping between the rows and the set of hash functions. Each of these hash functions $h_k{:}\{x_1 \ldots x_N\} \rightarrow \{1 \ldots w\}, 1 \leq k \leq d$, takes an item from the input stream and maps it into a counter indexed by the corresponding hash function. For example, $h_3(x) = 8$ indicates that the item "x" is mapped to the 8th position in the third row of the sketch.

Update Procedure: When a new item "x" with count c, the sketch is updated by:

$$\text{sketch}[k,h_k(x)] \leftarrow \text{sketch}[k,h_k(x)] + c, \quad \forall 1 \leq k \leq d$$

Query Procedure: Since multiple items can be hashed to the same position, the stored frequency in any one row is guaranteed to *overestimate* the true count. Thus, to answer the point query, we return the minimum over all the positions indexed by the k hash functions. The answer to Query(x) is: $\hat{c} = \min_k \text{sketch}[k, h_k(x)]$.

2.4 CU sketch

The Count-Min sketch with conservative update (CU sketch) (Goyal et al., 2010) is similar to CM sketch except the update operation. It is based on the idea of conservative update (Estan and Varghese, 2002) introduced in the context of networking. It is used with CM sketch to further improve the estimate of a point query. To update an item, x with frequency c, we first compute the frequency $\hat{c}$ of this item from the existing data structure and the counts are updated according to:

$$\hat{c} = min_k \text{ sketch}[k,h_k(x)], \quad \forall 1 \leq k \leq d$$

$$\text{sketch}[k,h_k(x)] \leftarrow \max\{\text{sketch}[k,h_k(x)], \hat{c} + \text{c}\}$$

The intuition is that, since the point query returns the minimum of all the d values, we will update a counter only if it is necessary as indicated by the above equation.

3 Generating Polarity Lexicon

Our framework to generate lexicon has three main steps: First, we compute Semantic Orientation (SO) of words using a formula defined in Section 2.2 using a large corpus. Second, we use a thesaurus (like Roget) to constrain all synonym words in a group to have the same polarity. Third, we discard words which do not follow the above constraints. The three steps are discussed in the following subsections.

3.1 Computing SO of a word

We use CM sketch to store counts of word pairs (except word pairs involving stop words and numbers) within a sliding window of size[1] 7 using a large corpus: GWB66 of size 64GB (see Section 4.3). We fix the number of counters of the sketch to 2 billion ($2B$) (8GB of memory) with conservative update (CU) as it performs the best for (Goyal et al., 2010) with $d = 5$ (see Section 2.3) hash functions. We store exact counts of words in hash table.

Once, we have stored the counts for all words and word pairs, we can compute the SO of a word using a formula defined in Section 2.2. Moreover, a word can have multiple senses, hence it can belong to multiple paragraphs. To assign a single label to a word, we combine all its SO scores. We use positive SO scores to label words as positive and negative SO to label words as negative. We discard words with SO equal to zero. We apply this strategy to all the words in a thesaurus (like Roget) (refer to Section 3.2), we call the lexicon constructed using SO scores using thesaurus words as "SO" lexicon.

3.2 Using Thesaurus structure

Thesaurus like Roget[2], Macquarie are available in several languages. We use freely available version of Roget thesaurus which has 1046 categories, each containing on average 64 words and phrases. Terms within a category are closely related to one another, and they are further grouped into near-synonymous words and phrases called paragraphs. There are about 3117 paragraphs in Roget thesaurus. One of the examples of paragraphs from the Roget thesaurus is shown in Table 1. All the words appears to be near-synonymous with positive polarity.

[1]Window size 7 is chosen from intuition and not tuned.

[2]http://www.nzdl.org/ELKB/

pure undefiled modest delicate decent decorous cherry chaste continent virtuous honest platonic virgin unsullied simonpure

Table 1: A paragraph from the Roget thesaurus

We assign semantic orientation (SO) score to a thesaurus paragraph[3] ($SO(TP)$) by averaging over SO scores over all the words in it. The $SO(TP)$ score constrains all the words in a paragraph to have same polarity. If $SO(TP) > 0$, all the words in a paragraph are marked as positive. If $SO(TP) < 0$, all the words in a group are marked as negative. For $SO(TP) = 0$, we discard all the words of a paragraph. For the paragraph in Table 1, the $SO(TP)$ for the paragraph is 8.72. Therefore, all the words in this paragraph are labeled as positive. However, the SO scores for "virgin" and "decorous" are negative, therefore they are marked as negative by previous lexicon "SO", however they seem to be more positive than negative. Therefore, using the structure of the lexicon helps us in correcting the polarity of these words to negative. We apply this strategy to all the 3117 Roget thesaurus paragraphs and construct "SO-TP" lexicon using $SO(TP)$ scores.

3.3 Words and Thesaurus Consensus

Since near-synonymous words could have different connotation or polarity. Hence, here we use both SO of word and $SO(TP)$ of its paragraph to assign polarity to a word. If $SO(w) > 0$ and $SO(TP) > 0$, then we mark that word as positive. If $SO(w) < 0$ and $SO(TP) < 0$, then we mark that word as negative. In other cases, we discard the word.

We refer to the lexicon constructed using this strategy on Roget thesaurus paragraphs as "SO-WTP" lexicon. The motivation behind this is to generate precision orientated lexicon by having consensus over both individual and paragraph scores. For the paragraph in Table 1, we discard words "virgin" and "decorous" from the lexicon, as they have conflicting $SO(w)$ and $SO(TP)$ scores. In experiments in Section 5.2.1, we also examine existing lexicons to constrain the polarity of thesaurus paragraphs.

4 Evaluating SO computed using sketch

We compare the accuracy of computed SO using different sized corpora. We also compare exact counts with approximate counts using sketch.

[3]We do not assign polarity to phrases and stop words.

4.1 Data

We use Gigaword corpus (Graff, 2003) and a 66% portion of a copy of web crawled by (Ravichandran et al., 2005). For both the corpora, we split the text into sentences, tokenize and convert into lower-case. We generate words and word pairs over a sliding window of size 7. We use four different sized corpora: Gigaword (GW), GigaWord + 16% of web data (GWB16), GigaWord + 50% of web data (GWB50), and GigaWord + 66% of web data (GWB66). Corpus Statistics are shown in Table 2. We store exact counts of words in a hash table and store approximate counts of word pairs in the sketch.

4.2 Test Set

We use General Inquirer lexicon[4] (Stone et al., 1966) as a benchmark to evaluate the semantic orientation scores similar to (Turney and Littman, 2003) work. Our test set consists of 1597 positive and 1980 negative words. Accuracy is used as an evaluation metric.

Corpus	GW	GWB16	GWB50	GWB66
Unzipped Size (GB)	9.8	22.8	49	64
# of sentences (Million)	56.78	191.28	462.60	608.74
# of Tokens (Billion)	1.8	4.2	9.1	11.8
Stream Size (Billion)	2.67	6.05	13.20	17.31

Table 2: Corpus Description

4.3 Effect of Increasing Corpus Size

We evaluate SO of words on four different sized corpora (see Section 4.1): GW (9.8GB), GWB20 (22.8GB), GWB50 (49GB) and GWB66 (64GB). First, we will fix number of counters to 2 billion ($2B$) (CU-2B) as it performs the best for (Goyal et al., 2010). Second, we will compare the CU-2B model with the Exact over increasing corpus size.

We can make several observations from the Figure 1: • It shows that increasing the amount of data improves the accuracy of identifying the SO of a word. We get an absolute increase of 5.5 points in accuracy when we add 16% Web data to GigaWord (GW). Adding 34% more Web data (GWB50), gives a small increase of 1.3 points. Adding 16% more Web data (GWB66), give an increase of 0.5 points. • Second, CU-2B performs as good as Exact. • These results are also comparable to Turney's (2003) state-of-the-art work where they report an accuracy of 82.84%. Note, they use a 100 billion tokens corpus which is larger than GWB66 (12 billion tokens).

This experiments shows that using unzipped corpus size $\geq$ 50 GB (12 billion tokens), we get performance comparable to the state-of-the-art. Hence, this approach is applicable for any language which has large collection of monolingual data available in it. Note that these results compared to best results of (Goyal et al., 2010) that is 77.11 are 4.5 points better; however in their work their goal was to show their approach scales to large data. We suspect the difference in results is due to difference in pre-processing and choosing the window size. We used counts from GWB66 (64GB) to generate lexicons in Section 3.

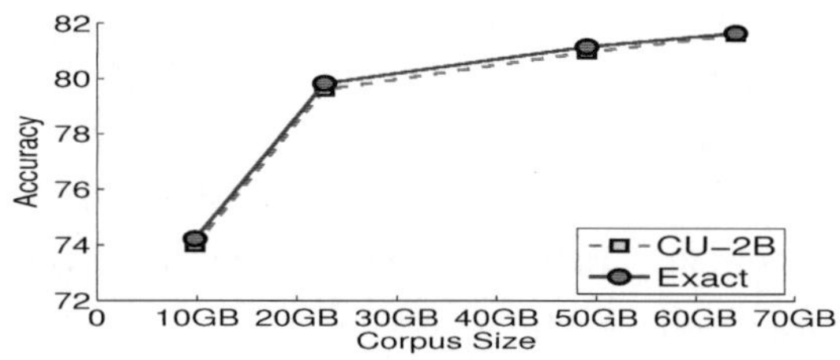

Figure 1: Evaluating Semantic Orientation of words with Exact and CU counts with increase in corpus size

5 Lexicon evaluation

We evaluate the lexicons proposed in Section 3 both intrinsically (by comparing their lexicon entries against General Inquirer (GI) lexicon) and extrinsically (by using them in a phrase polarity annotation task). We remove stop words and phrases for comparison from existing lexicons as our framework does not assign polarity to them.

5.1 Intrinsic evaluation

We compare the lexicon entries of "SO", "SO-TP" , and "SO-WTP" against entries of GI Lexicon. This evaluation is similarly used by other authors (Turney and Littman, 2003; Mohammad et al., 2009) to evaluate sentiment lexicons.

Table 3 shows the percentage of GI positive (Pos), negative (Neg) and all (All) lexicon entries that

[4]The General Inquirer lexicon which is freely available at `http://www.wjh.harvard.edu/~inquirer/`

Lexicon (size)	**Pos** (1597)	**Neg** (1980)	**All** (3577)
SO (32.2*K*)	0.79	**0.73**	**0.76**
SO-TP (33.1*K*)	**0.88**	0.64	0.75
SO-WTP (22.6*K*)	0.78	0.65	0.71
Roget-ASL (27.8*K*)	0.79	0.40	0.57

Table 3: The percentage of GI entries (positive, negative, and all) that match those of the automatically generated lexicons

match the proposed lexicons. The recall of our precision orientated lexicon SO-WTP is only 5 and 4 % less compared to SO and SO-TP respectively which are more recall oriented. We evaluate these lexicons against Roget-ASL (discussed in Section 5.2.1). Even, Our SO-WTP precision oriented lexicon has more recall than Roget-ASL.

5.2 Extrinsic evaluation

In this section, we compare the effectiveness of our lexicons on a task of phrase polarity identification. We use the MPQA corpus which contains news articles from a wide variety of news sources manually annotated for opinions and other private states (like beliefs, emotions, sentiments, speculations, etc.). Moreover, it has polarity annotations (positive/negative) at the phrase level. We use MPQA[5] version 2.0 collection of 2789 positive and 6079 negative phrases. We perform an extrinsic evaluation of our automatic generated lexicons (using large data and thesaurus) against existing automated and manually generated lexicons by using them to automatically determine the phrase polarity. This experimental setup is similar to Mohammad et al. (2009). However, in their work, they used MPQA version 1.0.

We use a similar algorithm as used by Mohammad et al. (2009) to determine the polarity of the phrase. If any of the words in the target phrase is labeled in the lexicon as having negative SO, then the phrase is marked as negative. If there are no negative words in the target phrase and it contains one or more positive words, then the phrase is marked as positive. In all other cases, do not assign any tag.

The only difference with respect to Mohammad et al. (2009) is that we use a list of 58 negation words used in OpinionFinder[6] (Wilson et al., 2005b) (Version 1.4) to flip the polarity of a phrase if it contains odd number of negation words. We can get better accuracies on phrase polarity identification using supervised classifiers (Wilson et al., 2005a). However, the goal of this work is only to show the effectiveness of large data and thesaurus learned lexicons.

Lexicon	**# of positives**	**# of negatives**	**# of all**
GI	1597	1980	3577
MPQA	2666	4888	7554
ASL	2320	2616	4936
Roget (ASL)	21637	6161	27798
Roget (GI)	10804	16319	27123
Roget (ASL+GI)	16168	12530	28698
MSOL	22088	32712	54800
SO	16620	15582	32202
SO-TP	22959	10117	33076
SO-WTP	14357	8257	22614
SO+GI	8629	9936	18565
SO-TP+GI	12049	9317	21366

Table 4: Summarizes all lexicons size

5.2.1 Baselines

We compare our method against the following baselines: First, MPQA Lexicon[7] ((Wilson et al., 2005a)). Second, we use Affix seed lexicon (ASL) seeds used by Mohammad et al. (2009) to assign labels to Roget thesaurus paragraphs. ASL was constructed using 11 affix patterns, e.g. honest-dishonest (X-disX pattern). If ASL matches more positive words than negative words in a paragraph then all the words in the paragraph are labeled as positive. However, if ASL matches more negative words than positive words in a paragraph, then all words in the paragraph are labeled as negative. For other cases, we do not assign any labels. The generated lexicon is referred as Roget (ASL). Third, we use GI Lexicon instead of ASL and generate Roget (GI) Lexicon. Fourth, we use ASL + GI, and generate Roget (ASL+GI) Lexicon. Fifth, MSOL[8] generated by Mohammad et al. (2009) using ASL+GI lexicon on Macquarie Thesaurus. Note that Macquarie Thesaurus is not freely available and its size is larger than the freely available Roget's thesaurus.

5.2.2 GI seeds information with SO Lexicon

We combine the GI seed lexicon with semantic orientation of word computed using large corpus to mark the words positive or negative in thesaurus paragraphs. We combine the information

[5]http://www.cs.pitt.edu/mpqa/databaserelease/

[6]www.cs.pitt.edu/mpqa/opinionfinderrelease

[7]www.cs.pitt.edu/mpqa/lexiconrelease/collectinfo1.html

[8]`http://www.umiacs.umd.edu/~saif/Release/MSOL-June15-09.txt`

Polarity	+ (2789)			- (6079)			**All** (8868)		
SO Lexicon	*R*	*P*	*F*	*R*	*P*	*F*	*R*	*P*	*F*
MPQA	.48	**.73**	.58	.48	**.95**	.64	.48	**.87**	.62
Roget (ASL)	**.64**	.45	.53	.32	.90	.47	.42	.60	.49
Roget (GI)	.50	.60	.55	.55	.86	.67	.53	.76	.62
Roget (ASL+GI)	.62	.57	.59	.49	.91	.64	.53	.75	.62
MSOL	.51	.58	.54	**.60**	.84	.70	**.57**	.74	.64
SO	.63	**.54**	.58	**.50**	.90	.64	**.54**	**.73**	.62
SO-TP	**.68**	.51	.58	.44	**.93**	.60	.52	.69	.59
SO-WTP	.65	**.54**	.59	.44	**.93**	60	.51	.72	.60
SO+GI	.60	.57	.58	**.46**	**.93**	.62	.50	.75	.60
SO-TP+GI	**.62**	**.58**	.60	.45	**.93**	.61	**.51**	**.76**	.61

Table 5: Results on marking polarity of phrases using various lexicons. The # in parentheses is the # of gold +/-/all phrases.

from large corpus with GI in two forms: • SO+GI: If GI matches more number of positive words than negative words in a paragraph and SO of a word > 0, then that word is labeled as positive. However, if GI matches more number of negative words than positive words in a paragraph and SO of a word < 0, that word is labeled as negative. For other cases, we do not assign any labels to words. • SO-TP+GI: Here, we use $SO(TP)$ scores instead of SO scores and use the same strategy as in previous bullet to generate the lexicon.

Table 4 summarizes the size of all lexicons. MPQA has the largest size among manually created lexicons. It is build on top of GI Lexicon. Roget (ASL) has 78% positive entries. MSOL is the biggest lexicon and it is about 2.5 times bigger than our precision oriented SO-WTP lexicon.

5.2.3 Results

Table 5 demonstrates the performance of the algorithm (discussed in Section 5.2) when using different lexicons. The performance of existing lexicons is shown in the top part of the table. The performance of large data and thesaurus lexicons is shown in the middle of the table. The bottom of the table combines GI information with large data and thesaurus.

In the first part of the Table 5, our results demonstrate that MPQA in the first row of the table has the best precision on this task for both positive and negative phrases. Roget (ASL) in the second row has the best recall for positives which is double the recall for negatives. Hence, this indicates that ASL is biased towards positive words. Using GI with Roget gives more balanced recall for both positives and negatives in third row. Roget (ASL+GI) are more biased towards positive words. MSOL has the best recall for negatives; however it comes at an expense of equal drop in precision with respect to MPQA.

In the second part of the Table using large data, "SO" lexicon has same F-score as MPQA with precision and recall trade-offs. Using thesaurus along with large data has comparable F-score; however it again gives some precision and recall trade-offs with noticeable 6 points drop in recall for negatives. The small decrease in F-score for SO-WTP precision-oriented lexicon ($22,614$ entries) is due to its small size in comparison to SO lexicon ($32,202$ entries). We are currently working with a small sized freely available thesaurus which is smaller than Macquarie, hence MSOL performs the best.

Using GI lexicon in bottom part of the Table, we incorporate another form of information, which provides overall better precision than SO, SO-TP, and SO-WTP approaches. Even for languages, where we have only large amounts of data available, "SO" can be beneficial. If we have thesaurus available for a language, it can be combined with large data to produce precision oriented lexicons.

6 Discussion and Conclusion

We constructed lexicons automatically using large data and a thesaurus and evaluated its quality both intrinsically and extrinsically. This framework can easily scale to any language with a thesaurus and a unzipped corpus size of $\geq$ 50 GB (12 billion tokens). However, if a language does not have thesaurus, word similarity between words can be used to generate word clusters. Currently we are exploring using word clusters instead of using thesaurus in our framework. Moreover, if a language does not have large collection of data, we like to explore bilingual lexicons to compute semantic orientation of a word in another language. Another promising direction would be to explore the idea of word similarity combined with CM sketch (stores the approximate counts of all word pairs in a bounded space of 8GB) in graph propagation setting without explicitly representing the graph structure between words.

Acknowledgments

We thank the anonymous reviewers for helpful comments. This work is partially funded by NSF grant IIS-0712764 and Google Research Grant Grant for Large-Data NLP.

References

Eneko Agirre, Enrique Alfonseca, Keith Hall, Jana Kravalova, Marius Paşca, and Aitor Soroa. 2009. A study on similarity and relatedness using distributional and wordnet-based approaches. In *NAACL '09: Proceedings of HLT-NAACL*.

Graham Cormode and S. Muthukrishnan. 2004. An improved data stream summary: The count-min sketch and its applications. *J. Algorithms*.

S. R. Das and M. Y. Chen. 2001. Yahoo! for Amazon: Opinion extraction from small talk on the Web. In *Proceedings of the 8th Asia Pacific Finance Association Annual Conference (APFA)*, Bangkok, Thailand.

Cristian Estan and George Varghese. 2002. New directions in traffic measurement and accounting. *SIGCOMM Comput. Commun. Rev.*, 32(4).

Amit Goyal, Jagadeesh Jagarlamudi, Hal Daumé III, and Suresh Venkatasubramanian. 2010. Sketching techniques for Large Scale NLP. In *6th WAC Workshop at NAACL-HLT*.

Amit Goyal, Ellen Riloff, and Hal Daume III. 2010b. Automatically producing plot unit representations for narrative text. In *Proceedings of the 2010 Conference on Empirical Methods in Natural Language Processing*, pages 77–86. Association for Computational Linguistics, October.

D. Graff. 2003. English Gigaword. Linguistic Data Consortium, Philadelphia, PA, January.

Saif Mohammad, Cody Dunne, and Bonnie Dorr. 2009. Generating high-coverage semantic orientation lexicons from overtly marked words and a thesaurus. In *Proceedings of the 2009 Conference on Empirical Methods in Natural Language Processing*, pages 599–608. Association for Computational Linguistics.

Satoshi Morinaga, Kenji Yamanishi, Kenji Tateishi, and Toshikazu Fukushima. 2002. Mining product reputations on the Web. In *Proceedings of the 8th Association for Computing Machinery SIGKDD International Conference on Knowledge Discovery and Data Mining (KDD-2002)*, pages 341–349, Edmonton, Canada.

Tetsuya Nasukawa and Jeonghee Yi. 2003. Sentiment analysis: Capturing favorability using natural language processing. In *Proceedings of the 2nd International Conference on Knowledge Capture (K-CAP 2003)*, pages 70–77, Sanibel Island, Florida.

Bo Pang and Lillian Lee. 2008. Opinion mining and sentiment analysis. *Foundations and Trends in Information Retrieval*, Vol. 2(1-2):pp. 1–135.

Bo Pang, Lillian Lee, and Shivakumar Vaithyanathan. 2002. Thumbs up? Sentiment classification using machine learning techniques. pages 79–86, Philadelphia, Pennsylvania.

Patrick Pantel, Eric Crestan, Arkady Borkovsky, Ana-Maria Popescu, and Vishnu Vyas. 2009. Web-scale distributional similarity and entity set expansion. In *Proceedings of EMNLP*.

Delip Rao and Deepak Ravichandran. 2009. Semi-supervised polarity lexicon induction. In *Proceedings of the 12th Conference of the European Chapter of the ACL (EACL 2009)*, pages 675–682, Athens, Greece, March. Association for Computational Linguistics.

Deepak Ravichandran, Patrick Pantel, and Eduard Hovy. 2005. Randomized algorithms and nlp: using locality sensitive hash function for high speed noun clustering. In *Proceedings of ACL*.

Philip J. Stone, Dexter C. Dunphy, Marshall S. Smith, and Daniel M. Ogilvie. 1966. *The General Inquirer: A Computer Approach to Content Analysis*. MIT Press.

Richard Tong. 2001. An operational system for detecting and tracking opinions in on-line discussions. In *Working Notes of the Special Interest Group on Information Retrieval (SIGIR) Workshop on Operational Text Classification*, pages 1–6, New Orleans, Louisianna.

Peter D. Turney and Michael L. Littman. 2003. Measuring praise and criticism: Inference of semantic orientation from association. *ACM Trans. Inf. Syst.*, 21:315–346, October.

Leonid Velikovich, Sasha Blair-Goldensohn, Kerry Hannan, and Ryan McDonald. 2010. The viability of web-derived polarity lexicons. In *Human Language Technologies: The 2010 Annual Conference of the North American Chapter of the Association for Computational Linguistics*, pages 777–785, Los Angeles, California, June. Association for Computational Linguistics.

Theresa Wilson, Janyce Wiebe, and Paul Hoffmann. 2005a. Recognizing contextual polarity in phrase-level sentiment analysis. In *Proceedings of Human Language Technology Conference and Conference on Empirical Methods in Natural Language Processing*, pages 347–354. Association for Computational Linguistics.

T. Wilson, P. Hoffmann, S. Somasundaran, J. Kessler, J. Wiebe, Y. Choi, C. Cardie, E. Riloff, and S. Patwardhan. 2005b. OpinionFinder: A system for subjectivity analysis. In *Proceedings of Human Language Technology Conference and Conference on Empirical Methods in Natural Language Processing Interactive Demonstrations*, pages 34–35.

Developing Robust Models for Favourability Analysis

Daoud Clarke **Peter Lane**
School of Computer Science
University of Hertfordshire
Hatfield, UK
daoud@metrica.net
peter.lane@bcs.org.uk

Paul Hender
Metrica
London, UK
paul@metrica.net

Abstract

Locating documents carrying positive or negative favourability is an important application within media analysis. This paper presents some empirical results on the challenges facing a machine-learning approach to this kind of opinion mining. Some of the challenges include: the often considerable imbalance in the distribution of positive and negative samples; changes in the documents over time; and effective training and quantification procedures for reporting results. This paper begins with three datasets generated by a media-analysis company, classifying documents in two ways: detecting the presence of favourability, and assessing negative vs. positive favourability. We then evaluate a machine-learning approach to automate the classification process. We explore the effect of using five different types of features, the robustness of the models when tested on data taken from a later time period, and the effect of balancing the input data by undersampling. We find varying choices for the optimum classifier, feature set and training strategy depending on the task and dataset.

1 Introduction

Media analysis is a discipline closely related to content analysis (Krippendorff, 2004), with an emphasis on analysing content with respect to:

Favourability how favourable an article is with respect to an entity. This will typically be on a five point scale: very negative, negative, neutral, positive or very positive.

Key messages topics or areas that a client is interested in. This allows the client to gain feedback on the success of particular public relations campaigns, for example.

Media analysis has traditionally been done manually, however the explosion of content on the world-wide web, in particular social media, has led to the introduction of automatic techniques for performing media analysis, e.g. Tatzl and Waldhauser (2010).

In this paper, we discuss our recent findings in applying machine learning techniques to favourability analysis. The work is part of a two-year collaboration between Gorkana Group, which includes one of the foremost media analysis companies, Metrica, and the University of Hertfordshire. The goal is to develop ways of automating media analysis, especially for social media. The data used are from traditional media (newspapers and magazines) since at the time of starting the experiment there was more manually analysed data available. We discuss the typical problems that arise in this kind of text mining, and the practical results we have found.

The documents are supplied by Durrants, the media monitoring company within the Gorkana Group, and consist of text from newspaper and magazine articles in electronic form. Each document is analysed by trained human analysts, given scores for favourability, as well as other characteristics which the client has requested. This dataset is used to provide feedback to the clients about how they are portrayed in the media, and is summarised by Metrica for clients' monthly reports.

Favourability analysis is very closely related to sentiment analysis, with the following distinction:

Proceedings of the 2nd Workshop on Computational Approaches to Subjectivity and Sentiment Analysis, ACL-HLT 2011, pages 44–52,
24 June, 2011, Portland, Oregon, USA ©2011 Association for Computational Linguistics

sentiment analysis generally focuses on a (subjective) sentiment implying an opinion of the author, for example:[1]

(1) Microsoft is the greattteesssst at EVERYTHING

expresses the author's opinion (which others may not share) whereas favourability analysis, whilst also taking into account sentiment, also measures favourable **objective** mentions of entities. For example:[2]

(2) Halloween Eve Was The Biggest Instagram Day Ever, Doubling Its Traffic

is an objective statement (no one can doubt that the traffic doubled) that is favourable with respect to the organisation, Instagram. Since the task is so similar to that of sentiment analysis, we hypothesise that similar techniques will be useful.

The contributions of this paper are as follows: (1) whilst automated sentiment analysis has received a lot of attention in the academic literature, favourability analysis has so far not benefited from an in-depth analysis. (2) We provide results on a wide variety of different classifiers, whereas previous work on sentiment analysis typically considers at most two or three different classifiers. (3) We discuss the problem of imbalanced data, looking at how this impacts on the training and evaluation techniques. (4) We show that both attribute selection and balancing the classifier's training set can improve performance.

2 Background

There is a very large body of literature on both sentiment analysis and machine learning; for space reasons, we will mention only a small sample.

2.1 Favourability Analysis

The most closely related task to ours is arguably opinion mining, i.e. determining sentiment with respect to a particular target. Balahur et al. (2010) examine this task for newspaper articles. They show that separating out the objective favourability from the expressed sentiment led to an increase in inter-annotator agreement, which they report as 81%, after implementing improvements to the process. Melville et al. (2009) report on an automated system for opinion mining applied to blogs, which achieves between 64% and 91% accuracy, depending on the domain, while Godbole et al. (2007) describe a system applied to news and blogs.

Pang et al. (2002) introduced machine learning to perform sentiment analysis. They used naïve bayes, support vector machines (SVMs) and maximum entropy on the movie review domain, and report accuracies between 77% and 83% depending on the feature set, which included unigrams, bigrams, and part-of-speech tagged unigrams. More recent work along these lines is described in (Pang and Lee, 2008; Prabowo and Thelwall, 2009).

One approach to sentiment analysis is to build up a lexicon of sentiment carrying words. Turney (2002) described a way to automatically build such a lexicon based on looking at co-occurrences of words with other words whose sentiment is known. This idea was extended by Gamon et al. (2005) who also considered the lack of co-occurrence as useful information.

Koppel and Schler (2006) show that it is important to distinguish the two tasks of determining neutral from non-neutral sentiment, and positive versus negative sentiment, and that doing so can significantly improve the accuracy of automated systems.

2.2 Machine Learning Approaches

Document classification is an ideal domain for machine learning, because the raw data, the text, are easily manipulated, and often large amounts of text can be obtained, making the problems amenable to statistical analysis.

A classification model is essentially a mapping, from a document described as a set of feature values to a class label. In most cases, this class label is a simple yes-no choice, such as whether the document is favourable or not. In the experimental section of this paper we describe results from applying a range of different classification algorithms.

In general, two issues that affect machine-learning approaches are the selection of features, and the presence of imbalanced data.

[1] Actually, this is an ironic comment on a blog post at TechCrunch.

[2] A headline from TechCrunch

2.2.1 Features

Useful features for constructing classification models from text documents include sets of unigrams, bigrams or trigrams, dependency relationships or selected words: we review these features in the next section. From a machine-learning perspective, it is useful for the features to include only relevant information, and also to be independent of each other. This feature-selection problem has been tackled by several authors in different ways, e.g. (Blum and Langley, 1997; Forman, 2003; Green et al., 2010; Mladenić, 1998; Rogati and Yang, 2002). In our experiments, we evaluate a technique to reduce the number of features using attribute selection.

Alternative approaches to understanding the sentiment of text attempt to go beyond the simple labelling of the presence of a word. Some authors have described experiments augmenting the above feature sets with additional information. Mullen and Collier (2004), for example, uses WordNet to add information about words found within text, and consequently reports improved classification performance in a sentiment analysis task.

2.3 Imbalanced Data

Our datasets, as is usual in many real-world applications, present varying degrees of imbalance between the two classes. Imbalanced data must be dealt with at two parts of the process: during *training*, to ensure the model is capable of working with both classes, and in *evaluation*, to ensure a model with the best performance is selected for use on novel data. These two elements are often treated together, but need to be considered separately. In particular, the appropriate training method to handle imbalanced data can vary between algorithm and domain.

First considering *evaluation*, the standard measure of accuracy (proportion of correctly classified examples) is inappropriate if 90% of the documents are within one class. A simple ZeroR classifier (selecting the majority class) will score highly, but it will never get any examples of the minority class correct. A better evaluation technique uses a combination of the separate accuracy measures on the two classes (a_1 and a_2), where a_i denotes the proportion of instances from class i that were judged correctly. For example, the geometric mean, as proposed by Kubat et al. (1998), computes $\sqrt{a_1 \times a_2}$. This has the property that it strongly penalises poor performance in any one class: if either a_1 or a_2 is zero then the geometric mean will be zero. This characteristic is important for our purposes, since it is "easy" to get high accuracy on the majority class, the measure will favour classifiers that perform well on the minority class without significant loss of accuracy in the majority class. In addition, the geometric mean does not give preference to any one class, unlike, for example, the F-measure. Measures such as the average precision and recall, or F-measure, may also prove useful, especially if preference is being given to one class.

Second considering the *training* process. An imbalanced training set can lead to *bias* in the construction of a machine-learning model. Such effects are well-known in the literature, and various approaches have been proposed to address this problem, such as balancing the training set using under or over sampling, and altering the weighting of the classifier based on the proportion of the expected class. In our experiments we used undersampling (where a random sample is taken from the majority class to balance the size of the minority class); this technique has the disadvantage of discarding training data. In contrast, the SMOTE (Chawla et al., 2004) algorithm is a technique for creating new instances of the minority class, to balance the number in the majority class. We also used geometric-mean as the evaluation measure for algorithms such as SVMs, when selecting parameters.

3 Our Approach

3.1 Description of Data

The source documents have been tagged by analysts for favourability and unfavourability, both of which are given a non-negative score that is indicative both of the number of favourable/unfavourable mentions of the organisation and the degree of favourability/unfavourability. Neutral documents are assigned a score of zero for both favourability and unfavourability. We assign each document a class based on its favourability f and unfavourability u scores. Documents are categorised as follows:

Dataset	Mixed	V. Neg.	Negative	Neutral	Positive	V. Pos.
A	472	86	138	1610	1506	1664
C	7	0	5	2824	852	50
S	522	94	344	9580	2057	937

Table 1: Number of documents in each class for the datasets A, C and S.

Dataset	Neutral	Non-neutral
A	1610	3866
C	2824	914
S	9580	3954

Table 2: Class distributions for pseudo-subjectivity task

Dataset	Positive	Negative
A	3170	224
C	902	5
S	2994	438

Table 3: Class distributions for pseudo-sentiment task

$f > 0$ and $u > 0$: **mixed**
$f = 0$ and $u > 1$: **very negative**
$f = 0$ and $u = 1$: **negative**
$f = 0$ and $u = 0$: **neutral**
$f = 1$ and $u = 0$: **positive**
$f > 1$ and $u = 0$: **very positive**

Table 1 shows the number of documents in each category for three datasets A, C and S, which are anonymised to protect Metrica's clients' privacy. A and S are datasets for high-tech companies, whereas C is for a charity. This is reflected in the low occurence of negative favourability with dataset C. Datasets A and C contain only articles that are relevant to the client, whereas S contains articles for the client's competitors. We only make use of favourability judgments with respect to the client, however, so those that are irrelevant to the client we simply treat as neutral. This explains the overwhelming bias towards neutral sentiment in dataset S.

In our experiments, we consider only those documents which have been manually analysed and for which the raw text is available. Duplicates were removed from the dataset. Duplicate detection was performed using a modified version of Ferret (Lane et al., 2006) which compares occurrences of character trigrams between documents. We considered two documents to be duplicates if they had a similarity score higher than 0.75.

This paper describes experiments for two tasks:

Pseudo-subjectivity — detecting the presence or absence of favourability. This is thus a two-class problem with **neutral** documents in one class, and all other documents in the other.

Pseudo-sentiment — distinguishing between documents with generally positive and negative favourability. In our experiments, we treat this as a two class problem, with **negative** and **very negative** documents in one class and **positive** and **very positive** documents in the other (ignoring mixed sentiment).

3.2 Method

We follow a similar approach to Pang et al. (2002): we generate features from the article text, and train a classifier using the manually analysed data.

We sorted the documents by time, and then selected the earliest two thirds as a training set, and kept the remainder as a held out test set. This allows us to get an idea of how the system will perform when it is in use, since the system will necessarily be trained on documents from an earlier time period. We performed cross validation on the randomised training set, giving us an upper bound on the performance of the system, and we also measured the accuracy of every system on the held out dataset. We hypothesised that new topics would be discussed in the later time frame, and thus the accuracy would be lower, since the system would not be trained on data for these topics.

We also experimented with balancing the input data to the classifiers; each system was run twice, once with all the input data, and once with data which had been undersampled so that the number of documents in each class was the same. And also we experimented with attribute selection: reducing the number of features used to describe the dataset.

Type	Relation	Term
governor	det	the
governor	rcmod	sued
governor	nn	leader
dependent	poss	conference
dependent	nsubj	bullish
dependent	dep	beat

Table 4: Example dependency relations extracted from the data. "Type" indicates whether the term referring to the organisation is the governor or the dependent in the expression.

3.2.1 Features for documents

We used five types of features:

Unigrams, bigrams and trigrams: produced using the WEKA tokenizer with the standard settings.[3]

EntityWords: unigrams of words occurring within a sentence containing a mention of the organisation in question. Mentions of the organisation were detected using manually constructed regular expressions, based on datasets for organisations collected elsewhere in the company. Sentence boundary detection was performed using an OpenNLP[4] tool.

Dependencies: we extract dependencies using the Stanford dependency parser. For the purpose of this experiment, we only considered dependencies directly connecting the term relating to the organisation. Table 4 gives example dependencies extracted from the data. For example, the phrase "...prompted [organisation name] to be bullish..." led to the extraction of the term *bullish*, where the organisation name is the subject of the verb and the organisation name is a dependent of the verb *bullish*. For each dependency, all this information is combined into a single feature.

3.3 Classification Algorithms

We used the following classifiers in our experiments: naïve Bayes, Support Vector Machines (SVMs), k-nearest neighbours with $k = 1$ and $k = 5$, radial basis function (RBF) networks, Bayesian networks, decision trees (J48) and a propositional rule learner, Repeated Incremental Pruning to Produce Error Reduction (JRip). We also included two baseline classifiers, ZeroR, which simply chooses the most frequent class in the training set, and Random, which chooses classes at random based on their frequencies in the training set.

These are taken from the WEKA toolkit (Witten and Frank, 2005), with the exception of SVMs, for which we used the LibSVM implementation, naïve Bayes (since the Weka implementation does not appear to treat the value occurring with a feature as a frequency) and Random, both of which we implemented ourselves. We used WEKA's default settings for classifiers where appropriate.

3.3.1 Parameter search for SVMs

We used a radial-basis kernel for our SVM algorithm which requires two parameters to be optimised experimentally. This was done for each fold of cross validation. Each fold was further divided, and three-fold cross validation was performed for each parameter combination. We varied the gamma parameter exponentially between 10^{-5} and 10^{5} in multiples of 100, and varied cost between 1 and 15 in increments of 2. We used the geometric mean of the accuracies on the two classes to choose the best combination of parameters; using the geometric mean enables us to train and evaluate the SVM from either balanced or imbalanced datasets.

3.3.2 Attribute Selection

Because of the long training time of many of the classifiers with numbers of features, we also looked at whether reducing the dimensionality of the data before training by performing attribute selection would enhance or hinder performance. The attribute selection was done by ranking the features using the Chi-squared measure and taking the top 250 with the most correlation with the class. The exception to this was k-nearest neighbours, for which we used random projections with 250 dimensions. For the RBF network we tried both attribute selection and random projections, and naïve Bayes was run both with and without attribute selection.

3.4 Results

Tables 5 and 6 show the best classifier on the cross-validation evaluation for each dataset and feature set for the pseudo-subjectivity and pseudo-sentiment tasks respectively, together with the Random clas-

[3] We used the StringToWordVectorClass constructed with an argument of 5,000.

[4] `http://opennlp.sourceforge.net`

Dataset	Features	Best Classifier	Att. Sel.	Balance	Cross val. acc.	Held out acc.
S		*Random*			*0.465 ± 0.008*	*0.461 ± 0.007*
S	EntityWords	SVM	X		**0.912** ± 0.002	**0.952** ± 0.001
S	Unigrams	JRip	X	X	0.907 ± 0.002	**0.952** ± 0.002
S	Bigrams	SVM	X	X	0.875 ± 0.007	0.885 ± 0.004
S	Trigrams	Naïve Bayes			0.791 ± 0.003	0.759 ± 0.003
S	Dependencies	RBFNet		X	0.853 ± 0.005	0.766 ± 0.054
C		*Random*			*0.417 ± 0.017*	*0.419 ± 0.027*
C	EntityWords	Naïve Bayes	X		0.704 ± 0.011	0.640 ± 0.018
C	Unigrams	Naïve Bayes	X		0.735 ± 0.007	0.659 ± 0.032
C	Bigrams	Naïve Bayes			**0.756** ± 0.012	0.640 ± 0.014
C	Trigrams	Naïve Bayes			**0.757** ± 0.004	**0.679** ± 0.017
A		*Random*			*0.453 ± 0.004*	*0.453 ± 0.017*
A	EntityWords	BayesNet	X		0.691 ± 0.008	**0.625** ± 0.019
A	Unigrams	SVM	X	X	**0.696** ± 0.005	0.619 ± 0.010
A	Bigrams	SVM	X	X	0.680 ± 0.012	0.609 ± 0.026
A	Trigrams	Naïve Bayes		X	0.610 ± 0.011	0.536 ± 0.019

Table 5: Results for the pseudo-subjectivity task, distinguishing documents neutral with respect to favourability from those which are not neutral. The accuracy was computed as the geometric mean of accuracy on the neutral documents and the accuracy on the non-neutral documents. The best-performing classifier on cross-validation is shown for each feature set, along with the Random classifier as a baseline. An indication is given of whether the best-performing system used attribute selection and/or balancing on the input data.

Dataset	Features	Best Classifier	Balance	Cross val. acc.	Held out acc.
S		*Random*		*0.332 ± 0.023*	*0.365 ± 0.03*
S	EntityWords	Naïve Bayes	X	0.738 ± 0.008	0.552 ± 0.033
S	Unigrams	Naïve Bayes	X	0.718 ± 0.017	0.650 ± 0.024
S	Bigrams	Naïve Bayes	X	0.748 ± 0.013	0.682 ± 0.023
S	Trigrams	Naïve Bayes	X	**0.766** ± 0.014	**0.716** ± 0.038
S	Dependencies	Naïve Bayes		0.566 ± 0.014	0.523 ± 0.060
A		*Random*		*0.253 ± 0.026*	*0.111 ± 0.072*
A	EntityWords	Naïve Bayes	X	0.737 ± 0.016	0.656 ± 0.067
A	Unigrams	Naïve Bayes	X	0.769 ± 0.008	**0.756** ± 0.031
A	Bigrams	Naïve Bayes		0.755 ± 0.009	0.618 ± 0.157
A	Trigrams	Naïve Bayes		**0.800** ± 0.02	**0.739** ± 0.088

Table 6: Results for the pseudo-sentiment task, distinguishing positive and negative favourability. See the preceding table for details. None of the best performing systems used attribute selection on this task. No data is shown for dataset C since there were not enough negative documents in the test set to compute the accuracies.

sifier baseline. The accuracies shown were computed using the geometric mean of the accuracy on the two classes. This was computed for each cross-validation fold; the value shown is the (arithmetic) mean of the accuracies on the five folds, together with an estimate of the error in this mean. The values for the held out data were computed in the same way, dividing the data into five, allowing us to estimate the error in the accuracy.

4 Discussion

4.1 Overall accuracy

The most notable difference between the two tasks, pseudo-subjectivity and pseudo-sentiment, is that the best classifier for the sentiment task was naïve Bayes in every case, whereas the best classifier varies with dataset and feature set for the pseudo-subjectivity task. This is presumably because the independence assumption on which the naïve Bayes classifier is based holds very well for the pseudo-sentiment task, at least with our datasets.

The level of accuracy we report for the pseudo-sentiment task is lower than that typically reported for sentiment analysis, e.g. Pang et al. (2002), but in line with that from other results, such as Melville et al. (2009). This could be because favourability is harder to determine than sentiment. For example it may require world knowledge in addition to linguistic knowledge, in order to determine whether the reporting of a particular event is good news for a company, even if reported objectively.

Accuracy on the held out dataset is up to 10% lower than the cross-validation accuracy on the pseudo-subjectivity task, and up to 6% lower on the pseudo-sentiment task. This is probably due to a change in topics over time. This degradation in performance could be reduced by techniques such as those used to improve cross-domain sentiment analysis (Li et al., 2009; Wan, 2009).

4.2 Features

Trigrams proved the most effective feature type in 3 out of the 5 different experiments, with unigrams and entity words proving the best in 1 case each. However, in many cases, there is not a significant difference between the results for different datasets.

Although we only computed dependencies for one dataset, S, we found that they did not provide significant benefit on their own. This may be due to the sparseness of the data, since we only extracted dependencies with respect to the organisation in question. Dependencies may be useful when combined with other features, such as unigrams.

Attribute selection was not always effective in improving classification, even with the high-dimensionality of the data. In the pseudo-sentiment task, none of the best classifiers used attribute selection. In the pseudo-subjectivity task, 8 out of 13 results showed a benefit in using attribute selection. This issue deserves further exploration, not least because reducing the number of attributes can considerably speed-up the training process.

4.3 Imbalance

Finally, we look at our results considering the imbalanced data problem. Within some of the algorithms, balance is actively taken account during the training process: e.g. naïve Bayes has a weighting on its class output to compensate for different frequencies, and the SVM training process uses geometric mean for computing performance, which encourages a good performance on imbalanced data. In addition, we have presented results on the difference between training with balanced and unbalanced datasets. Better results are obtained in 5 out of the 13 results for the pseudo-subjectivity task (Table 5), and in 6 out of 9 results for the pseudo-sentiment task (Table 6), suggesting that balancing the training data is a useful technique in most cases.

However, a surprising result is found in Table 7, which shows selected pseudo-subjectivity results for dataset S with and without balanced input data. This dataset has an approximately 70:30 imbalance in the class distribution. Interestingly, balancing the data shows mixed results for this dataset. In particular, the accuracy of the Bayesian network, and sometimes the naïve Bayes classifier, are severely reduced. We found similar behaviour with dataset C (with a 75:25 imbalance), however, as shown in Table 8, we found the converse on dataset A (with a 30:70 imbalance): nearly every classifier performed better with balanced data. Further, Table 6 shows that balancing data has proven effective for the naïve Bayes classifiers in the pseudo-sentiment task, where the imbalance is more severe (94:6 for

		Unbalanced			Balanced		
Features	Classifier	Neut.	Non.	Cross val. acc.	Neut.	Non.	Cross val. acc.
EntityWords	SVM	0.962	0.864	0.912 ± 0.003	0.959	0.864	0.911 ± 0.002
EntityWords	Naïve Bayes	0.969	0.850	0.908 ± 0.003	1	0	0 ± 0
Unigrams	SVM	0.959	0.857	0.907 ± 0.002	0.954	0.859	0.905 ± 0.002
Unigrams	Naïve Bayes	0.774	0.789	0.781 ± 0.006	0.910	0.581	0.727 ± 0.008
Bigrams	SVM	0.747	0.933	0.835 ± 0.006	0.849	0.901	0.875 ± 0.007
Bigrams	Naïve Bayes	0.883	0.716	0.795 ± 0.004	0.947	0.569	0.734 ± 0.005
Trigrams	BayesNet	0.620	0.883	0.739 ± 0.009	0.975	0.118	0.289 ± 0.086
Trigrams	J48	0.356	0.964	0.586 ± 0.012	0.441	0.942	0.644 ± 0.008
Trigrams	JRip	0.422	0.963	0.637 ± 0.003	0.388	0.963	0.605 ± 0.042
Trigrams	SVM	0.575	0.921	0.728 ± 0.008	0.604	0.909	0.740 ± 0.009
Trigrams	Naïve Bayes	0.810	0.758	0.784 ± 0.003	0.922	0.593	0.739 ± 0.005
Trigrams	RBFNet	0.459	0.949	0.659 ± 0.010	0.478	0.934	0.667 ± 0.013

Table 7: Selected balanced versus unbalanced cross validation accuracies (geometric mean) for dataset S, pseudo-subjectivity task, together with the accuracies on the individual classes, neutral and non-neutral. For consistency, only results where attribute selection was performed are shown.

		Unbalanced			Balanced		
Features	Classifier	Neut.	Non.	Cross val. acc.	Neut.	Non.	Cross val. acc.
EntityWords	SVM	0.872	0.394	0.587 ± 0.006	0.575	0.812	0.683 ± 0.007
EntityWords	Naïve Bayes	0.972	0.111	0.326 ± 0.021	0.944	0.192	0.426 ± 0.015
Unigrams	SVM	0.837	0.464	0.622 ± 0.011	0.694	0.698	0.696 ± 0.005
Unigrams	Naïve Bayes	0.896	0.318	0.531 ± 0.018	0.736	0.582	0.652 ± 0.012
Bigrams	SVM	0.852	0.36	0.553 ± 0.006	0.58	0.8	0.68 ± 0.012
Bigrams	Naïve Bayes	0.959	0.203	0.439 ± 0.017	0.86	0.433	0.605 ± 0.024
Trigrams	SVM	0.935	0.173	0.401 ± 0.018	0.407	0.851	0.588 ± 0.009
Trigrams	Naïve Bayes	0.938	0.249	0.481 ± 0.013	0.84	0.446	0.61 ± 0.011

Table 8: Selected balanced versus unbalanced cross validation accuracies (geometric mean) for dataset A, pseudo-subjectivity task (see the preceding table for details).

A, and 88:12 for S).

Given these results, we suggest that balancing the training datasets is usually an effective strategy, although sometimes the benefits are small if account of balancing is also part of the parameter-selection process for your learning algorithm.

5 Conclusion and Further Work

We have empirically analysed a range of machine-learning techniques for developing favourability classifiers in a commercial context. These techniques include different classification algorithms, use of attribute selection to reduce the feature sets, and treatment of the imbalanced data problem. Also, we used five different types of feature set to create the datasets from the raw text. We have found a wide variation, from less than 0.7 to over 0.9 geometric mean of accuracy, depending on the particular set of data analysed. We have shown how balancing the class distribution in training data can be beneficial in improving performance, but some algorithms (i.e. naïve Bayes) can be adversely affected. In future work we will apply these techniques to larger volumes of social media, and further explore the questions of balancing datasets, other features and feature selection, as well as embedding these algorithms within the workflow of the company.

References

A. Balahur, R. Steinberger, M. Kabadjov, V. Zavarella, E. Van Der Goot, M. Halkia, B. Pouliquen, and J. Belyaeva. 2010. Sentiment analysis in the news. In *Proceedings of LREC*.

A.L. Blum and P. Langley. 1997. Selection of relevant features and examples in machine learning. *Artificial intelligence*, 97:245–271.

N.V. Chawla, N. Japkowicz, and A. Kotcz. 2004. Editorial: special issue on learning from imbalanced data sets. *ACM SIGKDD Explorations Newsletter*, 6:1–6.

G. Forman. 2003. An extensive empirical study of feature selection metrics for text classification. *The Journal of Machine Learning Research*, 3:1289–1305.

M. Gamon, A. Aue, S. Corston-Oliver, and E. Ringger. 2005. Pulse: Mining customer opinions from free text. *Advances in Intelligent Data Analysis VI*, pages 121–132.

N. Godbole, M. Srinivasaiah, and S. Skiena. 2007. Large-scale sentiment analysis for news and blogs. In *Proceedings of the International Conference on Weblogs and Social Media (ICWSM)*.

P.D. Green, P.C.R. Lane, A.W. Rainer, and S. Scholz. 2010. Selecting measures in origin analysis. In *Proceedings of AI-2010, The Thirtieth SGAI International Conference on Innovative Techniques and Applications of Artificial Intelligence*, pages 379–392.

M. Koppel and J. Schler. 2006. The importance of neutral examples for learning sentiment. *Computational Intelligence*, 22:100–109.

K. Krippendorff. 2004. *Content analysis: An introduction to its methodology*. Sage Publications, Inc.

M. Kubat, R.C. Holte, and S. Matwin. 1998. Machine learning for the detection of oil spills in satellite radar images. *Machine Learning*, 30:195–215.

P.C.R. Lane, C. Lyon, and J.A. Malcolm. 2006. Demonstration of the Ferret plagiarism detector. In *Proceedings of the 2nd International Plagiarism Conference*.

T. Li, V. Sindhwani, C. Ding, and Y. Zhang. 2009. Knowledge transformation for cross-domain sentiment classification. In *Proceedings of the 32nd international ACM SIGIR conference on Research and development in information retrieval*, pages 716–717. ACM.

P. Melville, W. Gryc, and R. D. Lawrence. 2009. Sentiment analysis of blogs by combining lexical knowledge with text classification. In *Proceedings of the 15th ACM SIGKDD international conference on Knowledge discovery and data mining*, KDD '09, pages 1275–1284, New York, NY, USA. ACM.

D. Mladenić. 1998. Feature subset selection in text-learning. *Machine Learning: ECML-98*, pages 95–100.

T. Mullen and N. Collier. 2004. Sentiment analysis using support vector machines with diverse information sources. In *Proceedings of EMNLP*, volume 4, pages 412–418.

B. Pang and L. Lee. 2008. Opinion mining and sentiment analysis. *Foundations and Trends in Information Retrieval*, 2(1-2):1–135.

B. Pang, L. Lee, and S. Vaithyanathan. 2002. Thumbs up?: sentiment classification using machine learning techniques. In *Proceedings of the ACL-02 conference on Empirical methods in natural language processing-Volume 10*, pages 79–86. Association for Computational Linguistics.

R. Prabowo and M. Thelwall. 2009. Sentiment analysis: A combined approach. *Journal of Informetrics*, 3:143–157.

M. Rogati and Y. Yang. 2002. High-performing feature selection for text classification. In *Proceedings of the eleventh international conference on Information and knowledge management*, pages 659–661. ACM.

G. Tatzl and C. Waldhauser. 2010. Aggregating opinions: Explorations into Graphs and Media Content Analysis. *ACL 2010*, page 93.

P.D. Turney. 2002. Thumbs up or thumbs down?: Semantic orientation applied to unsupervised classification of reviews. In *Proceedings of the 40th Annual Meeting on Association for Computational Linguistics*, pages 417–424. Association for Computational Linguistics.

X. Wan. 2009. Co-training for cross-lingual sentiment classification. In *Proceedings of the Joint Conference of the 47th Annual Meeting of the ACL and the 4th International Joint Conference on Natural Language Processing of the AFNLP: Volume 1-Volume 1*, pages 235–243. Association for Computational Linguistics.

I. H. Witten and E. Frank. 2005. *Data Mining: Practical Machine Learning Tools and Techniques*. Morgan Kaufmann.

Detecting Implicit Expressions of Sentiment in Text Based on Commonsense Knowledge

Alexandra Balahur, Jesús M. Hermida, Andrés Montoyo
Department of Software and Computing Systems
University of Alicante
Apartado de correos 99, E-03080 Alicante, Spain
{abalahur, jhermida, montoyo}@dlsi.ua.es

Abstract

Sentiment analysis is one of the recent, highly dynamic fields in Natural Language Processing. Most existing approaches are based on word-level analysis of texts and are able to detect only explicit expressions of sentiment. In this paper, we present an approach towards automatically detecting emotions (as underlying components of sentiment) from contexts in which no clues of sentiment appear, based on commonsense knowledge. The resource we built towards this aim – EmotiNet - is a knowledge base of concepts with associated affective value. Preliminary evaluations show that this approach is appropriate for the task of implicit emotion detection, thus improving the performance of sentiment detection and classification in text.

1 Introduction

Research in affect has a long established tradition in many sciences - linguistics, psychology, socio-psychology, cognitive science, pragmatics, marketing or communication science. Recently, many closely related subtasks were developed also in the field of Natural Language Proceeing (NLP), such as emotion detection, subjectivity analysis, opinion mining to sentiment analysis, attitude and appraisal analysis or review mining (Pang and Lee, 2008).

Among these tasks, sentiment analysis aims at detecting the expressions of sentiment in text and subsequently classify them, according to their polarity (semantic orientation) among different categories (usually, among positive and negative). The problem is defined by Pang and Lee (2008) as "the binary classification task of labeling an opinionated document as expressing either an overall positive or an overall negative." (Pang and Lee, 2008)

According to the Webster dictionary (http://www.merriam-webster.com/), sentiment suggests a settled opinion reflective of one's feelings, where the term feeling is defined as the conscious subjective experience of emotion. (Van den Bos, 2006), "a single component of emotion, denoting the subjective experience process" (Scherer, 2005).

Most of the research performed in the field of sentiment analysis has aimed at detecting explicit expressions of sentiment (i.e. situations where specific words or word combinations are found in texts). Nevertheless, the expression of emotion is most of the times not achieved through the use of emotion-bearing words (Pennebaker et al., 2003), but indirectly, by presenting situations that based on commonsense knowledge can be interpreted in an affective manner (Balahur and Montoyo, 2008; Balahur and Steinberger, 2009).

In this paper, we present a method to build a commonsense knowledge base (EmotiNet) representing situations that trigger emotions. We demonstrate that by using this resource, we are

Proceedings of the 2nd Workshop on Computational Approaches to Subjectivity and Sentiment Analysis, ACL-HLT 2011, pages 53–60,
24 June, 2011, Portland, Oregon, USA ©2011 Association for Computational Linguistics

able to detect emotion from textual contexts in which no explicit mention of affect is present.

2 State of the Art

In Artificial Intelligence (AI), the term affective computing was first introduced by Picard (1995). Previous approaches to spot affect in text include the use of models simulating human reactions according to their needs and desires (Dyer, 1987), fuzzy logic (Subasic and Huettner, 2000), lexical affinity based on similarity of contexts – the basis for the construction of WordNet Affect (Strapparava and Valitutti, 2004) or SentiWord-Net (Esuli and Sebastiani, 2005), detection of affective keywords (Riloff et al., 2003) and machine learning using term frequency (Pang et al., 2002; Riloff and Wiebe, 2003), or term discrimination (Danisman and Alpkocak, 2008). Other proposed methods include the creation of syntactic patterns and rules for cause-effect modeling (Mei Lee et al., 2009). Significantly different proposals for emotion detection in text are given in the work by (Liu et al, 2003) and the recently proposed framework of sentic computing (Cambria et al., 2009), whose scope is to model affective reaction based on commonsense knowledge. For a survey on the affect models and their affective computing applications, see (Calvo and D'Mello, 2010).

3 Motivation and Contribution

The tasks of emotion detection and sentiment analysis have been approached by a large volume of research in NLP . Nevertheless, most of this research has concentrated on developing methods for detecting only explicit mentions of sentiment in text. Therefore, sentences such as "I'm going to a party", which express an underlying emotion, cannot be classified by most of the existing approaches. A method to overcome this issue is proposed in by *sentic* computing (Cambria et al., 2009) and by (Liu et al, 2003), whose main idea is acquiring knowledge on the emotional effect of different concepts. In this manner, the system would know that "going to a party" is something that produces "joy". However, more complex contexts, such as "I'm going to a party, although I should study for my exam.", where the emotion expressed is most probably "guilt", cannot be correctly detected and classified by present systems.

In the light of these considerations, our contribution relies in proposing and implementing a framework for modeling affect based on the appraisal theories, which can support the automatic processing of texts to extract:

- The components of the situation presented (which we denote by "action chains") and their relation (temporal, causal etc.)
- The elements on which the appraisal is done in each action of the chain (agent, action, object);
- The appraisal criteria that can automatically be determined from the text (modifiers of the action, actor, object in each action chain);

4 Modeling Affective Reaction Using Commonsense Knowledge

Our main idea is that emotion can be expressed in text by presenting a sequence of actions (situations in which different concepts appear), which, based on commonsense knowledge and previous experiences, trigger an emotional reaction. This idea is linked to the Appraisal Theories, which claim that emotions are elicited and differentiated on the basis of the subjective evaluation of the personal significance of a situation, object or event (De Rivera, 1977; Frijda, 1986; Johnson-Laird and Oatley, 1989 – among others). Viewed in a simpler manner, a situation is presented as a chain of actions, each with an actor and an object; the appraisal depends on the temporal and causal relationship between them, on the characteristics of the actors involved in the action and on the object of the action.

Given this insight, the general idea behind our approach is to model situations as chains of actions and their corresponding emotional effect using an ontological representation. According to the definition provided by Studer et al. (1998), an ontology captures knowledge shared by a community that can be easily sharable with other communities. These two characteristics are especially relevant if we want the recall of our approach to be increased. Knowledge managed in our approach has to be shared by a large community and it also needs to be fed by heterogeneous sources of common knowledge to avoid uncertainties. However, specific assertions can be introduced to account for the specificities of individuals or contexts. In this manner, we can model the interaction of different events in the context in which they take place.

5 Building a Knowledge Base for Detecting Implicit Expressions of Emotion

In order to build a resource that is capable of capturing emotional reaction to real-world situations in which commonsense knowledge plays a significant role in the affective interpretation, we aim at representing chains of actions and their corresponding emotional labels from several situations in such a way that we will be able to extract general patterns of appraisal. Our approach defines an action chain as a sequence of action links, or simply actions that trigger an emotion on an actor. Each specific action link can be described with a tuple (actor, action type, patient, emotional reaction).

In order to manage and store action chains, the approach we propose defines a new knowledge base, called EmotiNet, which aims to be a resource for detecting emotions in text, and a (semi)automatic, iterative process to build it, which is based on existing knowledge from different sources. This process extracts the action chains from a set of documents and adds them to the KB. Specifically, EmotiNet was built by following the next steps:

1. The design of an ontology, which contains the definitions of the main concepts of the domain.
2. The extension and population of this ontology using the situations stored in the ISEAR International Survey of Emotional Antecedents and Reactions (ISEAR, http://www.unige.ch/fapse/emotion/databanks/isear.html) – (Scherer and Wallbott, 1997) database.
3. The expansion of the ontology using existing commonsense knowledge bases – ConceptNet (Liu and Singh, 2004) and other resources – VerbOcean (Chklovski and Pantel, 2004).

5.1 Design of the Ontology

As mentioned before, the process of building the core of the EmotiNet knowledge base (KB) of action chains started with the design of the core ontology, whose design process was specifically divided in three stages:

1. Establishing the scope and purpose of the ontology. The EmotiNet ontology needs to capture and manage knowledge from three domains: kinship membership, emotions (and their relations) and actions (characteristics and relations between them).

2. Reusing knowledge from existing ontologies. In a second stage, we searched for other ontologies on the Web containing concepts related to the knowledge cores we specified. At the end of the process, we located two ontologies that are reused in our ontological representation: the ReiAction ontology (www.cs.umbc.edu/~lkagal1/rei/ontologies/ReiAction.owl), which represents actions between entities in a general manner, and the family ontology (www.dlsi.ua.es/~jesusmhc/emotinet/family.owl), which contains knowledge about family members and the relations between them.

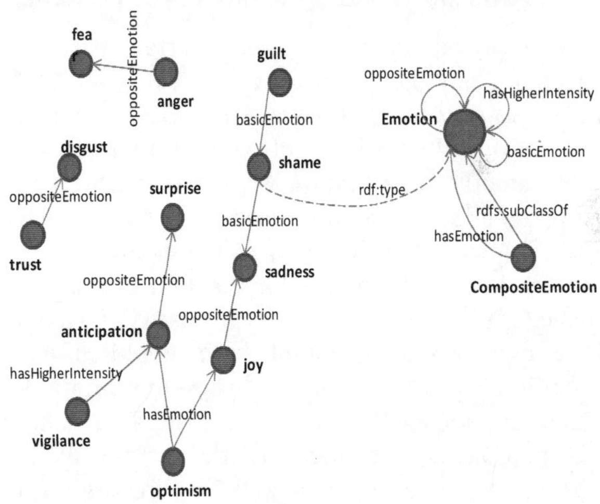

Figure 1. Partial RDF graph of the Emotion Ontology.

3. Creating the final knowledge core from the ontologies imported. This third stage involved the design of the last remaining core, i.e. emotion, and the combination of the different knowledge sources into a single ontology: EmotiNet. In order to describe the emotions and the way they relate and compose, we employ Robert Plutchik's wheel of emotion (Plutchik, 2001) and Parrot's tree-structured list of emotions (Parrot, 2001). These models contain an explicit modeling of the relations between the different emotions. At the end of the design process, the knowledge core included different types of relations between emotions and a collection of specific instances of emotion (e.g. anger, joy). In the last step, these three cores were combined using new classes and relations between the existing members of these ontologies (Fig. 2).

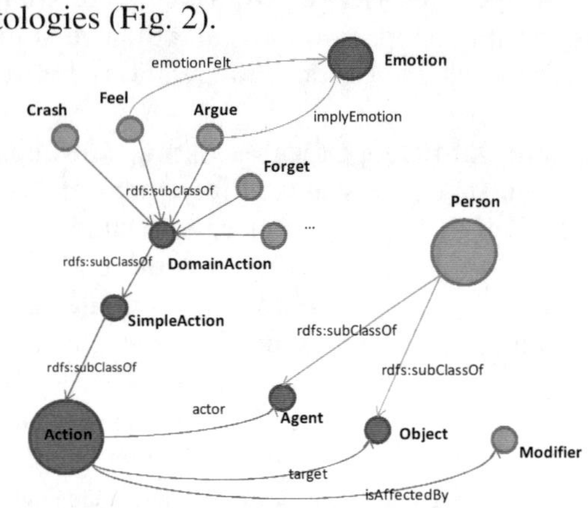

Figure 2. Main concepts of EmotiNet.

5.2 Extension and Population of the Ontology

In order to have a homogenous starting base, we selected from the 7667 examples in the ISEAR database only the 1081 cases that contained descriptions of situations between family members. Subsequently, the examples were POS-tagged using *TreeTagger*. Within each emotion class, we then computed the similarity of the examples with one another, using the implementation of the Lesk distance in Ted Pedersen's Similarity Package. This score was used to split the examples in each emotion class into six clusters using the Simple K-Means implementation in Weka. The idea behind this approach, confirmed by the output of the clusters, was to group examples that are similar, in vocabulary and structure. From this collection, we manually selected a subset of 175 documents with 25 expressions related to each of the emotions: anger, disgust, guilt, fear, sadness, joy and shame. The criteria for choosing this subset were the simplicity of the sentences and the variety of actions described.

The next step was to extract the actions chains described in each of the examples. For this, we employed *Semrol*, the semantic role labeling (SRL) system introduced by Moreda et al. (2007). For the core of knowledge in the EmotiNet KB, we need 100% accurate information. Therefore, we manually extract the agent, the verb and the patient (the surface object of the verb) from the output of Semrol. For example, if we use the input sentence "I'm going to a family party because my mother obliges me to", the system extracts two triples with the main actors of the sentences: (I, go, family party) and (mother, oblige, me), related by the causal adverb "because".

Further on, we resolve the anaphoric expressions automatically, using a heuristic selection of the family member mentioned in the text that is closest to the anaphoric reference and whose properties (gender, number) are compatible with the ones of the reference. The replacement of the references to the speaker, e.g. 'I', 'me', 'myself', is resolved by taking into consideration the entities mentioned in the sentence. In case of ambiguity, we choose the youngest, female member. Following the last example, the subject of the action would be assigned to the daughter of the family and the triples would be updated: (daughter, go, family_party) and (mother, oblige, daughter). Finally, the action links (triplets) are grouped and sorted in action chains. This process of sorting is determined by the adverbial expressions that appear within the sentence, which actually specify the position of each action on a temporal line (e.g. "although" "because", "when"). We defined pattern rules according to which the actions introduced by these modifiers happen prior to or after the current context.

Using our combined emotion model as a reference, we manually assigned one of the seven most basic emotions, i.e. anger, fear, disgust, shame, sadness, joy or guilt, or the neutral value to all the action links obtained, thus generating 4-tuples (subject, action, object, emotion), e.g. (daughter, go, family party, neutral) or (mother, oblige, daughter, disgust).

Once we carried out these processes on the chosen documents, we obtained 175 action chains (ordered lists of tuples). In order to be included in the EmotiNet knowledge base, all their action links needed to be mapped to existing concepts or instances within the KB. When these did not exist, they were added to it. We would like to highlight that in EmotiNet, each tuple (actor, action, patient, emotion) extracted has its own representation as an instance of the subclasses of *Action*. Each in-stance of *Action* is related to an instance of the class *Feel*, which represents the emotion felt in this action. Subsequently, these instances (action links) were grouped in sequences of actions (class *Sequence*) ended by an instance of the class Feel, which determine the final emotion felt by the main actor(s) of the chain.

In our example, we created two new classes *Go* and *Oblige* (subclasses of *DomainAction*) and two new instances of them: instance *act1* ("Go", "daughter", "family_party", "Neutral"); and instance *act2* ("Oblige", "mother", "daughter", "Angry"). The last action link already existed within EmotiNet from another chain so we reused it: instance *act3* ("Feel", "daughter", "anger"). The next step consisted in grouping these instances into sequences by means of instances of the class Sequence, which is a subclass of Action that can establish the temporal order between two actions (which one occurred first). Fig. 3 shows an example of a RDF graph with the action chain of our example. We used Jena (http://jena.sourceforge.net/) and MySQL for the management and storage of EmotiNet on a database.

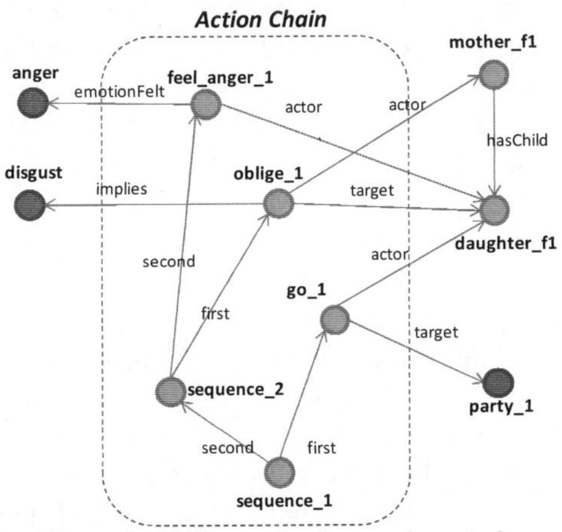

Figure 3. RDF graph of an action chain.

5.3 Ontology Expansion

In order to extend the coverage of the resource, we expanded the ontology with the actions and relations from VerbOcean. This process is essential for EmotiNet, since it adds new types of action and relations between actions, which might not have been analyzed before, thus reducing the degree of dependency between the resource and the initial set of examples. In particular, 299 new actions were automatically included as subclasses of *DomainAction*, which were directly related to any of the actions of our ontology through three new relations: *can-result-in, happens-before and similar*.

6 Experiments and Evaluation

The evaluation of our approach consists in testing if by employing the model we built and the knowledge contained in the core of EmotiNet (which we denote by "knowledge sets"), we are able to detect the emotion expressed in new examples pertaining to the categories in ISEAR. Therefore, we use a test set (marked with B) that contains 895 examples (ISEAR phrases corresponding to the seven emotions modeled, from which core examples were removed).

In order to assess the system performance on the two test sets, we followed the same process we used for building the core of EmotiNet, with the exception that the manual modeling of examples into tuples was replaced with the automatic extraction of (actor, verb, patient) triples from the output given by Semrol. Subsequently, we eliminated the stopwords in the phrases contained in these three roles and performed a simple coreference resolution. Next, we ordered the actions presented in the phrase, using the adverbs that connect the sentences, through the use of patterns (temporal, causal etc.). The resulted action chains for each of the examples in the two test sets will be used in carrying different experiments:

(1). In the first approach, for each of the situations in the test sets (represented now as action chains), we search the EmotiNet KB to encounter the sequences in which these actions in the chains are involved and their corresponding subjects. As a result of the search process, we obtain the emotion label corresponding to the new situation and the subject of the emotion based on a weighting function. This function takes into consideration the number of actions and the position in which they appear in the sequence contained in EmotiNet. The issue in this first approach is that many of the examples cannot be classified, as the knowledge they contain is not present in the ontology.

(2). A subsequent approach aimed at surpassing the issues raised by the missing knowledge in EmotiNet. In a first approximation, we aimed at introducing extra knowledge from VerbOcean, by adding the verbs that were similar to the ones in the core examples (represented in VerbOcean through the "similar" relation). Subsequently, each of the actions in the examples to be classified that was not already contained in EmotiNet, was sought in VerbOcean. In case one of the similar actions was already contained in the KB, the actions were considered equivalent. Further on, each action was associated with an emotion, using the ConceptNet relations and concepts (HasSubevent, Causes, ConceptuallyRelatedTo, HasPrerequisite). Finally, new examples were matched against chains of actions containing the same emotions, in the same order. While more complete than the first approximation, this approach was also affected by lack of knowledge about the emotional content of actions. To overcome this issue, we proposed two heuristics:

(2a) In the first one, actions on which no affect information was available, were sought in within the examples already introduced in the EmotiNet and were assigned the most frequent class of emotion labeling them. The corresponding results are marked with A2a and B2a, respectively.

(2b) In the second approximation, we used the most frequent emotion associated to the known links of a chain, whose individual emotions were obtained from ConceptNet. In this case, the core of action chains is not involved in the process. The corresponding results are marked with A2b and B2b.

We performed the steps described on test set B. The results are shown in Table 1 (results on classified examples) and Table 2 (results on all examples).

Emotion	Correct			Total			Accuracy		
	B1	B2a	B2b	B1	B2a	B2b	B1	B2a	B2b
disgust	16	16	21	44	42	40	36.36	38.09	52.50
shame	25	25	26	70	78	73	35.71	32.05	35.62
anger	31	47	57	105	115	121	29.52	40.86	47.11
fear	35	34	37	58	65	60	60.34	52.30	61.67
sadness	46	45	41	111	123	125	41.44	36.58	32.80
joy	13	16	18	25	29	35	52	55.17	51.43
guilt	59	68	64	158	165	171	37.34	41.21	37.43
Total	225	251	264	571	617	625	39.40	40.68	42.24

Table 1. Results of the emotion detection using EmotiNet on classified examples in test set B

Emotion	Correct			Total	Recall		
	B1	B2a	B2b	B1	B1	B2a	B2b
Disgust	16	16	21	59	27.11	27.11	35.59
Shame	25	25	26	91	27.47	27.47	28.57
Anger	31	47	57	145	21.37	32.41	39.31
Fear	35	34	37	85	60.34	52.30	61.67
Sadness	46	45	41	267	17.22	16.85	15.36
Joy	13	16	18	50	26	32	36.00
Guilt	59	68	64	198	29.79	34.34	32.32
Total	225	251	264	895	25.13	28.04	29.50
Baseline	126	126	126	895	14.0.7	14.07	14.07

Table 2. Results of the emotion detection using EmotiNet on all test examples in test set B

7 Discussion and conclusions

From the results in Table 1 and 2, we can conclude that the approach is valid and represents a method that is appropriate for the detection of emotions from contexts where no affect-related words are present. Nonetheless, much remains to be done to fully exploit the capabilities of EmotiNet. We showed that the approach has a high degree of flexibility, i.e. new information can be easily introduced from existing common-sense knowledge bases, such as ConceptNet, mainly due to its internal structure and degree of granularity.

The error analysis we performed shed some light on the causes of error of the system. The first finding is that extracting only the action, verb and patient semantic roles is not sufficient. There are other roles, such as the modifiers, which change the overall emotion in the text. Therefore, such modifiers should be included as attributes of the concepts identified in the roles. A further source of errors was that lack of knowledge on specific actions. Thus, the results of our approach can be practically limited by the structure, expressivity and degree of granularity of the imported resources. Therefore, to obtain the final, extended version of EmotiNet we should analyze the interactions between the core and the imported resources and among these re-sources as well.

Finally, other errors were produced by NLP processes and propagated at various steps of the processing chain (e.g. SRL, coreference resolution). Some of these errors cannot be eliminated; however, others can be partially solved by using alternative NLP tools.

Future work aims at extending the model by adding affective properties to the concepts included, so that more of the appraisal criteria can be introduced in the model, testing new methods to assign affective value to the concepts and adding new knowledge from sources such as CYC.

Acknowledgments

This paper has been supported by the Spanish Ministry of Science and Innovation (grant no. TIN2009-13391-C04-01), by the Spanish Ministry of Education under the FPU Program (AP2007-03076), and by the Valencian Ministry of Education (grant no. PROMETEO/2009/119 and ACOMP/ 2010/288).

References

A. Balahur and A. Montoyo. 2008. Applying a Culture Dependent Emotion Triggers Database for Text Valence and Emotion Classification, proceedings of the AISB 2008 Convention "Communication, Interaction and Social Intelligence".

A. Balahur and R. Steinberger. 2009. Rethinking Opinion Mining in Newspaper Articles: from Theory to Practice and Back, proceedings of the first workshop on Opinion Mining and Sentiment Analysis (WOMSA 2009).

A. Esuli and F. Sebastiani. 2005. Determining the semantic orientation of terms through gloss analysis", proceedings of CIKM 2005.

B. Pang and L. Lee. 2008. Opinion mining and sentiment analysis. Foundations and Trends in Information Retrieval, Vol 2, Nr. 1-2, 2008.

B. Pang, L. Lee and S. Vaithyanathan. 2002. Thumbs up? Sentiment classification using machine learning techniques, proceedings of EMNLP-02.

C. Strapparava and R. Mihalcea. 2007. Semeval 2007 task 14: Affective text, proceedings of ACL 2007.

E. Cambria, A. Hussain, C. Havasi and C. Eckl. 2009. Affective Space: Blending Common Sense and Affective Knowledge to Perform Emotive Reasoning, proceedings of the 1st Workshop on Opinion Mining and Sentiment Analysis (WOMSA).

E. Riloff and J. Wiebe. 2003. Learning extraction patterns for subjective expressions, proceedings of the 2003 Conference on Empirical Methods in Natural Language Processing.

E. Riloff, J. Wiebe and T. Wilson. 2003. Learning subjective nouns using extraction pattern bootstrapping. In Proceedings of the Conference on Natural Language Learning (CoNLL) 2003, pp.25-32, Edmonton, Canada.

G. Van den Bos. 2006. APA Dictionary of Psychology. Washington, DC: American Psychological Association.

H. Liu and P. Singh. 2004. ConceptNet: A Practical Commonsense Reasoning Toolkit, BT Technology Journal, Volume 22, Kluwer Academic Publishers.

H. Liu, H. Lieberman and T. Selker. 2003. A Model of Textual Affect Sensing Using Real-World Knowledge, proceedings of IUI 2003.

J. De Rivera. 1977. A structural theory of the emotions, Psychological Issues, 10 (4), Monograph 40.

J. W. Pennebaker, M. R. Mehl and K. Niederhoffer. 2003. Psychological aspects of natural language use: Our words, our selves, Annual Review of Psychology 54, 547-577.

K. Scherer and H. Wallbott. 1997. The ISEAR Questionnaire and Codebook, Geneva Emotion Research Group.

K. Scherer, K. 2005. What are emotions? and how can they be measured? Social Science Information, 3(44), 695-729.

M. Dyer. 1987. Emotions and their computations: three computer models, Cognition and Emotion, 1, 323-347.

N. Frijda. 1986. The emotions, Cambridge University Press.

P. Moreda, B. Navarro and M. Palomar. 2007. Corpus-based semantic role approach in information retrieval, Data Knowl. Eng. (DKE) 61(3):467-483.

P. N. Johnson-Laird and K. Oatley. 1989. The language of emotions: An analysis of a semantic field, Cognition and Emotion, 3, 81-123.

P. Subasic and A. Huettner. 2000. Affect Analysis of text using fuzzy semantic typing, IEEE Trasactions on Fuzzy System, 9, 483-496.

R. A. Calvo and S. D'Mello. 2010. Affect Detection: An Interdisciplinary Review of Models, Methods and Their Applications, IEEE Transactions on Affective Computing, Vol. 1, No. 1, Jan.-Jun.

R. Picard. 1995. Affective computing, Technical report, MIT Media Laboratory.

R. Plutchik. 2001. The Nature of Emotions. American Scientist. 89, 344.

R. Studer, R. V. Benjamins and D. Fensel. 1998. Knowledge engineering: Principles and methods, Data & Knowledge Engineering, 25(1-2):161–197.

S. Y. Mei Lee, Y. Chen and C.-R. Huang. 2009. Cause Event Representations of Happiness and Surprise, proceedings of PACLIC 2009.

T. Chklovski and P. Pantel. 2004. VerbOcean: Mining the Web for Fine-Grained Semantic Verb Relations", proceedings of EMNLP-04.

T. Danisman and A. Alpkocak. 2008. Feeler: Emotion Classification of Text Using Vector Space Model, proceedings of the AISB 2008 Convention, "Communication, Interaction and Social Intelligence".

W. Parrott. 2001. Emotions in Social Psychology, Psychology Press, Philadelphia.

A Link to the Past: Constructing Historical Social Networks

Matje van de Camp
Tilburg Centre for Cognition
and Communication
Tilburg University, The Netherlands
M.M.v.d.Camp@uvt.nl

Antal van den Bosch
Tilburg Centre for Cognition
and Communication
Tilburg University, The Netherlands
Antal.vdnBosch@uvt.nl

Abstract

To assist in the research of social networks in history, we develop machine-learning-based tools for the identification and classification of personal relationships. Our case study focuses on the Dutch social movement between 1870 and 1940, and is based on biographical texts describing the lives of notable people in this movement. We treat the identification and the labeling of relations between two persons into positive, neutral, and negative both as a sequence of two tasks and as a single task. We observe that our machine-learning classifiers, support vector machines, produce better generalization performance on the single task. We show how a complete social network can be built from these classifications, and provide a qualitative analysis of the induced network using expert judgements on samples of the network.

1 Introduction

The rapid growth of Social Networking Services such as Facebook, Myspace and Twitter over the last few years has made it possible to gather data on human interactions on a large scale, causing an increased interest in the field of Social Network Analysis and Extraction. Although we are now more interconnected than ever before due to technological advances, social networks have always been a vital part of human existence. They are prerequisite to the distribution of knowledge and beliefs among people and to the formation of larger entities such as organizations and communities. By applying the technology of today to the heritage of our past, it may be possible to uncover yet unknown patterns and provide a better insight into our society's development.

In this paper we present a case study based on historical biographical information, so-called secondary historical sources, describing people in a particular domain, region and time frame: the Dutch social movement between the mid-19th and mid-20th century. "Social movement" refers to the social-political-economical complex of ideologies, worker's unions, political organizations, and art movements that arose from the ideas of Karl Marx (1818–1883) and followers. In the Netherlands, a network of persons unfolded over time with leader figures such as Ferdinand Domela Nieuwenhuis (1846–1919) and Pieter Jelles Troelstra (1860–1930). Although this network is implicit in all the primary and secondary historical writings documenting the period, and partly explicit in the minds of experts studying the domain, there is no explicitly modeled social network of this group of persons. Yet, it would potentially benefit further research in social history to have this in the form of a computational model.

In our study we focus on detecting and labeling relations between two persons, where one of the persons, A, is the topic of a biographical article, and the other person, B, is mentioned in that article. The genre of biographical articles allows us to assume that person A is topical throughout the text. What remains is to determine whether the mention of person B signifies a relation between A and B, and if so, whether the relation in the direction of A to B can be labeled as positive, neutral, or negative. Many more fine-grained labels are possible (as discussed later in

Proceedings of the 2nd Workshop on Computational Approaches to Subjectivity and Sentiment Analysis, ACL-HLT 2011, pages 61–69,
24 June, 2011, Portland, Oregon, USA ©2011 Association for Computational Linguistics

the paper), but the primary aim of our case study is to build a basic network out of robustly recognized person-to-person relations at the highest possible accuracy. As our data only consists of several hundreds of articles describing an amount of people of roughly the same order of magnitude, we are facing data sparsity, and thus are limited in the granularity of the labels we wish to predict.

This paper is structured as follows. After a brief survey of related research in Section 2, we describe our method of research, our data, and our annotation scheme in Section 3. In Section 4 we describe how we implement relation detection and classification as supervised machine learning tasks. The outcomes of the experiments on our data are provided in Section 5. We discuss our findings, formulate conclusions, and identify points for future research in Section 6.

2 Related Research

Our research combines Social Network Extraction and Sentiment Analysis. We briefly review related research in both areas.

2.1 Social Network Extraction

A widely used method for determining the relatedness of two entities was first introduced by Kautz et al (1997). They compute the relatedness between two entities by normalizing their co-occurrence count on the Web with their individual hit counts using the Jaccard coefficient. If the coefficient reaches a certain threshold, the entities are considered to be related. For disambiguation purposes, keywords are added to the queries when obtaining the hit counts.

Matsuo et al (2004) apply the same method to find connections between members of a closed community of researchers. They gather person names from conference attendance lists to create the nodes of the network. The affiliations of each person are added to the queries as a crude form of named entity disambiguation. When a connection is found, the relation is labeled by applying minimal rules, based on the occurrence of manually selected keywords, to the contents of websites where both entities are mentioned.

A more elaborate approach to network mining is taken by Mika (2005) in his presentation of the *Flink* system. In addition to Web co-occurrence counts of person names, the system uses data mined from other—highly structured—sources such as email headers, publication archives and so-called Friend-Of-A-Friend (FOAF) profiles. Co-occurrence counts of a name and different interests taken from a predefined set are used to determine a person's expertise and to enrich their profile. These profiles are then used to resolve named entity co-reference and to find new connections.

Elson et al (2010) use quoted speech attribution to reconstruct the social networks of the characters in a novel. Though this work is most related regarding the type of data used, their method can be considered complementary to ours: where they relate entities based on their conversational interaction without further analysis of the content, we try to find connections based solely on the words that occur in the text.

Efforts in more general relation extraction from text have focused on finding recurring patterns and transforming them into triples (RDF). Relation types and labels are then deduced from the most common patterns (Ravichandran and Hovy, 2002; Culotta et al, 2006). These approaches work well for the induction and verification of straightforwardly verbalized factoids, but they are too restricted to capture the multitude of aspects that surround human interaction; a case in point is the kind of relationship between two persons, which people can usually infer from the text, but is rarely explicitly described in a single triple.

2.2 Sentiment Analysis

Sentiment analysis is concerned with locating and classifying the subjective information contained in a source. Subjectivity is inherently dependent on human interpretation and emotion. A machine can be taught to mimic these aspects, given enough examples, but the interaction of the two is what makes humans able to understand, for instance, that a sarcastic comment is not meant to be taken literally.

Although the general distinction between negative and positive is intuitive for humans to make, subjectivity and sentiment are very much domain and context dependent. Depending on the domain and context, a single sentence can have opposite meanings (Pang and Lee, 2008).

Many of the approaches to automatically solving tasks like these involve using lists of positively and negatively polarized words or phrases to calculate the overall sentiment of a clause, sentence or document (Pang et al, 2002). As shown by Kim and Hovy (2006), the order of the words potentially influences the interpretation of a text. Pang et al (2002) also found that the simple presence of a word is more important than the number of times it appears.

Word sense disambiguation can be a useful tool in determining polarity. Turney (2002) proposed a simple, but seemingly effective way to determine polarity at the word level. He calculates the difference between the mutual information gain of a phrase and the word 'excellent' and of the same phrase and the word 'poor'.

3 Method, Data, and Annotation

3.1 Method

In contrast to most previous work regarding social network extraction, we do not possess any explicit record of the network we are after. Although the documents we work with are available online, the number of hyperlinks between them is minimal and all personal relations are expressed only in running text. We aim to train a system able to extract these relations and classify their polarity automatically using as little information as possible that is not explicitly included in the text, thus keeping the reliance on external resources as limited as possible.

We take the same approach with regards to the sentiment analysis part of the task: no predefined lists are supplied to the system and no word sense disambiguation is performed.

We take a supervised machine learning approach to solving the problem, by training support vector machines on a limited number of preclassified examples. We chose to use SVMs as a baseline method that has been shown to be effective in text categorization tasks (Joachims, 1998). We compare performance between joint learning, using one multi-class classifier, and a pipeline, using a single class classifier to judge whether an instance describes a relation, and a second classifier to classify the relations according to their polarity.

3.2 Data

We use the Biographical Dictionary of Socialism and the Workers' Movement in the Netherlands (BWSA) as input for our system.[1] This digital resource consists of 574 biographical articles, in Dutch, relating to the most notable actors within the domain. The texts are accompanied by a database that holds such metadata as a person's full name and known aliases, dates of birth and death, and a short description of the role they played within the Workers' Movement. The articles were written by over 200 different authors, thus the use of vocabulary varies greatly across the texts. The length of the biographies also varies: the shortest text has 308 tokens, the longest has 7,188 tokens. The mean length is 1,546 tokens with a standard deviation of 784.

A biography can be seen as a summary of the most important events in a person's life. Therefore, this type of data suits our purpose well: any person that the main character was closely related to, can be expected to appear in his or her biography.

In training our relation extraction system we look only at the relation from A to B and its associated polarity. The assumption that we make here is that by processing the BWSA in its entirety, making each of the 574 main characters person A once and harvesting all of their relations, we will get a full view of the existing relations, including the relation from B to A if A and B have a relation and B also has a biography in the BWSA.

We create one data set focused on a particular person who is prevalent throughout the data, namely Ferdinand Domela Nieuwenhuis (FDN). He started his career as a Lutheran priest, but lost his faith and pursued a career in socialist politics. After a series of disappointments, however, he turned to anarchism and eventually withdrew himself from the political stage completely, though his ideas continued to inspire others. We expect that the turmoil of his life will be reflected in his social network and the variety of relationships surrounding him.

As a first step in recreating Domela Nieuwenhuis' network, we extract all sentences from the BWSA that mention the name 'Domela', by which he is generally known. We exclude Domela's own biography from the search. All but one of the ex-

[1] http://www.iisg.nl/bwsa/

tracted sentences, 447 in total, actually refer to Ferdinand Domela Nieuwenhuis. This sentence is removed, resulting in a total of 446 sentences spread over 153 biographies. Each sentence with a mention is expanded with additional context, to capture more clues than the sentence with the mention might hold. Preliminary tests showed that two sentences of context before the mention, and two sentences of context after the mention is sufficient. Often there is an introduction before a person is mentioned, and an elaboration on the relation after the mention. Figure 1 shows an example fragment.

However, since Domela was a rather controversial and a-typical figure, his network might not be a good representation of the actual relations in the data. Therefore, we create a second data set by randomly extracting another 534 sentences with their surrounding context from the BWSA that contain a named entity which is not the main entity of the biography. We aim to test which data set leads to better performance in finding and classifying relations across the entire community.

3.3 Annotation

All fragments in the Domela set were annotated by two human annotators, native speakers of Dutch, but unfamiliar with the domain of social history. They were asked to judge whether the fragment does in fact describe a relation between the two entities and, if so, whether the polarity of the relation from A to B is negative, neutral, or positive; i.e. whether person A has a negative, neutral or positive attitude towards person B.

With regards to the existence of a relation, the annotators reached an agreement of 74.9%. For the negative, neutral and positive classes they agreed on 60.8%, 24.2%, and 66.5%, respectively. All disagreements were resolved in discussion. The class distribution over the three polarities after resolution is shown in Table 1.

The generic set was annotated by only one of the annotators. The class distribution of this set is also shown in Table 1. It is roughly the same as the distribution for the A to B polarities from the Domela set.

Class	**Generic set**		**FDN set**	
	No.	%	No.	%
negative	86	16.1	74	16.6
neutral	134	25.1	87	19.5
positive	238	44.6	215	48.2
not related	76	14.2	70	15.7
total	534	100	446	100

Table 1: Class distribution

4 Relation Extraction and Classification

We train our system using LibSVM (Chang and Lin, 2001), an implementation of support vector machines. In training, the cost factor is set to 0.01 with a polynomial kernel type.

4.1 Preprocessing

First, all fragments and biographies are lemmatized and POS-tagged using Frog, a morpho-syntactic analyzer for Dutch (Van den Bosch et al, 2007). In a next step, Named Entity Recognition is performed with a classifier-based sequence processing tool trained on biographical data.

To identify the person to which a named entity refers, the name is split up into chunks representing first name, initials, infix and surname. These chunks, as far as they are included in the string, are then matched against the BWSA database. If no match is found, the name is added to the database as a new person. For now, however, we treat the network as a closed community by only extracting those fragments in which person B is one that already has a biography in the BWSA. At a later stage, biographies of people from outside the BWSA can be gathered and used to determine their position within the network.

4.2 Features

Co-occurrence counts: We calculate an initial measure of the relatedness of A to B using a method that is similar to Kautz et al (1997). The main difference is that we do not get our co-occurrence counts only from the Web, but also from the data itself. Since the domain of the data is so specific, Web counts do not accurately represent the actual distribution of people in the data. More famous people are likely to receive more attention on the Web than less famous people.

Ansing^{PER-A} and Domela Nieuwenhuis^{PER-B} were in written contact with each other since August 1878. Domela Nieuwenhuis probably wrote uplifting words in his letter to Ansing, which was not preserved, after reading Pekelharing's report of the program convention of the ANWV in *Vragen des Tijds*, which was all but flattering for Ansing.
In this letter, Domela also offered his services to Ansing and his friends.
Domela Nieuwenhuis used this opportunity to ask Ansing several questions about the conditions of the workers, the same that he had already asked in a letter to the ANWV in 1877, which had been left unanswered.
Ansing answered the questions extensively.

Figure 1: English translation of an example fragment from the FDN set.

This is illustrated by Figure 2, where the number of times each person's name is mentioned within the BWSA is compared to the number of times he or she is mentioned on the Web.

We collect all possible combinations of each person's first names, initials and surnames (some are known by multiple surnames) and their aliases from the database and get the number of hits, i.e. the number of articles or webpages that contain the name, by querying the BWSA and Yahoo!. For each we derive 6 scores:

- *A-B*: the maximum hit count of all combinations of A ∩ B divided by the maximum hit count of A;
- *A-B(25)*: the maximum hit count of all combinations of A ∩ B within 25 words divided by the maximum hit count of A;
- *B-A*: the maximum hit count of all combinations of A ∩ B divided by the maximum hit count of B;
- *B-A(25)*: the maximum hit count of all combinations of A ∩ B within 25 words divided by the maximum hit count of B;
- *AB*: the maximum hit count of all combinations of A ∩ B divided by the maximum hit count of A plus the maximum hit count of B;
- *AB(25)*: the maximum hit count of all combinations of A ∩ B within 25 words divided by the maximum hit count of A plus the maximum hit count of B.

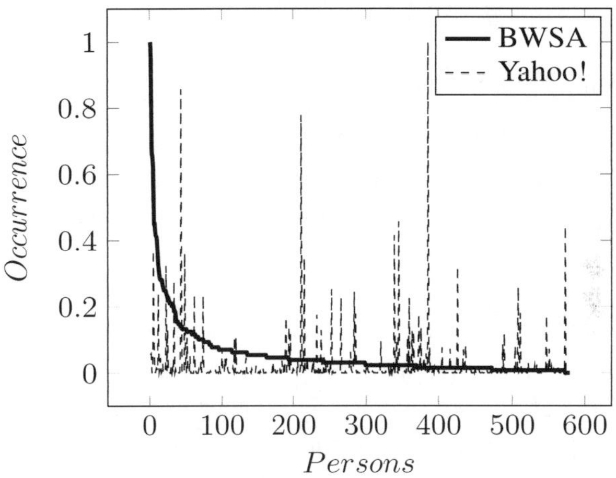

Figure 2: Fraction of maximum occurrence count for all 574 persons in the BWSA and on Yahoo!.

Set mention count: As an indication of the relatedness more specific to the text fragment under consideration, we add the number of times A or B is mentioned in the 5-sentence-context of the fragment, and the number of sentences in which both A and B are mentioned to the feature vector.

Lexical features: Preliminary tests revealed that keeping lemmatized verbs and nouns provided the best results, with mildly positive effects for prepositions and person names. All tokens outside these categories were not incorporated in the feature vector.

Person names are further processed in two ways: all mentions of person A and person B are replaced with labels 'PER-A' and 'PER-B'; all names of other persons mentioned in the fragment are replaced with label 'PER-X', where X is either the next available letter in the alphabet (anonymous) or the person's unique ID in the database (identified).

We create four variants of both the generic data set and the FDN data set: one that represents only verbs and nouns (VN), one that also includes prepositions (VNPr), one that includes anonymous person names (VNP-a) and a last one that includes identified person names (VNP-i). Each set is split into a training and a test set of respectively 90% and 10% of the total size. We test our system both with binary features and with tf.idf weighted features.

5 Results and Evaluation

5.1 Binary versus Tf.idf

Figure 3 shows the 10-fold cross-validation accuracy scores on the joint learning task for each of the training vector sets using binary and tf.idf weighted features. We take the majority class of the training set as our baseline. In all cases we observe that unweighted binary features outperform weighted features. These results are in line with the findings of Pang et al (2002), who found that the occurrence of a word is more important than its frequency in determining the sentiment of a text.

Regarding the different feature sets, the addition of prepositions or person names, either anonymous or identified, does not have a significant effect on the results. Only for the VNP-a set the score is raised from 47.86 % to 48.53 % by the inclusion of anonymous person names.

5.2 Co-occurrence

We perform a second experiment to assess the influence of adding any of the co-occurrence measures to the feature vectors. Figure 4 displays the results for the VN set on its own and with inclusion of the set mention counts (M), the BWSA co-occurrence scores (B) and the Yahoo! co-occurrence scores (Y).

For the generic set, we observe in all cases that the co-occurrence measures have a negative effect on the overall score. For the FDN set this is not always the case. The set mention counts slightly improve the score, though this is not significant. The remainder of the experiments is performed on the vectors without any co-occurrence scores.

5.3 Joint Learning versus Pipeline

Table 2 lists the accuracy scores on the training sets on both the joint learning task and the pipeline. Only for the FDN set does the system perform better on the two-step task than on the single task. In fact, the FDN set reaches an accuracy of 53.08 % in the two-step task, which is 6.55 % higher than the majority class baseline and the highest score so far.

The system consistently performs better on the joint learning task for the generic set. Further investigation into why the pipeline does not do well on the generic set reveals that in the first step of the task, where instances are classified on whether they describe a relation or not, all instances always get classified as 'related'. This immediately results in an error rate of approximately 15%. In the second step, when classifying relations into negative, neutral or positive, we observe that in most cases the system again resorts to majority class voting and thus does not exceed the baseline.

Even for the FDN set, where the pipeline does outperform the joint learning task, the difference in accuracy between both tasks is minor (0.22-0.96 %). We conclude that it is preferable to approach our classification problem as a single, rather than a two-step task. If the system already resorts to majority class voting in the first step, every occurrence of a name in a biography will be flagged as a relation, which is detrimental to the precision of the system.

5.4 Generic versus FDN

Although the classifiers trained on both sets do not perform particularly well, the FDN set provides a greater gain in accuracy over the baseline. The same is shown when we train the system on the training sets for both data sets and test them on the held out test sets. For the generic set, the VNP-a feature set provides the best results. It results in an accuracy of 50% on the test set, with a baseline of 48.2%.

For the FDN data set, none of the different feature sets performs better than the others on the joint learning task. In testing, however, the VNP-a set proves to be most successful. It results in an accuracy of 66.7%, which is a gain of 4.5% over the baseline of 62.2%.

To test how well each of the sets generalizes over the entire community, we test both sets on each

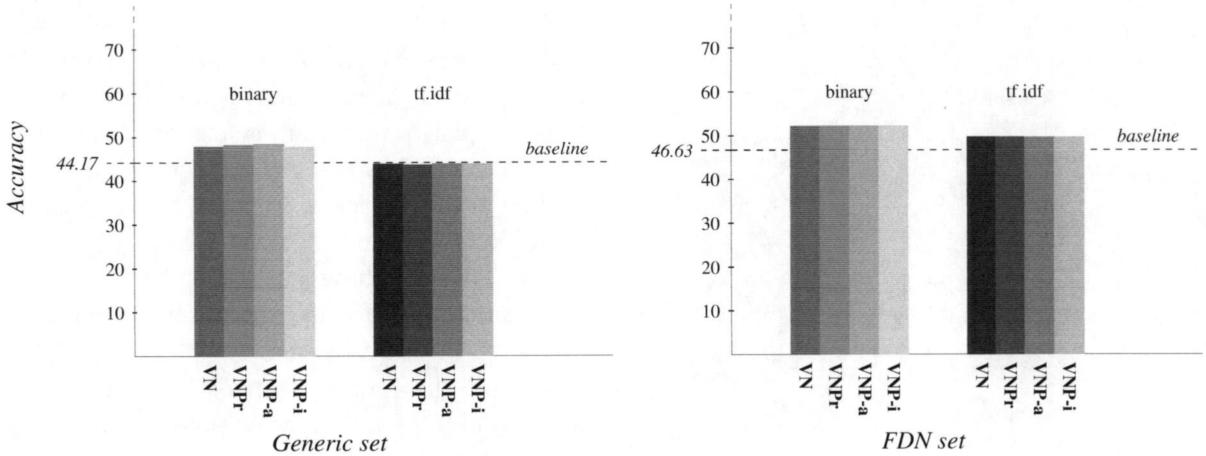

Figure 3: Binary versus weighted features.

	Generic set			FDN set		
	joint	*pipeline*	*baseline*	*joint*	*pipeline*	*baseline*
VN	47.92	45.83	44.17	52.12	52.83	46.63
VNPr	48.33	46.88	44.17	52.12	**53.08**	46.63
VNP-a	**48.54**	46.88	44.17	52.12	52.34	46.63
VNP-i	47.71	45.83	44.17	52.12	52.59	46.63

Table 2: Accuracy scores on training sets (10-fold cross-validation) for both the joint learning task and the pipeline.

other. Training on the generic set and testing on the FDN set results in an accuracy of 45.3% with a baseline of 48.2%. Doing the same experiment vice versa results in an accuracy of 44.8% with a baseline of 44.6%. Examining the output reveals that both systems resort to selecting the majority class ('positive') in most cases. The system that was trained on the FDN set correctly selects the 'negative' class in a few cases, but never classifies a fragment as 'neutral' or 'not related'. The distribution of classes in the output of the generic system shows a bit more variety: 0.2% is classified as 'negative', 10.1% is classified as 'neutral' and 89.7% is classified as 'positive'. None of the fragments are classified as 'not related'. A possible explanation for this is the fact that the 'not related' fragments in the FDN set specifically describe situations where the main entity is not related to Ferdinand Domela Nieuwenhuis; these fragments could still describe a relation from the main entity to another person mentioned in the fragment and therefore be miss-classified.

5.5 Evaluation

To evaluate our system, we process the entire BWSA, extracting from each biography all fragments that mention a person from any of the other biographies. We train the system on the best performing feature set of the generic data set, VNP-a. In order to filter out some of the errors, we remove all relations of which only one instance is found in the BWSA.

The resulting network is evaluated qualitatively by a domain expert on a sample of the network. For this we extracted the top-five friends and foes for five persons. Both rankings are based on the frequency of the relation in the system's output. The lists of friends are judged to be mostly correct. This is probably due to the fact that the positive relation is the majority class, to which the classifiers easily revert.

The generated lists of foes are more controversial. Some of the lists contain names which are also included in the list of friends. Of course, this is not

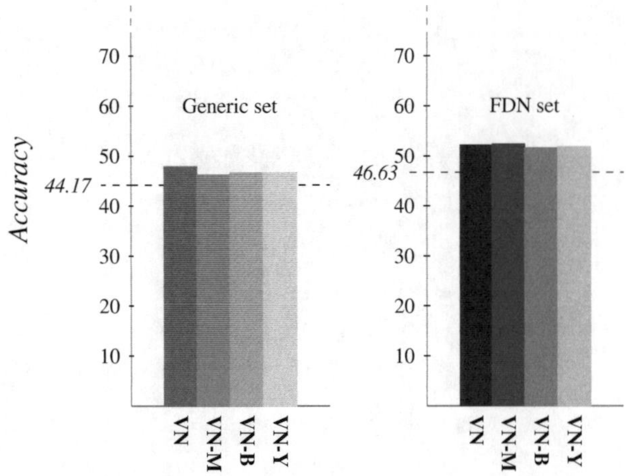

Figure 4: Comparison of co-occurrence features: M = set mention counts, B = BWSA co-occurrence, Y = Yahoo! co-occurrence.

necessarily a sign of bad system performance: we do not count time as a factor in this experiment and relationships are subject to change. 25% of the listed foes are judged to be completely wrong by the expert judge. 10% are not so much enemies of the main entity, but did have known political disagreements with them. The remaining 65% are considered to be plausible as foes, though the expert would not have placed them in the top five.

6 Discussion and Future Research

Our case study has demonstrated that relations between persons can be identified and labeled by their polarity at an above-baseline level, though the improvements are minor. Yet, the utility of the classifications is visible in the higher-level task of constructing a complete social network from all the classified pairwise relations. After filtering out relations with only one attestation, a qualitative analysis by a domain expert on frequency-ranked top-five lists of friends and foes yielded mostly correct results on the majority class, 'positive', and approximately 65% correct on the harder 'negative' class. If we would not have used the classifier and guessed only the majority 'positive' class, we would not have been able to build ranked lists of foes.

In discussions with domain experts, several extensions to our current annotation scheme have been proposed, some of which may be learnable to some usable extent (i.e. leading to qualitatively good labelings in the overall social network) with machine learning tools given sufficient annotated material. First, we plan to include more elaborate annotations by domain experts that discriminate between types of relationships, such as between family members, co-workers, or friends. Second, relationships are obviously not static throughout time; their polarity and type can change, and they have a beginning and an end.

We aim at working with other machine learning methods in future expansions of our experimental matrix, including the use of rule learning methods because of their interpretable output. Another direction of research, related to the idea of the improved annotation levels, is the identification of sub-networks in the total social network. Arguably, certain sub-networks identify ideologically like-minded people, and may correspond to what eventually developed into organizations such as workers unions or political organizations. When we are able to link automatically detected temporal expressions to initializations, changes, and endings of relationships, we may be able to have enough ingredients for the automatic identification of large-scale events such as the emergence of a political movement.

References

Antal van den Bosch, Bertjan Busser, Sander Canisius and Walter Daelemans. 2007. *An efficient memory-based morphosyntactic tagger and parser for Dutch.* Selected Papers of the 17th Computational Linguistics in the Netherlands Meeting, Leuven, Belgium, 99–114.

Chih-Chung Chang and Chih-Jen Lin. 2001. *LIBSVM: a library for support vector machines.* Software available at `http://www.csie.ntu.edu.tw/~cjlin/libsvm`.

Aron Culotta, Andrew McCallum and Jonathan Betz. 2006. *Integrating probabilistic extraction models and data mining to discover relations and patterns in text.* Proceedings of the main conference on Human Language Technology Conference of the North American Chapter of the Association of Computational Linguistics (HLT-NAACL) 2006, 296–303.

Walter Daelemans, Jakub Zavrel, Ko van der Sloot and Antal van den Bosch. 2010. *TiMBL: Tilburg Memory*

Based Learner, version 6.3, Reference Guide. ILK Research Group Technical Report Series no. 10-01.

David K. Elson, Nicholas Dames, Kathleen R. McKeown. 2010. *Extracting social networks from literary fiction*. Proceedings of the 48th Annual Meeting of the Association for Computational Linguistics 2010, 138–147.

Thorsten Joachims. 1998. *Text categorization with support vector machines: Learning with many relevant features*. Proceedings of ECML-98, 10th European Conference on Machine Learning 1998, 137-142.

Henry Kautz, Bart Selman and Mehul Shah. 1997. *The hidden web*. AI Magazine, volume 18, number 2, 27–36.

Soo-Min Kim and Eduard Hovy. 2006. *Automatic identification of pro and con reasons in online reviews*. Proceedings of the COLING/ACL Main Conference Poster Sessions, 483–490.

Yutaka Matsuo, Hironori Tomobe, Koiti Hasida and Mitsuru Ishizuka. 2004. *Finding social network for trust calculation*. European Conference on Artificial Intelligence - ECAI 2004.

Peter Mika. 2005. *Flink: Semantic web technology for the extraction and analysis of social networks*. Web Semantics: Science, Services and Agents on the World Wide Web, volume 3, number 2-3, 211–223.

Bo Pang, Lillian Lee and Shivakumar Vaithyanathan. 2002. *Thumbs up? Sentiment classification using machine learning techniques*. Proceedings of the Conference on Empirical Methods in Natural Language Processing (EMNLP), 79–86.

Bo Pang and Lillian Lee. 2008. *Opinion mining and sentiment analysis*. Foundations and Trends in Information Retrieval, vol. 2, number 1-2, 1–135.

Deepak Ravichandran and Eduard Hovy. 2002. *Learning Surface Text Patterns for a Question Answering System*. Proceedings of the 40th Annual Meeting on Association for Computational Linguistics (ACL) 2002.

Peter D. Turney. 2002. *Thumbs up or thumbs down? Semantic orientation applied to unsupervised classification of reviews*. Proceedings of the Association for Computational Linguistics (ACL), 417-424.

Tracking Sentiment in Mail: How Genders Differ on Emotional Axes

Saif M. Mohammad† and **Tony (Wenda) Yang**†⋆
Institute for Information Technology, National Research Council Canada†.
Ottawa, Ontario, Canada, K1A 0R6.
School of Computing Science, Simon Fraser University⋆
Burnaby, British Columbia, V5A 1S6.
saif.mohammad@nrc-cnrc.gc.ca, wenday@sfu.ca

Abstract

With the widespread use of email, we now have access to unprecedented amounts of text that we ourselves have written. In this paper, we show how sentiment analysis can be used in tandem with effective visualizations to quantify and track emotions in many types of mail. We create a large word–emotion association lexicon by crowdsourcing, and use it to compare emotions in love letters, hate mail, and suicide notes. We show that there are marked differences across genders in how they use emotion words in work-place email. For example, women use many words from the joy–sadness axis, whereas men prefer terms from the fear–trust axis. Finally, we show visualizations that can help people track emotions in their emails.

1 Introduction

Emotions are central to our well-being, yet it is hard to be objective of one's own emotional state. Letters have long been a channel to convey emotions, explicitly and implicitly, and now with the widespread usage of email, people have access to unprecedented amounts of text that they themselves have written and received. In this paper, we show how sentiment analysis can be used in tandem with effective visualizations to track emotions in letters and emails.

Automatic analysis and tracking of emotions in emails has a number of benefits including:

1. Determining risk of repeat attempts by analyzing suicide notes (Osgood and Walker, 1959; Matykiewicz et al., 2009; Pestian et al., 2008).[1]
2. Understanding how genders communicate through work-place and personal email (Boneva et al., 2001).
3. Tracking emotions towards people and entities, over time. For example, did a certain managerial course bring about a measurable change in one's inter-personal communication?
4. Determining if there is a correlation between the emotional content of letters and changes in a person's social, economic, or physiological state. Sudden and persistent changes in the amount of emotion words in mail may be a sign of psychological disorder.
5. Enabling affect-based search. For example, efforts to improve customer satisfaction can benefit by searching the received mail for snippets expressing anger (Díaz and Ruz, 2002; Dubé and Maute, 1996).
6. Assisting in writing emails that convey only the desired emotion, and avoiding misinterpretation (Liu et al., 2003).
7. Analyzing emotion words and their role in persuasion in communications by fervent letter writers such as Francois-Marie Arouet Voltaire and Karl Marx (Voltaire, 1973; Marx, 1982).[2]

In this paper, we describe how we created a large word–emotion association lexicon by crowdsourcing with effective quality control measures (Section

[1]The 2011 Informatics for Integrating Biology and the Bedside (i2b2) challenge by the National Center for Biomedical Computing is on detecting emotions in suicide notes.

[2]Voltaire: http://www.whitman.edu/VSA/letters
Marx: http://www.marxists.org/archive/marx/works/date

Proceedings of the 2nd Workshop on Computational Approaches to Subjectivity and Sentiment Analysis, ACL-HLT 2011, pages 70–79,
24 June, 2011, Portland, Oregon, USA ©2011 Association for Computational Linguistics

3). In Section 4, we show comparative analyses of emotion words in love letters, hate mail, and suicide notes. This is done: (a) To determine the distribution of emotion words in these types of mail, as a first step towards more sophisticated emotion analysis (for example, in developing a depression–happiness scale for Application 1), and (b) To use these corpora as a testbed to establish that the emotion lexicon and the visualizations we propose help interpret the emotions in text. In Section 5, we analyze how men and women differ in the kinds of emotion words they use in work-place email (Application 2). Finally, in Section 6, we show how emotion analysis can be integrated with email services such as Gmail to help people track emotions in the emails they send and receive (Application 3).

The emotion analyzer recognizes words with positive polarity (expressing a favorable sentiment towards an entity), negative polarity (expressing an unfavorable sentiment towards an entity), and no polarity (neutral). It also associates words with joy, sadness, anger, fear, trust, disgust, surprise, anticipation, which are argued to be the eight basic and prototypical emotions (Plutchik, 1980).

2 Related work

Over the last decade, there has been considerable work in sentiment analysis, especially in determining whether a term has a positive or negative polarity (Lehrer, 1974; Turney and Littman, 2003; Mohammad et al., 2009). There is also work in more sophisticated aspects of sentiment, for example, in detecting emotions such as anger, joy, sadness, fear, surprise, and disgust (Bellegarda, 2010; Mohammad and Turney, 2010; Alm et al., 2005; Alm et al., 2005). The technology is still developing and it can be unpredictable when dealing with short sentences, but it has been shown to be reliable when drawing conclusions from large amounts of text (Dodds and Danforth, 2010; Pang and Lee, 2008).

Automatically analyzing affect in emails has primarily been done for automatic gender identification (Cheng et al., 2009; Corney et al., 2002), but it has relied on mostly on surface features such as exclamations and very small emotion lexicons. The WordNet Affect Lexicon (WAL) (Strapparava and Valitutti, 2004) has a few hundred words annotated with associations to a number of affect categories including the six Ekman emotions (joy, sadness, anger, fear, disgust, and surprise).[3] General Inquirer (GI) (Stone et al., 1966) has 11,788 words labeled with 182 categories of word tags, including positive and negative polarity.[4] Affective Norms for English Words (ANEW) has pleasure (happy–unhappy), arousal (excited–calm), and dominance (controlled–in control) ratings for 1034 words.[5] Mohammad and Turney (2010) compiled emotion annotations for about 4000 words with eight emotions (six of Ekman, trust, and anticipation).

3 Emotion Analysis

3.1 Emotion Lexicon

We created a large word–emotion association lexicon by crowdsourcing to Amazon's mechanical Turk.[6] We follow the method outlined in Mohammad and Turney (2010). Unlike Mohammad and Turney, who used the *Macquarie Thesaurus* (Bernard, 1986), we use the *Roget Thesaurus* as the source for target terms.[7] Since the 1911 US edition of *Roget's* is available freely in the public domain, it allows us to distribute our emotion lexicon without the burden of restrictive licenses. We annotated only those words that occurred more than 120,000 times in the Google n-gram corpus.[8]

The *Roget's Thesaurus* groups related words into about a thousand categories, which can be thought of as coarse senses or concepts (Yarowsky, 1992). If a word is ambiguous, then it is listed in more than one category. Since a word may have different emotion associations when used in different senses, we obtained annotations at word-sense level by first asking an automatically generated word-choice question pertaining to the target:

Q1. Which word is closest in meaning to *shark* (target)?

- *car*
- *tree*
- *fish*
- *olive*

The near-synonym is taken from the thesaurus, and the distractors are randomly chosen words. This

[3]WAL: http://wndomains.fbk.eu/wnaffect.html

[4]GI: http://www.wjh.harvard.edu/~inquirer

[5]ANEW: http://csea.phhp.ufl.edu/media/anewmessage.html

[6]Mechanical Turk: www.mturk.com/mturk/welcome

[7]Macquarie Thesaurus: www.macquarieonline.com.au
Roget's Thesaurus: www.gutenberg.org/ebooks/10681

[8]The Google n-gram corpus is available through the LDC.

question guides the annotator to the desired sense of the target word. It is followed by ten questions asking if the target is associated with positive sentiment, negative sentiment, anger, fear, joy, sadness, disgust, surprise, trust, and anticipation. The questions are phrased exactly as described in Mohammad and Turney (2010).

If an annotator answers Q1 incorrectly, then we discard information obtained from the remaining questions. Thus, even though we do not have correct answers to the emotion association questions, likely incorrect annotations are filtered out. About 10% of the annotations were discarded because of an incorrect response to Q1.

Each term is annotated by 5 different people. For 74.4% of the instances, all five annotators agreed on whether a term is associated with a particular emotion or not. For 16.9% of the instances four out of five people agreed with each other. The information from multiple annotators for a particular term is combined by taking the majority vote. The lexicon has entries for about 24,200 word–sense pairs. The information from different senses of a word is combined by taking the union of all emotions associated with the different senses of the word. This resulted in a word-level emotion association lexicon for about 14,200 word types. These files are together referred to as the *NRC Emotion Lexicon version 0.92*.

3.2 Text Analysis

Given a target text, the system determines which of the words exist in our emotion lexicon and calculates ratios such as the number of words associated with an emotion to the total number of emotion words in the text. This simple approach may not be reliable in determining if a particular sentence is expressing a certain emotion, but it is reliable in determining if a large piece of text has more emotional expressions compared to others in a corpus. Example applications include detecting spikes in anger words in close proximity to mentions of a target product in a twitter stream (Díaz and Ruz, 2002; Dubé and Maute, 1996), and literary analyses of text, for example, how novels and fairy tales differ in the use of emotion words (Mohammad, 2011b).

4 Love letters, hate mail, and suicide notes

In this section, we quantitatively compare the emotion words in love letters, hate mail, and suicide notes. We compiled a *love letters corpus (LLC) v 0.1* by extracting 348 postings from lovingyou.com.[9] We created a *hate mail corpus (HMC) v 0.1* by collecting 279 pieces of hate mail sent to the *Millenium Project*.[10] The *suicide notes corpus (SNC) v 0.1* has 21 notes taken from Art Kleiner's website.[11] We will continue to add more data to these corpora as we find them, and all three corpora are freely available.

Figures 1, 2, and 3 show the percentages of positive and negative words in the love letters corpus, hate mail corpus, and the suicide notes corpus. Figures 5, 6, and 7 show the percentages of different emotion words in the three corpora. Emotions are represented by colours as per a study on word–colour associations (Mohammad, 2011a). Figure 4 is a bar graph showing the difference of emotion percentages in love letters and hate mail. Observe that as expected, love letters have many more joy and trust words, whereas hate mail has many more fear, sadness, disgust, and anger.

The bar graph is effective at conveying the extent to which one emotion is more prominent in one text than another, but it does not convey the source of these emotions. Therefore, we calculate the *relative salience* of an emotion word w across two target texts T_1 and T_2:

$$\text{RelativeSalience}(w|T_1, T_2) = \frac{f_1}{N_1} - \frac{f_2}{N_2} \quad (1)$$

Where, f_1 and f_2 are the frequencies of w in T_1 and T_2, respectively. N_1 and N_2 are the total number of word tokens in T_1 and T_2. Figure 8 depicts a relative-salience word cloud of joy words in the love letters corpus with respect to the hate mail corpus. As expected, love letters, much more than hate mail, have terms such as *loving, baby, beautiful, feeling,* and *smile*. This is a nice sanity check of the manually created emotion lexicon. We used Google's freely available software to create the word clouds shown in this paper.[12]

[9]LLC: http://www.lovingyou.com/content/inspiration/loveletters-topic.php?ID=loveyou

[10]HMC: http://www.ratbags.com

[11]SNC: http://www.well.com/ art/suicidenotes.html?w

[12]Google WordCloud: http://visapi-gadgets.googlecode.com/svn/trunk/wordcloud/doc.html

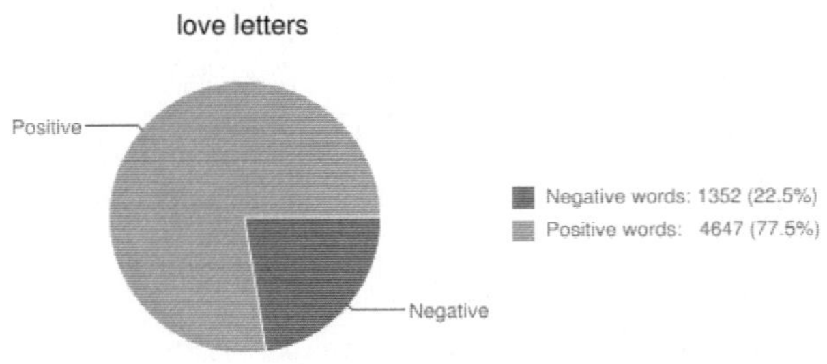

Figure 1: Percentage of positive and negative words in the love letters corpus.

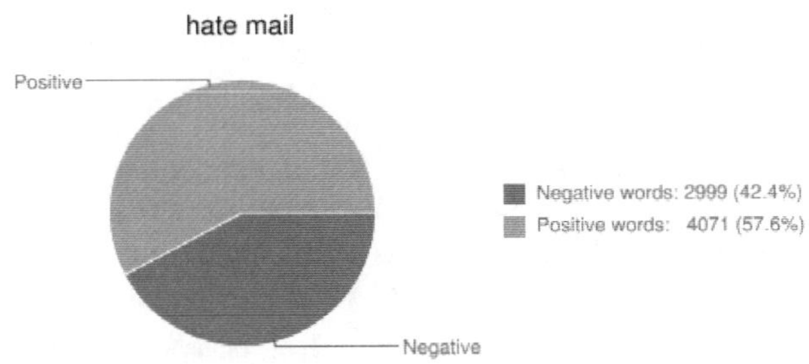

Figure 2: Percentage of positive and negative words in the hate mail corpus.

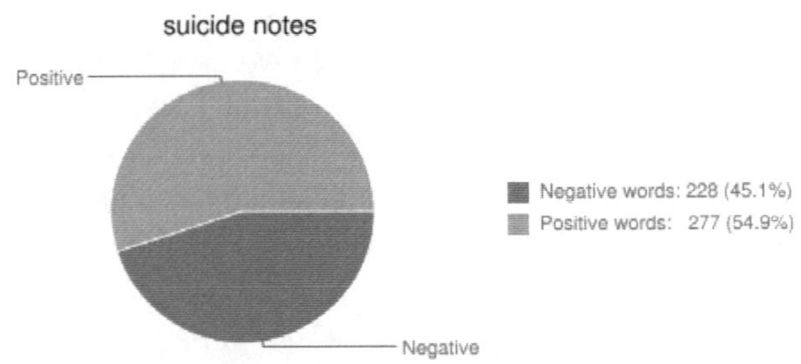

Figure 3: Percentage of positive and negative words in the suicide notes corpus.

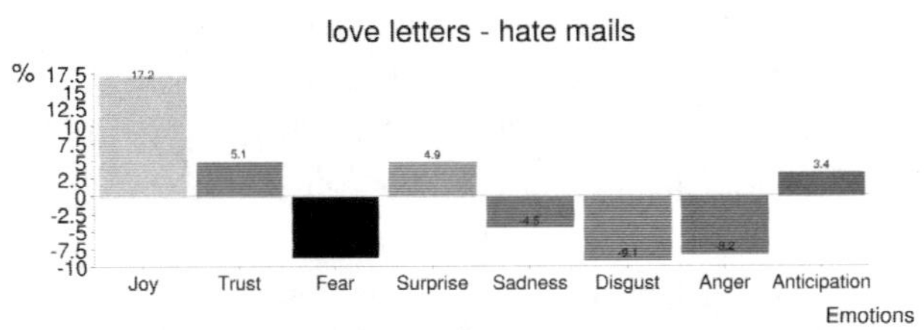

Figure 4: Difference in percentages of emotion words in the love letters corpus and the hate mail corpus. The relative-salience word cloud for the joy bar is shown in the figure to the right (Figure 8).

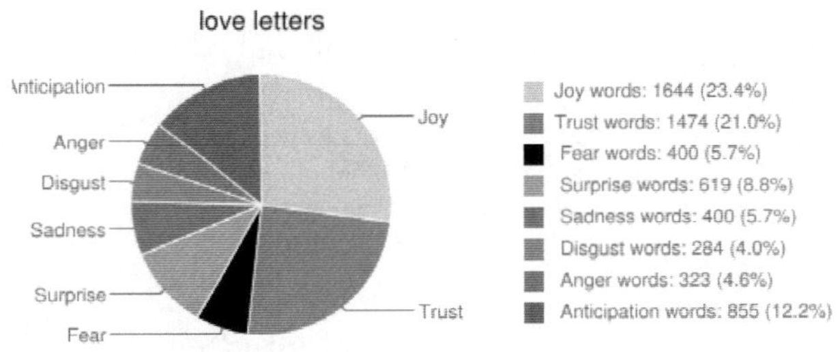

Figure 5: Percentage of emotion words in the love letters corpus.

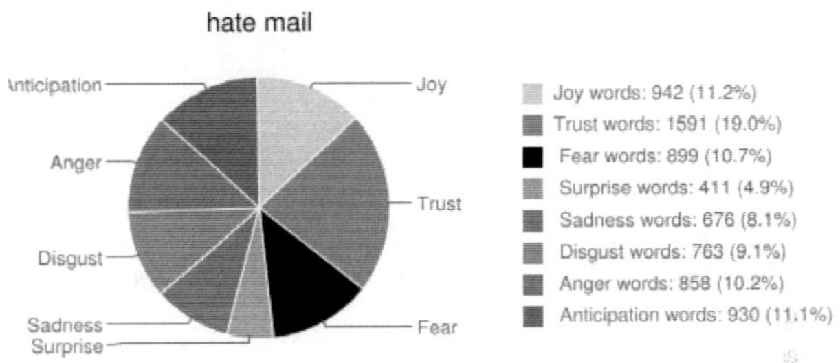

Figure 6: Percentage of emotion words in the hate mail corpus.

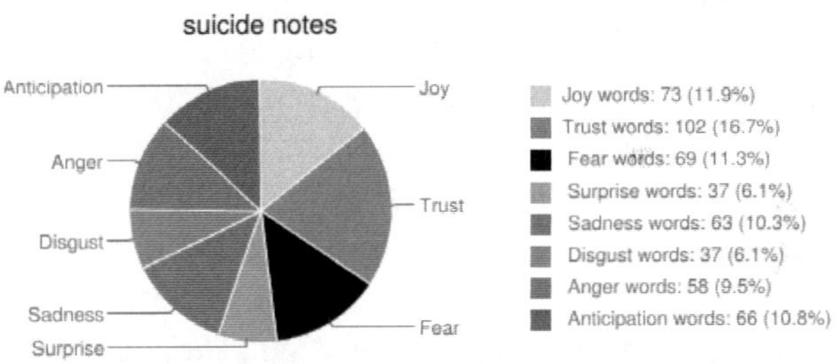

Figure 7: Percentage of emotion words in the suicide notes corpus.

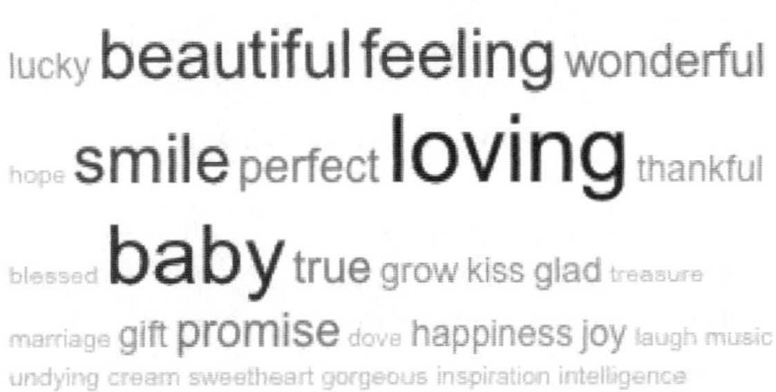

Figure 8: Love letters corpus - hate mail corpus: relative-salience word cloud for **joy**.

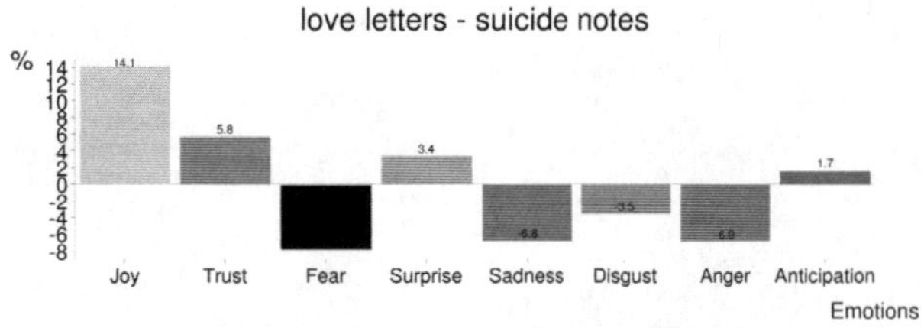

Figure 9: Difference in percentages of emotion words in the love letters corpus and the suicide notes corpus.

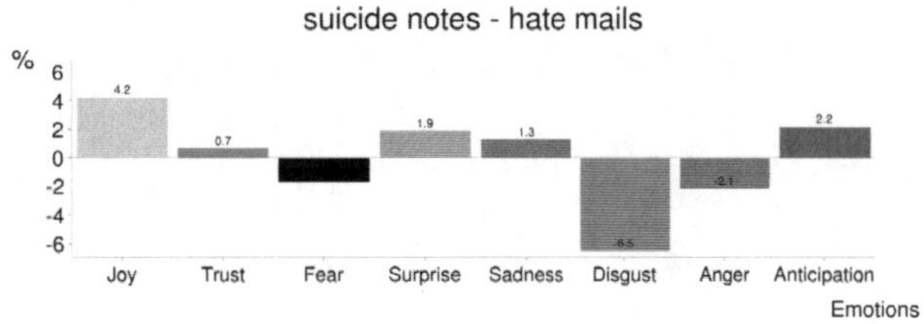

Figure 10: Difference in percentages of emotion words in the suicide notes corpus and the hate mail corpus.

Figure 9 is a bar graph showing the difference in percentages of emotion words in love letters and suicide notes. The most salient fear words in the suicide notes with respect to love letters, in decreasing order, were: *hell, kill, broke, worship, sorrow, afraid, loneliness, endless, shaking,* and *devil.*

Figure 10 is a similar bar graph, but for suicide notes and hate mail. Figure 11 depicts a relative-salience word cloud of disgust words in the hate mail corpus with respect to the suicide notes corpus. The cloud shows many words that seem expected, for example *ignorant, quack, fraudulent, illegal, lying,* and *damage*. Words such as *cancer* and *disease* are prominent in this hate mail corpus because the *Millenium Project* denigrates various alternative treatment websites for cancer and other diseases, and consequently receives angry emails from some cancer patients and physicians.

5 Emotions in email: men vs. women

There is a large amount of work at the intersection of gender and language (see bibliographies compiled by Schiffman (2002) and Sunderland et al. (2002)). It is widely believed that men and women use language differently, and this is true even in computer mediated communications such as email (Boneva et al., 2001). It is claimed that women tend to foster

Figure 11: Suicide notes - hate mail: relative-salience word cloud for **disgust**.

personal relations (Deaux and Major, 1987; Eagly and Steffen, 1984) whereas men communicate for social position (Tannen, 1991). Women tend to share concerns and support others (Boneva et al., 2001) whereas men prefer to talk about activities (Caldwell and Peplau, 1982; Davidson and Duberman, 1982). There are also claims that men tend to be more confrontational and challenging than women.[13]

Otterbacher (2010) investigated stylistic differences in how men and women write product reviews. Thelwall et al. (2010) examine how men and women communicate over social networks such as MySpace. Here, for the first time using an emotion lexicon of more than 14,000 words, we investigate if there are gender differences in the use of emotion words in work-place communications, and if so, whether they support some of the claims mentioned in the above paragraph. The analysis shown here, does not prove the propositions; however, it provides empirical support to the claim that men and women use emotion words to different degrees.

We chose the Enron email corpus (Klimt and Yang, 2004)[14] as the source of work-place communications because it remains the only large publicly available collection of emails. It consists of more than 200,000 emails sent between October 1998 and June 2002 by 150 people in senior managerial posi-

[13] http://www.telegraph.co.uk/news/newstopics/howaboutthat/6272105/Why-men-write-short-email-and-women-write-emotional-messages.html

[14] The Enron email corpus is available at http://www-2.cs.cmu.edu/ enron

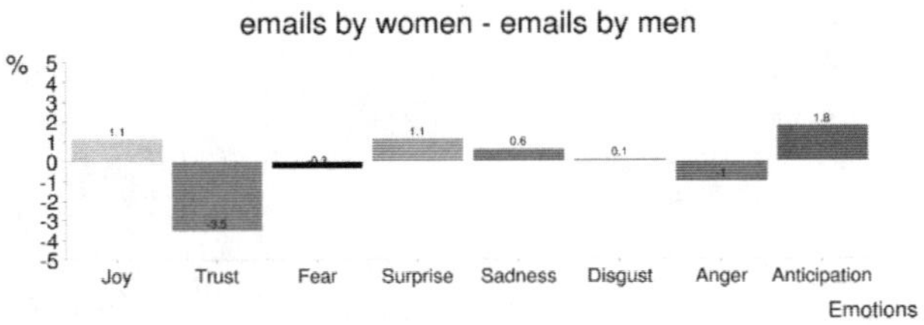

Figure 12: Difference in percentages of emotion words in emails sent by women and emails sent by men.

Figure 13: Emails by women - emails by men: relative-salience word cloud of **trust**.

tions at the Enron Corporation, a former American energy, commodities, and services company. The emails largely pertain to official business but also contain personal communication.

In addition to the body of the email, the corpus provides meta-information such as the time stamp and the email addresses of the sender and receiver. Just as in Cheng et al. (2009), (1) we removed emails whose body had fewer than 50 words or more than 200 words, (2) the authors manually identified the gender of each of the 150 people solely from their names. If the name was not a clear indicator of gender, then the person was marked as "gender-untagged". This process resulted in tagging 41 employees as female and 89 as male; 20 were left gender-untagged. Emails sent from and to gender-untagged employees were removed from all further analysis, leaving 32,045 mails (19,920 mails sent by men and 12,125 mails sent by women). We then determined the number of emotion words in emails written by men, in emails written by women, in emails written by men to women, men to men, women to men, and women to women.

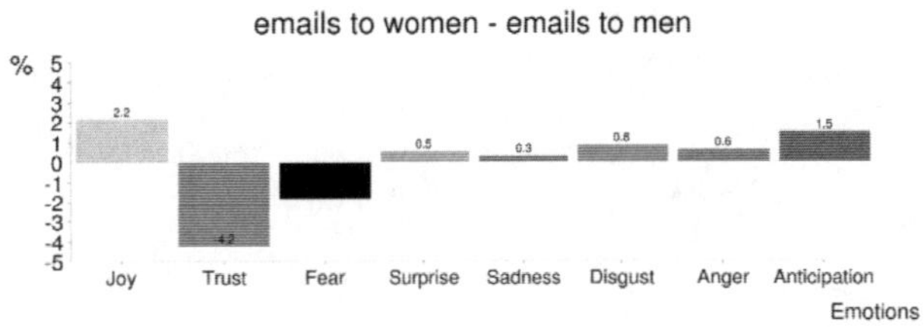

Figure 14: Difference in percentages of emotion words in emails sent to women and emails sent to men.

Figure 15: Emails to women - emails to men: relative-salience word cloud of **joy**.

5.1 Analysis

Figure 12 shows the difference in percentages of emotion words in emails sent by men from the percentage of emotion words in emails sent by women. Observe the marked difference is in the percentage of trust words. The men used many more trust words than women. Figure 13 shows the relative-salience word cloud of these trust words.

Figure 14 shows the difference in percentages of emotion words in emails sent *to* women and the percentage of emotion words in emails sent *to* men. Observe the marked difference once again in the percentage of trust words and joy words. The men receive emails with more trust words, whereas women receive emails with more joy words. Figure 15 shows the relative-salience word cloud of joy.

Figure 16 shows the difference in emotion words in emails sent by men to women and the emotions in mails sent by men to men. Apart from trust words, there is a marked difference in the percentage of anticipation words. The men used many more anticipation words when writing to women, than when writing to other men. Figure 17 shows the relative-

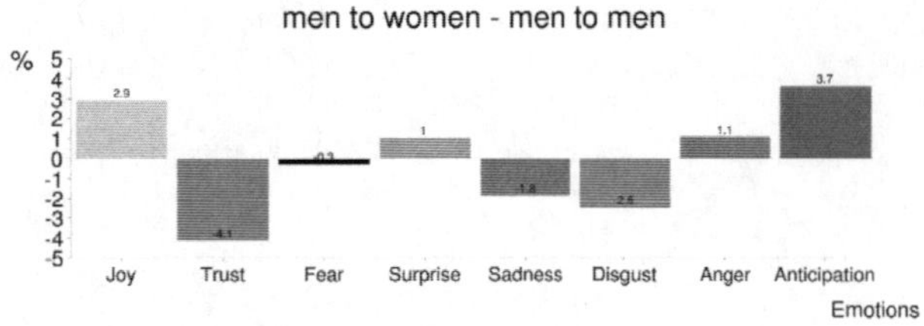

Figure 16: Difference in percentages of emotion words in emails sent by men to women and by men to men.

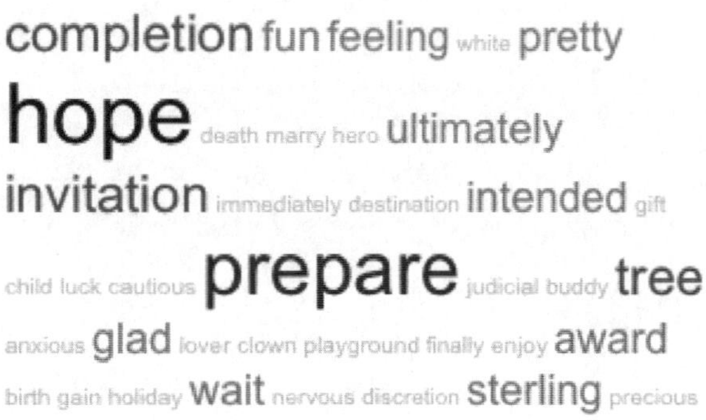

Figure 17: Emails by men to women - email by men to men: relative-salience word cloud of **anticipation**.

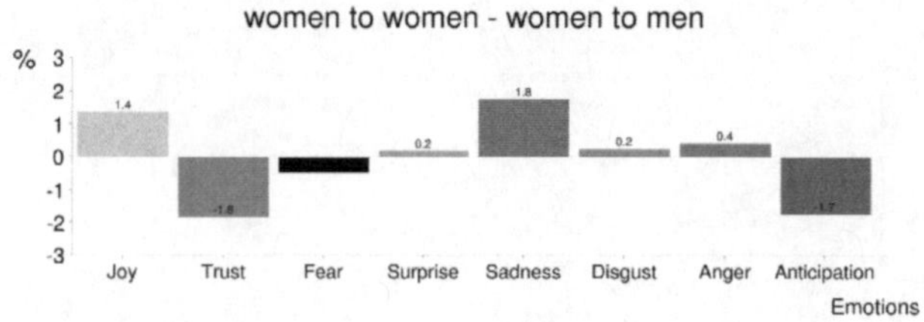

Figure 18: Difference in percentages of emotion words in emails sent by women to women and by women to men.

Figure 19: Emails by women to women - emails by women to men: relative-salience word cloud of **sadness**.

salience word cloud of these anticipation words.

Figures 18, 19, 20, and 21 show difference bar graphs and relative-salience word clouds analyzing some other possible pairs of correspondences.

5.2 Discussion

Figures 14, 16, 18, and 20 support the claim that when writing to women, both men and women use more joyous and cheerful words than when writing to men. Figures 14, 16 and 18 show that both men and women use lots of trust words when writing to men. Figures 12, 18, and 20 are consistent with the notion that women use more cheerful words in emails than men. The sadness values in these figures are consistent with the claim that women tend to share their worries with other women more often than men with other men, men with women, and women with men. The fear values in the Figures 16 and 20 suggest that men prefer to use a lot of fear words, especially when communicating with other men. Thus, women communicate relatively more on the joy–sadness axis, whereas men have a preference for the trust–fear axis. It is interesting how there is a markedly higher percentage of anticipation words in cross-gender communication than in same-sex communication (Figures 16, 18, and 20).

6 Tracking Sentiment in Personal Email

In the previous section, we showed analyses of sets of emails that were sent across a network of individuals. In this section, we show visualizations catered toward individuals—who in most cases have access to only the emails they send and receive. We are using Google Apps API to develop an application that integrates with Gmail (Google's email service), to provide users with the ability to track their emotions towards people they correspond with.[15] Below we show some of these visualizations by selecting John Arnold, a former employee at Enron, as a stand-in for the actual user.

Figure 22 shows the percentage of positive and negative words in emails sent by John Arnold to his colleagues. John can select any of the bars in the figure to reveal the difference in percentages of emotion words in emails sent to that particular person and all the emails sent out. Figure 23 shows the graph pertaining to Andy Zipper. Figure 24 shows the percentage of positive and negative words in each of the emails sent by John to Andy.

In the future, we will make a public call for vol-

[15]Google Apps API: http://code.google.com/googleapps/docs

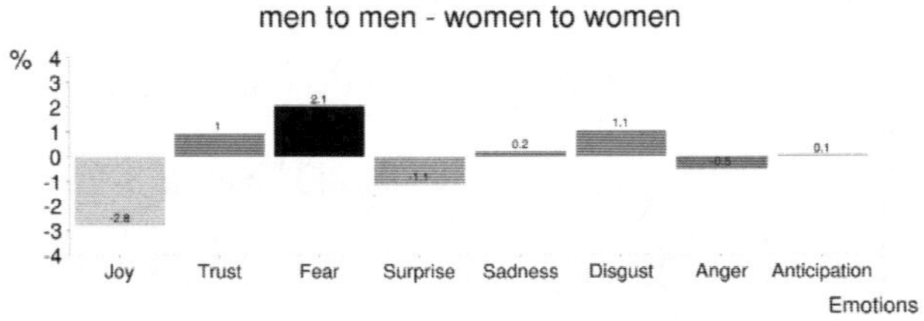

Figure 20: Difference in percentages of emotion words in emails sent by men to men and by women to women.

Figure 21: Emails by men to men - emails by women to women: relative-salience word cloud of **fear**.

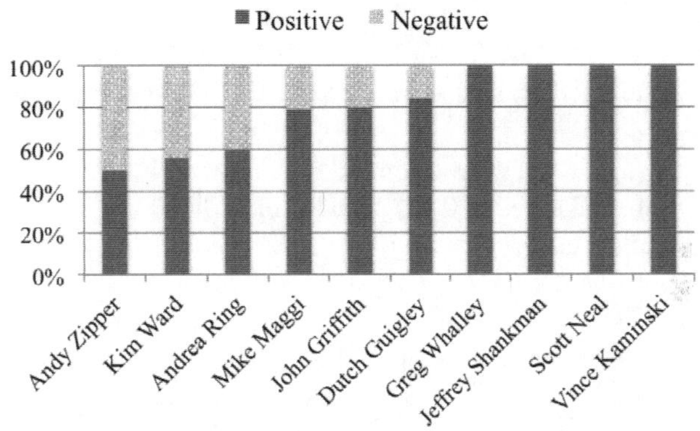

Figure 22: Emails sent by John Arnold.

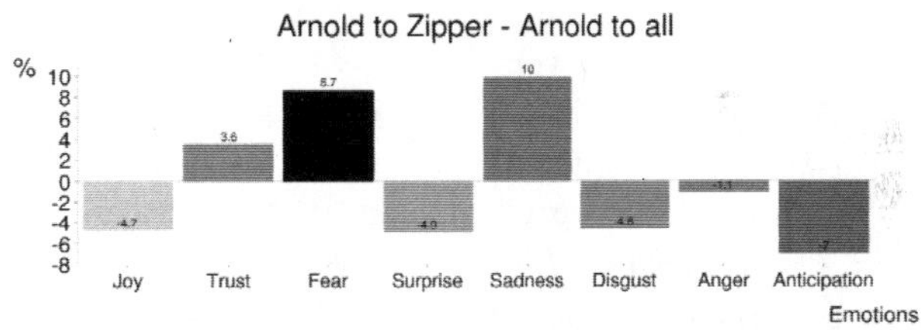

Figure 23: Difference in percentages of emotion words in emails sent by John Arnold to Andy Zipper and emails sent by John to all.

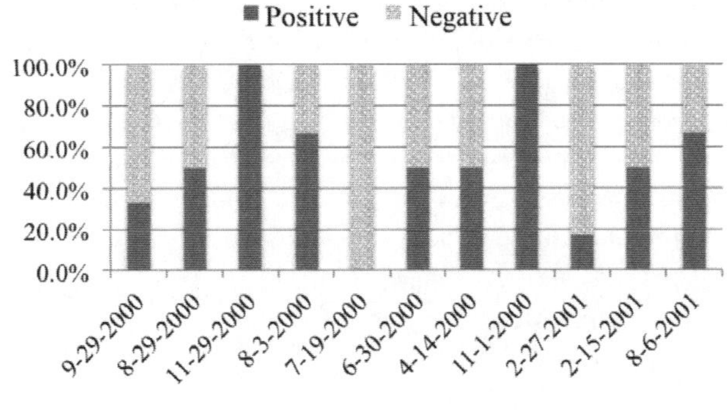

Figure 24: Emails sent by John Arnold to Andy Zipper.

unteers interested in our Gmail emotion application, and we will request access to numbers of emotion words in their emails for a large-scale analysis of emotion words in personal email. The application will protect the privacy of the users by passing emotion word frequencies, gender, and age, but no text, names, or email ids.

7 Conclusions

We have created a large word–emotion association lexicon by crowdsourcing, and used it to analyze and track the distribution of emotion words in mail.[16] We compared emotion words in love letters, hate mail, and suicide notes. We analyzed work-place email and showed that women use and receive a relatively larger number of joy and sadness words, whereas men use and receive a relatively larger number of trust and fear words. We also found that there is a markedly higher percentage of anticipation words in cross-gender communication (men to women and women to men) than in same-sex communication. We showed how different visualizations and word clouds can be used to effectively interpret the results of the emotion analysis. Finally, we showed additional visualizations and a Gmail application that can help people track emotion words in the emails they send and receive.

Acknowledgments

Grateful thanks to Peter Turney and Tara Small for many wonderful ideas. Thanks to the thousands of people who answered the emotion survey with diligence and care. This research was funded by National Research Council Canada.

[16]Please send an e-mail to saif.mohammad@nrc-cnrc.gc.ca to obtain the latest version of the NRC Emotion Lexicon, suicide notes corpus, hate mail corpus, love letters corpus, or the Enron gender-specific emails.

References

Cecilia Ovesdotter Alm, Dan Roth, and Richard Sproat. 2005. Emotions from text: Machine learning for text-based emotion prediction. In *Proceedings of the Joint Conference on HLT–EMNLP*, Vancouver, Canada.

Jerome Bellegarda. 2010. Emotion analysis using latent affective folding and embedding. In *Proceedings of the NAACL-HLT 2010 Workshop on Computational Approaches to Analysis and Generation of Emotion in Text*, Los Angeles, California.

J.R.L. Bernard, editor. 1986. *The Macquarie Thesaurus*. Macquarie Library, Sydney, Australia.

Bonka Boneva, Robert Kraut, and David Frohlich. 2001. Using e-mail for personal relationships. *American Behavioral Scientist*, 45(3):530–549.

Mayta A. Caldwell and Letitia A. Peplau. 1982. Sex differences in same-sex friendships. *Sex Roles*, 8:721–732.

Na Cheng, Xiaoling Chen, R. Chandramouli, and K.P. Subbalakshmi. 2009. Gender identification from e-mails. In *Computational Intelligence and Data Mining, 2009. CIDM '09. IEEE Symposium on*, pages 154 –158.

Malcolm Corney, Olivier de Vel, Alison Anderson, and George Mohay. 2002. Gender-preferential text mining of e-mail discourse. *Computer Security Applications Conference, Annual*, 0:282–289.

Lynne R. Davidson and Lucile Duberman. 1982. Friendship: Communication and interactional patterns in same-sex dyads. *Sex Roles*, 8:809–822. 10.1007/BF00287852.

Kay Deaux and Brenda Major. 1987. Putting gender into context: An interactive model of gender-related behavior. *Psychological Review*, 94(3):369–389.

Ana B. Casado Díaz and Francisco J. Más Ruz. 2002. The consumers reaction to delays in service. *International Journal of Service Industry Management*, 13(2):118–140.

Peter Dodds and Christopher Danforth. 2010. Measuring the happiness of large-scale written expression: Songs, blogs, and presidents. *Journal of Happiness Studies*, 11:441–456. 10.1007/s10902-009-9150-9.

Laurette Dubé and Manfred F. Maute. 1996. The antecedents of brand switching, brand loyalty and verbal responses to service failure. *Advances in Services Marketing and Management*, 5:127–151.

Alice H. Eagly and Valerie J. Steffen. 1984. Gender stereotypes stem from the distribution of women and men into social roles. *Journal of Personality and Social Psychology*, 46(4):735–754.

Bryan Klimt and Yiming Yang. 2004. Introducing the enron corpus. In *CEAS*.

Adrienne Lehrer. 1974. *Semantic fields and lexical structure*. North-Holland, American Elsevier, Amsterdam, NY.

Hugo Liu, Henry Lieberman, and Ted Selker. 2003. A model of textual affect sensing using real-world knowledge. In *Proceedings of the 8th international conference on Intelligent user interfaces*, IUI '03, pages 125–132, New York, NY. ACM.

Karl Marx. 1982. *The Letters of Karl Marx*. Prentice Hall.

Pawel Matykiewicz, Wlodzislaw Duch, and John P. Pestian. 2009. Clustering semantic spaces of suicide notes and newsgroups articles. In *Proceedings of the Workshop on Current Trends in Biomedical Natural Language Processing*, BioNLP '09, pages 179–184, Stroudsburg, PA, USA. Association for Computational Linguistics.

Saif M. Mohammad and Peter D. Turney. 2010. Emotions evoked by common words and phrases: Using mechanical turk to create an emotion lexicon. In *Proceedings of the NAACL-HLT 2010 Workshop on Computational Approaches to Analysis and Generation of Emotion in Text*, LA, California.

Saif Mohammad, Cody Dunne, and Bonnie Dorr. 2009. Generating high-coverage semantic orientation lexicons from overtly marked words and a thesaurus. In *Proceedings of Empirical Methods in Natural Language Processing (EMNLP-2009)*, pages 599–608, Singapore.

Saif M. Mohammad. 2011a. Even the abstract have colour: Consensus in wordcolour associations. In *Proceedings of the 49th Annual Meeting of the Association for Computational Linguistics: Human Language Technologies*, Portland, OR, USA.

Saif M. Mohammad. 2011b. From once upon a time to happily ever after: Tracking emotions in novels and fairy tales. In *Proceedings of the ACL 2011 Workshop on Language Technology for Cultural Heritage, Social Sciences, and Humanities (LaTeCH)*, Portland, OR, USA.

Charles E. Osgood and Evelyn G. Walker. 1959. Motivation and language behavior: A content analysis of suicide notes. *Journal of Abnormal and Social Psychology*, 59(1):58–67.

Jahna Otterbacher. 2010. Inferring gender of movie reviewers: exploiting writing style, content and metadata. In *Proceedings of the 19th ACM international conference on Information and knowledge management*, CIKM '10, pages 369–378, New York, NY, USA. ACM.

Bo Pang and Lillian Lee. 2008. Opinion mining and sentiment analysis. *Foundations and Trends in Information Retrieval*, 2(1–2):1–135.

John P. Pestian, Pawel Matykiewicz, and Jacqueline Grupp-Phelan. 2008. Using natural language processing to classify suicide notes. In *Proceedings of the Workshop on Current Trends in Biomedical Natural Language Processing*, BioNLP '08, pages 96–97, Stroudsburg, PA, USA. Association for Computational Linguistics.

Robert Plutchik. 1980. A general psychoevolutionary theory of emotion. *Emotion: Theory, research, and experience*, 1(3):3–33.

Harold Schiffman. 2002. Bibliography of gender and language. In *http://www.sas.upenn.edu/~haroldfs/popcult/bibliogs/gender/genbib.htm*.

Philip Stone, Dexter C. Dunphy, Marshall S. Smith, Daniel M. Ogilvie, and associates. 1966. *The General Inquirer: A Computer Approach to Content Analysis*. The MIT Press.

Carlo Strapparava and Alessandro Valitutti. 2004. Wordnet-Affect: An affective extension of WordNet. In *Proceedings of the 4th International Conference on Language Resources and Evaluation (LREC-2004)*, pages 1083–1086, Lisbon, Portugal.

Jane Sunderland, Ren-Feng Duann, and Paul Baker. 2002. Gender and genre bibliography. In *http://www.ling.lancs.ac.uk/pubs/clsl/clsl122.pdf*.

Deborah Tannen. 1991. *You just don't understand : women and men in conversation*. Random House.

Mike Thelwall, David Wilkinson, and Sukhvinder Uppal. 2010. Data mining emotion in social network communication: Gender differences in myspace. *J. Am. Soc. Inf. Sci. Technol.*, 61:190–199, January.

Peter Turney and Michael Littman. 2003. Measuring praise and criticism: Inference of semantic orientation from association. *ACM Transactions on Information Systems (TOIS)*, 21(4):315–346.

Francois-Marie Arouet Voltaire. 1973. *The selected letters of Voltaire*. New York University Press, New York.

David Yarowsky. 1992. Word-sense disambiguation using statistical models of Roget's categories trained on large corpora. In *Proceedings of the 14th International Conference on Computational Linguistics (COLING-92)*, pages 454–460, Nantes, France.

Developing Japanese WordNet Affect for Analyzing Emotions

Yoshimitsu Torii[1] **Dipankar Das**[2] **Sivaji Bandyopadhyay**[2] **Manabu Okumura**[1]
[1]Precision and Intelligence Laboratory, Tokyo Institute of Technology, Japan
[2]Computer Science and Engineering Department, Jadavpur University, India
torii@lr.pi.titech.ac.jp, dipankar.dipnil2005@gmail.com
sivaji_cse_ju@yahoo.com, oku@pi.titech.ac.jp

Abstract

This paper reports the development of Japanese *WordNet Affect* from the English *WordNet Affect* lists with the help of English *SentiWordNet* and Japanese *WordNet*. Expanding the available synsets of the English *WordNet Affect* using *SentiWordNet*, we have performed the translation of the expanded lists into Japanese based on the synsetIDs in the Japanese *WordNet*. A baseline system for emotion analysis of Japanese sentences has been developed based on the Japanese *WordNet Affect*. The incorporation of morphology improves the performance of the system. Overall, the system achieves average *precision*, *recall* and *F-scores* of 32.76%, 53% and 40.49% respectively on 89 sentences of the Japanese judgment corpus and 83.52%, 49.58% and 62.22% on 1000 translated Japanese sentences of the *SemEval 2007* affect sensing test corpus. Different experimental outcomes and morphological analysis suggest that irrespective of the google translation error, the performance of the system could be improved by enhancing the Japanese *WordNet Affect* in terms of coverage.

1 Introduction

Emotion analysis, a recent sub discipline at the crossroads of information retrieval (Sood *et al.*, 2009) and computational linguistics (Wiebe *et al.*, 2006) is becoming increasingly important from application view points of affective computing.

The majority of subjective analysis methods that are related to emotion is based on textual keywords spotting that use specific lexical resources. *SentiWordNet* (Baccianella *et al.*, 2010) is a lexical resource that assigns *positive*, *negative* and *objective* scores to each *WordNet* synset (Miller, 1995). Subjectivity wordlist (Banea *et al.*, 2008) assigns words with the strong or weak subjectivity and prior polarities of types *positive*, *negative* and *neutral*. Affective lexicon (Strapparava and Valitutti, 2004), one of the most efficient resources of emotion analysis, contains emotion words. To the best of our knowledge, these lexical resources have been created for English. A recent study shows that non-native English speakers support the growing use of the Internet[1]. Hence, there is a demand for automatic text analysis tools and linguistic resources for languages other than English.

In the present task, we have prepared the Japanese *WordNet Affect* from the already available English *WordNet Affect* (Strapparava and Valitutti, 2004). Entries in the English *WordNet Affect* are annotated using Ekman's (1993) six emotional categories (*joy, fear, anger, sadness, disgust, surprise*). The collection of the English *WordNet Affect*[2] synsets that are used in the present work was provided as a resource in the "*Affective Text*" shared task of *SemEval-2007* Workshop.

The six *WordNet Affect* lists that were provided in the shared task contain only 612 synsets in total with 1536 words. The words in each of the six emotion lists have been observed to be not more than 37.2% of the words present in the corresponding *SentiWordNet* synsets. Hence, these six lists are expanded with the synsets retrieved from the

[1] http://www.internetworldstats.com/stats.htm
[2] http://www.cse.unt.edu/~rada/affectivetext/

Proceedings of the 2nd Workshop on Computational Approaches to Subjectivity and Sentiment Analysis, ACL-HLT 2011, pages 80–86,
24 June, 2011, Portland, Oregon, USA

English *SentiWordNet* (Baccianella *et al.*, 2010). We assumed that the new sentiment bearing words in English *SentiWordNet* might have some emotional connotation in Japanese even keeping their part-of-speech (POS) information unchanged. The numbers of entries in the expanded word lists are increased by 69.77% and 74.60% at synset and word levels respectively. We have mapped the synsetID of the *WordNet Affect* lists with the synsetID of the WordNet 3.0[3]. This mapping helps in expanding the *WordNet Affect* lists with the recent version of *SentiWordNet 3.0* [4] as well as translating with the Japanese *WordNet* (Bond *et al.*, 2009). Some affect synsets (e.g., 00115193-a *huffy, mad, sore*) are not translated into Japanese as there are no equivalent synset in the Japanese *WordNet*.

Primarily, we have developed a baseline system based on the Japanese *WordNet Affect* and carried out the evaluation on a Japanese judgement corpus of 89 sentences. The system achieves the average *F-score* of 36.39% with respect to six emotion classes. We have also incorporated an open source Japanese morphological analyser[5]. The performance of the system has been increased by 4.1% in average *F-score* with respect to six emotion classes.

Scarcity of emotion corpus in Japanese motivated us to apply an open source google translator[6] to build the Japanese emotion corpus from the available English *SemEval-2007* affect sensing corpus. The baseline system based on the Japanese *WordNet Affect* achieves average *precision*, *recall* and *F-score* of 83.52%, 49.58% and 62.22% respectively on 1000 translated test sentences. The inclusion of morphological processing improves the performance of the system. Different experiments have been carried out by selecting different ranges of annotated emotion scores. Error analysis suggests that though the system performs satisfactorily in identifying the sentential emotions based on the available words of the Japanese *WordNet Affect*, the system suffers from the translated version of the corpus. In addition to that, the Japanese *WordNet Affect* also needs an improvement in terms of coverage.

The rest of the paper is organized as follows. Different developmental phases of the Japanese *WordNet Affect* are described in Section 3. Preparation of the translated Japanese corpus, different experiments and evaluations based on morphology and the annotated emotion scores are elaborated in Section 4. Finally Section 5 concludes the paper.

2 Related Works

The extraction and annotation of subjective terms started with machine learning approaches (Hatzivassiloglou and McKeown, 1997). Some well known sentiment lexicons have been developed, such as subjective adjective list (Baroni and Vegnaduzzo, 2004), English *SentiWordNet* (Esuli *et. al.*, 2006), Taboada's adjective list (Voll and Taboada, 2007), SubjectivityWord List (Banea *et al.*, 2008) etc. Andreevskaia and Bergler (2006) present a method for extracting *positive* or *negative* sentiment bearing adjectives from *WordNet* using the Sentiment Tag Extraction Program (STEP). The proposed methods in (Wiebe and Riloff, 2006) automatically generate resources for subjectivity analysis for a new target language from the available resources for English. On the other hand, an automatically generated and scored sentiment lexicon, *SentiFul* (Neviarouskaya *et al.*, 2009), its expansion, morphological modifications and distinguishing sentiment features also shows the contributory results.

But, all of the above mentioned resources are in English and have been used in coarse grained sentiment analysis (e.g., *positive*, *negative* or *neutral*). The proposed method in (Takamura *et al.*, 2005) extracts semantic orientations from a small number of seed words with high accuracy in the experiments on English as well as Japanese lexicons. But, it was also aimed for sentiment bearing words. Instead of English *WordNet Affect* (Strapparava and Valitutti, 2004), there are a few attempts in other languages such as, Russian and Romanian (Bobicev *et al.*, 2010), Bengali (Das and Bandyopadhyay, 2010) etc. Our present approach is similar to some of these approaches but in contrast, we have evaluated our Japanese *WordNet Affect* on the *SemEval 2007* affect sensing corpus translated into Japanese. In recent trends, the application of mechanical turk for generating emotion lexicon (Mohammad and Turney, 2010) shows promising results. In the present task, we have incorporated the open source, available and accessible resources to achieve our goals.

[3] http://wordnet.princeton.edu/wordnet/download/

[4] http://sentiwordnet.isti.cnr.it/

[5] http://mecab.sourceforge.net/

[6] http://translate.google.com/#

3 Developmental Phases

3.1 *WordNet Affect*

The English *WordNet Affect*, based on Ekman's six emotion types is a small lexical resource compared to the complete *WordNet* but its affective annotation helps in emotion analysis. Some collection of *WordNet Affect* synsets was provided as a resource for the shared task of *Affective Text* in *SemEval-2007*. The whole data is provided in six files named by the six emotions. Each file contains a list of synsets and one synset per line. An example synset entry from *WordNet Affect* is as follows.

a#00117872 angered enraged furious infuriated maddened

The first letter of each line indicates the part of speech (POS) and is followed by the *affectID*. The representation was simple and easy for further processing. We have retrieved and linked the compatible synsetID from the recent version of *WordNet 3.0* with the *affectID* of the *WordNet Affect* synsets. We have searched each *WordNet Affect* synset in *WordNet 3.0*. If a matching *WordNet 3.0* synset is found, the *WordNet 3.0 synsetID* is mapped to the *WordNet Affect affectID*. The linking between two synsets of *WordNet Affect* and *WordNet 3.0* is shown in Figure 1.

WordNet Affect:
n#05587878 anger choler ire
a#02336957 annoyed harassed harried pestered vexed
WordNet:
07516354-n anger, ire, choler
02455845-a annoyed harassed harried pestered vexed
Linked Synset ID with Affect ID:
n#05587878 ←→ 07516354-n anger choler ire
a#02336957 ←→ 02455845-a annoyed harassed harried pestered vexed

Figure 1: Linking between the synsets of *WordNet Affect* and *WordNet*

3.2 Expansion of *WordNet Affect* using *SentiWordNet*

It has been observed that the *WordNet Affect* contains fewer number of emotion word entries. The six lists provided in the *SemEval 2007* shared task contain only 612 synsets in total with 1536 words. The detail distribution of the emotion words as well as the synsets in the six different lists according to their POS is shown in Table 1. Hence, we have expanded the lists with adequate number of emotion words using *SentiWordNet* before attempting any translation of the lists into Japanese. *SentiWordNet* assigns each synset of *WordNet* with two coarse grained subjective scores such as *positive* and *negative* along with an *objective* score. *SentiWordNet* contains more number of coarse grained emotional words than *WordNet Affect*. We assumed that the translation of the coarse grained emotional words into Japanese might contain more or less fine-grained emotion words. One example entry of the *SentiWordNet* is shown below. The POS of the entry is followed by a *synset ID*, *positive* and *negative* scores and synsets containing sentiment words.

SentiWordNet:
a 121184 0.25 0.25 infuriated#a#1 furious#a#2 maddened#a#1 enraged#a#1 angered#a#1

Our aim is to increase the number of emotion words in the *WordNet Affect* using *SentiWordNet*, both of which are developed from the *WordNet*. Hence, each word of the *WordNet Affect* is replaced by the equivalent synsets retrieved from *SentiWordNet* if the synset contains that emotion word. The POS information in the *WordNet Affect* is kept unchanged during expansion. A related example is shown in Figure 2. The distributions of expanded synsets and words for each of the six emotion classes based on four different POS types (*noun N*, *verb V*, *adjective Adj.* and *adverb Adv.*) are shown in Table 1. But, we have kept the duplicate entries at synset level for identifying the emotion related scores in our future attempts by utilizing the already associated *positive* and *negative* scores of *SentiWordNet*. The percentage of entries in the updated word lists are increased by 69.77 and 74.60 at synset and word levels.

3.3 Translation of Expanded *WordNet Affect* into Japanese

We have mapped the *affectID* of the *WordNet Affect* to the corresponding *synsetID* of the *WordNet 3.0*. This mapping helps to expand the *WordNet Affect* with the recent version of *SentiWordNet* 3.0 as well as translating the expanded lists into Japanese using the Japanese *WordNet* (Bond *et al.*, 2009).

Emotion Classes	*WordNet Affect* **Synset (*S*)** and **Word (*W*)** [*After SentiWordNet updating*]							
	N		*V*		*Adj*		*Adv*	
	S	*W*	*S*	*W*	*S*	*W*	*S*	*W*
Anger	48 [198]	99 [403]	19 [103]	64 [399]	39 [89]	120 [328]	21 [23]	35 [50]
Disgust	3 [17]	6 [21]	6 [21]	22 [62]	6 [38]	34 [230]	4 [5]	10 [19]
Fear	23[89]	45 [224]	15 [48]	40 [243]	29 [62]	97 [261]	15 [21]	26 [49]
Joy	73 [375]	149 [761]	40 [252]	122 [727]	84 [194]	203 [616]	30 [45]	65 [133]
Sadness	32 [115]	64 [180]	10 [43]	33 [92]	55 [129]	169 [779]	26 [26]	43 [47]
Surprise	5 [31]	8 [28]	7 [42]	28 [205]	12 [33]	41 [164]	4 [6]	13 [28]

Table 1: Number of POS based Synsets and Words in six *WordNet Affect* lists before and after updating using *SentiWordNet*

Linked *Affect* word:
n#05587878 ←→ 07516354-n *anger choler ire*

SentiWordNet synsets containing "*anger*":
07516354-n anger, ire, choler
14036539-n angriness, anger
00758972-n anger, ira, ire, wrath
01785971-v anger
01787106-v see_red, anger

SentiWordNet synsets containing "choler":
07552729-n fretfulness, fussiness, crossness, petulance, peevishness, irritability, choler
05406958-n choler, yellow_bile

Expanded *Affect* word:
n#05587878 ←→ 07516354-n anger choler ire 14036539-n angriness anger 00758972-n anger ira, ire wrath 01785971-v anger … 05406958-n choler

Figure 2: Expansion of *WordNet Affect* synset using *SentiWordNet*

As the Japanese *WordNet*[7] is freely available and it is being developed based on the English *WordNet*, the synsets of the expanded lists are automatically translated into Japanese equivalent synsets based on the *synsetIDs*. The number of translated Japanese words and synsets for six affect lists are shown in Table 2 and Table 3 respectively. The following are some translated samples that contain word as well as phrase level translations.

07510348-n surprise → 愕き, 驚き

07503260-n disgust → むかつき, 嫌悪

07532440-n unhappiness, sadness → 不仕合せさ, 哀情, 悲しみ, 不幸せさ, 不幸さ…

07527352-n joy, joyousness, joyfulness → ジョイ, 愉楽, うれしいこと, 慶び, うれしさ, 歓び, 悦楽, 歓, 嬉しさ, 欣び, 楽しいこと…

Emotion Classes	Translated *WordNet Affect* list in Japanese (#Words)			
	N	*V*	*Adj*	*Adv*
Anger	861	501	231	9
Disgust	49	63	219	10
Fear	375	235	334	104
Joy	1959	1831	772	154
Sadness	533	307	575	39
Surprise	144	218	204	153

Table 2: Number of POS based translated word entries in six Japanese *WordNet Affect* lists

Emotion Classes	Japanese *WordNet Affect* list			
	Trans (*#Syn*)	*Non-Trans* (*#Syn*)	*Translated Morphemes*	
			(*#W*)	(*#P*)
Anger	254	159	1033	450
Disgust	57	24	218	97
Fear	146	74	615	315
Joy	628	238	2940	1273
Sadness	216	97	846	519
Surprise	112	25	456	216

Table 3: Number of translated (*Trans*) and non-translated (*Non-Trans*) synsets (*Syn*), words (*W*) and phrases (*P*) in six Japanese *WordNet Affects*.

3.4 Analyzing Translation Errors

Some *SentiWordNet* synsets (e.g., 00115193-a *huffy, mad, sore*) are not translated into Japanese as there are no equivalent synset entries in the Japanese *WordNet*. There were a large number of word combinations, collocations and idioms in the Japanese *WordNet Affect*. These parts of synsets show problems during translation and therefore manual

[7] http://nlpwww.nict.go.jp/wn-ja/index.en.html

translation is carried out for these types. Some of the English synsets ('07517292-n *lividity*') were not translated into Japanese. But, an equivalent gloss of the word '*lividity*' that is present in the Japanese *WordNet* is *"a state of fury so great the face becomes discolored"*. One of the reasons of such translation problems may be that no equivalent Japanese word sense is available for such English words.

4 Evaluation and Analysis

We have evaluated the lexical coverage of the developed Japanese *WordNet Affect* on a small emotional judgment corpus and *SemEval 2007* affect sensing corpus.

4.1 Evaluation on Judgment Corpus

The judgment corpus that is being developed by the Japan System Applications Co. Ltd. [8] contains only 100 sentences of emotional judgments. But, this corpus is not an open source till date. We have evaluated our Japanese *WordNet Affect* based baseline system on these 100 sentences and the results for each of the six emotion classes are shown in Table 4. We have also incorporated an open source morphological analyzer[9] in our baseline system.

The algorithm is that, if a word in a sentence is present in any of the Japanese *WordNet Affect* lists; the sentence is tagged with the emotion label corresponding to that affect list. But, if any word is not found in any of the six lists, each word of the sentence is passed through the morphological process to identify its root form which is searched through the Japanese *WordNet Affect* lists again. If the root form is found in any of the six Japanese *WordNet Affect* lists, the sentence is tagged accordingly. Otherwise, the sentence is tagged as non-emotional or *neutral*. The average *F-Score* of the baseline system has been improved by 4.1% with respect to the six emotion classes. Due to the fewer number of sentential instances in some emotion classes (e.g., *joy*, *sadness*, *surprise*), the performance of the system gives poor results even after including the morphological knowledge. One of the reasons may be the less number of words and synset entries in some *WordNet Affect* lists (e.g., *fear*). Hence, we have aimed to translate the English *SemEval 2007* affect sensing corpus into Japanese and evaluate our system on the translated corpus.

Emotion Classes (#Sentences)	Judgment Corpus (in %) Before Morphology [***After Morphology***]		
	Precision	Recall	F-Score
Anger (#32)	51.61 [***64.29***]	50.00 [***68.12***]	50.79 [***66.14***]
disgust (#18)	25.00 [***45.00***]	5.56 [***10.56***]	9.09 [***17.10***]
fear (#33)	NULL		
joy (#3)	3.45 [***8.08***]	66.67 [***100.00***]	6.56 [***14.95***]
Sadness (#5)	NULL		
surprise (#9)	6.90 [***13.69***]	22.22 [***33.33***]	10.53 [***19.41***]

Table 4: Precision, Recall and F-Scores (in %) of the system per emotion class on the Judgment corpus by including and excluding morphology.

4.2 Evaluation on Translated SemEval 2007 Affect Sensing Corpus

The English *SemEval 2007* affect sensing corpus consists of news headlines only. Each of the news headlines is tagged with a valence score and scores for all the six Ekman's emotions. The six emotion scores for each sentence are in the range of 0 to 100. We have considered that each sentence is assigned a single sentential emotion tag based on the maximum emotion score out of six annotated emotion scores. We have used the Google translator API [10] to translate the 250 and 1000 sentences of the trial and test sets of the *SemEval 2007* corpus respectively. The experiments regarding morphology and emotion scores are conducted on the trial corpus. We have carried out different experiments on 1000 test sentences by selecting different ranges of emotion scores. The corresponding experimental results are also shown in Table 5. Incorporation of morphology improves the performance of the system. On the other hand, it is observed that the performance of the system decreases by increasing the range of Emotion Scores (ES). The reason may be that the numeric distribution of the sentential instances in each of the emotion classes decreases as the range in emotion scores increases.

[8] http://www.jsa.co.jp/

[9] http://mecab.sourceforge.net/

[10] http://translate.google.com/#

Emotion Classes	Japanese Translated *SemEval 2007* Test Corpus (in %)					
	Before Morphology [***After Morphology***]					
	Emotion Score (ES) ≥ 0			**Emotion Score (ES) ≥ 10**		
	Precision	Recall	F-Score	Precision	Recall	F-Score
Anger	61.01[***68.75***]	18.83[***31.16***]	28.78[***42.88***]	44.65[***52.08***]	25.54[***33.32***]	32.49[***40.35***]
disgust	79.55[***85.05***]	8.35[***16.06***]	15.12[***27.01***]	40.91[***41.46***]	9.89[***18.07***]	15.93[***24.97***]
Fear	93.42[***95.45***]	10.26[***16.77***]	18.49[***28.52***]	77.63[***81.82***]	13.32[***21.42***]	22.74[***34.03***]
Joy	69.07[***72.68***]	57.03[***80.30***]	62.48[***76.29***]	53.89[***55.61***]	56.50[***96.22***]	55.17[***70.40***]
sadness	83.33[***84.29***]	10.58[***19.54***]	18.77[***31.67***]	67.78[***69.87***]	11.78[***19.88***]	20.07[***30.86***]
surprise	94.94[***94.94***]	7.84[***13.65***]	14.48[***23.99***]	72.15[***74.58***]	8.25[***15.87***]	14.81[***26.30***]
	Emotion Score (ES) ≥ 30			**Emotion Score (ES) ≥ 50**		
Anger	21.38[***28.12***]	39.08[***62.45***]	27.64[***38.59***]	6.92[***10.42***]	57.89[**78.02**]	12.36[***18.26***]
disgust	2.27[***5.04***]	3.70[***6.72***]	2.82[***6.15***]	NIL	NIL	NIL
Fear	44.74[***56.82***]	16.67[***28.76***]	24.29[***38.45***]	21.05[***29.55***]	17.98[***31.26***]	19.39[***30.79***]
Joy	31.48[***33.42***]	56.86[***97.08***]	40.52[***50.53***]	12.04[***24.98***]	61.32[***87.66***]	20.12[***39.10***]
sadness	37.78[***69.86***]	15.60[**25.31**]	22.08[***37.22***]	13.33[***23.07***]	12.12[***22.57***]	12.70[***18.71***]
surprise	17.72[***20.34***]	8.14[***18.56***]	11.16[***20.35***]	3.80[***8.50***]	7.50[***12.50***]	5.04[***10.11***]

Table 6: Precision, Recall and F-Scores (in %) of the system per emotion class on the translated Japanese *SemEval 2007* test corpus before and after including morphology on different ranges of Emotion Scores.

4.3 Analysis of Morphology

Japanese affect lists include words as well as phrases. We deal with phrases using Japanese morphology tool to find affect words in a sentence and substitute an affect word into its original conjugated form. One of the main reasons of using a morphology tool is to analyze the conjugated form and to identify the phrases. For example, the Japanese word for the equivalent English word '*anger*' is "怒る (*o ko ru*)" but there are other conjugated word forms such as "怒った(*o ko tta*)" that means '*angered*' and it is used in past tense. Similarly, other conjugated form "怒っていた (*o ko tte i ta*)" denotes the past participle form '*have angered*' of the original word '*anger*'. The morphological form of its passive sense is "怒られる (*o ko ra re ru*)" that means '*be angered*'. We identify the word forms from their corresponding phrases by using the morpheme information. For example, the phrase "怒られる (*o ko ra re ru*)" consists of two words, one is "怒ら (*o ko ra*) that is in an imperfective form and other word is "れる (*re ru*) which is in an original form. The original form of the imperfective word 怒ら (*o ko ra*) is "怒る (*o ko ru*)". It has been found that some of the English multi-word phrases have no equivalent Japanese phrase available. Only the equivalent Japanese words are found in Japanese *WordNet*. For example, the following synset contains a multi-word phrase '*see-red*'. Instead of any equivalent phrases, only words are found in Japanese *WordNet*. *01787106-v anger, see -red* → 怒る, 憤る, 立腹

5 Conclusion

The present paper describes the preparation of Japanese *WordNet Affect* containing six types of emotion words in six separate lists. The automatic approach of expanding, translating and sense disambiguation tasks reduces the manual effort. The resource is still being updated with more number of emotional words to increase the coverage. The sense disambiguation task needs to be improved further in future by incorporating more number of translators and considering their agreement into account. In future we will adopt a corpus-driven approach for updating the resource with more number of emotion words and phrases for extending the emotion analysis task in Japanese.

Acknowledgments

The work reported in this paper is supported by a grant from the India-Japan Cooperative Programme (DST-JST) 2009 Research project entitled "Sentiment Analysis where AI meets Psychology" funded by Department of Science and Technology (DST), Government of India.

References

Andreevskaia A. and Bergler Sabine. 2007. CLaC and CLaC-NB: Knowledge-based and corpus-based approaches to sentiment tagging. *4th International Workshop on Semantic Evaluations (SemEval-2007)*, pp. 117–120, Prague.

Baccianella Stefano, Esuli Andrea and Sebas-tiani Fabrizio. 2010. SentiWordNet 3.0: An Enhanced Lexical Re-source for Sentiment Analysis and Opinion Mining. *In Proceedings of the 7th Conference on Language Resources and Evaluation*, pp. 2200-2204.

Banea, Carmen, Mihalcea Rada, Wiebe Janyce. 2008. A Bootstrapping Method for Building Subjectivity Lexicons for Languages with Scarce Resources. *The Sixth International Conference on Language Resources and Evaluation (LREC 2008).*

Baroni M. and Vegnaduzzo S. 2004. Identifying subjective adjectives through web-based mutual information. *Proceedings of the German Conference on NLP.*

Bobicev Victoria, Maxim Victoria, Prodan Tatiana, Burciu Natalia, Anghelus Victoria. 2010. Emotions in words: developing a multilingual WordNet-Affect. *CICLING 2010.*

Bond, Francis, Hitoshi Isahara, Sanae Fujita, Kiyotaka Uchimoto, Takayuki Kuribayashi and Kyoko Kanzaki. 2009. Enhancing the Japanese WordNet. *7th Workshop on Asian Language Resources, ACL-IJCNLP 2009*, Singapore.

Das Dipankar and Bandyopadhyay Sivaji. 2010. Developing Bengali WordNet Affect for Analyzing Emotion. *23rd International Conference on the Computer Processing of Oriental Languages (ICCPOL-2010)*, pp. 35-40, California, USA.

Ekman Paul. 1992. An argument for basic emotions, *Cognition and Emotion*, 6(3-4):169-200.

Esuli, Andrea. and Sebastiani, Fabrizio. 2006. SENTIWORDNET: A Publicly Available Lexical Resource for Opinion Mining, *LREC*.

Hatzivassiloglou V. and McKeown K. R. 1997. Predicting the semantic orientation of adjectives. *35th Annual Meeting of the ACL and the 8th Conference of the European Chapter of the ACL*, pp. 174–181.

Miller, A. G. 1995. WordNet: a lexical database for English. In *Communications of the ACM*, vol. 38 (11), November, pp. 39-41.

Mohammad, S. and Turney, P.D. 2010. Emotions evoked by common words and phrases: Using Mechanical Turk to create an emotion lexicon. *Proceedings of the NAACL-HLT 2010 Workshop on Computational Approaches to Analysis and Generation of Emotion in Text*, LA, California, 26-34.

Neviarouskaya, Alena, Prendinger Helmut, and Ishizuka Mitsuru. 2009. SentiFul: Generating a Reliable Lexicon for Sentiment Analysis. *International Conference on Affective Computing and Intelligent Interaction (ACII'09)*, IEEE, pp. 363-368.

Sood S. and Vasserman, L. 2009. ESSE: Exploring Mood on the Web. *3rd International AAAI Conference on Weblogs and Social Media (ICWSM) Data Challenge Workshop.*

Strapparava Carlo and Valitutti, A. 2004. Wordnet-affect: an affective extension of wordnet, *In 4th International Conference on Language Resources and Evaluation*, pp. 1083-1086.

Strapparava Carlo and Mihalcea Rada. 2007. SemEval-2007 Task 14: Affective Text. *45th Aunual Meeting of Association for Computational linguistics.*

Takamura Hiroya, Inui Takashi, Okumura Manabu. 2005. Extracting Semantic Orientations of Words using Spin Model. *43rd Annual Meeting of the Association for Computational Linguistics*, pp.133-140.

Voll, K. and M. Taboada. 2007. Not All Words are Created Equal: Extracting Semantic Orientation as a Function of Adjective Relevance. In *Proceedings of the 20th Australian Joint Conference on Artificial Intelligence.* pp. 337-346, Gold Coast, Australia.

Wiebe Janyce and Riloff Ellen. 2006. Creating Subjective and Objective Sentence Classifiers from Unannotated Texts. *International Conference on Intelligent Text Processing and Computational Linguistics*, Mexico City, pp. 475–486.

Improving a Method for Quantifying Readers' Impressions of News Articles with a Regression Equation

Tadahiko Kumamoto
Chiba Institute of Technology
2-17-1, Tsudanuma, Narashino,
Chiba 275-0016, Japan
kumamoto@net.it-chiba.ac.jp

Yukiko Kawai
Kyoto Sangyo University
Motoyama, Kamigamo,
Kita-Ku, Kyoto 603-8555,
Japan

Katsumi Tanaka
Kyoto University
Yoshida-Honmachi,
Sakyo-Ku, Kyoto 606-8501,
Japan

Abstract

In this paper, we focus on the impressions that people gain from reading articles in Japanese newspapers, and we propose a method for extracting and quantifying these impressions in real numbers. The target impressions are limited to those represented by three bipolar scales, "Happy – Sad," "Glad – Angry," and "Peaceful – Strained," and the strength of each impression is computed as a real number between 1 and 7. First, we implement a method for computing impression values of articles using an impression lexicon. This lexicon represents a correlation between the words appearing in articles and the influence of these words on the readers' impressions, and is created from a newspaper database using a word co-occurrence based method. We considered that some gaps would occur between values computed by such an unsupervised method and those judged by the readers, and we conducted experiments with 900 subjects to identify what gaps actually occurred. Consequently, we propose a new approach that uses regression equations to correct impression values computed by the method. Our investigation shows that accuracy is improved by a range of 23.2% to 42.7% by using regression equations.

1 Introduction

In recent years, many researchers have been attempting to model the role of emotion in interactions between people or between people and computers, and to establish how to make computers recognize and express emotions (Picard, 1997; Massaro, 1998; Bartneck, 2001). However, there have not been many studies that have extracted the impressions that people form after seeing or listening to text and multimedia content. For multimedia content such as music and images, several impression-based retrieval methods have been proposed for locating paintings and pieces of music that convey impressions similar to those registered by users (Sato et al., 2000; Kumamoto, 2005; Takayama et al., 2005). By comparison, there are only a few studies that have extracted the readers' impressions gained from text such as news articles, novels, and poems (Kiyoki et al., 1994; Kumamoto and Tanaka, 2005; Lin et al., 2008).

In this paper, we focus on the impressions that people gain from reading articles in Japanese newspapers, and we propose a method for extracting and quantifying these impressions in real numbers. The target impressions are limited to those represented by three bipolar scales, "Happy – Sad," "Glad – Angry," and "Peaceful – Strained," and the strength of each impression is computed as a real number between 1 and 7 denoting a position on the corresponding scale. Then, interpretation of the position is grounded based on a seven-point scale. For example, on the scale "Happy – Sad," the score 1 equals "Happy," the middle score 4 denotes "Neither happy nor sad," and the score 7 equals "Sad." If the impression value of an article is 2.5, then the average reader will experience an intermediate impression between "Comparatively happy (2)" and "A little happy (3)" from reading the article.

First, we assumed that words causing a certain impression from articles co-occur often with impres-

Proceedings of the 2nd Workshop on Computational Approaches to Subjectivity and Sentiment Analysis, ACL-HLT 2011, pages 87–95,
24 June, 2011, Portland, Oregon, USA ©2011 Association for Computational Linguistics

sion words that express that impression, and do not co-occur very often with impression words that express the opposite impression. Proceeding with this assumption, we implemented a method for analyzing co-occurrence relationships between words in every article extracted from a newspaper database. We then created an impression lexicon. This lexicon represents a correlation between the words appearing in articles and the influence of these words on the readers' impressions. We then implemented a method that computes impression values of articles using the lexicon. We considered that some gaps occur between values computed by such an unsupervised method and those judged by the readers, and we conducted experiments with 900 subjects to identify what gaps actually occurred. In these experiments, each subject read ten news articles and estimated her/his impressions of each article using the three bipolar scales. Thereafter, for each scale, we drew a scatter diagram to identify the potential correspondence relationships between the values computed by the method and those judged by the subjects. As a result, we found that the correspondence relationships could be approximately represented by cubic and quintic regression equations. We, therefore, propose a new approach that uses regression equations to correct impression values computed by the method.

The rest of this paper is organized as follows. In Section 2, we present related work. In Section 3, we present the design of the three bipolar scales, a method for the automated construction of an impression lexicon, and a method for computing impression values of articles using this lexicon. In Section 4, we analyze the correspondence relationships between values computed using the lexicon and those judged by the readers, and based on the results of this analysis, we propose a method of using regression equations to correct impression values computed using the lexicon. In Section 5, we investigate how far accuracy can be improved by using the regression equations. Finally, in Section 6, we conclude the paper.

2 Related Work

There are many studies that identify information givers' emotions from some sort of information that they have transmitted (Cowie et al., 2001; Forbes-Riley and Litman, 2004; Kleinsmith and Bianchi-Berthouze, 2007). On the other hand, there are only a few studies that have extracted the impressions which information receivers gain from the text that they have received (Kiyoki et al., 1994; Kumamoto and Tanaka, 2005; Lin et al., 2008).

Kiyoki et al. (1994) have proposed a mathematical model of meanings, and this model allows a semantic relation to be established between words according to a given context. Their method uses a mathematical model and creates a semantic space for selecting the impression words that appropriately express impressions of text according to a given context. In other words, this method does not quantify impressions of text, but just selects one or more impression words expressing the impressions. Thus, their aim differs from ours.

Lin et al. (2008) have proposed a method for classifying news articles into emotion categories from the reader's perspective. They have adopted a machine learning approach to build a classifier for the method. That is, they obtained Chinese news articles from a specific news site on the web which allows a user to cast a vote for one of eight emotions, "happy," "sad," "angry," "surprising," "boring," "heartwarming," "awesome," and "useful." They collected 37,416 news articles along with their voting statistics, and developed a support vector machine-based classifier using 25,975 of them as training data. However, their method just classifies articles into emotion classes and does not quantify the reader's emotions. Thus, their aim also differs from ours.

Kumamoto and Tanaka (2005) have proposed a word co-occurrence-based method for quantifying readers' impressions of news articles in real numbers. However, this method is similar to Turney's method (Turney, 2002), and it is considered to be a Japanese version of this method in the broad sense. Turney's method is one for classifying various genres of written reviews into "recommended" or "not recommended." His method extracts phrases with specific patterns from text, and calculates pointwise mutual information *PMI*(i, "excellent") between a phrase i and the reference word "excellent," and *PMI*(i, "poor") between the same phrase i and the reference word "poor." Then, *PMI*(i, w) is calculated based on a co-occurrence relationship between i and w. Next, the semantic orientation (*SO*) of the phrase i is obtained by calculating the difference between *PMI*(i, "excellent") and *PMI*(i, "poor"). Finally, *SO* of the text is determined by averaging the *SO* of all the phrases. In contrast, Kumamoto et al.'s method quantifies impressions in real numbers, and it can deal with impressions represented by two bipolar scales, "Sad – Glad" and "Angry – Pleased." For that purpose, reference words are selected for each scale. Since all the reference words are Japanese, Kumamoto et al,'s method extracts readers' impressions from Japanese articles only. Also, conditional probabilities are used instead of *PMI*. Since these methods fit our assumption that words causing a certain impression of articles co-occur often with the impression words that express that impression, and do not co-occur very often with impression words that express the opposite impression, we decided to implement a new method based on Kumamoto et al.'s method.

3 Computing impression values of news articles using an impression lexicon

3.1 Determining target impressions

Kumamoto (2010) has designed six bipolar scales suitable for representing impressions of news articles: "Happy – Sad," "Glad – Angry," "Interesting – Uninteresting," "Optimistic – Pessimistic," "Peaceful – Strained," and "Surprising – Common." First, he conducted nine experiments, in each of which 100 subjects read ten news articles and estimated their impressions on a scale from 1 to 5 for each of 42 impression words. These 42 impression words were manually selected from a Japanese thesaurus (Ohno and Hamanishi, 1986) as words that can express impressions of news articles. Next, factor analysis was applied to the data obtained in the experiments, and consequently the 42 words were divided into four groups: negative words, positive words, two words that were "uninteresting" and "common," and two words that were "surprising" and "unexpected." In the meantime, after cluster analysis of the data, the 42 words were divided into ten groups. Based on the results of both analyses, the author created the six bipolar scales presented above. However, he showed that impressions on the "Surprising – Common" scale differed greatly among individuals in terms of their perspective. In addition, he insisted that processing according to the background knowledge, interest, and character of individuals was required to deal with the impressions represented by the two scales "Interesting – Uninteresting" and "Optimistic – Pessimistic." Therefore, we decided not to use these three scales at the present stage, and adopted the remaining three scales, "Happy – Sad," "Glad – Angry," and "Peaceful – Strained."

3.2 Constructing an impression lexicon

An impression lexicon plays an important role in computing impressions of news articles. In this paper, we describe the implementation of a method for automatically constructing an impression lexicon based on Kumamoto et al.'s method as described earlier.

First, while two contrasting reference words are used for each scale in their method, two contrasting sets, each consisting of multiple reference words, are used in this paper.

Next, let the set of reference words which expresses an impression at the left of a scale be S_L, and let the set of reference words which expresses an impression at the right of the scale be S_R. Articles including one or more reference words in S_L or S_R are all extracted from a newspaper database, and the number of reference words belonging to each set is counted in each article. For this we used the 2002 to 2006 editions of the Yomiuri Newspaper Text Database as the newspaper database. Then, let the articles in each of which the number of reference words belonging to S_L is larger than the number of reference words belonging to S_R be A_L, and let the number of articles in A_L be N_L. Let the articles in each of which the number of reference words belonging to S_L is smaller than the number of reference words belonging to S_R be A_R, and let the number of articles in A_R be N_R. Next, all words are extracted from each of A_L and A_R except for particles, adnominal words[1], and demonstratives, and the document frequency of each word is measured. Then, let the document frequency in A_L of a word w

[1]This part of speech exists only in Japanese, not in English. For example, "that," "so called," and "of no particular distinction" are dealt with as adnominal words in Japanese.

Table 1: Specifications of our impression lexicon.

Scales	# of entries	W_L	W_R
Happy – Sad	387,428	4.90	3.80
Glad – Angry	350,388	4.76	3.82
Peaceful – Strained	324,590	3.91	4.67

be $N_L(w)$, and let the document frequency in A_R of a word w be $N_R(w)$. The revised conditional probabilities of a word w are defined as follows.

$$P_L(w) = \frac{N_L(w)}{N_L}, \qquad P_R(w) = \frac{N_R(w)}{N_R}$$

These formula are slightly different from the conditional probabilities used in their method, and only articles that satisfy the assumptions described above are used in order to calculate $P_L(w)$ and $P_R(w)$.

Finally, the impression value $v(w)$ of a word w is calculated using these $P_L(w)$ and $P_R(w)$ as follows.

$$v(w) = \frac{P_L(w) * W_L}{P_L(w) * W_L + P_R(w) * W_R}$$

$$W_L = \log_{10} N_L, \qquad W_R = \log_{10} N_R$$

That is, a weighted interior division ratio $v(w)$ of $P_L(w)$ and $P_R(w)$ is calculated using these formulas, and stored as an impression value of w in the scale "S_L – S_R" in an impression lexicon. Note that W_L and W_R denote weights, and the larger N_L and N_R are, the heavier W_L and W_R are.

The numbers of entries in the impression lexicon constructed as above are shown in Table 1 together with the values of W_L and W_R obtained. Further, the two contrasting sets of reference words[2], which were used in creating the impression lexicon, are enumerated in Table 2 for each scale. These words were determined after a few of trial and error and are based on two criteria, namely (i) it is a verb or adjective that expresses either of two contrasting impressions represented by a scale, and (ii) as far as possible, it does not suggest other types of impressions.

[2]These words were translated into English by the authors.

Table 2: Reference words prepared for each scale.

Scales	Reference words
Happy	tanoshii (happy), tanoshimu (enjoy), tanosimida (look forward to), tanoshigeda (joyous)
– Sad	kanashii (sad), kanashimu (suffer sadness), kanashimida (feel sad), kanashigeda (look sad)
Glad	ureshii (glad), yorokobashii (blessed), yorokobu (feel delight)
– Angry	ikaru/okoru (get angry), ikidooru (become irate), gekidosuru (get enraged)
Peaceful	nodokada (peaceful), nagoyakada (friendly), sobokuda (simple), anshinda (feel easy)
– Strained	kinpakusuru (strained), bukimida (scared), fuanda (be anxious), osoreru (fear)

3.3 Computing impression values of articles

For each scale, the impression value of an article is calculated as follows. First, the article is segmented into words using "Juman" (Kurohashi et al., 1994)[3], one of the most powerful Japanese morphological analysis systems, and an impression value for each word is obtained by consulting the impression lexicon constructed as described in 3.2. Seventeen rules that we designed are then applied to the Juman output. For example, there is a rule that a phrase of a negative form like "sakujo-shi-nai (do not erase)" should not be divided into a verb "shi (do)," a suffix "nai (not)," and an action noun "sakujo (erasion)" but should be treated as a single verb "sakujo-shi-nai (do-not-erase)." There is also a rule that an assertive phrase such as "hoomuran-da (is a home run)" should not be divided into a copula "da (is)" and a noun "hoomuran (a home run)" but should form a single copula "hoomuran-da (is-a-home-run)." Further, there is a rule that a phrase with a prefix, such as "sai-charenji (re-challenge)" should not be divided into a prefix "sai (re)" and an

[3]Since there are no boundary markers between words in Japanese, word segmentation is needed to identify individual words.

action noun "charenji (challenge)" but should form a single action noun "sai-charenji (re-challenge)." All the rules are applied to the Juman output in creating an impression lexicon and computing the impression values of news articles. Finally, an average of the impression values obtained for all the words except for particles, adnominal words, and demonstratives is calculated and presented as an impression value of the article.

4 Correcting computed impression values

4.1 Analyzing a correspondence relationship between computed and manually rated values

We considered that some gaps would occur between impression values computed by an unsupervised method such as the one we used and those of the readers. We, therefore, conducted experiments in which a total of 900 people participated as subjects, and identified what gaps actually occurred.

First, we conducted experiments with 900 subjects, and obtained data that described correspondence relationships between news articles and impressions to be extracted from the articles. That is, the 900 subjects were randomly divided into nine equal groups, each group consisting of 50 males and 50 females, and 90 articles which were selected from the 2002 edition of the Mainichi Newspaper Text Database[4] were randomly divided into nine equal parts. Then, each subject was asked to read the ten articles presented in a random order and rate each of them using three seven-point bipolar scales presented in a random order. The scales we used were "Happy – Sad," "Glad – Angry," and "Peaceful – Strained," and the subjects were asked to assess, on a scale of 1 to 7, the intensity of each impression, represented by each scale, from reading a target article. For example, on the scale "Happy – Sad," the score 1 equaled "Happy," the middle score 4 denoted "Neither happy nor sad," and the score 7 equaled "Sad." After the experiments, for each scale, we calculated an average of the 100 values rated for every article. We regarded this average as the impression value to be extracted from the article. Note that, in these experiments, we presented only the first paragraphs of the original news articles to the subjects. This procedure was derived from the fact that people can understand the outline of a news article by just reading the first paragraph of the article, as well as the fact that impressions of an article may change in every paragraph. Development of a method for following the change of impressions in an article will be a future project.

Next, impression values for the first paragraphs of the 90 articles were computed by the method we implemented in 3.3, where the first paragraphs were identical to those presented to the subjects in the experiments. Note that, according to the definition of our equations, these impression values are close to 1 when impressions on the left of a scale are felt strongly, and are close to 0 when impressions on the right of a scale are felt strongly. We therefore used the following formula and converted the computed value into a value between 1.0 and 7.0.

$$Converted = (1 - Computed) * 6 + 1$$

Next, for each scale, we drew a scatter diagram to identify the potential correspondence relationship between these converted values and the averages obtained in the experiments, as illustrated in Figure 1. We can see from any of the scatter diagrams that the impression values manually rated by the subjects are positively correlated with those automatically computed by the method we implemented. In fact, their coefficients of correlation are 0.76, 0.84, and 0.78 from the case at the top of the figure, which are all high. This not only means that, as an overall trend, the underlying assumption of this paper is satisfied, but also indicates that the correspondence relationships can be represented by regression equations.

4.2 Correcting computed impression values with regression equations

Next, we applied regression analysis to the converted values and the averages, where the converted values were used as the explanatory variable, and the averages were used as the objective variable. In this regression analysis, various regression models (Kan, 2000) such as linear function, logarithmic function, logistic curve, quadratic function, cubic function, quartic function, and quintic function were used on

[4]This database is different from the Yomiuri newspaper database we used in creating an impression lexicon.

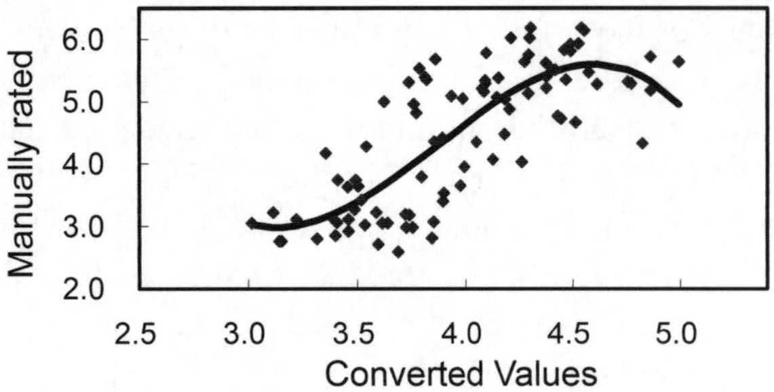

(a) In the case of "Happy – Sad"

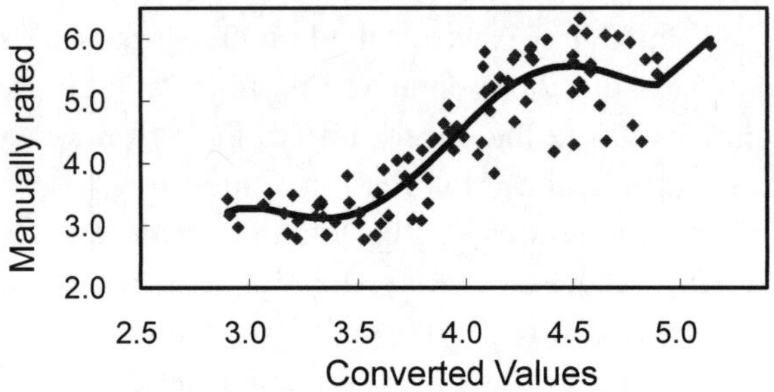

(b) In the case of "Glad – Angry"

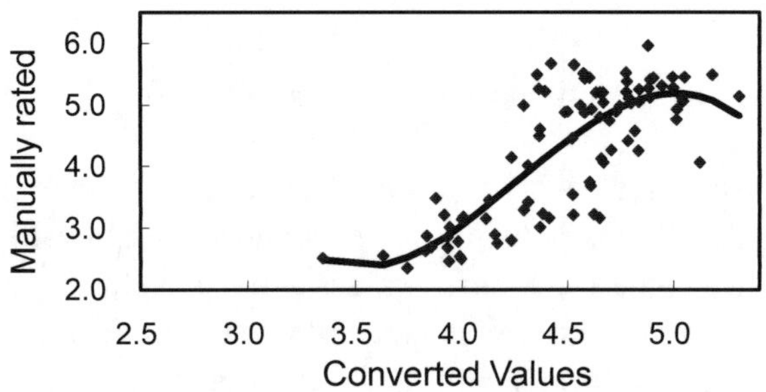

(c) In the case of "Peaceful – Strained"

Figure 1: Scatter diagrams and regression equations.

a trial basis. As a result, the regression equation, which had the highest coefficient of determination, was determined as an optimal function denoting the correspondence relationship between the converted values and the averages in each scale. This means that, for each scale, the impression value of an article was more accurately obtained by correcting a value computed by the method we implemented using the corresponding regression equation.

The regression equations obtained here were "$-1.636x^3 + 18.972x^2 - 70.686x + 88.515$" for the "Happy – Sad," "$2.385x^5 - 46.872x^4 + 363.660x^3 - 1391.589x^2 + 2627.063x - 1955.306$" for the "Glad – Angry," and "$-1.714x^3 + 21.942x^2 - 90.792x + 124.822$" for the "Peaceful –Strained," and they are already illustrated on the corresponding scatter diagrams in Figure 1. Their coefficients of determination were 0.63, 0.81, 0.64, respectively, which were higher than 0.5 in all scales. This means that the results of regression analysis were good. In addition, we can see from Figure 1 that each regression equation fits the shape of the corresponding scatter diagram.

Table 3: Change of the Euclidean distance by using regression equations.

Scales	D_{Before}	D_{After}	*Rate1*
Happy – Sad	0.94	0.67	29.0%
Glad – Angry	0.83	0.47	42.7%
Peaceful – Strained	0.82	0.63	23.2%

5 Performance Evaluation

First, we estimated the accuracy of the proposed method for learned data. For that, we used the data obtained in the experiments described in 4.1, and investigated how far gaps between the computed values and the averages of the manually rated values were reduced by using the regression equations. The results are shown in Table 3. In this table, D_{Before} denotes the Euclidean distance between the computed values without correction and the averages for the 90 articles, and D_{After} denotes the Euclidean distance between the values corrected with the corresponding regression equation and the averages for the 90 articles. Then *Rate1* was calculated as an improvement rate by the following formula:

$$Rate1 = \frac{D_{Before} - D_{After}}{D_{Before}} \times 100$$

Table 3 shows fairly high improvement rates in all the scales, and hence we find that accuracy is improved by using the regression equations. In particular, D_{After} for the scale "Glad – Angry" is less than 0.5 or a half of a step and is sufficiently small.

Next, we calculated the accuracy of the method (Kumamoto and Tanaka, 2005) on which the proposed method is based, and compared it with that of the proposed method. The results are shown in Table 4. In this table, $D_{Baseline}$ denotes the Euclidean

Table 4: Comparison with a baseline method.

Scales	$D_{Baseline}$	$D_{Proposed}$	*Rate2*
Happy – Sad	0.99	0.67	32.3%
Glad – Angry	0.82	0.47	42.7%
Peaceful – Strained	1.00	0.63	37.0%

distance between the values computed by the baseline method and the averages for the 90 articles, and $D_{Proposed}$ is equivalent to D_{After} in Table 3. Then *Rate2* is calculated as an improvement rate by the following formula:

$$Rate2 = \frac{D_{Baseline} - D_{Proposed}}{D_{Baseline}} \times 100$$

Table 4 also shows that fairly high improvement rates were obtained in all the scales. Note that the baseline method was implemented in the following way. First, a pair of reference words was prepared for each scale. Actually, the pair "tanoshii (happy)" and "kanashii (sad)" was used for the scale "Happy – Sad"; the pair "ureshii (glad)" and "ikaru/okoru (get angry)" for the scale "Glad – Angry"; and "nodokada (peaceful)" and "kinpakusuru (strained)" for the scale "Peaceful – Strained." Next, an impression lexicon for the baseline method was constructed from the news articles which were used to construct our impression lexicon.

The results shown in Tables 3 and 4 prove that the proposed method has a high level of accuracy for the articles used in obtaining the regression equations.

As the next step, we estimated the accuracy of the proposed method for unlearned data. For that, we performed five-fold cross-validation using the data obtained in 4.1. First, the data were randomly divided into five equal parts, each part consisting of data for 18 articles. Next, a learned data set was created arbitrarily from four of the five parts, or data for 72 articles, and an unlearned data set was created from the remaining part, or data for 18 articles. Regression analysis was then applied to the learned data set. As a result, an optimal regression equation that expressed a correspondence relationship between the computed values and the averages of the manually rated values in the learned data set was obtained for each scale. Next, we calculated the Euclidean distance between the averages for 18 articles in the unlearned data set and the values which were computed from the 18 articles themselves and corrected with the corresponding optimal regression equation. The results are shown in Table 5. In this table, D_{Mean}, D_{Max}, and D_{Min} denote the mean, maximum, and minimum values of the five Euclidean distances calculated from a total of five unlearned data sets, respectively. Comparing $D_{Proposed}$ in Table 4 and D_{Mean} in Table 5, we find that they are almost equivalent. This means that the proposed method is also effective for unlearned data.

Table 5: Estimation of overall accuracy based on five-fold cross-validation.

Scales	D_{Mean}	D_{Max}	D_{Min}
Happy – Sad	0.69	0.78	0.57
Glad – Angry	0.49	0.58	0.42
Peaceful – Strained	0.64	0.81	0.50

Table 6: Influence of size of target newspaper database to Euclidean distance.

	Editions		
Scales	2002-2006	2005-2006	2006
Happy – Sad	0.67	0.69	0.73
Glad – Angry	0.47	0.50	0.54
Peaceful – Strained	0.63	0.65	0.69

Finally, we investigated how the accuracy of the proposed method was influenced by the size of the newspaper database used in constructing an impression lexicon. First, using each of the 2002 to 2006 editions, the 2005 to 2006 editions, and the 2006 edition only, impression lexicons were constructed. Three regression equations were then obtained for each lexicon in the same way. Next, for each scale, we calculated the Euclidean distance between the values which were computed from all the 90 articles using each lexicon and corrected with the corresponding regression equation, and the averages obtained in 4.1. The results are shown in Table 6. Table 6 shows that the accuracy of the proposed method is reduced slightly as the size of newspaper database becomes smaller. Conversely, this suggests that the accuracy of the proposed method can be improved as the size of newspaper database increases. We would like to verify this suggestion in the near future.

6 Conclusion

This paper has proposed a method for quantitatively identifying the impressions that people gain from reading Japanese news articles. The key element of the proposed method lies in a new approach that uses regression equations to correct impression values computed from news articles by an unsupervised method. Our investigation has shown that accuracy for learned data is improved by a range of 23.2% to 42.7% by using regression equations, and that accuracy for unlearned data is almost equivalent to the accuracy for learned data. Note that, in this paper, the target impressions are limited to those represented by three bipolar scales, "Happy – Sad," "Glad – Angry," and "Peaceful – Strained," and the strength of each impression is computed as a real number between 1 and 7 denoting a position on the corresponding scale.

Our main future work is described below. Since the proposed method uses a word co-occurrence based method to construct an impression lexicon, it may not be effective for other types of scale. We therefore need to examine and consider what kinds of scales are suitable for the proposed method. Personal adaptation is important in methods dealing with impressions created by such artworks as music and paintings. In order to develop a method for more accurately quantifying readers' impressions of news articles, we will also tackle this personal adaptation problem. Further, we plan to integrate the proposed method into a search engine, a recommendation system, and an electronic book reader, and to verify the effectiveness of readers' impressions of news articles in creating a ranking index for information retrieval and recommendation, or in determining the type of emotional speech used in reading an e-paper.

Acknowledgments

A part of this work was sponsored by National Institute of Information and Communications Technology (NICT), Japan, and was achieved under the project named "Evaluating Credibility of Web Information."

References

Christoph Bartneck. 2001. How convincing is Mr. Data's smile: Affective expressions of machines. *User Modeling and User-Adapted Interaction*, 11:279–295.

R. Cowie, E. Douglas-Cowie, N. Tsapatsoulis, G. Votsis, S. Kollias, W. Fellenz, and J. G. Taylor. 2001. Emotion recognition in human-computer interaction. *IEEE Signal Processing Magazine*, 18:32–80.

Kate Forbes-Riley and Diane J. Litman. 2004. Predicting emotion in spoken dialogue from multiple knowledge sources. In *Proc. of Human Language Technology Conf. of the NAACL*, pages 201–208.

Tamio Kan. 2000. *Multivariate Statistical Analysis*. Gendai-Sugakusha, Kyoto, Japan.

Yasushi Kiyoki, Takashi Kitagawa, and Takanari Hayama. 1994. A metadatabase system for semantic image search by a mathematical model of meaning. *SIGMOD Rec.*, 23:34–41.

Andrea Kleinsmith and Nadia Bianchi-Berthouze. 2007. Recognizing affective dimensions from body posture. In *Proc. of the Int. Conf. on Affective Computing and Intelligent Interaction*, volume LNCS 4738, pages 48–58, September.

Tadahiko Kumamoto and Katsumi Tanaka. 2005. Proposal of impression mining from news articles. In *Proc. of Int. Conf. on Knowledge-Based Intelligent Information and Engineering Systems*, volume LNAI 3681, pages 901–910. Springer.

Tadahiko Kumamoto. 2005. Design and evaluation of a music retrieval scheme that adapts to the user's impressions. In *Proc. of Int. Conf. on User Modeling*, volume LNAI 3538, pages 287–296. Springer.

Tadahiko Kumamoto. 2010. Design of impression scales for assessing impressions of news articles. In *Proc. of DASFAA Workshop on Social Networks and Social Media Mining on the Web*, volume LNCS 6193, pages 285–295.

Sadao Kurohashi, Toshihisa Nakamura, Yuji Matsumoto, and Makoto Nagao. 1994. Improvements of Japanese morphological analyzer JUMAN. In *Proc. of the Int. Workshop on Sharable Natural Language Resources*, pages 22–28, Nara, Japan.

Kevin Hsin-Yih Lin, Changhua Yang, and Hsin-Hsi Chen. 2008. Emotion classification of online news articles from the reader's perspective. In *Proc. of the IEEE/WIC/ACM Int. Conf. on Web Intelligence and Intelligent Agent Technology*, pages 220–226, Washington, DC, USA. IEEE Computer Society.

Dominic W. Massaro. 1998. *Perceiving Talking Faces: From Speech Perception to a Behavioral Principle*. MIT Press, USA.

Susumu Ohno and Masando Hamanishi, editors. 1986. *Ruigo-Kokugo-Jiten*. Kadokawa Shoten Publishing Co.,Ltd., Tokyo, Japan.

Rosalind W. Picard. 1997. *Affective Computing*. MIT Press.

Akira Sato, Jun Ogawa, and Hajime Kitakami. 2000. An impression-based retrieval system of music collection. In *Proc. of the Int. Conf. on Knowledge-Based Intelligent Information Engineering Systems & Allied Technologies*, volume 2, pages 856–859, Brighton, UK.

Tsuyoshi Takayama, Hirotaka Sasaki, and Shigeyuki Kuroda. 2005. Personalization by relevance ranking feedback in impression-based retrieval for multimedia database. *Journal of Systematics, Cybernetics and Informatics*, 3(2):85–89.

Peter D. Turney. 2002. Thumbs up or thumbs down? semantic orientation applied to unsupervised classification of reviews. In *Proc. of the Annual Meeting of the Association for Computational Linguistics*, pages 417–424, Philadelphia, USA.

Feature Selection for Sentiment Analysis Based on Content and Syntax Models

Adnan Duric and Fei Song
School of Computer Science, University of Guelph, 50 Stone Road East,
Guelph, Ontario, N1G 2W1, Canada
{aduric, fsong}@uoguelph.ca

Abstract

Recent solutions for sentiment analysis have relied on feature selection methods ranging from lexicon-based approaches where the set of features are generated by humans, to approaches that use general statistical measures where features are selected solely on empirical evidence. The advantage of statistical approaches is that they are fully automatic, however, they often fail to separate features that carry sentiment from those that do not. In this paper we propose a set of new feature selection schemes that use a Content and Syntax model to automatically learn a set of features in a review document by separating the entities that are being reviewed from the subjective expressions that describe those entities in terms of polarities. By focusing only on the subjective expressions and ignoring the entities, we can choose more salient features for document-level sentiment analysis. The results obtained from using these features in a maximum entropy classifier are competitive with the state-of-the-art machine learning approaches.

1 Introduction

As user generated data become more commonplace, we seek to find better approaches to extract and classify relevant content automatically. This gives users a richer, more informative, and more appropriate set of information in an efficient and organized manner. One way for organizing such data is *text classification*, which involves mapping documents into *topical* categories based on the occurrences of particular features. Sentiment Analysis (SA) can be framed as a text classification task where the categories are *polarities* such as *positive* and *negative*. However, the similarities end here. Whereas general text classification is concerned with features that distinguish different topics, sentiment analysis deals with features about subjectivity, affect, emotion, and points-of-view that *describe* or *modify* the related entities. Since user-generated review documents contain both kinds of features, SA solutions ultimately face the challenge of separating the factual content from the subjective content describing it.

For example, taking a segment from a randomly chosen document in Pang et al.'s movie review corpus[1], we see how entities and modifiers are related to each other:

> ... Of course, it helps that **Kaye** has an **actor** as *talented* as **Norton** to play **this part**. It's *astonishing* how *frightening* **Norton** looks with a shaved head and a swastika on his chest. ... Visually, **the film** is *very powerful*. **Kaye** indulges in a lot of *interesting* **artistic choices**, and most of **them** *work nicely*.

Indeed, most of the information about an entity that relates it to a particular polarity comes from the *modifying* words. In the example above, these words are adjectives such as *talented*, *frightening*, *interesting*, and *powerful*. They can also be verbs such as *work* and adverbs such as *nicely*. The entities are

[1] http://www.cs.cornell.edu/people/pabo/movie-review-data/

Proceedings of the 2nd Workshop on Computational Approaches to Subjectivity and Sentiment Analysis, ACL-HLT 2011, pages 96–103,
24 June, 2011, Portland, Oregon, USA ©2011 Association for Computational Linguistics

represented by various nouns and pronouns such as: *Kaye*, *Norton*, *actor* and *them*.

Therefore, the task of classifying a review document can be explored by taking into account a mixture of entities and their modifiers. An important characteristic of review documents is that the reviewers tend to discuss the whole set of entities throughout the entire document, whereas the modifiers for those entities tend to be more localized at the sentence or phrase level. In other words, each entity can be *polymorphous* within the document, with a long-range *semantic* relationship between its forms while the modifiers in each case are bound to the entity in a short-range, *syntactic* relationship. Generalizing a single entity to all the entities that are found in a document, and taking all their respective modifiers into account, we can start to infer the polarity of the entire document based on the set of all the modifiers. This reduces to finding all the syntactic words in the document and disregarding the entities.

Taking another look at the example modifiers, we might assume that all of the relevant indicators for SA come from specific parts of speech categories such as *adjectives* and *adverbs*, while other parts of speech classes such as nouns are more relevant for general text classification, and can be discarded. However, as demonstrated by Pang et al. (2002), Pang and Lee (2004), Hu and Liu (2004), and Riloff et al. (2003), there are some nouns and verbs that are useful sentiment indicators as well. Therefore, a clear distinction cannot be made along parts of speech categories.

To address this issue, we propose a *feature selection* scheme in which we can obtain important sentiment indicators that:

1. Do not rely on specific parts of speech classes while maintaining the focus on syntax words.

2. Separate semantic words that do not indicate sentiment while keeping nouns that do.

3. Reflect the domain for the set of documents.

By using feature selection schemes that focus on the outlined sentiment indicators as a basis for our machine learning approach, we should achieve competitive accuracy results when classifying document polarities.

The rest of this paper is organized as follows. Section 2 discusses some important work and results for SA and outlines the modelling and classification techniques used by our approach. Section 3 provides details about our feature selection methods. Our experiments and analyses are given in section 4, and conclusions and future directions are presented in section 5.

2 Related Work

2.1 Feature Selection in Sentiment Analysis

The majority of the approaches for SA involve a two-step process:

1. Identify the parts of the document that will likely contribute to *positive* or *negative* sentiments.

2. Combine these parts of the document in ways that increase the odds of the document falling into one of these two polar categories.

The simplest approach for (1) by Pang et al. (2002) is to use the most frequently-occurring words in the corpus as polarity indicators. This approach is commonly used with general text classification, and the results achieved indicate that simple document frequency cutoffs can be an effective feature selection scheme. However, this scheme picks up on many entity words that do not contain any subjectivity.

The most common approach, used by researchers such as Das and Chen (2007), starts with a manually created lexicon specific to their particular domain whereas others (Hurst and Nigam, 2004; Yi et al., 2003) attempt to craft a general-purpose opinion lexicon that can be used across domains. More recent lexicon-based approaches (Ding et al., 2008; Hu and Liu, 2004; Kim and Hovy, 2004; Riloff et al., 2003) begin with a small set of 'seed' words and bootstrap this set through synonym detection or various on-line resources to obtain a larger lexicon. However, lexicon-based approaches have several key difficulties. First, they take time to compile. Whitelaw et al. (2005) report that their feature selection process took 20 person-hours, since it involves work done by human annotators. In separate qualitative experiments done by Pang et al. (2002),

Wilson et al. (2005) and Kim and Hovy (2004), the agreement between human judges when given a list of sentiment-bearing words is as low as 58% and no higher than 76%. In addition, some words may not be frequent enough for a classification algorithm.

2.2 Topic Modelling and HMM-LDA

Topic models such as *Latent Dirichlet Allocation* (LDA) are generative models that allow documents to be explained by a set of unobserved (latent) topics. Hidden Markov Model LDA (HMM-LDA) (Griffiths et al., 2005) is a topic model that simultaneously models topics and syntactic structure in a collection of documents. The idea behind the model is that a typical word can play different roles. It can either be part of the content and serve in a semantic (topical) purpose or it can be used as part of the grammatical (syntactic) structure. It can also be used in both contexts. HMM-LDA models this behavior by inducing syntactic classes for each word based on how they appear together in a sentence using a Hidden Markov Model. Each word gets assigned to a syntactic class, but one class is reserved for the semantic words. Words in this class behave as they would in a regular LDA topic model, participating in different topics and having certain probabilities of appearing in a document. More formally, the model is defined in terms of three sets of variables and a *generative process*. Let $\mathbf{w} = \{w_1, ..., w_n\}$ be a sequence of words where each word w_i is one of V words; $\mathbf{z} = \{z_1, ..., z_n\}$, a sequence of topic assignments where each z_i is one of K topics; and $\mathbf{c} = \{c_1, ..., c_n\}$, a sequence of class assignments where each c_i is one of C classes. One class, $c_i = 1$ is designated as the 'semantic class', and the rest, the 'syntactic' classes.

Since we are dealing with a Hidden Markov Model, we require a variable representing the *transition probabilities* between the classes, given by a $C \times C$ *transition matrix* π that models transitions between classes c_{i-1} and c_i. The generative process is described as follows:

1. Sample $\theta^{(d)}$ from a Dirichlet prior $Dir(\alpha)$

2. For each word w_i in document d:

   (a) Draw $z_i \sim \theta^{(d)}$

   (b) Draw $c_i \sim \pi^{(c_i-1)}$

   (c) If $c_i = 1$, then draw $w_i \sim \phi^{(z_i)}$, else draw $w_i \sim \phi^{(c_i)}$

where $\phi^{(z_i)} \sim Dir(\beta)$ and $\phi^{(c_i)} \sim Dir(\delta)$, both from *Dirichlet* distributions.

2.3 Text Classification Based on Maximum Entropy Modelling

Maximum Entropy Modelling (Manning and Schütze, 1999) is a framework whereby the features represent constraints on the overall model and the idea is to incorporate the knowledge that we have while preserving as much uncertainty as possible about the knowledge we do not have. The features f_i are binary functions where there is a vector x representing input elements (unigram features in our case) and c, the class label for one of the possible categories. More specifically, a feature function is defined as follows:

$$f_{i,c'}(x, c) = \begin{cases} 1 & \text{if } x \text{ contains } w_i \text{ and } c = c' \\ 0 & \text{otherwise} \end{cases} \tag{2.1}$$

where word w_i and category c' correspond to a specific feature.

Employing the feature functions described above, a Maximum Entropy model takes the following form:

$$P(x, c) = \frac{1}{Z} \prod_{i=1}^{K} \alpha_i^{f_i(x,c)} \tag{2.2}$$

where K is the number of features, α_i is the weight for feature f_i, and Z is a normalizing constant. By taking the logarithm on both sides, we get the log-linear model:

$$\log P(x, c) = -\log Z + \sum_{i=1}^{K} f_i(x, c) \log \alpha_i \tag{2.3}$$

To classify a document, we compute $P(c|x)$ so that the c with the highest probability will be the category for the given document.

3 Feature Selection (FS) Based on HMM-LDA

3.1 Characteristics of Salient Features

To motivate our approach, we first describe criteria that are useful in selecting salient features for SA:

1. *Features should be expressive enough to add useful information to the classification process.* As discussed in section 1, the most expressive features in terms of polarity are the *modifying* words that describe an entity in a certain way. These are usually, but not restricted to, adjectives, adverbs, subjective verbs and nouns.

2. *All features together should form a broad and comprehensive viewpoint of the entire corpus.* In a corpus of many documents, some features can represent a subset of the corpus very accurately, while other features may represent another subset of the corpus. The problem arises when representing the whole corpus with a specific feature set (Sebastiani, 2002).

3. *Features should be as domain-dependent as possible.* Examples from Hurst and Nigam (2004) and Das and Chen (2007) as well as many other approaches indicate that SA is a domain-dependant task, and the final features should reflect the domain of the corpus that they are representing.

4. *Features must be frequent enough.* Rare features do not occur in many documents and make it difficult to train a machine learning algorithm. Experiments by Pang et al. (2002) indicate that having more features does not help learning, and the best accuracy was achieved by selecting features based on *document frequency*.

5. *Features should be discriminative enough.* A learning system needs to be able to pick up on their presence in certain documents for one outcome and absence in other documents for another outcome in classification.

3.2 FS Based on Syntactic Classes

Our proposed FS scheme is to utilize HMM-LDA to obtain words that, for the most part, follow the criteria we set out in subsection 3.1. We train an HMM-LDA model to give us the syntactic classes that we further combine to form our final features. Let word $w_i \in V$ where V is the vocabulary. Also let $c_j \in C$ be a class. We define $P_{c_j}(w_i)$ as the probability of word w_i in class c_j, and one class, $c_j = 1$ indicates the semantic class. Since each class (syntactic and semantic) has a probability distribution over all words, we need to select words that offer a good *representation* of the class. The representative words in each class have a much higher probability than the other words. Therefore, we can select the representative words by the *cumulative probability*. Specifically, we select the top percentage of the words in a class whereby the sum of their probabilities will be within some pre-defined range. This is necessary since there are many words in each class with low probabilities in which we are not interested (Steyvers and Griffiths, 2006). The cumulative distribution function is defined as:

$$F_j(w_i) = \sum_{P_{c_j}(w) \geq P_{c_j}(w_i)} P_{c_j}(w) \qquad (3.1)$$

Then, we can define the set of words in class c_j as:

$$W_{c_j} = \{w_i | F_j(w_i) \leq \eta\} \qquad (3.2)$$

where η is a pre-defined threshold such that $0 \leq \eta \leq 1$. Next, we define the set of words in all the syntactic classes W_{syn} as:

$$W_{syn} = \{w_i | w_i \in W_{c_j} \text{ and } c_j \neq 1\} \qquad (3.3)$$

and the set of words in the semantic class W_{sem} as:

$$W_{sem} = \{w_i | w_i \in W_{c_j} \text{ and } c_j = 1\} \qquad (3.4)$$

Since modifying words for sentiment typically fall into syntactic classes, we could use words in W_{syn} as features for SA. However, as observed by Pang et al. (2002), the best classification performance is achieved by a subset of features (typically around 2500). As a general step, we can apply a document frequency (DF) cutoff to select the most frequent features. Let $df(w_i)$ denote the document frequency of word w_i, indicating the number of documents in which w_i occurs in the corpus. Then the resulting features selected based on *df* can be defined as:

$$cut(W_{syn}, \epsilon) = \{w_i | w_i \in W_{syn} \text{ and } df(w_i) \geq \epsilon\} \quad (3.5)$$

where ϵ is the minimum document frequency required for feature selection.

3.3 FS Based on Set Difference between Syntactic and Semantic Classes

The main characteristic of using HMM-LDA classes for feature selection is that the set of words in the syntactic classes and the set of words in the semantic class are not disjoint. In fact, there is quite a large overlap. In this and the next subsections, we discuss ways to remedy and even exploit this situation to get a higher level of accuracy. In the Pang et al. movie review data, there is about 35% overlap between words in the syntactic and semantic classes for $\eta = 0.9$. Our first systematic approach attempts to gain better accuracy by lowering the ratio of semantic words in the final feature set.

More formally, given the set of syntactic words W_{syn}, we can reduce the overlap with W_{sem} by doing a set difference operation:

$$W_{syn} - W_{sem} \quad (3.6)$$

This will give us all the words that are more favoured in the syntactic classes. However, as we shall see shortly, and also as we earlier speculated, by subtracting all the words in the semantic class, we are actually getting rid of some useful features. This is because (a) it is possible for the semantic class to contain words that are syntactic, and as a result are useful, and (b) there exist some semantic words that are good indicators of polarity. Therefore, we seek to 'lessen' the influence of the semantic class by cutting only a certain portion of it out, but not all of them.

For the above scheme, we outline Algorithm 1 that enables us to select features from W_{syn} by applying a percentage cutoff for W_{sem} and then doing a set difference operation. We define $top(W_{sem}, \delta)$ to be the $\delta\%$ of the words with top probabilities in W_{sem}.

Note that when $\delta = 1.0$, we get the same result as $W_{syn} - W_{sem}$. In our experiments, we try a range of δ values for SA.

Algorithm 1 Syntactic-Semantic Set Difference

Require: W_{syn} and W_{sem} as input

1: $W'_{sem} = top(W_{sem}, \delta)$
2: $W_{diff} = W_{syn} - W'_{sem}$
3: $W'_{syn} = cut(W_{diff}, \epsilon)$

3.4 FS Based on Max Scores of Syntactic Features

The running theme through the HMM-LDA feature selection schemes is that if a word is highly ranked (has a high probability of occurring) in a syntactic class, we should use that word in our feature set. Moreover, if a word is highly ranked in the semantic class, we usually do not want to use that word in our feature set because the word usually indicates a frequent noun. Therefore, the desirable words are those that occur with high probability in the syntactic classes, but do not occur with high probability in the semantic class, or do not occur there at all.

To this end, we have formulated a scheme that adds such words to our feature set. For each word, we obtain its highest probability in the set of syntactic classes. Comparing this probability with the probability of the same word in the semantic class, we disregard the word if the probability in the semantic class is greater.

We define the max scores for word w_i for both the syntactic and semantic classes and describe how we select features based on the max scores in Algorithm 2.

Algorithm 2 Max Scores of Syntactic Features

Require: $c_j \in C$ where $1 \leq j \leq |C|$

1: **for all** $w_i \in V$ **do**
2: $S_{syn}(w_i) = max_{c_j \neq 1} P_{c_j}(w_i)$
3: $S_{sem}(w_i) = P_{c_1}(w_i)$
4: $W_{max} = \{w_i | S_{syn}(w_i) > S_{sem}(w_i)\}$
5: **end for**
6: $W'_{syn} = cut(W_{max}, \epsilon)$

4 Experiments

This section describes the steps taken to generate some experimental results for each scheme described in the previous section. Before we can analyze these sets of results, we take a look at some baselines.

4.1 Evaluation

We use the corpus of 2000 movie reviews (Pang and Lee, 2004) that consists of 1000 positive and 1000 negative documents selected from on-line forums. In our experiments, we randomize the documents and split the data into 1800 for training / testing purposes and 200 as the validation set. For the 1800 documents, we run a 3-fold cross validation procedure where we train on 1200 documents and test on 600. We compare the resultant feature sets after each FS scheme using the OpenNLP[2] Maximum Entropy classifier.

Throughout these experiments, we are interested in the *classification accuracy*. This is evaluated simply by comparing the resultant class from the classifier and the actual class annotated by Pang and Lee (2004). The number of matches is divided by the number of documents in the *test* set. Thus, given an *annotated* test set $d_{test_A} = \{(d_1, o_1), (d_2, o_2), \ldots (d_S, o_S)\}$ and the classified set, $d_{test_B} = \{(d_1, q_1), (d_2, q_2), \ldots (d_S, q_S)\}$, we calculate the accuracy as follows:

$$\frac{\sum_{i=1}^{S} I(o_i = q_i)}{S} \tag{4.1}$$

where $I(\cdot)$ is the indicator function.

4.2 Baseline Results

After replicating the results from Pang et al. (2002), we varied the number of iterations per fold by using a held-out validation set 'eval'. The higher accuracy achieved suggests that the model was not fully trained after 10 iterations.

In order to compare with our HMM-LDA based schemes, we ran experiments to explore a basic POS-based feature selection scheme. In this approach, we first tagged the words in each document with POS tags and selected the most frequently-occurring unigrams that were not tagged as 'NN', 'NNP', 'NNS' or 'NNPS' (the 'noun' categories). This corresponds to **POS (-NN*)** in Table 1. Next, we tagged all the words and only selected the words that were tagged as 'JJ*', 'RB*', and 'VB*' categories (the 'syntactic' categories). The idea is to include as part of the feature set all the words that are not 'semantically oriented'. This corresponds to **POS (JJ* + RB* + VB*)** in Table 1.

Iterations	DF cutoff	POS (-NN*)	POS (JJ*+RB* +VB*)
10	0.821	0.827	0.811
25	0.836	0.831	0.824
eval	0.845	0.848	0.826

Table 1: Baseline results with a different number of iterations. Each column represents a different feature selection method.

4.3 HMM-LDA Training

Our feature selection methods involve training an HMM-LDA model on the Pang et al. corpus of movie reviews, taking the class assignments, and combining the resultant unigrams to create features for the MaxEnt classifier. Since HMM-LDA is an *unsupervised* topic model, we can train it on the entire corpus. We trained the model using the Topic Modelling Toolbox[3] MATLAB package on the 2000 movie reviews. Since the HMM-LDA model requires sentences to be outlined, we used the usual end-of-sentence markers ('.', '!', '?', ':'). The training parameters are **T = 50** topics, **S = 20** classes, **ALPHA = 1.0**, **BETA = 0.01**, and **GAMMA = 0.1**. We found that 1000 iterations is sufficient as we tracked the log-likelihood of every 10 iterations.

After training, we have both the topic assignments **z** and the class assignments **c** for each word in each of the samples.

4.4 Selecting Features Based on Syntactic Classes

In this experiment we fix $\eta = 0.9$ to get the top words in each class having a cumulative probability under 0.9. These are the *representative* words in each class which we merge into W_{syn}. Finally, we select 2500 words by the *df* cutoff method. This list of words is then used as features for the MaxEnt classifier. We run the classifier for 10, 25 and 'eval' number of iterations in order to compare with the baseline results.

[2] http://incubator.apache.org/opennlp/

[3] http://psiexp.ss.uci.edu/research/programs_data/toolbox.htm

Iterations	FS Based on Syntactic Features
10	0.823
25	0.839
eval	0.863

Table 2: Results for FS Based on Syntactic Classes at 10, 25 and 'eval' iterations.

At $\eta = 0.9$, there are 6,189 words in W_{syn} before we select the top 2500 using the *df* cutoff. From Table 2, we see that the accuracy has increased from 0.845 to 0.863 at the 'eval' number iterations.

In all of our experiments, we use *df* cutoff to get a manageable number of features for the classifier. This is partly based on Pang et al. (2002) and partly based on calculating the *Pearson correlation* for each class between the document frequency and word probability at $\eta = 0.9$. Since every class has a positive correlation in the range of [0.313938, 0.888160] where the average is 0.576, we can say that there is a correlation between the two values.

4.5 Selecting Features Based on Set Difference

The result for Set Difference is derived by varying the percentage of top semantic words that should be excluded in the final feature set. For example, some words in $W_{syn} \cap W_{sem}$ that have a higher probability in W_{sem} are: *'hollywod'*, *'war'*, and *'fiction'* while some words that have a higher probability in W_{syn} include: *'good'*, *'love'* and *'funny'*. The δ value is defined by the percentage of the words in W_{sem} that we exclude from W_{syn}. The results for $0.0 \leq \delta \leq 1.0$ for increments of $\delta \times |W_{sem}|$, are summarized in Table 3.

δ	FS Based on Set Difference	δ	FS Based on Set Difference
0.0	0.861	0.5	0.852
0.1	0.862	0.6	0.846
0.2	0.865	0.7	0.849
0.3	0.858	0.8	0.847
0.4	0.857	0.9	0.840
		1.0	0.831

Table 3: Results for FS Based on Syntactic-Semantic set difference method. Each row represents the accuracy achieved at a particular δ value.

From the results, we can see that as we remove more and more words from W_{sem}, the accuracy level decreases. This suggests that $W_{sem} \cap W_{syn}$ contains some important features and if we subtract W_{sem} entirely, we essentially eliminate them. At each cutoff level, we are eliminating 10% until we have eliminated the whole set. Clearly, a more fine-grained approach is needed, and that leads us to the Max-Score results.

4.6 Selecting Features Based on Max Scores

For the method based on Max Scores, we may select features that are in both W_{sem} and W_{syn} sets as long as their max scores in W_{syn} are higher than those in W_{sem}.

Iterations	FS Based on Max Scores
eval	0.875

Table 4: Result for FS Based on Max Scores.

Comparing the accuracy in Table 4 with those in the previous subsections, we can say that using the fine-grained Max-Score algorithm improves the classification accuracy. This means that iteratively removing words that have a relatively higher probability in W_{sem} compared to W_{syn} does not eliminate important words occurring in both sets, but lessens the influence of some high probability words in W_{sem}.

4.7 Discussion of the Results

For our experiments, the best accuracy is achieved by utilizing the Max-Score algorithm (outlined in subsection 3.4) after a further selection of 2500 with the *df* cutoff. As discussed in subsection 3.4, the Max-Score algorithm enables us to select words that have a higher score in W_{syn} than in W_{sem}. This approach has the dual advantage of keeping the words that are present in both W_{syn} and W_{sem} but have higher scores in W_{syn} and ignoring the words that are also present in both sets but have higher scores in W_{sem}. Ultimately, this decreases the influence of the frequent and overlapped words that have a high probability in W_{sem}.

Finally, to quantify the significance level of our best approach against the baseline methods in subsection 4.2, we calculated the p-values for the one-tailed t-tests comparing our best approach based on Max Scores with the DF and POS (-NN*) baselines, respectively. The resulting p-values of 0.011 and 0.014 suggest that our best approach is *significantly* better than the baseline approaches.

5 Conclusions and Future Directions

In this paper, we have described a method for feature selection based on long-range and short-range dependencies given by the HMM-LDA topic model. By modelling review documents based on the combinations of syntactic and semantic classes, we have devised a method of separating the topical content that describes the *entities* under review from the opinion context (given by sentiment *modifiers*) about that entity in each case. By grouping all the sentiment modifiers for each entity in a document, we are selecting the features that are intuitively in line with the outlined characteristics of salient features for SA (see subsection 3.1). This is backed up by our experiments where we achieve competitive results for document polarity classification.

One avenue for future development of this framework could include identifying and extracting *aspects* from a review document. So far, we have not identified aspects from the entities, choosing instead to classify a document as a whole. However, this framework can be readily applied to extract relevant (most probable) aspects using the LDA topic model and then restrict the syntactic modifiers to the range of sentences where an aspect occurs. This would give us an *unsupervised* aspect extraction scheme that we can combine with a classifier to predict polarities for each aspect.

References

Sanjiv R. Das and Mike Y. Chen. 2007. Yahoo! for Amazon: Sentiment extraction from small talk on the Web. *Management Science*, 53(9):1375–1388.

Xiaowen Ding, Bing Liu, and Philip S. Yu. 2008. A holistic lexicon-based approach to opinion mining. In *Proceedings of the Conference on Web Search and Web Data Mining (WSDM)*.

Thomas L. Griffiths, Mark Steyvers, David M. Blei, and Joshua B. Tenenbaum. 2005. Integrating topics and syntax. In *In Advances in Neural Information Processing Systems 17*, pages 537–544. MIT Press.

Minqing Hu and Bing Liu. 2004. Mining opinion features in customer reviews. In *Proceedings of AAAI*, pages 755–760.

Matthew Hurst and Kamal Nigam. 2004. Retrieving topical sentiments from online document collections. In *Document Recognition and Retrieval XI*, pages 27–34.

Soo-Min Kim and Eduard Hovy. 2004. Determining the sentiment of opinions. In *Proceedings of the International Conference on Computational Linguistics (COLING)*.

Christopher D. Manning and Hinrich Schütze. 1999. *Foundations of statistical natural language processing*. MIT Press, Cambridge, MA, USA.

Bo Pang and Lillian Lee. 2004. A sentimental education: Sentiment analysis using subjectivity summarization based on minimum cuts. In *Proceedings of the Association for Computational Linguistics (ACL)*, pages 271–278.

Bo Pang, Lillian Lee, and Shivakumar Vaithyanathan. 2002. Thumbs up? Sentiment classification using machine learning techniques. In *Proceedings of the Conference on Empirical Methods in Natural Language Processing (EMNLP)*, pages 79–86.

Ellen Riloff, Janyce Wiebe, and Theresa Wilson. 2003. Learning subjective nouns using extraction pattern bootstrapping. In *Proceedings of the Conference on Natural Language Learning (CoNLL)*, pages 25–32.

Fabrizio Sebastiani. 2002. Machine learning in automated text categorization. *ACM Computing Surveys*, 34(1):1–47.

Mark Steyvers and Tom Griffiths. 2006. Probabilistic topic models. In T. Landauer, D. Mcnamara, S. Dennis, and W. Kintsch, editors, *Latent Semantic Analysis: A Road to Meaning*. Laurence Erlbaum.

Casey Whitelaw, Navendu Garg, and Shlomo Argamon. 2005. Using appraisal groups for sentiment analysis. In *Proceedings of the ACM SIGIR Conference on Information and Knowledge Management (CIKM)*, pages 625–631. ACM.

Theresa Wilson, Janyce Wiebe, and Paul Hoffmann. 2005. Recognizing contextual polarity in phrase-level sentiment analysis. In *Proceedings of the Human Language Technology Conference and the Conference on Empirical Methods in Natural Language Processing (HLT/EMNLP)*, pages 347–354.

Jeonghee Yi, Tetsuya Nasukawa, Razvan Bunescu, and Wayne Niblack. 2003. Sentiment analyzer: Extracting sentiments about a given topic using natural language processing techniques. In *Proceedings of the IEEE International Conference on Data Mining (ICDM)*.

Automatic Emotion Classification for Interpersonal Communication

Frederik Vaassen
CLiPS - University of Antwerp
S.L.202, Lange Winkelstraat 40-42
B-2000 Antwerpen, Belgium
frederik.vaassen@ua.ac.be

Walter Daelemans
CLiPS - University of Antwerp
S.L. 203, Lange Winkelstraat 40-42
B-2000 Antwerpen, Belgium
walter.daelemans@ua.ac.be

Abstract

We introduce a new emotion classification task based on Leary's Rose, a framework for interpersonal communication. We present a small dataset of 740 Dutch sentences, outline the annotation process and evaluate annotator agreement. We then evaluate the performance of several automatic classification systems when classifying individual sentences according to the four quadrants and the eight octants of Leary's Rose. SVM-based classifiers achieve average F-scores of up to 51% for 4-way classification and 31% for 8-way classification, which is well above chance level. We conclude that emotion classification according to the Interpersonal Circumplex is a challenging task for both humans and machine learners. We expect classification performance to increase as context information becomes available in future versions of our dataset.

1 Introduction

While sentiment and opinion mining are popular research topics, automatic emotion classification of text is a relatively novel –and difficult– natural language processing task. Yet it immediately speaks to the imagination. Being able to automatically identify and classify user emotions would open up a whole range of interesting applications, from in-depth analysis of user reviews and comments to enriching social network environments according to the user's emotions.

Most experiments in emotion classification focus on a set of basic emotions such as "happiness", "sadness", "fear", "anger", "surprise" and "disgust". The interpretation of "emotion" we're adopting in this paper, however, is slightly more specific. We concentrate on the emotions that are at play in interpersonal communication, more specifically in the dynamics between participants in a conversation: is one of the participants taking on a dominant role? Are the speakers working towards a common goal, or are they competing? Being able to automatically identify these power dynamics in interpersonal communication with sufficient accuracy would open up interesting possibilities for practical applications. This technology would be especially useful in e-learning, where virtual agents that accept (and interpret) natural language input could be used by players to practice their interpersonal communication skills in a safe environment.

The emotion classification task we present in this paper involves classifying individual sentences into the quadrants and octants of Leary's Rose, a framework for interpersonal communication.

We give a brief overview of related work in section 2 and the framework is outlined in section 3. Section 4 introduces the dataset we used for classification. Section 5 outlines the methodology we applied, and the results of the different experiments are reported on in section 6. We discuss these results and draw conclusions in section 7. Finally, section 8 gives some pointers for future research.

2 Related Work

The techniques that have been used for emotion classification can roughly be divided into pattern-based methods and machine-learning methods. An often-

Proceedings of the 2nd Workshop on Computational Approaches to Subjectivity and Sentiment Analysis, ACL-HLT 2011, pages 104–110,
24 June, 2011, Portland, Oregon, USA ©2011 Association for Computational Linguistics

used technique in pattern-based approaches is to use pre-defined lists of keywords which help determine an instance's overall emotion contents. The AESOP system by Goyal et al. (2010), for instance, attempts to analyze the affective state of characters in fables by identifying affective verbs and by using a set of projection rules to calculate the verbs' influence on their patients. Another possible approach –which we subscribe to– is to let a machine learner determine the appropriate emotion class. Mishne (2005) and Keshtkar and Inkpen (2009), for instance, attempt to classify LiveJournal posts according to their mood using Support Vector Machines trained with frequency features, length-related features, semantic orientation features and features representing special symbols. Finally, Rentoumi et al. (2010) posit that combining the rule-based and machine learning approaches can have a positive effect on classification performance. By classifying strongly figurative examples using Hidden Markov Models while relying on a rule-based system to classify the mildly figurative ones, the overall performance of the classification system is improved.

Whereas emotion classification in general is a relatively active domain in the field of computational linguistics, little research has been done regarding the automatic classification of text according to frameworks for interpersonal communication. We have previously carried out a set of classification experiments using Leary's Rose on a smaller dataset (Vaassen and Daelemans, 2010), only taking the quadrants of the Rose into account. To our knowledge, this is currently the only other work concerning automatic text classification using any realization of the Interpersonal Circumplex. We expand on this work by using a larger dataset which we evaluate for reliability. We attempt 8-way classification into the octants of the Rose, and we also evaluate a broader selection of classifier setups, including one-vs-all and error-correcting systems.

3 Leary's Rose

Though several frameworks have been developed to describe the dynamics involved in interpersonal communication (Wiggins, 2003; Benjamin, 2006), we have chosen to use the Interpersonal Circumplex, better known as "Leary's Rose" (Leary, 1957).

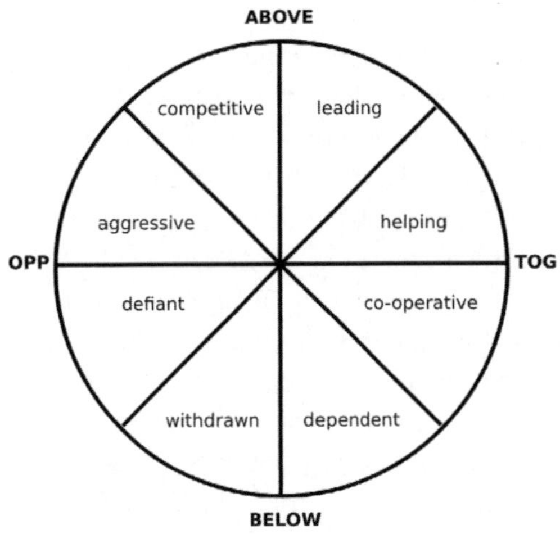

Figure 1: Leary's Rose

Leary's Rose (Figure 1) is defined by two axes: the *above-below* axis (vertical), which tells us whether the speaker is being dominant or submissive towards the listener; and the *together-opposed* axis (horizontal), which says something about the speaker's willingness to co-operate with the listener. The axes divide the Rose into four quadrants, and each quadrant can again be divided into two octants.

What makes the Circumplex especially interesting for interpersonal communication training is that it also allows one to predict (to some extent) what position the listener is most likely going to take in reaction to the way the speaker positions himself. Two types of interactions are at play in Leary's Rose, one of complementarity and one of similarity. *Above*-behavior triggers a (complementary) response from the *below* zone and vice versa, while *together*-behavior triggers a (similar) response from the *together* zone and *opposed*-behavior triggers a (similar) response from the *opposed* area of the Rose. The speaker can thus influence the listener's emotions (and consequently, his response) by consciously positioning himself in the quadrant that will likely trigger the desired reaction.

4 Dataset

To evaluate how difficult it is to classify sentences –both manually and automatically– according to Leary's Rose, we used an expanded version of the dataset described in Vaassen and Daelemans (2010).

The dataset[1] contains a total of 740 Dutch sentences labeled according to their position on the Interpersonal Circumplex. The majority of the sentences were gathered from works specifically designed to teach the use of Leary's Rose (van Dijk, 2000; van Dijk and Moes, 2005). The remaining sentences were specifically written by colleagues at CLiPS and by e-learning company Opikanoba. 31 sentences that were labeled as being purely neutral were removed from the dataset for the purposes of this classification experiment, leaving a set of 709 Dutch sentences divided across the octants and quadrants of the Interpersonal Circumplex. Table 1 shows the class distribution within the dataset and also lists the statistical random baselines for both 8-class and 4-class classification tasks.

709 sentences	TOG_A: 165 sentences	leading: 109 sentences
		helping: 56 sentences
	TOG_B: 189 sentences	co-operative: 92 sentences
		dependent: 97 sentences
	OPP_B: 189 sentences	withdrawn: 73 sentences
		defiant: 116 sentences
	OPP_A: 166 sentences	aggressive: 71 sentences
		competitive: 95 sentences
Baseline	25.4%	13.1%

Table 1: Distribution of classes within the dataset[2]

Below are a few example sentences with their corresponding position on the Rose.

- Please have a seat and we'll go over the options together. - **helping (TOG_A)**
- So what do you think I should do now? - **dependent (TOG_B)**
- That's not my fault, administration's not my responsibility! - **defiant (OPP_B)**
- If you had done your job this would never have happened! - **aggressive (OPP_A)**

4.1 Agreement Scores

Placing sentences on Leary's Rose is no easy task, not even for human annotators. An added complication is that the sentences in the dataset lack any form of textual or situational context. We therefore expect agreement between annotators to be relatively low.

To measure the extent of inter-annotator disagreement, we had four annotators label the same random subset of 50 sentences. The annotators were given a short introduction to the workings of Leary's Rose, and were then instructed to label each of the sentences according to the octants of the Rose using the following set of questions:

- Is the current sentence task-oriented (*opposed*) or relationship-oriented (*together*)?
- Does the speaker position himself as the dominant partner in the conversation (*above*) or is the speaker submissive (*below*)?
- Which of the above two dimensions (affinity or dominance) is most strongly present?

Annotators were also given the option to label a sentence as being purely neutral should no emotional charge be present.

Table 2 shows Fleiss' kappa scores calculated for 4 and 8-class agreement.

# of classes	κ
4	0.37
8	0.29

Table 2: Inter-annotator agreement, 4 annotators

Though the interpretation of kappa scores is in itself subjective, scores between 0.20 and 0.40 are usually taken to indicate "fair agreement".

The full dataset was also annotated a second time by the initial rater six months after the first annotation run. This yielded the intra-annotator scores in Table 3. A score of 0.5 is said to indicate "moderate agreement".

# of classes	κ
4	0.50
8	0.37

Table 3: Intra-annotator agreement

The relatively low kappa scores indicate that the classification of isolated sentences into the quadrants or octants of Leary's Rose is a difficult task even for humans.

As an upper baseline for automatic classification, we take the average of the overlaps between the

[1]Dataset available on request.

[2]"TOG" and "OPP" stand for *together* and *opposed* respectively, while "A" and "B" stand for *above* and *below*.

main annotator and each of the other annotators on the random subset of 50 sentences. This gives us an upper baseline of 51.3% for 4-way classification and 36.0% for the 8-class task.

5 Methodology

Our approach falls within the domain of automatic text categorization (Sebastiani, 2002), which focuses on the classification of text into predefined categories. Starting from a training set of sentences labeled with their position on the Rose, a machine learner should be able to pick up on cues that will allow the classification of new sentences into the correct emotion class. Since there are no easily identifiable keywords or syntactic structures that are consistently used with a position on Leary's Rose, using a machine learning approach is a logical choice for this emotion classification task.

5.1 Feature Extraction

The sentences in our dataset were first syntactically parsed using the Frog parser for Dutch (Van den Bosch et al., 2007). From the parsed output, we extracted token, lemma, part-of-speech, syntactic and dependency features using a "bag-of-ngrams" approach, meaning that for each n-gram (up to trigrams) of one of the aforementioned feature types present in the training data, we counted how many times it occurred in the current instance. We also introduced some extra features, including average word and sentence length, features for specific punctuation marks (exclamation points, question marks...) and features relating to (patterns of) function and content words.

Due to efficiency and memory considerations, we did not use all of the above feature types in the same experiment. Instead, we ran several experiments using combinations of up to three feature types.

5.2 Feature Subset Selection

Whereas some machine learners (e.g. Support Vector Machines) deal relatively well with large numbers of features, others (e.g. memory-based learners) struggle to achieve good classification accuracy when too many uninformative features are present. For these learners, we go through an extra feature selection step where the most informative features are identified using a filter metric (see also Vaassen and Daelemans (2010)), and where only the top n features are selected to be included in the feature vectors.

5.3 Classification

We compared the performance of different classifier setups on both the 4-way and 8-way classification tasks. We evaluated a set of native multiclass classifiers: the memory-based learner TiMBL (Daelemans and van den Bosch, 2005), a Naïve Bayes classifier and SVM Multiclass (Tsochantaridis et al., 2005), a multiclass implementation of Support Vector Machines. Further experiments were run using SVM light classifiers (Joachims, 1999) in a one-vs-all setup and in an Error-Correcting Output Code setup (ECOCs are introduced in more detail in section 5.3.1). Parameters for SVM Multiclass and SVM light were determined using Paramsearch's two-fold pseudo-exhaustive search (Van den Bosch, 2004) on vectors containing only token unigrams. The parameters for TiMBL were determined using a genetic algorithm designed to search through the parameter space[3].

5.3.1 Error-Correcting Output Codes

There are several ways of decomposing multiclass problems into binary classification problems. Error-Correcting Output Codes (ECOCs) (Dietterich and Bakiri, 1995) are one of these techniques. Inspired by *distributed output coding* in signal processing (Sejnowski and Rosenberg, 1987), ECOCs assign a distributed output code –or "codeword"– to each class in the multiclass problem. These codewords, when taken together, form a code matrix (Table 4).

Class 1	0	1	0	1	0	1	0
Class 2	0	0	0	0	1	1	1
Class 3	1	1	1	1	1	1	1
Class 4	0	0	1	1	0	0	1

Table 4: Example code matrix

Each column of this code matrix defines a binary classification task, with a 0 indicating that the instances with the corresponding class label should be part of a larger negative class, and a 1 indicat-

[3]The fitness factor driving evolution was the classification accuracy of the classifier given a set of parameters, using token unigram features in a 10-fold cross-validation experiment.

ing the positive class. A binary classifier (or "dichotomizer") is trained for each column. When a new instance is to be classified, it is first classified by each of these dichotomizers, which each return their predicted class (1 or 0). The combined output from each dichotomizer forms a new codeword. The final class is determined by choosing the codeword in the code matrix that has the smallest distance (according to some distance metric) to the predicted codeword.

This method offers one important advantage compared to other, simpler ensemble methods: because the final class label is determined by calculating the distance between the predicted codeword and the class codewords, it is possible to correct a certain number of bits in the predicted codeword if the distance between the class codewords is large enough.

Formally, a set of ECOCs can correct $\lfloor \frac{d-1}{2} \rfloor$ bits, where d is the minimum Hamming distance (the number of differing bits) between codewords in the code matrix. The error-correcting capacity of an ECOC setup is thus entirely dependent on the code matrix used, and a great deal of attention has been devoted to the different ways of constructing such code matrices (Ghani, 2000; Zhang et al., 2003; Álvarez et al., 2007).

In our ECOC classification setup, we used code matrices artificially constructed to maximize their error-correcting ability while keeping the number of classifiers within reasonable bounds. For 4-class classification, we constructed 7-bit codewords using the exhaustive code construction technique described in Dietterich and Bakiri (1995). For the 8-class classification problem, we used a Hadamard matrix of order 8 (Zhang et al., 2003), which has optimal row (and column) separation for the given number of columns. Both matrices have an error-correcting capacity of 1 bit.

6 Results

All results in this section are based on 10-fold cross-validation experiments. Table 5 shows accuracy scores and average F-scores for both 4-way and 8-way classification using classifiers trained on token unigrams only, using optimal learner parameters. For TiMBL, the number of token unigrams was limited to the 1000 most predictive according to the Gini coëfficient[4]. All other learners used the full range of token unigram features. The Naïve Bayes approach performed badly on the 8-way classification task, wrongly classifying all instances of some classes, making it impossible to calculate an F-score.

	4-class		8-class	
	accuracy	F-score	accuracy	F-score
SVM Multiclass	47.3%	46.8%	31.6%	28.3%
Naïve Bayes	42.6%	40.1%	26.1%	NaN
TiMBL	41.3%	41.3%	23.6%	22.9%
SVM / one-vs-all	46.0%	45.4%	29.3%	27.2%
SVM / ECOCs	48.1%	47.8%	31.3%	26.3%
Random baseline	25.4%		13.1%	
Upper baseline	51.3%		36.0%	

Table 5: Accuracy and average F-scores - token unigrams

All classifiers performed better than the random baseline (25.4% for 4-class classification, 13.1% for classification into octants) to a very significant degree. We therefore take these token unigram scores as a practical baseline.

	feature types	accuracy	avg. F-score
SVM Multiclass	w1, l3, awl	49.4%	49.4%
TiMBL	w1, w2, l1	42.0%	42.0%
SVM / one-vs-all	l2, fw3, c3	51.1%	51.0%
SVM / ECOCs	l2, c3	52.1%	51.2%

Table 6: Best feature type combinations - quadrants[5]

	feature types	accuracy	avg. F-score
SVM / one-vs-all	w1, l1, c1	34.0%	30.9%
SVM / ECOCs	w2, fw3, c3	34.8%	30.2%

Table 7: Best feature type combinations - octants

We managed to improve the performance of some of the classifier systems by including more and different features types. Tables 6 and 7 show performance for 4-way and 8-way classification respectively, this time using the best possible combination

[4]The filter metric and number of retained features was determined by testing the different options using 10-fold CV and by retaining the best-scoring combination (Vaassen and Daelemans, 2010).

[5]The "feature types" column indicates the types of features that were used, represented as a letter followed by an integer indicating the size of the n-gram: w: word tokens, l: lemmas, fw: function words, c: characters, awl: average word length (based on the number of characters)

of up to three feature types[6] for every classifier setup where an improvement was noted.

We used McNemar's test (Dietterich, 1998) to compare the token unigram scores with the best feature combination scores for each of the above classifiers. For both 4-way and 8-way classification, the one-vs-all and ECOC approaches produced significantly different results[7]. The improvement is less significant for TiMBL and SVM Multiclass in the 4-way classification experiments.

Note that for classification into quadrants, the performance of the SVM-based classifiers is very close to the upper baseline of 50.3% we defined earlier. It is unlikely that performance on this task will improve much more unless we add context information to our interpersonal communication dataset. The 8-way classification results also show promise, with scores up to 30%, but there is still room for improvement before we reach the upper baseline of 36%.

In terms of classifiers, the SVM-based systems perform better than their competitors. Naïve Bayes especially seems to be struggling, performing significantly worse for the 4-class classification task and making grave classification errors in the 8-way classification task. The memory-based learner TiMBL fares slightly better on the 8-class task, but isn't able to keep up with the SVM-based approaches.

When we examine the specific features that are identified as being the most informative, we see that most of them seem instinctively plausible as important cues related to positions on Leary's Rose. Question marks and exclamation marks, for instance, are amongst the 10 most relevant features. So too are the Dutch personal pronouns "u", "je" and "we" – "u" being a second person pronoun marking politeness, while "je" is the unmarked form, and "we" being the first person plural pronoun. Of course, none of these features on their own are strong enough to accurately classify the sentences in our dataset. It is only through complex interactions between many features that the learners are able to identify the correct class for each sentence.

[6]The best feature type combination for each setup was determined experimentally by running a 10-fold cross-validation test for each of the possible combinations.

[7]4-class SVM one-vs-all: P=0.0014, 4-class SVM ECOCs: P=0.0170, 8-class SVM one-vs-all: P=0.0045, 8-class SVM ECOCs: P=0.0092

7 Conclusions

We have introduced a new emotion classification task based on the Interpersonal Circumplex or "Leary's Rose", a framework for interpersonal communication. The goal of the classification task is to classify individual sentences (outside of their textual or situational context), into one of the four quadrants or eight octants of Leary's Rose. We have outlined the annotation process of a small corpus of 740 Dutch sentences, and have shown the classification task to be relatively difficult, even for human annotators. We evaluated several classifier systems in a text classification approach, and reached the best results using SVM-based systems. The SVM learners achieved F-scores around 51% on the 4-way classification task, which is close to the upper baseline (based on inter-annotator agreement), and performance on 8-class classification reached F-scores of almost 31%.

8 Future Research

The initial results of the emotion classification tasks described in this paper are promising, but there is a clear sense that without some contextual information, it is simply too difficult to correctly classify sentences according to their interpersonal emotional charge. For this reason, we are currently developing a new version of the dataset, which will no longer contain isolated sentences, but which will instead consist of full conversations. We expect that having the sentences in their textual context will make the classification task easier for both human annotators and machine learners. It will be interesting to see if and how the classification performance improves on this new dataset.

Acknowledgments

This study was made possible through financial support from the IWT (the Belgian government agency for Innovation by Science and Technology, TETRA-project deLearyous). Many thanks go out to our colleagues at the e-Media Lab (Groep T, Leuven, Belgium) and Opikanoba, partners in the deLearyous project. We would also like to thank the WASSA 2.011 reviewers for their helpful feedback.

References

Victor Álvarez, Jose A. Armario, Maria D. Frau, Elena Martin and Amparo Osuna. 2007. Error Correcting Codes from Quasi-Hadamard Matrices. *Lecture Notes in Computer Science*, volume 4547/2007.

Lorna S. Benjamin, Jeffrey C. Rothweiler and Kenneth L. Critchfield. 2006. The Use of Structural Analysis of Social Behavior (SASB) as an Assessment Tool. *Annual Review of Clinical Psychology*, Vol. 2, No. 1.

Walter Daelemans and Antal van den Bosch. 2005. *Memory-Based Language Processing*. Cambridge University Press, Cambridge, UK.

Thomas G. Dietterich and Ghulum Bakiri. 1995. Solving Multiclass Learning Problems via Error-Correcting Output Codes. *Journal of Artificial Intelligence Research*.

Thomas G. Dietterich. 1998. Approximate Statistical Tests for Comparing Supervised Classification Learning Algorithms. *Neural Computing*, volume 10.

Rayid Ghani. 2000. Using Error-Correcting Codes for Text Classification. *Proceedings of the Seventeenth International Conference on Machine Learning*.

Amit Goyal, Ellen Riloff, Hal Daume III and Nathan Gilbert. 2010. Toward Plot Units: Automatic Affect State Analysis. *Workshop on Computational Approaches to Analysis and Generation of Emotion in Text*.

Thorston Joachims. 1999. *Making large-scale support vector machine learning practical.* MIT Press, Cambridge, MA.

Fazel Keshtkar and Diana Inkpen. 2009. Using Sentiment Orientation Features for Mood Classification in Blogs. *Proceedings of the IEEE International Conference on Natural Language Processing and Knowledge Engineering (IEEE NLP-KE 2009)*.

Timothy Leary. 1957. *Interpersonal Diagnosis of Personality: Functional Theory and Methodology for Personality Evaluation*. Ronald Press Company, New York.

Kim Luyckx. 2011. The Effect of Author Set Size and Data Size in Authorship Attribution. *Literary and Linguistic Computing*, volume 26/1.

Francesco Masulli and Giorgio Valentini. 2004. An Experimental Analysis of the Dependence Among Codeword Bit Errors in ECOC Learning Machines. *Neurocomputing*, volume 57.

Gilad Mishne. 2005. Experiments with Mood Classification in Blog Posts. *Proceedings of the 1st Workshop on Stylistic Analysis of Text for Information Access*.

Vassiliki Rentoumi, Stefanos Petrakis, Manfred Klenner, George A. Vouros and Vangelis Karkaletsis. 2010. United we Stand: Improving Sentiment Analysis by Joining Machine Learning and Rule Based Methods. *Proceedings of the Seventh conference on International Language Resources and Evaluation (LREC'10)*.

Fabrizio Sebastiani. 2002. Machine Learning in Automated Text Categorization. *ACM Comput. Surv.*, volume 34/1.

Terrence J. Sejnowski and Charles R. Rosenberg. 1987. Parallel Networks that Learn to Pronounce English Text. *Complex Systems*.

Ioannis Tsochantaridis, Thorsten Joachims, Thomas Hofmann and Yasemin Altun. 2005. Large Margin Methods for Structured and Interdependent Output Variables. *Journal of Machine Learning Research*, 6:1453-1484 (2005).

Frederik Vaassen and Walter Daelemans. 2010. Emotion Classification in a Serious Game for Training Communication Skills. *Computational Linguistics in the Netherlands 2010: selected papers from the twentieth CLIN meeting*.

Antal van den Bosch. 2004. Wrapped Progressive Sampling Search for Optimizing Learning Algorithm Parameters. *Proceedings of the 16th Belgian-Dutch Conference on Artificial Intelligence (BNAIC2004)*.

Antal van den Bosch, Bertjan Busser, Walter Daelemans and Sander Canisius. 2007. An Efficient Memory-based Morphosyntactic Tagger and Parser for Dutch. *Selected Papers of the 17th Computational Linguistics in the Netherlands Meeting (CLIN17)*.

Bert van Dijk. 2000. *Beïnvloed anderen, begin bij jezelf. Over gedrag en de Roos van Leary*, 4th edition. Thema.

Bert van Dijk and Fenno Moes. 2005. *Het grote beïnvloedingsspel*. Thema.

Jerry S. Wiggins. 2003. *Paradigms of Personality Assessment*. Guilford Press.

Aijun Zhang, Zhi-Li Wu, Chun-Hung Li and Kai-Tai Fang. 2003. On Hadamard-Type Output Coding in Multiclass Learning. *Lecture Notes in Computer Science*, volume 2690/2003. Springer Berlin / Heidelberg.

Automatic Sentiment Classification of Product Reviews Using Maximal Phrases Based Analysis

Maria Tchalakova
Textkernel BV
Nieuwendammerkade
28A-17
NL-1022 AB Amsterdam
The Netherlands
maria.tchalakova@gmail.com

Dale Gerdemann
University of Tübingen
Wilhelmstr. 19-23
72074 Tübingen
Germany
dale.gerdemann@googlemail.com

Detmar Meurers
University of Tübingen
Wilhelmstr. 19-23
72074 Tübingen
Germany
dm@sfs.uni-tuebingen.de

Abstract

In this paper we explore the use of phrases occurring maximally in text as features for sentiment classification of product reviews. The goal is to find in a statistical way representative words and phrases used typically in positive and negative reviews. The approach does not rely on predefined sentiment lexicons, and the motivation for this is that potentially every word could be considered as expressing something positive and/or negative in different situations, and that the context and the personal attitude of the opinion holder should be taken into account when determining the polarity of the phrase, instead of doing this out of particular context.

1 Introduction

As human beings we use different ways to express opinions or sentiments. The field of sentiment analysis tries to identify the ways, in which people express opinions or sentiments towards a particular target or entity. The entities could be persons, products, events, etc. With the development of the Internet technologies and robust search engines in the last decade, people nowadays have a huge amount of free information. Because of this huge amount, however, the data needs to be first effectively processed so that it could be used in a helpful way. The automatic identification of sentiments would make possible the processing of large amounts of such opinionated data.

The focus of this paper is sentiment classification at document-level, namely classification of product reviews in the categories positive polarity or negative polarity. Training and testing data for our experiments is the Multi-Domain Sentiment Dataset (Blitzer et al., 2007), which consists of product reviews of different domains, downloaded from Amazon[1]. We explore the use of phrases occurring maximally in text as features for sentiment classification of product reviews. In contrast to many related works on sentiment classification of documents, we do not use general polarity lexicons, which contain predefined positive and negative words. Very often the same word or phrase could express something positive in one situation and something negative in another. We identify words and phrases, which are typically used in positive and negative documents of some specific domains, based on the frequencies of the words and phrases in the domain-specific corpora. After that we use these phrases to classify new sentiment documents from the same type of documents, from which the phrases are extracted.

[1] http://www.amazon.com/

Proceedings of the 2nd Workshop on Computational Approaches to Subjectivity and Sentiment Analysis, ACL-HLT 2011, pages 111–117,
24 June, 2011, Portland, Oregon, USA

2 Phrase Extraction

In order to extract distinctive phrases we use the approach of Burek and Gerdemann (2009), who try to identify phrases, which are distinctive for each of the four different categories of documents in their medical data. With distinctive they mean phrases, which occur predominantly in one category of the documents or another. The algorithm extracts phrases of any length. The idea is that if a phrase is distinctive for a particular category, it does not matter how long the phrase is. The algorithm looks for repeats of phrases of any length, and could also count different types of occurrences of phrases, e.g. maximal, left-maximal, or right maximal. Considering such types of occurrences, it is possible to restrict the use of certain phrases, which might not be much distinctive and therefore might not be representative for a category. Similar to Burek and Gerdemann (2009) we experiment with using all types of occurrences of a phrase as long as the phrase occurs maximally at least one time in the text.

2.1 Distinctiveness of Phrases

Distinctive phrases are phrases, which predominantly occur in one particular type of documents (Burek and Gerdemann, 2009). The presence of such phrases in a document is a good indicator of the category (or type) of the document. The general rule, as Burek and Gerdemann (2009) point out, is that if some phrases are uniformly distributed in a set of documents with different categories, then these phrases are not distinctive for any of the categories in the collection. On the other hand, if particular phrases appear more often in one category of documents than in another, they are good representatives for the documents of this type, and consequently are said to be distinctive[2].

There are different weighting schemes, which one can use to determine the importance of a term for the semantics of a document. Burek and Gerdemann (2009) implement their own scoring function for weighting the extracted phrases. One of their reasons not to use the standard weighting function tf-idf is that the idf measure does not take into account what the category of the documents is, in which the term occurs. This is important in their case, because their data consist of four categories, which could be grouped in two main classes, namely *excellent* and *good* on the one hand, and *fair* and *poor* on the other hand. A problem when using tf-idf will appear, if there is a rare phrase, which occurs in a small number of documents, however, it clusters in documents from the two different classes, for example, in *excellent* and *fair*, or in *good* and *poor*. This will not be a good distinctive phrase for this categorization of the data. Another motivation to develop their own scoring function is to cope with the problem of *burstiness* (see section 2.2.1).

2.2 Extraction of Phrases

This section describes the algorithm of Burek and Gerdemann (2009) for extracting distinctive phrases and how we have modified and used it in the context of our work. We first show how the phrases are ranked, so that one knows what phrases are more or less distinctive than others.

2.2.1 The Scoring Algorithm

The extracted phrases are represented by occurrence vectors. These vectors have two elements - one for the number of documents with category *positive polarity*, and another for the *negative polarity*. Each element of the vector stores the number of distinct documents, in which the phrase occurs. For example, if a phrase occurs in 10 positive reviews, and 1 negative review, the occurrence vector of this phrase is <10, 1> . This shows that for the representation of the phrases we take into account the document frequency of the phrase, and not its term frequency. The motivation behind this choice is to cope with the problem of burstiness of terms. Madsen et al. (2005) explain burstiness in the following way: *The term burstiness (Church and Gale, 1995; Katz, 1996) describes the behavior of a rare word appearing many times in a single document. Because of the large number of possible words, most words do not appear in a given document. However, if a*

[2]If the number of occurrences of such phrase in the whole collection of documents is very small, however, the clustering of the phrase in some documents of a specific category, may be purely accidental. (Burek and Gerdemann, 2009)

word does appear once, it is much more likely to appear again, i.e. words appear in bursts.

We assign a score to a phrase by giving the phrase one point, if the phrase occurs in a document with positive polarity and zero points, if it occurs in a document with negative polarity.

Let us take again the occurrence vector of <10, 1> . According to the way the points are given, the vector will be assigned a score of 10 ((1 point * 10) + (0 points * 1) = 10). Is this a good score, which indicates that the phrase is distinctive for documents of category positive polarity? We can answer this question, if we randomly choose another phrase, which occurs in 11 documents, and see what the probability is, that this phrase would have a score, which is higher than or equally high to the score of the phrase in question (Burek and Gerdemann, 2009). In order to calculate this probability, the scoring method performs a simulation, in which occurrence vectors for randomly chosen phrases are created. Let us pick randomly one phrase, which hypothetically occurs in 11 reviews. Let also, have a data of 600 positive reviews and 600 negative reviews. The probability then, that the random phrase would occur in a positive or a negative review is 0.5. Based on these probabilities, the simulation process constructs random vectors for the random phrase, indicating whether the phrase occurs in a positive or in negative review. For example, if in a particular run, the simulation says that the random phrase occurs in a positive review, then we have a random vector of <1, 0>. Otherwise, <0, 1> for a negative review. The program calculates as many random vectors as the number of reviews, in which the random phrase is said to occur. In this example, the number of documents is 11. Therefore, 11 random vectors will be constructed. They may look like this: <1, 0>, <1, 0>, <0, 1> , <1, 0>, <1, 0>, <0, 1>, <0, 1>, <0, 1>, <1, 0>, <1, 0>, <0, 1>. These vectors are then summed up, and the result vector <6, 5> is the random occurrence vector for the random phrase. It tells us that the phrase, hypothetically, occurs in 6 positive and in 5 negative reviews. The score for the random phrase is now calculated in the same way as for the non-random phrases: 1 point is given for each occurrence of the phrase in a positive review, and 0 points otherwise. So, the score for this phrase is 6 (((1 point * 6) + (0 points * 5) = 6)). This process is performed a certain number of times. For the experiments presented in section 3.2, we run the simulation 10,000 times for each extracted phrase. This means that 10,000 random vectors per phrase are created.

The last step is to compare the scores of the random phrase with the score of the actual phrase, and to see how many of the 10,000 random vectors give a score higher than or equally high to the score of the actual phrase. If the number of random vectors, which give a higher than or equally high score to the actual phrase, is bigger than the number of random vectors, which give a score lower than the actual phrase, then the actual phrase is assigned a positive score, and the value of this score is the approximate number of random vectors, from which higher than or equally high scores to the actual phrase score are calculated. If the number is lower, the phrase is assigned the approximate number of random vectors, from which lower scores than the actual phrase score are calculated, and a minus sign is attached to the number, making the score negative.

2.2.2 The Phrase Extraction Algorithm

The main idea of the algorithm is that if a phrase is distinctive for a particular category, it does not matter how long the phrase is - as long as it helps for distinguishing one type of document from another, it should be extracted. In order to extract phrases in this way, the whole collection of documents is represented as one long string. Each phrase is then a substring of this string. It will be very expensive to compute statistics (i.e. tf and df) and to run the simulation process (see 2.2.1) for each substring in the text. The reason is that the amount of substrings might be huge - there are a total of N(N + 1) / 2 substrings in a corpus (Yamamoto and Church, 2001). Yamamoto and Church (2001) show how this problem can be overcome by grouping the substrings into equivalence classes and performing operations (i.e. computing statistics) on these classes instead of on the individual elements of the classes. They use for this the suffix array data structure. The number of the classes is at most 2N – 1.

2.2.3 Maximal Occurrence of a Phrase

The suffix array data structure allows for easy manipulation of the strings. The algorithm extracts phrases if they repeat in text, and if the phrases occur maximally at least once in the text. If the phrase do not occur maximally at least one time, then it may not be a good linguistic unit, which could stand on its own. Example of such words might be the different parts of certain named entities. For instance, the name *Bugs Bunny*. If *Bugs* or *Bunny* never appear apart from each other in the text, then this imply that they comprise a single entity and they should always appear together in the text. In this case it does not make sense, for example, to count only *Bugs* or only *Bunny* and calculate statistics (e.g. tf or df) for each of them. They should be grouped instead into a class.

Burek and Gerdemann (2009) mention three different types of occurrences of a phrase: left maximal, right maximal, and maximal. A left maximal occurrence of a phrase S[i,j] means that the longer phrase S[i-1,j] does not repeat in the corpus (Burek and Gerdemann, 2009). For example, in the sentences below, the phrase *recommend* is not left maximal, because it can be extended to the left with the word *highly*:

I highly *recommend* the book.
You *highly recommend* this camera.

On the other hand the phrase *highly recommend* is left maximal.

In a similar way we define the notion of right maximal occurrence of a phrase. A maximal occurrence of a phrase is when the occurrence of the phrase is both left maximal and right maximal (Burek and Gerdemann, 2009). The phrase *highly recommend* in the example sentences above is in this sense maximal.

It is not clear a priori which of these types should be taken into account for the successful realization of a given application. One could consider only the left maximal, only the right maximal, only the maximal occurrences of the phrases, or all occurrences. We experimented with *all* occurrences. Our motivation is that using all phrases would give us a big enough number of distinctive phrases and we will most probably not have a problem with data sparseness.

3 Sentiment Classification of Product Reviews

For the experiments presented below we used a supervised machine learning approach, and different sets of features. Reviews from two domains, *books* and *cameras & photos*, are used as training and testing data.

3.1 Choosing Distinctive Phrases for Classification

Once the phrases with which we would like to represent the documents are extracted, we need to consider two things in the very beginning. On the one hand, the phrases should be as much distinctive as possible. On the other hand, even though a phrase might occur predominantly in negative reviews, it occurs very often also in positive reviews (once or at least several times), and vice versa. Should we consider such phrases? If yes, what would be the least acceptable number of occurrences of the phrases in the opposite type of reviews? We might choose as distinctive phrases those which occur only in positive or only in negative reviews, however, these phrases will be very few, and we might have the problem of data sparseness. On the other hand, using all extracted phrases might bring a lot of noise, because many of the phrases will not be very good characteristics of the data. We experimented with several different subsets of the set of all extracted phrases.

In order to decide what subsets of extracted phrases to use, we analyzed the set of all extracted phrases paying attention to their vectors and the scores, trying to find a trade-off between the two mentioned considerations above.

3.2 Experiments

SVM is used as a machine learning algorithm for the experiments (the implementation of the SVM package LibSVM[3] in GATE[4]).

[3]Libsvm: a library for support vector machines, 2001. software available at http://www.csie.ntu.edu.tw/ cjlin/libsvm.
[4]http://gate.ac.uk/

For each experiment we first divide the reviews of each domain into training and testing data with ratio two to one. From this training data we extract the distinctive phrases, which are later used as features to the learning algorithm. As evaluation method we apply the k-fold cross validation test, with k=10. For all experiments we used the default tf-idf weight for the n-grams. For each domain we conduct five different experiments, each time using different subsets of distinctive phrases. All experiments were performed with GATE.

For each domain the training data from which the phrases are extracted consists of about 665 negative and 665 positive reviews. The testing data consists of 333 negative and 333 positive reviews.

It is interesting to notice that although the results of the experiments are different, they are very close to each other, regardless of the big difference in the number of phrases used as features. Therefore, we decided to experiment with all extracted phrases. It turned out that the results of that experiment are the best. This would imply that the bigger number of phrases is helpful and it compensates for the use of phrases that are not much distinctive.

The results of all experiments for domain *books* are summarized in Table 1. The best achieved results of 81% precision, recall, and F-measure are given in bold. The rightmost column gives the number of negative (n.) and positive (p.) phrases used in each experiment.

Experiment	Reviews	P	R	F-m	Phrases used
Exp1	Negative	0.77	0.80	0.79	1685 n.
	Positive	0.80	0.77	0.78	1116 p.
	Overall	0.78	0.78	0.78	
Exp2	Negative	0.75	0.80	0.77	924 n.
	Positive	0.80	0.74	0.76	568 p.
	Overall	0.77	0.77	0.77	
Exp3	Negative	0.76	0.78	0.77	349 n.
	Positive	0.78	0.76	0.77	178 p.
	Overall	0.77	0.77	0.77	
Exp4	Negative	0.77	0.79	0.78	10552 n.
	Positive	0.79	0.77	0.78	9084 p.
	Overall	0.78	0.78	0.78	
Exp5	Negative	0.80	0.81	0.80	All:
	Positive	0.81	0.80	0.80	24107 n.
	Overall	**0.81**	**0.81**	**0.81**	21149 p.

Table 1: Domain *books*

Table 2 summarizes the results for domain *camera&photos*, showing the best results of 86% precision, recall, and F-measure in bold.

Similar to the experiments with reviews of domain *books*, the results for *camera&photos* in all five experiments are very close. Again the best results are obtained when all extracted distinctive phrases are considered.

Experiment	Reviews	P	R	F-m	Phrases used
Exp1	Negative	0.85	0.83	0.84	1746n. 1883
	Positive	0.83	0.85	0.84	p.
	Overall	0.84	0.84	0.84	
Exp2	Negative	0.84	0.81	0.82	1013n. 1053
	Positive	0.81	0.85	0.83	p.
	Overall	0.83	0.83	0.83	
Exp3	Negative	0.86	0.83	0.85	384 n.
	Positive	0.83	0.87	0.85	432 p.
	Overall	0.85	0.85	0.85	
Exp4	Negative	0.85	0.83	0.84	7572 n.
	Positive	0.83	0.86	0.84	9821 p.
	Overall	0.84	0.84	0.84	
Exp5	Negative	0.86	0.85	0.86	All:
	Positive	0.85	0.87	0.86	16378 n.
	Overall	**0.86**	**0.86**	**0.86**	17951 p.

Table 2: Domain *camera&photos.*

In order to evaluate how well the results of the experiments are we performed several more experiments, in which the texts were represented with unigrams (1-grams) and bigrams (2-grams). Pang and Lee (2008) note that: *whether higher-order n-grams are useful features appears to be a matter of some debate. For example, Pang et al. (2002) report that unigrams outperform bigrams when classifying movie reviews by sentiment polarity, but Dave et al. (2003) find that in some settings, bigrams and trigrams yield better product-review polarity classification*. Bekkerman and Allan (2004) review the results of different experiments on text categorization in which n-gram approaches were used, and conclude that the use of bigrams for the representation of texts does not show general improvement (Burek and Gerdemann, 2009). It seems intuitive that when bigrams are used, we would have a better representation of the texts, because we would know what words combine with what other words in the texts. However, there is a data sparseness problem.

It seems interesting to compare the results obtained by representing the texts as unigrams, bigrams, and distinctive (maximally occurring) phrases, because the model based on phrases might use both unigrams and bigrams, and it allows also any other higher n-grams, that is, more context (and semantics) of the text is preserved.

Tables 3 and 4 present the results of the experiments using bag-of-tokens (1-gram) models, while Tables 5 and 6 present the experiments with the 2-gram models. GATE was used as a working environment, and SVM as learning algorithm.

Reviews	**Precision**	**Recall**	**F-measure**
Negative	0.77	0.82	0.79
Positive	0.82	0.75	0.78
Overall	0.79	0.79	0.79

Table 3: Domain *books*, 1-gram.

Reviews	**Precision**	**Recall**	**F-measure**
Negative	0.86	0.84	0.85
Positive	0.84	0.86	0.85
Overall	0.85	0.85	0.85

Table 4: Domain *camera&photos,* 1-gram.

Reviews	**Precision**	**Recall**	**F-measure**
Negative	0.72	0.80	0.75
Positive	0.78	0.69	0.73
Overall	0.75	0.75	0.75

Table 5: Domain *books,* 2-gram.

Reviews	**Precision**	**Recall**	**F-measure**
Negative	0.84	0.83	0.83
Positive	0.83	0.84	0.83
Overall	0.83	0.83	0.83

Table 6: Domain *camera&photos,* 2-gram.

Features	Precision	Recall	F-measure
All phrases	**0.81**	**0.81**	**0.81**
1-gram	0.79	0.79	0.79
2-gram	0.75	0.75	0.75

Table 7: Comparison, Domain *books.*

Features	Precision	Recall	F-measure
All phrases	**0.86**	**0.86**	**0.86**
1-gram	0.85	0.85	0.85
2-gram	0.83	0.83	0.83

Table 8: Comparison, Domain *camera&photos.*

Tables 7 and 8 summarize the overall results using 1-gram and 2-gram models and a model based on distinctive phrases for the representation of the texts. For both domains the best results are achieved with the model based on phrases (all phrases). For the domain *books* the overall precision, recall and F-measure results achieved with that model (81%) are 2% higher than the results obtained using the 1-gram model, and 6% higher than the results obtained using the 2-gram model. For domain *cameras & photos*, an improvement of 1% and 3% is achieved with the phrase model in comparison with the 1-gram and 2-gram models, respectively.

4 Related Work

Close to our work seems to be Funk et al. (2008). They classify product and company reviews into one of the 1-star to 5-star categories. The features to the learning algorithm (also SVM) are simple linguistic features of single tokens. They report best results with the combinations *root & orthography*, and *only root*. Another interesting related work is that of Turney (2002). He uses an unsupervised learning algorithm to classify a review as *recommended* or *not recommended*. The algorithm extracts phrases from a given review, and determines their pointwise mutual information with the words *excellent* and *poor*. Turney (2002) points out that the contexual information is very often necessary for the correct determination of the sentiment polarity of a certain word.

5 Conclusion

This paper presented different experiments on classifying product reviews of domains *books* and *cameras & photos* under the categories *positive polarity* and *negative polarity* using distinctive (maximally occurring) phrases as features. For both domains best results were achieved with all extracted distinctive phrases as features. This approach outperforms slightly the 1-gram and 2-gram experiments on this data and shows that the use of phrases occurring maximally in text could be successfully applied in the classification of sentiment data and that it is worth experimenting with classifying sentiment data without necessarily relying on general predefined sentiment lexicons.

References

Ron Bekkerman and James Allan. 2004. Using bigrams in text categorization. *Technical Report IR-408*, Center of Intelligent Information Retrieval, UMass Amherst.

John Blitzer, Mark Dredze, and Fernando Pereira. 2007. Biographies, bollywood, boomboxes and blenders: Domain adaptation for sentiment classification. In *Proceedings of the 45th Annual Meeting of the Association of Computational Linguistics*, pp. 440-447, Prague, Czech Republic. Association for Computational Linguistics.

Gaston Burek and Dale Gerdemann. 2009. Maximal phrases based analysis for prototyping online discussion forums postings. In *Proceedings of the workshop on Adaptation of Language Resources and Technologies to New Domains (AdaptLRTtoND)*, Borovets, Bulgaria.

Kenneth W. Church and William A. Gale. 1995. Poisson mixtures. *Natural Language Engineering*, 1:163-190.

Kushal Dave, Steve Lawrence and David M. Pennock. 2003. Mining the peanut gallery: Opinion extraction and semantic classification of product reviews. In *Proceedings of WWW,* pp. 519-528.

Adam Funk, Yaoyong Li, Horacio Saggion, Kalina Bontcheva, and Christian Leibold. 2008. Opinion analysis for business intelligence applications. In *Proceedings of First International Workshop on Ontology-supported Business Intelligence (OBI2008)* at the *7th International Semantic Web Conference (ISWC)*, Karlsruhe, Germany.

Slava M. Katz. 1996. Distribution of content words and phrases in text and language modelling. *Natural Language Engineering*, 2(1):15-59.

Rasmus E. Madsen, David Kauchak, and Charles Elkan. 2005. Modeling word burstiness sing the dirichlet distribution. In *Proceedings of the 22nd International Conference on Machine Learning*, pp. 545-552.

Bo Pang and Lillian Lee. 2008. Opinion mining and sentiment analysis. *Foundations and Trends in Information Retrieval*, Vol. 2, Nos. 1-2 (2008) 1-135.

Bo Pang, Lillian Lee., and Shivakumar Vaithyanathan. 2002. Thumbs up? Sentiment classification using machine learning techniques. In *Proceedings of the Conference on Empirical Methods in Natural Language Processing (EMNLP)*, pp. 79-86.

Peter D. Turney. 2002. Thumbs up or thumbs down? Semantic orientation applied to unsupervised classification of reviews. In *Proceedings of the 40th Annual Meeting on Association for Computational Linguistics*, pp. 417-424.

Mikio Yamamoto and Kenneth W. Church. 2001. Using suffix arrays to compute term frequency and document frequency for all substrings in a corpus. In *Computational Linguistics*, 27(1):1-30.

Mining Subjective Knowledge from Customer Reviews: A Specific Case of Irony Detection

Antonio Reyes and **Paolo Rosso**
Natural Language Engineering Lab - ELiRF
Departamento de Sistemas Informáticos y Computación
Universidad Politécnica de Valencia, Spain
{areyes,prosso}@dsic.upv.es

Abstract

The research described in this work focuses on identifying key components for the task of irony detection. By means of analyzing a set of customer reviews, which are considered as ironic both in social and mass media, we try to find hints about how to deal with this task from a computational point of view. Our objective is to gather a set of discriminating elements to represent irony. In particular, the kind of irony expressed in such reviews. To this end, we built a freely available data set with ironic reviews collected from Amazon. Such reviews were posted on the basis of an online viral effect; i.e. contents whose effect triggers a chain reaction on people. The findings were assessed employing three classifiers. The results show interesting hints regarding the patterns and, especially, regarding the implications for sentiment analysis.

1 Introduction

Verbal communication is not a trivial process. It implies to share a common code as well as being able to infer information beyond the semantic meaning. A lot of communicative acts imply information not grammatically expressed to be able to decode the whole sense: if the hearer is not capable to infer that information, the communicative process is incomplete. Let us consider a joke. The amusing effect sometimes relies on not given information. If such information is not filled, the result is a bad, or better said, a misunderstood joke. This information, which is not expressed with "physical" words, supposes a great challenge, even from a linguistic analysis, because it points to social and cognitive layers quite difficult to be computationally represented. One of the communicative phenomena which better represents this problem is irony. According to Wilson and Sperber (2007), irony is essentially a communicative act which expresses an opposite meaning of what was literally said.

Due to irony is common in texts that express subjective and deeply-felt opinions, its presence represents a significant obstacle to the accurate analysis of sentiment in such texts (cf. Councill et al. (2010)). In this research work we aim at gathering a set of discriminating elements to represent irony. In particular, we focus on analyzing a set of customer reviews (posted on the basis of an online viral effect) in order to obtain a set of key components to face the task of irony detection.

This paper is organized as follows. Section 2 introduces the theoretical problem of irony. Section 3 presents the related work as well as the evaluation corpus. Section 4 describes our model and the experiments that were performed. Section 5 assesses the model and presents the discussion of the results. Finally, Section 6 draws some final remarks and addresses the future work.

2 Pragmatic Theories of Irony

Literature divides two primaries classes of irony: verbal and situational. Most theories agree on the main property of the former: verbal irony conveys an opposite meaning; i.e. a speaker says something that seems to be the opposite of what s/he means (Colston and Gibbs, 2007). In contrast, situational irony is a state of the world which is perceived as ironical (Attardo, 2007); i.e. situations that should not be (Lucariello, 2007). Our work focuses on verbal irony. This kind of irony is defined as a way of intentionally denying what it is literally expressed (Curcó, 2007); i.e. a kind of indirect negation (Giora, 1995). On the basis of some pragmatic frameworks, authors focus on certain fine-grained aspects of this term. For instance, Grice (1975) con-

Proceedings of the 2nd Workshop on Computational Approaches to Subjectivity and Sentiment Analysis, ACL-HLT 2011, pages 118–124,
24 June, 2011, Portland, Oregon, USA ©2011 Association for Computational Linguistics

siders that an utterance is ironic if it intentionally violates some conversational maxims. Wilson and Sperber (2007) assume that verbal irony must be understood as echoic; i.e. as a distinction between use and mention. Utsumi (1996), in contrast, suggests an ironic environment which causes a negative emotional attitude. According to these points of view, the elements to conceive a verbal expression as ironic point to different ways of explaining the same underlying concept of opposition, but specially note, however, that most of them rely on literary studies (Attardo, 2007); thus, their computational formalization is quite challenging. Furthermore, consider that people have their own concept of irony, which often does not match with the rules suggested by the experts. For instance, consider the following expressions retrieved from the web:

1. "If you find it hard to laugh at yourself, I would be happy to do it for you."
2. "Let's pray that the human race never escapes from Earth to spread its iniquity elsewhere."

These examples, according to some user-generated tags, could be either ironic, or sarcastic, or even satiric. However, the issue we want to focus does not lie on what tag should be the right for every expression, but on the fact that there is not a clear distinction about the boundaries among these terms. For Colston (2007), sarcasm is a term commonly used to describe an expression of verbal irony; whereas for Gibbs (2007), sarcasm along with jocularity, hyperbole, rhetorical questions, and understatement, are types of irony. Attardo (2007) in turn, considers that sarcasm is an overtly aggressive type of irony. Furthermore, according to Gibbs and Colston (2007), irony is often compared to satire and parody.

In accordance with these statements, the limits among these figurative devices are not clearly differentiable. Their differences rely indeed on matters of usage, tone, and obviousness, which are not so evident in ordinary communication acts. Therefore, if there are no formal boundaries to separate these concepts, even from a theoretical perspective, people will not be able to produce ironic expressions as the experts suggest. Instead, there will be a mixture of expressions pretending to be ironic but being sarcastic, satiric, or even humorous. This get worse when dealing with non prototypical examples. Observe the following fragment from our corpus:

3. "I am giving this product [a t-shirt] 5 stars because not everyone out there is a ladies' man. In the hands of lesser beings, it can help you find love. In the hands of a playa like me, it can only break hearts. That's why I say use with caution. I am passing the torch onto you, be careful out there folks."

In this text irony is perceived as a mixture of sarcasm and satire, whose effect is not only based on expressing an opposite or negative meaning, but a humorous one as well.

Taking into account these assumptions, we begin by defining irony as a *verbal subjective expression whose formal constituents attempt to communicate an underlying meaning, focusing on negative or humorous aspects, which is opposite to the one expressed.* Based on this definition, we consider sarcasm, satire, and figures such as the ones suggested in (Gibbs, 2007), as specific extensions of a general concept of irony, and consequently, we will not make any fine-grained distinction among them; i.e. irony will include them.

3 Approaching Irony Detection

As far as we know, very few attempts have been carried out in order to integrate irony in a computational framework. The research described by Utsumi (1996) was one of the first approaches to computationally formalize irony. However, his model is too abstract to represent irony beyond an idealized hearer-listener interaction. Recently, from a computational creativity perspective, Veale and Hao (2009) focused on studying irony by analyzing humorous similes. Their approach gives some hints to explain the cognitive processes that underly irony in such structures. In contrast, Carvalho et al. (2009) suggested some clues for automatically identifying ironic sentences by means of identifying features such as emoticons, onomatopoeic expressions, punctuation and quotation marks. Furthermore, there are others approaches which are focused on particular devices such as sarcasm and satire, rather than on the whole concept of irony. For instance, Tsur et al. (2010) and Davidov et al. (2010) address the problem of finding linguistic elements that mark the use of sarcasm in online product reviews and tweets, respectively. Finally, Burfoot and Baldwin (2009) explore the task of automatic satire detection by evaluating features related to headline elements, offensive language and slang.

3.1 Evaluation Corpus

Due to the scarce work on automatic irony processing, and to the intrinsic features of irony, it is quite difficult and subjective to obtain a corpus with ironic data. Therefore, we decided to rely on the wisdom of the crowd and use a collection of customer reviews from the Amazon web site. These reviews are considered as ironic by customers, as well as by many journalists, both in mass and social media. According to such means, all these reviews deal with irony, sarcasm, humor, satire and parody (hence, they are consistent with our definition of irony). All of them were posted by means of an online viral effect, which in most cases, increased the popularity and sales of the reviewed products. The *Three Wolf Moon T-shirt* is the clearest example. This item became one of the most popular products, both in Amazon as well as in social networks, due to the ironic reviews posted by people[1].

Our positive data are thus integrated with reviews of five different products published by Amazon. All of them were posted through the online viral effect. The list of products is: i) *Three Wolf Moon T-shirt* (product id: B002HJ377A); ii) *Tuscan Whole Milk* (product id: B00032G1S0); iii) *Zubaz Pants* (product id: B000WVXM0W); iv) *Uranium Ore* (product id: B000796XXM); and v) *Platinum Radiant Cut 3-Stone* (product id: B001G603AE). A total of 3,163 reviews were retrieved. Then, in order to automatically filter the ones more likely to be ironic without performing a manual annotation (which is planned to be carried out in the near feature), we removed the reviews whose customer rating, according to the Amazon rating criteria, was lesser than four stars. The assumptions behind this decision rely on two facts: i) the viral purpose, and ii) the ironic effect. The former caused that people to post reviews whose main purpose, and perhaps the only one, was to exalt superficial properties and non-existent consequences; thus the possibilities to find *real* reviews were minimal. Considering this scenario, the latter supposes that, if someone ironically wants to reflect properties and consequences such as the previous ones, s/he will not do it by rating the products with one or two stars, instead, s/he will rate them with the highest scores.

After applying this filter, we obtained an ironic set integrated with 2,861 documents. On the other hand, two negative sets were automatically collected from two sites: Amazon.com (**AMA**) and Slashdot.com (**SLA**). Each contains 3,000 documents. The products selected from AMA were: Bananagrams (toy), The Help by Kathryn Stockett (book), Flip UltraHD Camcorder (camera), I Dreamed A Dream (CD), Wii Fit Plus with Balance Board (Videogame console). Finally, the data collected from SLA contain web comments categorized as funny in a community-driven process. The whole evaluation corpus is integrated with 8,861 documents. It is available at http://users.dsic.upv.es/grupos/nle.

4 Model

We define a model with six categories which attempts to represent irony from different linguistic layers. These categories are: *n-grams, POS n-grams, funny profiling, positive/negative profiling, affective profiling*, and *pleasantness profiling*.

4.1 N-grams

This category focuses on representing the ironic documents in the simplest way: with sequences of n-grams (from order 2 up to 7) in order to find a set of recurrent words which might express irony. Note that all the documents were preprocessed. Firstly, the stopwords were removed, and then, all the documents were stemmed. The next process consisted in removing irrelevant terms by applying a $tf-idf$ measure. This measure assesses how relevant a word is, given its frequency both in a document as in the entire corpus. Irrelevant words such as *t-shirt, wolf, tuscan, milk,* etc., were then automatically eliminated. The complete list of filtered words, stopwords included, contains 824 items. Examples of the most frequent sequences are given in Table 1.

4.2 POS n-grams

The goal of this category is to obtain recurrent sequences of morphosyntactic patterns. According to

[1]According to results obtained with Google, apart from the more than one million of results retrieved when searching this product, there are more than 10,000 blogs which comment the effect caused by these reviews.

Table 1: Statistics of the most frequent word n-grams.

Order	Sequences	Examples
2-grams	160	opposit sex; american flag; alpha male
3-grams	82	sex sex sex; fun educ game
4-grams	78	fun hit reload page; remov danger reef pirat
5-grams	76	later minut custom contribut product
6-grams	72	fals function player sex sex sex
7-grams	69	remov danger reef pirat fewer shipwreck surviv

Table 2: Statistics of the most frequent POS-grams.

Order	Sequences	Examples
2-grams	300	dt nn; nn in; jj nn; nn nn
3-grams	298	dt nn in; dt jj nn; jj nn nn
4-grams	282	nn in dt nn; vb dt jj nn
5-grams	159	vbd dt vbg nn jj
6-grams	39	nnp vbd dt vbg nn jj
7-grams	65	nns vbd dt vbg nn jj fd

our definition, irony looks for expressing an opposite meaning; however, the ways of transmitting that meaning are enormous. Therefore, we pretend to symbolize an abstract structure through sequences of POS tags (hereafter, POS-grams) instead of only words. It is worth highlighting that a statistical substring reduction algorithm (Lü et al., 2004) was employed in order to eliminate redundant sequences. For instance, if the sequences "he is going to look so hot in this shirt" and "he is going to look hot in this shirt" occur with similar frequencies in the corpus, then, the algorithm removes the last one because is a substring of the first one. Later on, we labeled the documents employing the FreeLing resource (Atserias et al., 2006). The N-best sequences of POS-grams, according to orders 2 up to 7, are given in Table 2.

4.3 Funny profiling

Irony takes advantage of humor aspects to produce its effect. This category intends to characterize the documents in terms of humorous properties. In order to represent this category, we selected some of the best humor features reported in the literature: *stylistic features, human centeredness*, and *keyness*. The stylistic features, according to the experiments reported in (Mihalcea and Strapparava, 2006), were obtained by collecting all the words labeled with the tag "sexuality" in WordNet Domains (Bentivogli et al., 2004). The second feature focuses on social relationships. In order to retrieve these words, the elements registered in WordNet (Miller, 1995), which belong to the synsets $relation$, $relationship$ and $relative$, were retrieved. The last feature is represented by obtaining the keyness value of the words (cf. (Reyes et al., 2009)). This value is calculated comparing the word frequencies in the ironic documents against their frequencies in a reference corpus. Google N-grams (Brants and Franz, 2006) was used as the reference corpus. Only the words whose keyness was ≥ 100 were kept.

4.4 Positive/Negative Profiling

As we have already pointed out, one of the most important properties of irony relies on the communication of negative information through positive one. This category intends to be an indicator about the correlation between positive and negative elements in the data. The Macquarie Semantic Orientation Lexicon (MSOL) (Saif et al., 2009) was used to label the data. This lexicon contains 76,400 entries (30,458 positive and 45,942 negative ones).

4.5 Affective Profiling

In order to enhance the quality of the information related to the expression of irony, we considered to represent information linked to psychological layers. The affective profiling category is an attempt to characterize the documents in terms of words which symbolize subjective contents such as emotions, feelings, moods, etc. The WordNet-Affect resource (Strapparava and Valitutti, 2004) was employed for obtaining the affective terms. This resource contains 11 classes to represent affectiveness. According to the authors, these classes represent how speakers convey affective meanings by means of selecting certain words and not others.

4.6 Pleasantness Profiling

The last category is an attempt to represent ideal cognitive scenarios to express irony. This means that, like words, the contexts in which irony appears are enormous. Therefore, since it is impossible to make out all the possibilities, we pretend to define a schema to represent favorable and unfavorable ironic contexts on the basis of pleasantness values. In order to represent those values, we used the Dictionary of Affect in Language (Whissell, 1989). This dictionary assigns a score of pleasantness to

$\sim$ 9,000 English words. The scores were obtained from human ratings. The range of scores goes from 1 (unpleasant) to 3 (pleasant).

5 Evaluation

In order to verify the effectiveness of our model, we evaluated it through a classification task. Two underlying goals were analyzed: a) feature relevance; and b) the possibility of automatically finding ironic documents.

The classifiers were evaluated by comparing the positive set against each of the two negative subsets (AMA and SLA, respectively). All the documents were represented as frequency-weighted term vectors according to a representativeness ratio. This ratio was estimated using Formula 1:

$$\delta(d_k) = \frac{\sum_{i,j} fdf_{i,j}}{|d|} \quad (1)$$

where i is the i-th conceptual category ($i = 1 \ldots 6$); j is the j-th feature of i; $fdf_{i,j}$ (*feature dimension frequency*) is the frequency of features j of category i; and $|d|$ is the length of the k-th document d_k. For categories funny, positive/negative, affective, and pleasantness, we determined an empirical threshold of representativeness ≥ 0.5. A document was assigned the value = 1 (presence) if its δ exceeded the threshold, otherwise a value = 0 (absence) was assigned. A different criterion was determined for the n-grams and POS-grams because we were not only interested in knowing whether or not the sequences appeared in the corpus, but also in obtaining a measure to represent the degree of similarity among the sets. In order to define a similarity score, we used the Jaccard similarity coefficient.

The classification accuracy was assessed employing three classifiers: Naïve Bayes (NB), support vector machines (SVM), and decision trees (DT). The sets were trained with 5,861 instances (2,861 positive and 3,000 negative ones). 10-fold cross validation method was used as test. Global accuracy as well as detailed performance in terms of $precision$, $recall$, and $F-measure$, are given in Table 3.

Table 3: Classification results.

		Accuracy	Precision	Recall	F-Measure
NB	AMA	72,18%	0,745	0,666	0,703
	SLA	75,19%	0,700	0,886	0,782
SVM	AMA	75,75%	0,771	0,725	0,747
	SLA	73,34%	0,706	0,804	0,752
DT	AMA	74,13%	0,737	0,741	0,739
	SLA	75,12%	0,728	0,806	0,765

5.1 Discussion

Regarding the first goal (feature relevance), our a-priori aim of representing some irony features in terms of six general categories seems to be acceptable. According to the results depicted in Table 3, the proposed model achieves good rates of classification which support this assumption: from 72% up to 89%, whereas a classifier that labels all texts as non-ironic would achieve an accuracy around 54%. Moreover, both precision and recall, as well as F-measure rates corroborate the effectiveness of such performance: most of classifiers obtained scores > 0.7. This means that, at least regarding the data sets employed in the experiments, the capabilities for differentiating an ironic review from a non-ironic one, or a web comment, are satisfactory.

With respect to the second goal, an information gain filter was applied in order to verify the relevance of the model for finding ironic documents regarding the different $discourses$ profiled in each negative subset. In Table 4 we detailed the most discriminating categories per subset according to their information gain scores. On the basis of the results depicted in this table, it is evident how the relevance of the categories varies in function of the negative subset. For instance, when classifying the AMA subset, it is clear how the POS-grams (order 3), pleasantness and funny categories, are the most informative ones; in contrast, the pleasantness, n-grams (order 5) and funny categories, are the most relevant ones regarding the SLA subset. Moreover, it is important to note how the negative words, without being the most differentiable ones, function as discriminating elements.

Table 4: The 5 most discriminating categories regarding information gain results.

AMA	POS 3-grams	Pleasantness	Funny	POS 2-grams	POS 4-grams
SLA	Pleasantness	5-grams	Funny	Affectiveness	6-grams

Taking into consideration all previous remarks, we would like to stress some observations with respect to each category. Regarding the **n-grams**, it is important to note the presence of some interesting sequences which are not common to the three subsets. For instance: *pleasantly surprised*. However, we cannot define irony only in terms of these sequences because they might represent domain-specific information such as the bigram: *customer service*.

With respect to the **POS-grams**, the fact of focusing on morphosyntactic templates instead of only on words seem to be more affective. For instance, the sequence *noun* + *verb* + *noun* + *adjective* would represent more information than the sum of simple words: *[grandpa/hotel/bed]* + *[looks/appears/seems]* + *[years/days/months]* + *[younger/bigger/dirtier]*. These sequences of POS tags show how an abstract representation could be more useful than a simple word representation.

The **funny** category seems to be a relevant element to express irony. However, its relevance might be supported by the kind of information profiled in the positive set. Considering the comic trend in the reviews posted by Amazon's customers, it is likely that many of the words belonging to this category appeared in such reviews. For instance, in the following example the words in italics represent funny elements: "I am an attractive *guy*. Slender, weak, and I have never shaved in my 19 years, but *sexy* as hell, and I cannot tell you how many *women* have flocked to me since my purchase". Regardless, it is important to stress that this category is equally discriminating for all sets, funny web comments included.

Concerning the **positive/negative profiling**, it is necessary to emphasize that, despite the greater number of negative words in the MSOL (more than 15,000 words of difference; cf. Section 4.4), the positive elements are the most representative in the ironic documents. This fact corroborates the assumption about the use of positive information in order to express an underlying negative meaning: "The cool_{POS}, $\text{refreshing}_{\text{POS}}$ $\text{taste}_{\text{POS}}$ of the milk_{POS} washed away my pain_{NEG} and its $\text{kosher}_{\text{POS}}$ $\text{source}_{\text{POS}}$ of $\text{calcium}_{\text{POS}}$ wash away my fear_{NEG}".

Regarding the **affective** category, its relevance is not as important as we have a-priori considered, despite it is one of the categories used to discriminate the SLA subset: "Man, that was *weird* ... I think is *funny*, because there's a *good* overlap". However, if we take into account the whole accuracy for this subset, then we can conclude that its relevance is minor. Nonetheless, we still consider that the affective information is a valuable factor which must be taken into account in order to provide rich knowledge related to subjective layers of linguistic representation.

The role played by the **pleasantness** category on the classifications is significant. Despite the category is not the most discriminating, its effectiveness for increasing the classification accuracy is remarkable. For instance, consider the following ironic sentence: "I *became* the *man* I *always dreamed* I *could be all* those *nights staying up* late watching *wrestling*", where most of its constituents are words whose pleasantness score is ≥ 2.5; i.e. these words (in italics) should communicate information related to favorable pleasant contexts.

6 Conclusions and Future Work

Irony is one of the most subjective phenomena related to linguistic analysis. Its automatic processing is a real challenge, not only from a computational perspective but from a linguistic one as well. In this work we have suggested a model of six categories which attempts to describe salient characteristics of irony. They intend to symbolize low and high level properties of irony on the basis of formal linguistic elements. This model was assessed by creating a freely available data set with ironic reviews. The results achieved with three different classifiers are satisfactory, both in terms of classification accuracy, as well as precision, recall, and F-measure. Further work consists of improving the quality of every category, as well as of identifying new ones in order to come up with an improved model capable to detect better ironic patterns in different kinds of texts.

Acknowledgments

The National Council for Science and Technology (CONACyT - México) has funded the research of the first author. This work was carried out in the framework of the MICINN Text-Enterprise (TIN2009-13391-C04-03) research project and the Microcluster VLC/Campus (International Campus of Excellence) on Multimodal Intelligent Systems.

References

J. Atserias, B. Casas, E. Comelles, M. González, L. Padró, and M Padró. 2006. Freeling 1.3: Syntactic and semantic services in an open-source nlp library. In *Proceedings of the 5th International Conference on Language Resources and Evaluation*, pages 48–55.

S. Attardo. 2007. Irony as relevant inappropriateness. In R. Gibbs and H. Colston, editors, *Irony in Language and Thought*, pages 135–174. Taylor and Francis Group.

L. Bentivogli, P. Forner, B. Magnini, and E. Pianta. 2004. Revising the wordnet domains hierarchy: semantics, coverage and balancing. In Gilles Sérasset, editor, *Multilingual Linguistic Resources*, pages 94–101.

T. Brants and A. Franz. 2006. Web 1t 5-gram corpus version 1.

C. Burfoot and T. Baldwin. 2009. Automatic satire detection: Are you having a laugh? In *ACL-IJCNLP '09: Proceedings of the ACL-IJCNLP 2009 Conference Short Papers*, pages 161–164.

P. Carvalho, L. Sarmento, M. Silva, and E. de Oliveira. 2009. Clues for detecting irony in user-generated contents: oh...!! it's "so easy" ;-). In *TSA '09: Proceeding of the 1st international CIKM workshop on Topic-sentiment analysis for mass opinion*, pages 53–56.

H. Colston and R. Gibbs. 2007. A brief history of irony. In R. Gibbs and H. Colston, editors, *Irony in Language and Thought*, pages 3–24. Taylor and Francis Group.

H. Colston. 2007. On necessary conditions for verbal irony comprehension. In R. Gibbs and H. Colston, editors, *Irony in Language and Thought*, pages 97–134. Taylor and Francis Group.

I. Councill, R. McDonald, and L. Velikovich. 2010. What's great and what's not: learning to classify the scope of negation for improved sentiment analysis. In *Proceedings of the Workshop on Negation and Speculation in Natural Language Processing*, pages 51–59, July.

C. Curcó. 2007. Irony: Negation, echo, and metarepresentation. In R. Gibbs and H. Colston, editors, *Irony in Language and Thought*, pages 269–296. Taylor and Francis Group.

D. Davidov, O. Tsur, and A. Rappoport. 2010. Semi-supervised recognition of sarcastic sentences in Twitter and Amazon. In *Proceeding of the 23rd international conference on Computational Linguistics*, July.

R. Gibbs and H. Colston. 2007. The future of irony studies. In R. Gibbs and H. Colston, editors, *Irony in Language and Thought*, pages 339–360. Taylor and Francis Group.

R. Gibbs. 2007. Irony in talk among friends. In R. Gibbs and H. Colston, editors, *Irony in Language and Thought*, pages 339–360. Taylor and Francis Group.

R. Giora. 1995. On irony and negation. *Discourse Processes*, 19(2):239–264.

H. Grice. 1975. Logic and conversation. In Peter Cole and Jerry L. Morgan, editors, *Syntax and semantics*, volume 3, pages 41–58. New York: Academic Press.

X. Lü, L. Zhang, and J. Hu. 2004. Statistical substring reduction in linear time. In *Proceedings of IJCNLP-04, HaiNan island*.

J. Lucariello. 2007. Situational irony: A concept of events gone away. In R. Gibbs and H. Colston, editors, *Irony in Language and Thought*, pages 467–498. Taylor and Francis Group.

R. Mihalcea and C. Strapparava. 2006. Learning to Laugh (Automatically): Computational Models for Humor Recognition. *Journal of Computational Intelligence*, 22(2):126–142.

G. Miller. 1995. Wordnet: A lexical database for english. *Communications of the ACM*, 38(11):39–41.

A. Reyes, P. Rosso, and D. Buscaldi. 2009. Humor in the blogosphere: First clues for a verbal humor taxonomy. *Journal of Intelligent Systems*, 18(4):311–331.

M. Saif, D. Cody, and D. Bonnie. 2009. Generating high-coverage semantic orientation lexicons from overtly marked words and a thesaurus. In *Proceedings of the 2009 Conference on EMNLP*, pages 599–608, Morristown, NJ, USA. Association for Computational Linguistics.

C. Strapparava and A. Valitutti. 2004. WordNet-affect: an affective extension of WordNet. In *Proceedings of the 4th International Conference on Language Resources and Evaluation*, volume 4, pages 1083–1086.

O. Tsur, D. Davidov, and A. Rappoport. 2010. {ICWSM} — a great catchy name: Semi-supervised recognition of sarcastic sentences in online product reviews. In William W. Cohen and Samuel Gosling, editors, *Proceedings of the Fourth International AAAI Conference on Weblogs and Social Media*, pages 162–169, Washington, D.C., 23-26 May. The AAAI Press.

A. Utsumi. 1996. A unified theory of irony and its computational formalization. In *Proceedings of the 16th conference on Computational Linguistics*, pages 962–967, Morristown, NJ, USA. Association for Computational Linguistics.

T. Veale and Y. Hao. 2009. Support structures for linguistic creativity: A computational analysis of creative irony in similes. In *Proceedings of CogSci 2009, the 31st Annual Meeting of the Cognitive Science Society*, pages 1376–1381.

C. Whissell. 1989. The dictionary of affect in language. *Emotion: Theory, Research, and Experience*, 4:113–131.

D. Wilson and D. Sperber. 2007. On verbal irony. In R. Gibbs and H. Colston, editors, *Irony in Language and Thought*, pages 35–56. Taylor and Francis Group.

Automatic Expansion of Feature-Level Opinion Lexicons

Fermín L. Cruz, José A. Troyano, F. Javier Ortega, Fernando Enríquez
University of Seville
Avda. Reina Mercedes s/n.
41012 Seville, Spain
{fcruz,troyano,javierortega,fenros}@us.es

Abstract

In most tasks related to opinion mining and sentiment analysis, it is necessary to compute the semantic orientation (i.e., positive or negative evaluative implications) of certain opinion expressions. Recent works suggest that semantic orientation depends on application domains. Moreover, we think that semantic orientation depends on the specific targets (*features*) that an opinion is applied to. In this paper, we introduce a technique to build domain-specific, feature-level opinion lexicons in a semi-supervised manner: we first induce a lexicon starting from a small set of annotated documents; then, we expand it automatically from a larger set of unannotated documents, using a new graph-based ranking algorithm. Our method was evaluated in three different domains (headphones, hotels and cars), using a corpus of product reviews which opinions were annotated at the feature level. We conclude that our method produces feature-level opinion lexicons with better accuracy and recall that domain-independent opinion lexicons using only a few annotated documents.

1 Introduction

Sentiment analysis is a modern subdiscipline of natural language processing which deals with subjectivity, affects and opinions in texts (a good survey on this subject can be found in (Pang and Lee, 2008)). This discipline is also known as *opinion mining*, mainly in the context of text mining and information extraction. Many classification and extraction problems have been defined, with different levels of granularity depending on applications requirements: e.g. classification of text documents or smaller pieces of text into objective and subjective, classification of opinionated documents or individual sentences regarding the overall opinion (into "positive" and "negative" classes, or into a multi-point scale) or extraction of individual opinions from a piece of text (may include opinion target, holder, polarity or intensity of the opinions, among others). As a key in solving most of these problems, the *semantic orientation* of some opinion expressions should be computed: a numeric value, usually between -1 and 1, referring to the negative or positive affective implications of a given word or prhase. These values can be collected in an *opinion lexicon*, so this resource can be accessed when needed.

Many recent works (Popescu and Etzioni, 2005; Kanayama and Nasukawa, 2006; Cruz et al., 2010; Qiu et al., 2011) suggest the need for domain-specific opinion lexicons, containing semantic orientations of opinion expressions when used in a particular domain (e.g., the word "predictable" has opposite semantic orientations when used to define the driving experience of a car or the plot of a movie). Moreover, within a given domain, the specific target of the opinion is also important to induce the polarity and the intensity of the affective implications of some opinion expressions (consider for example the word "cheap" when referring to the *price* or to the *appearance* of an electronic device). This is especially important to extract opinions from product reviews, where users write their opinions about individual features of a product. These domain-specific, feature-level opinion lexicons can be manually collected, but it implies a considerable amount of time

Proceedings of the 2nd Workshop on Computational Approaches to Subjectivity and Sentiment Analysis, ACL-HLT 2011, pages 125–131,
24 June, 2011, Portland, Oregon, USA ©2011 Association for Computational Linguistics

and effort, especially if a large number of different domains are considered.

In this work, we propose a method to automatically induce feature-level, domain-specific opinion lexicons from an annotated corpus. As we are committed to reduce the time and effort, we research about the automatic expansion of this kind of lexicons, so we keep the number of required annotated documents as low as possible. In order to do so, we propose a graph-based algorithm which can be applied to other knowledge propagation problems.

In the next section, we review some related previous works to contextualize our approach. In section 3, we define the feature-level opinion lexicons and describe our method to induce and expand them in a semi-supervised manner. In section 4, we carry out some experiments over a dataset of reviews of three diferent domains. Finally, we discuss the results and draw some conclusions in section 5.

2 Related work

In this section, we briefly discuss some related works about semantic orientation induction and opinion lexicon expansion, pointing out the main differences with our contribution. We also introduce the feature-based opinion extraction task, since it is the natural application context for feature-level opinion lexicons.

2.1 Semantic orientation induction

Many methods for computing semantic orientations of words or phrases have been proposed over the last years. Some of them rely on a large set of text documents to compute semantic orientations of words in an unsupervised manner (Hatzivassiloglou and McKeown, 1997; Turney and Littman, 2003; Yu and Hatzivassiloglou, 2003). They all start from a few positive and negative seeds, and calculate the semantic orientation of target words based on conjunctive constructions (Hatzivassiloglou and McKeown, 1997) or co-occurrences (Turney and Littman, 2003; Yu and Hatzivassiloglou, 2003) of target words and seeds. These methods allow computing domain-specific semantic orientations, just using a set of documents of the selected domain, but they obtain modest values of recall and precision. We are using the observations about conjunctive constructions from (Hatzivassiloglou and McKeown, 1997) in our approach.

Other works use the lexical resource WordNet(Fellbaum, 1998) to compute the semantic orientation of a given word or phrase. For example, in (Kamps et al., 2004), a distance function between words is defined using WordNet synonymy relations, so the semantic orientation of a word is calculated from the distance to a positive seed ("good") and a negative seed ("bad"). Other works use a bigger set of seeds and the synonyms/antonyms sets from WordNet to build an opinion lexicon incrementally (Hu and Liu, 2004a; Kim and Hovy, 2004). In other works (Esuli and Sebastiani, 2006; Baccianella et al., 2010; Esuli and Sebastiani, 2005), the basic assumption is that if a word is semantically oriented in one direction, then the words in its gloss (i.e. textual definitions) tend to be oriented in the same direction. Two big sets of positive and negative words are built, starting from two initial sets of seed words and growing them using the synonymy and antonymy relations in WordNet. For every word in those sets, a textual representation is obtained by collecting all the glosses of that word. These textual representations are transformed into vectors by standard text indexing techniques, and a binary classifier is trained using these vectors. The same assumption about words and their glosses is made by Esuli and Sebastiani (2007), but the relation between words and glosses are used to build a graph representation of WordNet. Given a few seeds as input, two scores of positivity and negativity are computed, using a random-walk ranking algorithm similar to PageRank (Page et al., 1998). As a result of these works, an opinion lexicon named SentiWordNet (Baccianella et al., 2010) is publicly available. We are also using a ranking algorithm in our expansion method, but applying it to a differently built, domain-specific graph of terms.

The main weakness of the dictionary-based approaches is that they compute domain-independent semantic orientations. There are some manually-collected lexicons (Stone, 1966; Cerini et al., 2007), with semantic orientations of terms set by humans. However, they are also domain-independent resources.

2.2 Opinion lexicon expansion

There are a couple of works that deal with the more specific problem of opinion lexicon expansion. In (Kanayama and Nasukawa, 2006), the authors propose an algorithm to automatically expand an initial opinion lexicon based on *context coherency*, the tendency for same polarities to appear successively in contexts. In (Qiu et al., 2011), a method to automatically expand an initial opinion lexicon is presented. It consists of identifing the syntactic relations between opinion words and opinion targets, and using these relations to automatically identify new opinion words and targets in a bootstrapping process. Then, a polarity (positive or negative) is assigned to each of these new opinion words by applying some contextual rules. In both works, the opinion lexicons being expanded are domain-specific, but they are not taking into account the dependency between the specific targets of the opinions and the semantic orientations of terms used to express those opinions. To our knowledge, there are no previous works on inducing and expanding feature-level opinion lexicons.

2.3 Feature-based opinion extraction

Feature-based opinion extraction is a task related to opinion mining and information extraction. It consists of extracting individual opinions from texts, indicating the polarity and the specific target of each opinion; then, these opinions can be aggregated, summarized and visualized. It was first defined by Hu and Liu (2004b), and attemped by many others (Popescu and Etzioni (2005), Ding et al. (2008) and Cruz et al. (2010), among others), because of its practical applications. Being a key element in this task, most of these works propose algorithms to compute semantic orientations of terms, generally domain-specific orientations. We aim to build not only domain-specific but also feature-level opinion lexicons, in an attempt to improve the performance of a feature-based opinion extraction system (a description of our system can be found in (Cruz et al., 2010)).

3 Proposed method

In this section we define *feature-level opinion lexicons* and propose a semi-supervised method to obtain it. The method consists of two main steps. First, a small lexicon is induced from a set of annotated documents. Then, the lexicon is automatically expanded using a set of unannotated documents.

3.1 Definitions

A *domain* D is a class of entities with a fixed set of opinable features F_D. A *feature* is any component, part, attribute or property of an entity. A *feature-based opinion* is any piece of text with positive or negative implications on any feature of an entity. We name *opinion words* to the minimun set of words from an opinion from which you can decide the *polarity* (i.e., if it is a positive or a negative opinion). A *feature-level opinion lexicon* L_D for a given domain D is a function $T \times F_D \rightarrow [-1.0, 1.0]$, where T is a set of *terms* (i.e., individual words or phrases), and F_D is the set of opinable features for the domain D. L_D assign a semantic orientation to each term from T when used as opinion words in an opinion on a particular feature from F_D.

3.2 Induction

In order to generate a feature-based opinion lexicon to be used as seed in our expansion experiments, we collect a set of text reviews R_D on a particular domain D, and annotate all the feature-based opinions we encounter. Each opinion is a tuple $(polarity, f, opW)$, where $polarity$ is + (positive) or - (negative), f is a feature from F_D, and opW is a set of opinion words from the text. Each annotated opinion gives information about the semantic orientation of the opinion words. Most of the times, the polarity of the opinion implies the polarity of the opinion words. But sometimes, the opinion words include some *special expressions* that have to be considered to induce the polarity of the rest of opinion words, as *negation expressions*[1], which invert the polarity of the rest of opinion words; and *dominant polarity expressions*[2], which completely determine the polarity of an opinion, no matter which other opinion words take part. For each opinion term observed (individual words or phrases included as opinion words, once negation and dominant polarity

[1] *Negation expressions*: barely, hardly, lack, never, no, not, not too, scarcely.

[2] *Dominant polarity expressions*: enough, sufficient, sufficiently, reasonably, unnecessarily, insufficient, insufficiently, excessive, excessively, overly, too, at best, too much.

expressions been removed), the final semantic orientation for a given feature is the mean of the semantic orientations suggested by each annotated opinion on that feature containing the opinion expression (we take 1.0/-1.0 for each positive/negative annotation).

3.3 Expansion

Starting from a big set of unannotated text reviews R'_D, we use the information provided by conjunctive constructions to expand the lexicon previously induced. As explained by Hatzivassiloglou and McKeown (1997), two opinion terms appearing in a conjunctive constructions tend to have semantic orientations with the same or opposite directions, depending on the conjunction employed. Based on this principle, we build a graph linking those terms appearing in a conjunctive expression. We compute the semantic orientation of each term spreading the information provided by those terms in the initial lexicon through the graph. In order to do that, we propose a new random-walk ranking algorithm with the ability to deal with graphs containing positively and negatively weighted edges.

3.3.1 Building the graph

The graph is built from R'_D, searching for conjunctive constructions between terms. Two terms participate in a conjunctive construction if they appear consecutively in the text separated by a conjunction *and* or *but*, or the puntuation mark *comma* (,). There are two types of conjunctive constructions, *direct* and *inverse*, depending on the conjunction and the negation expressions participating. In a direct conjunctive construction, both terms seems to share the same semantic orientation; in a reverse one, they might have opposite semantic orientations. Some examples are shown next:

- **Direct conjunctive constructions**

  The camera has a **bright *and* accurate** len.
  It is a **marvellous**, really **entertaining** movie.
  ...**clear** *and* **easy to use** interface.
  ...**easy to understand**, **user-friendly** interface.

- **Inverse conjunctive constructions**

  The camera has a **bright** *but* **inaccurate** len.
  It is a **entertaining** *but* **typical** film.
  The driving is **soft** *and not* **aggresive**.

The terms observed in conjunctive constructions (in bold type in the previous examples) are the nodes of the graph. If two terms participate in a conjunctive cosntruction, the corresponding nodes are linked by an edge. Each edge is assigned a weight equal to the number of direct conjunctive constructions minus the number of inverse conjunctive constructions observed between the linked terms.

3.3.2 PolarityRank

We propose a new random-walk ranking algorithm, named PolarityRank. It is based on PageRank (Page et al., 1998). In summary, PageRank computes the relevance of each node in a graph based on the incoming edges and the relevance of the nodes participating in those edges; an edge is seen as a recommendation of one node to another. PolarityRank generalizes the concept of vote or recommendation, allowing edges with positive and negative weights. A positive edge still means a recommendation, more strongly the greater the weight of the edge. By contrast, a negative edge represents a negative feedback, more strongly the greater the absolute value of the weight. PolarityRank calculates two scores for each node, a positive and a negative one (PR^+ and PR^-, respectively). Both scores are mutually dependent: the positive score of a node n is increased in proportion to the positive score of the nodes linked to n with positively weighted edges; in addition, the positive score of n is also increased in proportion to the negative score of the nodes linked to n with negatively weighted edges. The same principles apply to the calculus of the negative scores of the nodes.

The algorithm definition is as follows. Let $G = (V, E)$ be a directed graph where V is a set of nodes and E a set of directed edges between pair of nodes. Each edge of E has an associated real value or weight, distinct from zero, being p_{ji} the weight associated with the edge going from node v_j to v_i. Let us define $Out(v_i)$ as the set of indices j of the nodes for which there exists an outgoing edge from v_i. Let us define $In^+(v_i)$ and $In^-(v_i)$ as the sets of indices j of the nodes for which there exists an incoming edge to v_i whose weight is positive or negative, respectively. We define the positive and negative PolarityRank of a node v_i (equation 1), where the values e^+ and e^- are greater than zero for certain nodes acting as positive or negative seeds, respectively. The parameter d is a damping factor that guarantees convergence; in our experiments we use a value of 0.85 (as recommended in the original definition of PageRank). The computation of PR^+ and PR^- is done iteratively as described by Page et al. (1998).

$$
\begin{aligned}
PR^+(v_i) &= (1-d)e_i^+ + \\
&+ d\Big(\sum_{j\in In^+(v_i)} \frac{p_{ji}}{\sum_{k\in Out(v_j)}|p_{jk}|}PR^+(v_j) + \\
&+ \sum_{j\in In^-(v_i)} \frac{-p_{ji}}{\sum_{k\in Out(v_j)}|p_{jk}|}PR^-(v_j)\Big) \\
PR^-(v_i) &= (1-d)e_i^- + \\
&+ d\Big(\sum_{j\in In^+(v_i)} \frac{p_{ji}}{\sum_{k\in Out(v_j)}|p_{jk}|}PR^-(v_j) + \\
&+ \sum_{j\in In^-(v_i)} \frac{-p_{ji}}{\sum_{k\in Out(v_j)}|p_{jk}|}PR^+(v_j)\Big)
\end{aligned} \tag{1}
$$

The sum of the values of e^+ and e^- must be equal to the number of nodes in the graph.

3.3.3 Extending the lexicon

Based on a seed lexicon L_D, and a set of unannotated reviews R'_D, the expanded lexicon L'_D is obtained following these steps:

1. Build a graph $G = (V, E)$ representing the conjunctive relations observed in R'_D.

2. For each feature f from F_D:
   (a) For each v_i from V with associated term t_i, such that $L_D(t_i, f)$ is defined, assign that value to e_i^+ if it is greater than 0, else assign it to e_i^-.
   (b) Linearly normalize the values of e_i^+ and e_i^-, so that the sum of the values is equal to $|V|$.
   (c) Compute PR^+ and PR^-.
   (d) For each v_i from V with associated term t_i, assign $SO(v_i)$ to $L'_D(t_i, f)$, where:

$$SO(v_i) = \frac{PR^+(v_i) - PR^-(v_i)}{PR^+(v_i) + PR^-(v_i)}$$

   Note that these values are contained in the interval $[-1.0, 1.0]$.

4 Experiments

In this section we report the results of some experiments aimed to evaluate the quality of the feature-level opinion lexicons obtained by our method.

4.1 Data

We used a set of reviews of three different domains (*headphones*, *hotels* and *cars*). We retrieved them from Epinions.com, a website specialized in product reviews written by customers. Some reviews from the dataset were labeled, including the polarity, the feature and the opinion words of each individual opinion found. Some information of the dataset is shown in table 1. The dataset is available for public use[3].

Domain	Reviews	Opinions	Features
Headphones	587 (2591)	3897	31
Hotels	988 (6171)	11054	60
Cars	972 (23179)	8519	91

Table 1: Information of the dataset. The number of unannotated reviews available for each domain is shown in parenthesis.

4.2 Experimental setup

All the experiments were done using 10-fold cross-validation. Each annotated dataset was randomly partitioned into ten subsets. The results reported for each experiment are the average results obtained in ten different runs, taking a different subset as testing set and the remaining nine subsets as training set (to induce seed lexicons). To evaluate the lexicons, we compute recall and precision over the terms participating as opinion words in the opinions annotated in the testing set. Recall is the proportion of terms which are contained in the lexicon; precision is the proportion of terms with a correct sentiment orientation in the lexicon.

4.3 Results

Table 2 shows the results of the evaluation of the induced and expanded lexicons. In order to figure out the gain in precision and recall obtained by our expansion method, we induced lexicons for each domain using different numbers of annotated reviews

[3]http://www.lsi.us.es/~fermin/index.php/Datasets

Domain	$\|R_D\|$	Induced Lexicon p	r	F_1	Expanded Lexicon p	r	F_1	$\delta(p)$	$\delta(r)$	$\delta(F_1)$
Headphones	9	0.9941	0.4479	0.6176	0.9193	0.7332	0.8158	-0.0748	**+0.2853**	**+0.1982**
	45	0.9821	0.7011	0.8181	0.9440	0.8179	0.8764	-0.0381	+0.1168	+0.0583
	108	0.9665	0.8038	0.8777	0.9525	0.8562	0.9018	-0.0140	+0.0524	+0.0241
	531	**0.9554**	0.9062	0.9302	0.9526	**0.9185**	**0.9352**	-0.0028	+0.0123	+0.0051
Hotels	9	0.9875	0.3333	0.4984	0.9416	0.8131	0.8726	-0.0459	**+0.4798**	**+0.3743**
	117	0.9823	0.7964	0.8796	0.9716	0.8802	0.9236	-0.0107	+0.0838	+0.0440
	324	0.9822	0.8732	0.9245	0.9775	0.9128	0.9440	-0.0047	+0.0396	+0.0195
	891	**0.9801**	0.9449	0.9622	0.9792	**0.9507**	**0.9647**	-0.0009	+0.0058	+0.0026
Cars	9	0.9894	0.4687	0.6361	0.9536	0.8262	0.8853	-0.0358	**+0.3575**	**+0.2493**
	117	0.9868	0.8008	0.8841	0.9712	0.8915	0.9296	-0.0156	+0.0907	+0.0455
	279	0.9849	0.8799	0.9294	0.9786	0.9116	0.9439	-0.0063	+0.0317	+0.0145
	882	**0.9847**	0.9300	0.9566	0.9831	**0.9408**	**0.9615**	-0.0016	+0.0108	+0.0049

Table 2: Results of expansion of lexicons induced from different numbers of annotated reviews. The second and third experiments for each domain are done selecting the number of annotated reviews needed to achieve F_1 scores for the induced lexicon similar to the F_1 scores for the expanded lexicon from the previous experiment.

and expanding them using the whole set of unannotated reviews. For each domain, we show the results of experiments using only nine annotated reviews (one from each subset of reviews of the cross-validation process), and using all the available annotated reviews. The second and third experiments for each domain are those where F_1 scores for the induced lexicon is similar to the F_1 scores for the expanded lexicon from the previous experiment. Thus, we can measure the number of additional annotated reviews needed to obtain similar results without expansion. Using only nine annotated reviews, the expanded feature-level opinion lexicon achieves 0.8158 of F_1 for the *headphones* domain, 0.8764 for the *hotels* domain and 0.8853 for the *cars* domain, a far better result that using a domain-independent opinion lexicon[4]. To obtain similar F_1 scores without using the expansion method, you should annotate between six and thirteen times more reviews.

5 Conclusions

There is evidence that the semantic orientation of an opinion term not only depends on the domain, but also on the specific feature which that term is applied to. In this paper, we propose a method to automatically induce domain-specific, feature-level opinion lexicons from annotated datasets. We research about the automatic expansion of this kind of lexicons, so we keep the number of required annotated documents as low as possible. The results of the experiments confirm the utility of feature-level opinion lexicons in opinion mining tasks such as feature-based opinion extraction, reaching 0.9538 as average of F_1 in three tested domains. Even though if only a few annotated reviews are available, the lexicons produced by our automatic expansion method reach an average F_1 of 0.8592, which is far better that using domain-independent opinion lexicon. Our expansion method is based on the representation of terms and their similarities and differences in a graph, and the application of a graph-based algorithm (PolarityRank) with the ability to deal with positively and negatively weighted graphs. The same algorithm can be applied to other knowledge propagation problems, whenever a small amount of information on some of the entities involved (and about the similarities and differences between the entities) is available. For example, we applied the same algorithm to compute trust and reputation in social networks(Ortega et al., 2011).

[4]We perform some experiment using the domain-independent opinion lexicon SentiWordNet (Baccianella et al., 2010), obtaining F_1 values equal to 0.7907, 0.8199 and 0.8243 for the *headphones*, *hotels* and *cars* domains.

References

Stefano Baccianella, Andrea Esuli, and Fabrizio Sebastiani. 2010. Sentiwordnet 3.0: An enhanced lexical resource for sentiment analysis and opinion mining. In Nicoletta Calzolari (Conference Chair),

Khalid Choukri, Bente Maegaard, Joseph Mariani, Jan Odijk, Stelios Piperidis, Mike Rosner, and Daniel Tapias, editors, *Proceedings of the Seventh conference on International Language Resources and Evaluation (LREC'10)*, Valletta, Malta, may. European Language Resources Association (ELRA).

S. Cerini, V. Compagnoni, A. Demontis, M. Formentelli, and G. Gandini, 2007. *Language resources and linguistic theory: Typology, second language acquisition, English linguistics.*, chapter Micro-WNOp: A gold standard for the evaluation of automatically compiled lexical resources for opinion mining. Franco Angeli Editore, Milano, IT.

Fermín L. Cruz, José A. Troyano, Fernando Enríquez, Javier Ortega, and Carlos G.Vallejo. 2010. A knowledge-rich approach to feature-based opinion extraction from product reviews. In *Proceedings of the 2nd International Workshop on Search and Mining User-Generated Contents*, pages 13–20. ACM.

Xiaowen Ding, Bing Liu, and Philip S. Yu. 2008. A holistic lexicon-based approach to opinion mining. In *WSDM '08: Proceedings of the international conference on Web search and web data mining*, pages 231–240, New York, NY, USA. ACM.

Andrea Esuli and Fabrizio Sebastiani. 2005. Determining the semantic orientation of terms through gloss analysis. In *Proceedings of the ACM SIGIR Conference on Information and Knowledge Management (CIKM)*.

Andrea Esuli and Fabrizio Sebastiani. 2006. Determining term subjectivity and term orientation for opinion mining. In *Proceedings of the European Chapter of the Association for Computational Linguistics (EACL)*.

Andrea Esuli and Fabrizio Sebastiani. 2007. Pageranking wordnet synsets: An application to opinion mining. In *Proceedings of ACL-07, the 45th Annual Meeting of the Association of Computational Linguistics*, pages 424–431. Association for Computational Linguistics.

Christiane Fellbaum, editor. 1998. *WordNet: An Electronic Lexical Database*. MIT Press.

Vasileios Hatzivassiloglou and Kathleen R. McKeown. 1997. Predicting the semantic orientation of adjectives. In *Proceedings of the eighth conference on European chapter of the Association for Computational Linguistics*, pages 174–181, Morristown, NJ, USA. Association for Computational Linguistics.

Minqing Hu and Bing Liu. 2004a. Mining and summarizing customer reviews. In *Proceedings of the ACM SIGKDD Conference on Knowledge Discovery and Data Mining (KDD)*, pages 168–177.

Minqing Hu and Bing Liu. 2004b. Mining and summarizing customer reviews. In *KDD '04: Proceedings of the tenth ACM SIGKDD international conference on Knowledge discovery and data mining*, pages 168–177, New York, NY, USA. ACM.

Jaap Kamps, Maarten Marx, Robert J. Mokken, and Maarten De Rijke. 2004. Using wordnet to measure semantic orientation of adjectives. In *National Institute for*, volume 26, pages 1115–1118.

Hiroshi Kanayama and Tetsuya Nasukawa. 2006. Fully automatic lexicon expansion for domain-oriented sentiment analysis. In *Proceedings of the Conference on Empirical Methods in Natural Language Processing (EMNLP)*, pages 355–363, Sydney, Australia, July. Association for Computational Linguistics.

Soo-Min Kim and Eduard Hovy. 2004. Determining the sentiment of opinions. In *Proceedings of the International Conference on Computational Linguistics (COLING)*.

Javier Ortega, José Troyano, Fermín Cruz, and Fernando Enríquez de Salamanca. 2011. PolarityTrust: measuring trust and reputation in social networks. In *Fourth International Conference on Internet Technologies and Applications (ITA 11)*, Wrexham, North Wales, United Kingdom, 9.

Lawrence Page, Sergey Brin, Rajeev Motwani, and Terry Winograd. 1998. The pagerank citation ranking: Bringing order to the web. Technical report, Stanford Digital Library Technologies Project.

Bo Pang and Lillian Lee. 2008. Opinion mining and sentiment analysis. *Foundations and Trends in Information Retrieval*, 2(1-2):1–135.

Ana-Maria Popescu and Oren Etzioni. 2005. Extracting product features and opinions from reviews. In *Proceedings of the Human Language Technology Conference and the Conference on Empirical Methods in Natural Language Processing (HLT/EMNLP)*.

Guang Qiu, Bing Liu, Jiajun Bu, and Chun Chen. 2011. Opinion word expansion and target extraction through double propagation. *Computational Linguistics*, 37(1).

Philip J. Stone. 1966. *The General Inquirer: A Computer Approach to Content Analysis*. The MIT Press.

Peter D. Turney and Michael L. Littman. 2003. Measuring praise and criticism: Inference of semantic orientation from association. *ACM Transactions on Information Systems*, 21:315–346.

Hong Yu and Vasileios Hatzivassiloglou. 2003. Towards answering opinion questions: Separating facts from opinions and identifying the polarity of opinion sentences. In *Proceedings of the Conference on Empirical Methods in Natural Language Processing (EMNLP)*.

Robust Sense-Based Sentiment Classification

Balamurali A R[1] **Aditya Joshi**[2] **Pushpak Bhattacharyya**[2]
[1] IITB-Monash Research Academy, IIT Bombay
[2]Dept. of Computer Science and Engineering, IIT Bombay
Mumbai, India - 400076
{balamurali,adityaj,pb}@cse.iitb.ac.in

Abstract

The new trend in sentiment classification is to use **semantic features** for representation of documents. We propose a semantic space based on WordNet senses for a supervised document-level sentiment classifier. Not only does this show a better performance for sentiment classification, it also opens opportunities for building a robust sentiment classifier. We examine the possibility of using **similarity metrics** defined on WordNet to address the problem of not finding a sense in the training corpus. Using three popular similarity metrics, we replace unknown synsets in the test set with a *similar* synset from the training set. An improvement of 6.2% is seen with respect to baseline using this approach.

1 Introduction

Sentiment classification is a task under Sentiment Analysis (SA) that deals with automatically tagging text as positive, negative or neutral from the perspective of the speaker/writer with respect to a topic. Thus, a sentiment classifier tags the sentence '*The movie is entertaining and totally worth your money!*' in a movie review as *positive* with respect to the movie. On the other hand, a sentence '*The movie is so boring that I was dozing away through the second half.*' is labeled as *negative*. Finally, '*The movie is directed by Nolan*' is labeled as neutral. For the purpose of this work, we follow the definition of Pang et al. (2002) & Turney (2002) and consider a binary classification task for output labels as positive and negative.

Lexeme-based (bag-of-words) features are commonly used for supervised sentiment classification (Pang and Lee, 2008). In addition to this, there also has been work that identifies the roles of different *parts-of-speech (POS)* like adjectives in sentiment classification (Pang et al., 2002; Whitelaw et al., 2005). Complex features based on parse trees have been explored for modeling high-accuracy polarity classifiers (Matsumoto et al., 2005). Text parsers have also been found to be helpful in modeling valence shifters as features for classification (Kennedy and Inkpen, 2006). In general, the work in the context of supervised SA has focused on (but not limited to) different combinations of bag-of-words-based and syntax-based models.

The focus of this work is to represent a document as a set of sense-based features. We ask the following questions in this context:

1. *Are WordNet senses better features as compared to words?*

2. *Can a sentiment classifier be made robust with respect to features unseen in the training corpus using similarity metrics defined for concepts in WordNet?*

We modify the corpus by Ye et al. (2009) for the purpose of our experiments related to sense-based sentiment classification. To address the first question, we show that the approach that uses senses (either manually annotated or obtained through automatic WSD techniques) as features performs better than the one that uses words as features.

Using senses as features allows us to achieve robustness for sentiment classification by exploiting the definition of concepts (sense) and hierarchical structure of WordNet. Hence to address the second question, we replace a synset not present in the test set with a similar synset from the training set using similarity metrics defined on WordNet. Our results show that replacement of this nature provides a boost to the classification performance.

The road map for the rest of the paper is as follows: Section 2 describes the sense-based features that we use for this work. We explain the similarity-based replacement technique using WordNet synsets

Proceedings of the 2nd Workshop on Computational Approaches to Subjectivity and Sentiment Analysis, ACL-HLT 2011, pages 132–138,
24 June, 2011, Portland, Oregon, USA ©2011 Association for Computational Linguistics

in section 3. Details about our experiments are described in Section 4. In section 5, we present our results and discussions. We contextualize our work with respect to other related works in section 6. Finally, section 7 concludes the paper and points to future work.

2 WordNet Senses as Features

In their original form, documents are said to be in lexical space since they consist of words. When the words are replaced by their corresponding senses, the resultant document is said to be in semantic space.

WordNet 2.1 (Fellbaum, 1998) has been used as the sense repository. Each word/lexeme is mapped to an appropriate synset in WordNet based on its sense and represented using the corresponding synset id of WordNet. Thus, the word *love* is disambiguated and replaced by the identifier *21758160* which consists of a POS category identifier *2* followed by synset offset identifier *1758160*. This paper refers to POS category identifier along with synset offset as synset identifiers or as senses.

2.1 Motivation

We describe three different scenarios to show the need of sense-based analysis for SA. Consider the following sentences as the first scenario.

1. *"Her face **fell** when she heard that she had been fired."*

2. *"The fruit **fell** from the tree."*

The word *'fell'* occurs in different senses in the two sentences. In the first sentence, *'fell'* has the meaning of '*assume a disappointed or sad expression*, whereas in the second sentence, it has the meaning of '*descend in free fall under the influence of gravity*'. A user will infer the negative polarity of the first sentence from the negative sense of *'fell'* in it. This implies that there is at least one sense of the word *'fell'* that carries sentiment and at least one that does not.

In the second scenario, consider the following examples.

1. *"The snake bite proved to be **deadly** for the young boy."*

2. *"Shane Warne is a **deadly** spinner."*

The word *deadly* has senses which carry opposite polarity in the two sentences and these senses assign the polarity to the corresponding sentence. The first sentence is negative while the second sentence is positive.

Finally in the third scenario, consider the following pair of sentences.

1. *"He speaks a **vulgar** language."*

2. *"Now that's real **crude** behavior!"*

The words *vulgar* and *crude* occur as synonyms in the synset that corresponds to the sense '*conspicuously and tastelessly indecent*'. The synonymous nature of words can be identified only if they are looked at as senses and not just words.

As one may observe, the first scenario shows that a word may have *some sentiment-bearing* and *some non-sentiment-bearing senses*. In the second scenario, we show that there may be *different senses of a word that bear sentiments of opposite polarity*. Finally, in the third scenario, we show how *a sense can be manifested using different words*, *i.e.*, words in a synset. The three scenarios motivate the use of semantic space for sentiment prediction.

2.2 Sense versus Lexeme-based Feature Representations

We annotate the words in the corpus with their senses using two sense disambiguation approaches.

As the first approach, **manual sense annotation** of documents is carried out by two annotators on two subsets of the corpus, the details of which are given in Section 4.1. The experiments conducted on this set determine the ideal case scenario- the skyline performance.

As the second approach, a state-of-art algorithm for domain-specific WSD proposed by Khapra et al. (2010) is used to obtain an automatically sense-tagged corpus. This algorithm called **iterative WSD or IWSD** iteratively disambiguates words by ranking the candidate senses based on a scoring function.

The two types of sense-annotated corpus lead us to four feature representations for a document:

1. A group of word senses that have been manually annotated (*M*)

2. A group of word senses that have been annotated by an automatic WSD (*I*)

3. A group of *manually* annotated word senses and words (both separately as features) (*Sense + Words(M)*)

4. A group of *automatically* annotated word senses and words (both separately as features) (*Sense + Words(I)*)

Our first set of experiments compares the four feature representations to find the feature representation with which sentiment classification gives the best performance. Sense + Words(M) and Sense + Words(I) are used to overcome non-coverage of WordNet for some noun synsets.

3 Similarity Metrics and Unknown Synsets

3.1 Synset Replacement Algorithm

Using WordNet senses provides an opportunity to use similarity-based metrics for WordNet to reduce the effect of unknown features. If a synset encountered in a test document is not found in the training corpus, it is replaced by one of the synsets present in the training corpus. The substitute synset is determined on the basis of its similarity with the synset in the test document. The synset that is replaced is referred to as an *unseen synset* as it is not known to the trained model.

For example, consider excerpts of two reviews, the first of which occurs in the training corpus while the second occurs in the test corpus.

1. " *In the night, it is a* ***lovely*** *city and...* "

2. " *The city has many* ***beautiful*** *hot spots for honeymooners.* "

The synset of '*beautiful*' is not present in the training corpus. We evaluate a similarity metric for all synsets in the training corpus with respect to the sense of *beautiful* and find that the sense of *lovely* is closest to it. Hence, the sense of *beautiful* in the test document is replaced by the sense of *lovely* which is present in the training corpus.

The replacement algorithm is described in Algorithm 1. The term *concept* is used in place of *synset* though the two essentially mean the same in this context. The algorithm aims to find a concept *temp_concept* for each concept in the test corpus. The *temp_concept* is the concept closest to some concept in the training corpus based on the similarity metrics. The algorithm follows from the fact that the similarity value for a synset with itself is maximum.

```
Input: Training Corpus, Test Corpus,
Similarity Metric
Output: New Test Corpus
T:= Training Corpus;
X:= Test Corpus;
S:= Similarity metric;
train_concept_list = get_list_concept(T) ;
test_concept_list = get_list_concept(X);
for each concept C in test_concept_list do
    temp_max_similarity = 0 ;
    temp_concept = C ;
    for each concept D in train_concept_list do
        similarity_value = get_similarity_value(C,D,S);
        if (similarity_value > temp_max_similarity) then
            temp_max_similarity= similarity_value;
            temp_concept = D ;
        end
    end
    replace_synset_corpus(C,temp_concept,X);
end
Return X ;
```

Algorithm 1: Synset replacement using similarity metric

The *for* loop over C finds a concept *temp_concept* in the training corpus with the maximum *similarity_value*. The method *replace_synset_corpus* replaces the concept C in the test corpus with *temp_concept* in the test corpus X.

3.2 Similarity Metrics Used

We evaluate the benefit of three similarity metrics, namely LIN's similarity metric, Lesk similarity metric and Leacock and Chodorow (LCH) similarity metric for the synset replacement algorithm stated. These runs generate three variants of the corpus. We compare the benefit of each of these metrics by studying their sentiment classification performance. The metrics can be described as follows:

LIN: The metric by Lin (1998) uses the information content individually possessed by two concepts in addition to that shared by them. The information content shared by two concepts A and B is given by their most specific subsumer (lowest superordinate(*lso*). Thus, this metric defines the similarity between two concepts as

$$sim_{LIN}(A,B) = \frac{2 \times \log Pr(lso(A,B))}{\log Pr(A) + \log Pr(B)} \quad (1)$$

Lesk: Each concept in WordNet is defined through gloss. To compute the Lesk similarity (Banerjee and Pedersen, 2002) between A and B, a scoring function based on the overlap of words in their individual glosses is used.

Leacock and Chodorow (LCH): To measure similarity between two concepts A and B, Leacock and Chodorow (1998) compute the shortest path through hypernymy relation between them under the constraint that there exists such a path. The final value is computed by scaling the path length by the overall taxonomy depth (D).

$$sim_{LCH}(A,B) = -\log\left(\frac{len(A,B)}{2D}\right) \quad (2)$$

4 Experimentation

We describe the variants of the corpus generated and the experiments in this section.

4.1 Data Preparation

We create different variants of the dataset by Ye et al. (2009). This dataset contains 600 positive and 591 negative reviews about seven travel destinations. Each review contains approximately 4-5 sentences with an average number of words per review being 80-85.

To create the manually annotated corpus, two human annotators annotate words in the corpus with senses for two disjoint subsets of the original corpus by Ye et al. (2009). The inter-annotation agreement for a subset(20 positive reviews) of the corpus showed 91% sense overlap. The manually annotated corpus consists of 34508 words with 6004 synsets.

The second variant of the corpus contains word senses obtained from automatic disambiguation using IWSD. The evaluation statistics of the IWSD is shown in Table 1. Table 1 shows that the F-score for noun synsets is high while that for adjective synsets is the lowest among all. The low recall for adjective POS based synsets can be detrimental to classification since adjectives are known to express direct sentiment (Pang et al., 2002).

POS	#Words	P(%)	R(%)	F-Score(%)
Noun	12693	75.54	75.12	75.33
Adverb	4114	71.16	70.90	71.03
Adjective	6194	67.26	66.31	66.78
Verb	11507	68.28	67.97	68.12
Overall	34508	71.12	70.65	70.88

Table 1: Annotation Statistics for IWSD; P- Precision,R-Recall

4.2 Experimental Setup

The experiments are performed using C-SVM (linear kernel with default parameters[1]) available as a part of LibSVM[2] package. We choose to use SVM since it performs the best for sentiment classification (Pang et al., 2002). All results reported are average of five-fold cross-validation accuracies.

To conduct experiments on words as features, we first perform stop-word removal. The words are not stemmed as per observations by (Leopold and Kindermann, 2002). To conduct the experiments based on the synset representation, words in the corpus are annotated with synset identifiers along with POS category identifiers. For automatic sense disambiguation, we used the trained IWSD engine (trained on tourism domain) from Khapra et al. (2010). These synset identifiers along with POS category identifiers are then used as features. For replacement using semantic similarity measures, we used WordNet::Similarity 2.05 package by Pedersen et al. (2004).

To evaluate the result, we use accuracy, F-score, recall and precision as the metrics. Classification accuracy defines the ratio of the number of true instances to the total number of instances. Recall is calculated as a ratio of the true instances found to the total number of false positives and true positives. Precision is defined as the number of true instances divided by number of true positives and false negatives. Positive Precision (PP) and Positive Recall (PR) are precision and recall for positive documents while Negative Precision (NP) and Negative Recall (NR) are precision and recall for negative documents. F-score is the weighted precision-recall

[1] C=0.0,ϵ=0.0010

[2] http://www.csie.ntu.edu.tw/ cjlin/libsvm

Feature Representation	Accuracy	PF	NF	PP	NP	PR	NR
Words	84.90	85.07	84.76	84.95	84.92	85.19	84.60
Sense (M)	89.10	88.22	89.11	91.50	87.07	85.18	91.24
Sense + Words (M)	90.20	89.81	90.43	92.02	88.55	87.71	92.39
Sense (I)	85.48	85.31	85.65	87.17	83.93	83.53	87.46
Sense + Words(I)	86.08	86.28	85.92	85.87	86.38	86.69	85.46

Table 2: Classification Results; M-Manual, I-IWSD, W-Words, PF-Positive F-score(%), NF-Negative F-score (%), PP-Positive Precision (%), NP-Negative Precision (%), PR-Positive Recall (%), NR-Negative Recall (%)

score.

5 Results and Discussions

5.1 *Comparison of various feature representations*

Table 2 shows results of classification for different feature representations. The baseline for our results is the unigram bag-of-words model (Words).

An improvement of 4.2% is observed in the accuracy of sentiment prediction when manually annotated sense-based features (M) are used in place of word-based features (Words). The precision of both the classes using features based on semantic space is also better than one based on lexeme space. Reported results suggest that it is more difficult to detect negative sentiment than positive sentiment (Gindl and Liegl, 2008). However, using sense-based representation, it is important to note that negative recall increases by around 8%.

The combined model of words and manually annotated senses (Sense + Words (M)) gives the best performance with an accuracy of 90.2%. This leads to an improvement of 5.3% over the baseline accuracy [3].

One of the reasons for improved performance is the feature abstraction achieved due to the synset-based features. The dimension of feature vector is reduced by a factor of 82% when the document is represented in synset space. The reduction in dimensionality may also lead to reduction in noise (Cunningham, 2008).

A comparison of accuracy of different sense representations in Table 2 shows that manual disambiguation performs better than using automatic algorithms like IWSD. Although overall classification accuracy improvement of IWSD over baseline is marginal, negative recall also improves. This benefit is despite the fact that evaluation of IWSD engine over manually annotated corpus gave an overall F-score of 71% (refer Table 1). For a WSD engine with a better accuracy, the performance of sense-based SA can be boosted further.

Thus, in terms of feature representation of documents, sense-based features provide a better overall performance as compared to word-based features.

5.2 *Synset replacement using similarity metrics*

Table 3 shows the results of synset replacement experiments performed using similarity metrics defined in section 3. The similarity metric value NA shown in the table indicates that synset replacement is not performed for the specific run of experiment. For this set of experiments, we use the combination of sense and words as features (indicated by *Senses+Words (M)*).

Synset replacement using a similarity metric shows an improvement over using words alone. However, the improvement in classification accuracy is marginal compared to sense-based representation without synset replacement (Similarity Metric=NA).

Replacement using LIN and LCH metrics gives marginally better results compared to the vanilla setting in a manually annotated corpus. The same phenomenon is seen in the case of IWSD based approach[4]. The limited improvement can be due to the fact that since LCH and LIN consider only IS-A

[3]The improvement in results of semantic space is found to be statistically significant over the baseline at 95% confidence level when tested using a paired t-test.

[4]Results based on LCH and LIN similarity metric for automatic sense disambiguation is not statistically significant with α=0.05

Features Representation	SM	A	PF	NF
Words (Baseline)	**NA**	84.90	85.07	84.76
Sense+Words (M)	**NA**	90.20	89.81	90.43
Sense+Words (I)	**NA**	86.08	86.28	85.92
Sense+Words (M)	**LCH**	90.60	90.20	90.85
Sense+Words (M)	**LIN**	90.70	90.26	90.97
Sense+Words (M)	**Lesk**	91.12	90.70	91.38
Sense+Words (I)	**LCH**	85.66	85.85	85.52
Sense+Words (I)	**LIN**	86.16	86.37	86.00
Sense+Words (I)	**Lesk**	86.25	86.41	86.10

Table 3: Similarity Metric Analysis using different similarity metrics with synsets and a combinations of synset and words; SM-Similarity Metric, A-Accuracy, PF-Positive F-score(%), NF-Negative F-score (%)

relationship in WordNet, the replacement happens only for verbs and nouns. This excludes adverb synsets which we have shown to be the best features for a sense-based SA system.

Among all similarity metrics, the best classification accuracy is achieved using Lesk. The system performs with an overall classification accuracy of 91.12%, which is a substantial improvement of 6.2% over baseline. Again, it is only 1% over the vanilla setting that uses combination of synset and words. However, the similarity metric is not sophisticated as LIN or LCH. A good metric which covers all POS categories can provide substantial improvement in the classification accuracy.

6 Related Work

This work deals with studying benefit of a word sense-based feature space to supervised sentiment classification. This work assumes the hypothesis that *word sense is associated with the sentiment* as shown by Wiebe and Mihalcea (2006) through human interannotator agreement.

Akkaya et al. (2009) and Martn-Wanton et al. (2010) study rule-based sentiment classification using word senses where Martn-Wanton et al. (2010) uses a combination of sentiment lexical resources. Instead of a rule-based implementation, our work leverages on benefits of a statistical learning-based methods by using a supervised approach. Rentoumi et al. (2009) suggest an approach to use word senses to detect sentence level polarity using graph-based similarity. While Rentoumi et al. (2009) targets using senses to handle metaphors in sentences, we deal with generating a general-purpose classifier.

Carrillo de Albornoz et al. (2010) create an emotional intensity classifier using affective class concepts as features. By using WordNet synsets as features, we construct feature vectors that map to a larger sense-based space.

Akkaya et al. (2009), Martn-Wanton et al. (2010) and Carrillo de Albornoz et al. (2010) deal with sentiment classification of sentences. On the other hand, we associate sentiment polarity to a document on the whole as opposed to Pang and Lee (2004) which deals with sentiment prediction of subjectivity content only. Carrillo de Albornoz et al. (2010) suggests expansion using WordNet relations which we perform in our experiments.

7 Conclusion & Future Work

We present an empirical study to show that sense-based features work better as compared to word-based features. We show how the performance impact differs for different automatic and manual techniques. We also show the benefit using WordNet based similarity metrics for replacing unknown features in the test set. Our results support the fact that not only does sense space improve the performance of a sentiment classification system but also opens opportunities for building robust sentiment classifiers that can handle unseen synsets.

Incorporation of syntactical information along with semantics can be an interesting area of work. Another line of work is in the context of cross-lingual sentiment analysis. Current solutions are based on machine translation which is very resource-intensive. Using a bi-lingual dictionary which maps WordNet across languages can prove to be an alternative.

References

Cem Akkaya, Janyce Wiebe, and Rada Mihalcea. 2009. Subjectivity word sense disambiguation. In *Proc. of EMNLP '09*, pages 190–199, Singapore.

Satanjeev Banerjee and Ted Pedersen. 2002. An adapted lesk algorithm for word sense disambiguation using wordnet. In *Proc. of CICLing'02*, pages 136–145, London, UK.

Jorge Carrillo de Albornoz, Laura Plaza, and Pablo Gervs. 2010. Improving emotional intensity classification using word sense disambiguation. *Special issue: Natural Language Processing and its Applications. Journal on Research in Computing Science*, 46:131–142.

Pdraig Cunningham. 2008. Dimension reduction. In *Machine Learning Techniques for Multimedia*, Cognitive Technologies, pages 91–112.

Christiane Fellbaum. 1998. *WordNet: An Electronic Lexical Database*. Bradford Books.

Stefan Gindl and Johannes Liegl, 2008. *Evaluation of different sentiment detection methods for polarity classification on web-based reviews*, pages 35–43.

Alistair Kennedy and Diana Inkpen. 2006. Sentiment classification of movie reviews using contextual valence shifters. *Computational Intelligence*, 22(2):110–125.

Mitesh Khapra, Sapan Shah, Piyush Kedia, and Pushpak Bhattacharyya. 2010. Domain-specific word sense disambiguation combining corpus basedand wordnet based parameters. In *Proc. of GWC'10*, Mumbai, India.

Claudia Leacock and Martin Chodorow. 1998. Combining local context with wordnet similarity for word sense identification. In *WordNet: A Lexical Reference System and its Application*.

Edda Leopold and Jörg Kindermann. 2002. Text categorization with support vector machines. how to represent texts in input space? *Machine Learning*, 46:423–444.

Dekang Lin. 1998. An information-theoretic definition of similarity. In *In Proc. of the 15th International Conference on Machine Learning*, pages 296–304.

Tamara Martn-Wanton, Alexandra Balahur-Dobrescu, Andres Montoyo-Guijarro, and Aurora Pons-Porrata. 2010. Word sense disambiguation in opinion mining: Pros and cons. In *Proc. of CICLing'10*, Madrid,Spain.

Shotaro Matsumoto, Hiroya Takamura, and Manabu Okumura. 2005. Sentiment classification using word sub-sequences and dependency sub-trees. In *Proc. of PAKDD'05,*, Lecture Notes in Computer Science, pages 301–311.

Bo Pang and Lillian Lee. 2004. A sentimental education: Sentiment analysis using subjectivity summarization based on minimum cuts. In *Proc. of ACL'04*, pages 271–278, Barcelona, Spain.

Bo Pang and Lillian Lee. 2008. Opinion mining and sentiment analysis. *Found. Trends Inf. Retr.*, 2:1–135.

Bo Pang, Lillian Lee, and Shivakumar Vaithyanathan. 2002. Thumbs up? sentiment classification using machine learning techniques. volume 10, pages 79–86.

Ted Pedersen, Siddharth Patwardhan, and Jason Michelizzi. 2004. Wordnet::similarity: measuring the relatedness of concepts. In *Demonstration Papers at HLT-NAACL'04*, pages 38–41.

Vassiliki Rentoumi, George Giannakopoulos, Vangelis Karkaletsis, and George A. Vouros. 2009. Sentiment analysis of figurative language using a word sense disambiguation approach. In *Proc. of the International Conference RANLP'09*, pages 370–375, Borovets, Bulgaria.

Peter Turney. 2002. Thumbs up or thumbs down? Semantic orientation applied to unsupervised classification of reviews. In *Proc. of ACL'02*, pages 417–424, Philadelphia, US.

Casey Whitelaw, Navendu Garg, and Shlomo Argamon. 2005. Using appraisal groups for sentiment analysis. In *Proc. of CIKM '05*, pages 625–631, New York, NY, USA.

Janyce Wiebe and Rada Mihalcea. 2006. Word sense and subjectivity. In *Proc. of COLING-ACL'06*, pages 1065–1072.

Qiang Ye, Ziqiong Zhang, and Rob Law. 2009. Sentiment classification of online reviews to travel destinations by supervised machine learning approaches. *Expert Systems with Applications*, 36(3):6527 – 6535.

Sentiment Classification Using Semantic Features Extracted from WordNet-based Resources

Yoan Gutiérrez
Department of Informatics
University of Matanzas, Cuba.
{yoan.gutierrez}@umcc.cu

Sonia Vázquez and Andrés Montoyo
Department of Software and Computing Systems
University of Alicante, Spain.
{svazquez, montoyo}@dlsi.ua.es

Abstract

In this paper, we concentrate on the 3 of the tracks proposed in the NTCIR 8 MOAT, concerning the classification of sentences according to their opinionatedness, relevance and polarity. We propose a method for the detection of opinions, relevance, and polarity classification, based on ISR-WN (a resource for the multidimensional analysis with Relevant Semantic Trees of sentences using different WordNet-based information sources). Based on the results obtained, we can conclude that the resource and methods we propose are appropriate for the task, reaching the level of state-of-the-art approaches.

1 Introduction

In recent years, textual information has become one of the most important sources of knowledge to extract useful and heterogeneous data. Texts can provide from factual information such as descriptions, lists of characteristics or instructions to opinionated information such as reviews, emotions or feelings. This heterogeneity has motivated that dealing with the identification and extraction of opinions and sentiments in texts require special attention. In fact, the development of different tools to help government information analysts, companies, political parties, economists, etc to automatically get feelings from news and forums is a challenging task (Wiebe et al., 2005). Many researchers such as Balahur et al., (2010), Hatzivassiloglou et al.(2000), Kim and Hovy (2006), Wiebe et al. (2005) and many others have been working in this way and related areas. Moreover, in the course of years we find a long tradition on developing Question Answering (QA) systems. However, in recent years, researchers have concentrated on the development of Opinion Questions Answering (OQA) systems (Balahur et al., 2010). This new task has to deal with different problems such as Sentiment Analysis where documents must be classified according to sentiments and subjectivity features. Therefore, a new kind of evaluation that takes into account this new issue is needed.

One of the competitions that establishes the benchmark for opinion question answering systems, in a monolingual and cross-lingual setting, is the NTCIR Multilingual Opinion Analysis Task (MOAT) [1]. In this competition, researchers work hard to achieve better results on Opinion Analysis, introducing different techniques.

In this paper, we only concentrate on three tracks proposed in the NTCIR 8 MOAT, concerning to the classification of sentences according to their opinionatedness, relevance and polarity. We propose a method for the detection of opinions, relevance and polarity classification, based on ISR-WN which is a resource for the multidimensional analysis with Relevant Semantic Trees of sentences using different WordNet-based information sources.

2 Related works

Related to Opinion Analysis task we can find many points of view. Some researchers say that adjectives combined with semantic characteristics provide vital information to the performance of Opinion Analysis (Hatzivassiloglou et al., 2000). Others like Zubaryeva and Savoy (2010) assume

[1] http://research.nii.ac.jp/ntcir/ntcir-ws8/meeting/

Proceedings of the 2nd Workshop on Computational Approaches to Subjectivity and Sentiment Analysis, ACL-HLT 2011, pages 139–145,
24 June, 2011, Portland, Oregon, USA ©2011 Association for Computational Linguistics

that the extraction of relevant terms on the documents could define their polarity, designing a method capable of selecting terms that clearly belong to one type of polarity. Another research based on features extraction was conducted by Lai et al. (2010), they developed a trained system on Japanese Opinionated Sentence Identification. And Balahur and Montoyo (2009) proposed a method to extract, classify and summarize opinions on products from web reviews. It was based on the prior building of product characteristics taxonomy and on the semantic relatedness given by the Normalized Google Distance (Cilibrasi and Vitányi, 2007) and SVM learning. As we can see, the usage of features extraction is a suitable mode to work on Opinion Analysis task. Apart from that other authors have used semantic resources, for example, Kim and Hovy (2006, 2005) used semantic resources to get an approach on Holder Detection and Opinion Extraction tasks.

In general, using semantic resources is one of the most applied procedures over different tasks such as Document Indexing, Document Classification, Word Sense Disambiguation, etc. In Natural Language Processing (NLP), one of the most used resources for WSD and other tasks is WordNet (WN) (Fellbaum, 1998). WN is a lexical dictionary with word senses and descriptions. In order to enrich the WN resource, it has been linked with different lexical resources such as WordNet Domains (WND) (Magnini and Cavaglia, 2000) a lexical resource containing the domains of the synsets in WordNet, SUMO (Niles, 2001) an ontology relating the concepts in WordNet, WordNet Affect (WNA) an extension of WN where different synsets are annotated with one of the six basic emotions proposed by Ekman (1999), SentiWordNet (Esuli and Sebastiani, 2006) a lexical resource where each synset is annotated with polarity, Semantic Classes (SC) (Izquierdo *et al.*, 2007) a set of Base Level Concepts (BLC) based on WN, etc. The usage of these resources allows the tackling of NLP tasks from different points of view, depending on the resource used.

Our approach proposes using different semantic dimensions according to different resources. In order to achieve this, we use the Integration of Semantic Resources based on WordNet, which we explain in the next section and the Semantic Classes (SC).

2.1 Integration of Semantic Resources based on WordNet (ISR-WN)

ISR-WN (Gutiérrez *et al.*, 2010b) is a new resource that allows the integration of several semantic resources mapped to WN. In ISR-WN, WordNet 1.6 or 2.0 is used as a core to link several resources: SUMO, WND and WNA. As Gutiérrez et al. (2010a) describe, the integrated resource allows navigate inside the semantic network.

2.2 Semantic Classes (SC)

The Semantic Classes resource (Izquierdo *et al.*, 2007) consists of a set of Base Level Concepts (BLC) from WN obtained before applying a bottom-up process using the chain of hypernym relations. For each synset in WN, the process selects as its Base Level Concept the first local maximum, according to the relative number of relations. As a result, a resource with a set of BLCs linked semantically to several synsets is obtained.

In order to apply the multidimensionality that ISR-WN and SC provide, we have analyzed related approaches like (Magnini *et al.*, 2002; 2008) ,(Vázquez *et al.*, 2004), (Villarejo *et al.*, 2005), (Zouaq *et al.*, 2009) and others that take into account semantic dimensionality. Then, we have decided to use Relevant Semantic Trees (Gutiérrez *et al.*, 2010a) because it is an approach capable of being applied over several dimensions (resources) at once.

2.3 Relevant Semantic Trees (RST)

RST (Gutiérrez *et al.*, 2010a) is a method able to disambiguate the senses of the words contained in a sentence by obtaining the Relevant Semantic Trees from different resources. In order to measure the association between concepts in each sentence according to a multidimensional perspective, *RST* uses the Association Ratio (*AR*) measure (Vázquez *et al.*, 2004). Our purpose is to include the Multidimensional Semantic Analysis into the Opinion Analysis using *RSTs*.

In order to evaluate our approach the rules and corpus that concern the English monolingual subtasks from MOAT were used.

2.4 English monolingual subtasks

In these tasks the participants were provided with twenty topics. For each one of the topics, a question was given with a short and concise query, the expected polarity of the answer and the period of time. For each of the topics, a set of documents were assigned and they had to be splitted into sentences for the opinionated and relevance judgements and into opinion units for the polarity, opinion target and source tasks. In this work, we describe twelve runs for the opinionated, relevance and polarity judgement tasks.

3 WSD method

We propose an unsupervised knowledge-based method that uses the RST technique combined with SentiWordNet 3.0 (Esuli and Sebastiani, 2006) to tackle 3 of the monolingual English tasks proposed in the NTCIR 8 MOAT. In this approach WN 2.0 version is used.

The aim of this method is to obtain a *RST* of each sentence and then associate the *RST* with polarity values. The process involves the following resources: WND, WNA, the WN taxonomy, SUMO and Semantic Classes (SC). Because of SC does not have a tree structure we simply obtain the Relevant Semantic Classes. Subsequently, we determine the polarities collected for each label of each *RST* obtained according to the analyzed sentence. Our proposal involves four steps presented on sections 3.1, 3.2, 3.3 and 3.4.

3.1 Obtaining the Relevant Semantic Trees

In this section, we use a fragment of the original RST method with the aim of obtaining Relevant Semantic Trees of the sentences. Notice that this step must be applied for each resource.

Once each sentence is analyzed, the *AR* value is obtained and related to each concept in the trees. Equation 1 is used to measure and to obtain the values of Relevant Concepts:

$$AR(C,f) = \sum_{i=1}^{n} AR(C,f_i); \qquad (1)$$

Where:

$$AR(C,w) = P(C,w) * \log_2 \frac{P(C,\ w)}{P(C)}; \qquad (2)$$

In both equations *C* is a concept; *f* is a sentence or set of words (w); f_i is the *i-th* word of the sentence *f*; *P (C, w)* is the joint probability distribution; *P (C)* is the marginal probability.

In order to illustrate the processing steps, we will consider the following example: *"But it is unfair to dump on teachers as distinct from the educational establishment".* Using the WND resource, we show the manner in which we obtain the RST.

The first stage involves the lemmatization of the words in the sentence. For the example considered, the obtained lemmas are:

Lemmas [*unfair; dump; teacher, distinct, educational; establishment*]

Next, each lemma is looked up in ISR-WN and it is correlated with the WND concepts. Table 1 shows the results after applying Equation 1 over the example.

Vector			
AR	Domain	*AR*	Domain
0.90	Pedagogy	0.36	Commerce
0.90	Administration	0.36	Quality
0.36	Buildings	0.36	Psychoanalysis
0.36	Politics	0.36	Economy
0.36	Environment		

Table 1. Initial Concept Vector of Domains

After obtaining the Initial Concept Vector of Domains we apply Equation 3 in order to obtain the Relevant Semantic Tree related to the sentence.

$$AR(PC,f) = AR(ChC,f) - ND(IC,PC) \quad ;(3)$$

Where:

$$ND(IC,PC) = \frac{MP(IC,PC)}{TD} \quad ;(4)$$

Here *AR(PC, f)* represents the *AR* value of *PC* related to the sentence *f*; $AR(ChC,f)$ is the *AR* value calculated with equation 1 in case of *ChC* was included in the Initial Vector, otherwise is calculated with the equation 3; *ChC* is the Child Concept of *PC*; *ND* is a Normalized Distance; *IC* is the Initial Concept from we have to add the ancestors; *PC* is Parent Concept; *TD* is Depth of the hierarchic tree of the resource to use; and *MP* is Minimal Path.

Applying the Equation 3, the algorithm to decide which parent concept will be added to the vector is shown here:

```
if (AR(PC,f) value > 0 ){
  if ( PC had not been added to vector)
    PC is added to the vector with AR(PC, f) value;
  else PC value = PC value + AR(PC, f) value; }
```

The result after processing is shown in Table 2. This vector represents the Domain tree associated to the sentence. After the Relevant Semantic Tree is obtained, the Factotum Domain is eliminated from the tree. Due to the fact that Factotum is a generic Domain associated to words that appear in general contexts it does not provide useful information and experimentally we confirmed that it introduced errors; so we eliminate it (Magnini and Cavaglia, 2000).

Vector			
AR	Domain	*AR*	Domain
1.63	Social_Science	0.36	Buildings
0.90	Administration	0.36	Commerce
0.90	Pedagogy	0.36	Environment
0.80	Root_Domain	0.11	Factotum
0.36	Psychoanalysis	0.11	Psychology
0.36	Economy	0.11	Architecture
0.36	Quality	0.11	Pure_Science
0.36	Politics		

Table 2. Final Domain Vector

3.2 Obtaining the Positive Semantic Trees

In order to obtain the Positive Semantic Trees (*PST*) of the sentence, we will follow the same process described in section 3.1. In this case, the *AR* values will be replaced by the polarity value pertaining to the analyzed sense. The polarity is obtained from the SentiWordNet 3.0 resource, where each given sense from ISR-WN for WordNet version 2.0 is mapped to WordNet version 3.0. Hence, we can find each given sense from ISR-WN in SentiWordNet 3.0 and obtain the respective polarities. This new value will be called Positive Association (*PosA*). The *PosA* value is calculated using Equation 4 .

$$PosA(C,f) = \sum_{i=1}^{n} PosA(C,f_i); \qquad (4)$$

Where:

$$PosA(C,w) = \sum_{i=1}^{n} PosA(C,\mathrm{w_i}); \qquad (5)$$

Where C is a concept; f is a sentence or set of words (w); f_i is a *i-th* word of the sentence f; $PosA(C, w_i)$ is the positive value of the sense (w_i) related to C.

The *PosA* is used to measure the positive value associated to the leaves of the Semantic Trees where Concepts are placed. Subsequently, using the same structure of RST we create new Semantic Trees without *AR* values. Instead, the leaves with Concepts of this new Semantic Trees will be annotated with the *PosA* value.

Later, to assign some Positive value to the parent Concepts, each parent Concept will accumulate the positive values from child Concepts. Equation 6 shows the bottom-up process.

$$PosA(PC) = \sum_{i=1}^{n} PosA(ChC); \qquad (6)$$

Where *PC* is the Parent Concept; *ChC* is the Child Concept of *PC;* and *PosA(ChC)* represents the positive value of the *ChC*.

3.3 Obtaining the Negative Semantic Trees (*NST*)

In this phase, we repeat the step described in Section 3.2, but for negative values. Table 3 shows the *PST* and *NST* obtained from the example.

Vectors Pos-Neg					
PosA	*NegA*	Domain	*PosA*	*NegA*	Domain
0.00	1.00	Social_Science	0.00	0.00	Buildings
0. 00	0.00	Administration	0.00	0.50	Commerce
0.00	0.00	Pedagogy	0.00	0.00	Environment
0.00	0.00	Root_Domain	0.375	0.375	Factotum
0.00	0.00	Psychoanalysis	0.00	0.00	Psychology
0.00	0.50	Economy	0.00	0.00	Architecture
0.375	0.375	Quality	0.00	0.00	Pure_Science
0.00	0.00	Politics			

Table 3. Final Domain Vectors Pos-Neg

As we can see, the analyzed sentence is more linked to the *Social_Science* domain and it accumulates a negative value of *1* and a positive value of *0*. This indicates that the sentence is more negative than positive.

3.4 Obtaining polarities of the sentences

In this step, we concentrate on detecting which polarity is more representative according to the Semantic Trees obtained for each resource (dimension). For that, we combine the *RST* with *PST* and *RST* with *NST*. Depending on the obtained results we classify the sentence as Positive, Negative or Neutral. Before performing this step, we have to normalize the three types of Semantic Trees (*RST, PST* and *NST*) for each dimension to work with values between *0* and*1*.

Our main goal is to assign more weight to the polarities related to the most relevant Concepts in each Relevant Semantic Tree. Equation 7 shows the steps followed in order to obtain the positive semantic value.

$$ACPosA(RST, PST) = \sum_{i=1} RST_i * PST_i ; \quad (7)$$

Where *ACPosA* is the Positive Semantic Value of the analyzed sentence obtained for one Dimension, *RST* is the Relevant Semantic Tree sorted with the format: *RST [Concept| AR]*; *PST* is the Positive Semantic Tree sorted according *RST* structure with format: *PST [Concept|PosA]*; RST_i RST_i is the *i-th AR* value of Concept *i;* PST_i PST_i is the *i-th PosA* value of the concept *i.*

In order to measure the negative semantic value (*ACNegA*), we employ a similar equation replacing *PST* with *NST.* After obtaining the semantic opinion requirements, we evaluate our approach over three of the tasks proposed in the NTCIR 8 MOAT, for the monolingual English setting.

3.5 Judging sentence opinionatedness

The "opinionated" subtask requires systems to assign the values *YES* or *NO* to each of the sentences in the document collection provided. This value is given depending on whether the sentence contains an opinion (*Y*) or it does not (*N*). In order to tackle this task, we analyze the *PST* and *NST* of all dimensions (WN, WSD, WNA, SUMO and SC). After reviewing the *PSTs* and *NSTs* if at least one Concept has assigned a value distinct from zero the result will be "YES" in other cases will be "NO".

3.6 Determining sentence relevance

In the sentence relevance judgement task, the systems have to decide whether a sentence is relevant to the given question or not (Y|N). We assume that the given question is related to each sentence per topic if it has a *RST* 50% similar (the similarity is obtained by quantity of Concept labels that match). The analyzed sentence is relevant only if the *PST* and the *NST* values of all dimensions that are taken into account contain at least a positive or a negative value.

3.7 Polarity and topic-polarity classification

The polarity judgment task requires the systems to assign a value of *"POS", "NEG"* or *"NEU"* (positive, negative or neutral) to each of the sentences in the documents provided.

Our proposal consists of accumulating the *ACPos* values and *ACNeg* values of all Dimensions and comparing them. These accumulated values will be named *ACPosD* and *ACNegD* respectively. In case *ACPosD* > *ACNegD* the assigned value is *POS*, if *ACPosD* < *ACNegD* the assigned value is *NEG*, otherwise, the assigned value is *NEU*.

4 Evaluation and analysis

In this section we concentrated on measuring the influence of each Dimension (resource) taken separately and jointly in our proposal. Also, we have compared our results with the best results obtained by the participant systems in the NTCIR 8 MOAT competition.

4.1 Influence of each dimension

In this section, we present the results of the three tasks described above using the combination of all dimensions and using each of the resources separately. Moreover, we describe the experiments we have performed. Exp1: Combining all Dimensions (WND, WNA, WN taxonomy, SUMO and SC). Exp2: Using WNA. Exp3: Using WND. Exp4: Using SC. Exp5: Using SUMO. Exp6: Using WN taxonomy. The results are presented in Table 4.

Exp	Opinion			Relevance			Polarity		
	P	R	F	P	R	F	P	R	F
1	20.6	87.8	33.3	78.8	86.8	**82.6**	39.4	34.5	36.8
2	23.8	57.2	33.6	77.9	55.8	65.1	39.7	22.2	28.5
3	22.6	69.5	**34.1**	79.4	69.2	74.0	40.3	27.5	32.7
4	20.1	88.5	33.3	78.8	87.3	**82.3**	39.7	34.9	**37.2**
5	21.3	86.5	**34.2**	79.0	85.8	**82.3**	40.6	33.7	36.8
6	21.1	87.6	**34.1**	78.8	86.6	**82.5**	40.5	34.2	**37.1**

Table 4. Results on each task. Precision (P), Recall (R) and F-Measure (F).

As we can see, the best results are obtained in Experiment 4 and 6, which use the WN taxonomy and SC to obtain the *RST, PST* and *NST*. However, the other experiments results are similar in performance level. This indicates that our proposal can be successfully applied to opinion mining tasks.

4.2 Influence of the semantic dimensions without normalizing the vector

In order to prove that the value normalization introduces noise, we performed the same experiments without normalizing vectors. In Table 5, we show in bold font the F-Measure obtained that constitutes an improvement to previous results. It is important to remark that not normalizing the vectors helps the Polarity Classification task. All the experiments presented in Table 5 improved the previous results and the SC obtained one of the best results for the Polarity and the Relevance task.

Exp	Opinion			Relevance			Polarity		
	P	R	F	P	R	F	P	R	F
7	20.1	88.5	33.3	78.8	87.3	**82.8**	39.7	34.9	**37.2**
8	23.3	61.1	**33.7**	78.4	60.0	**68.0**	42.3	25.5	**31.8**
9	21.9	77.9	**34.2**	79.2	77.3	**78.2**	39.4	30.5	**34.4**
10	20.6	87.7	**33.4**	78.9	86.7	**82.6**	44.6	38.9	**41.6**
11	20.6	85.0	33.2	78.5	83.6	81.0	44.6	37.7	**40.9**
12	20.5	85.5	33.1	78.7	84.4	81.5	43.7	37.0	**40.1**

Table 5. Results without normalized vectors. Precision (P), Recall (R) and F-Measure (F).

4.3 Comparison with other proposals

In this section, we present a comparison between our proposal and the best participating systems in NTCIR 8 MOAT. In the sentence opinionatedness judgement task , the only systems that obtained better results compared to our proposal are UNINE (Zubaryeva and Savoy, 2010) and NECLC systems. These systems obtained F-measure values of 40.1% and 36.52% respectively. These results are not so far from our results, with the simple difference of 5.9% and 2.32% respectively.

In comparison to our proposal, UNINE is based on selecting terms that clearly belong to one type of polarity compared to the others and the value types of polarities are defined summing the count number of terms that tend to be overused in positive, negative and neutral opinionated sentences possibilities (Zubaryeva and Savoy, 2010). The opinionated score is the sum of *Positive Scores* and *Negative Scores* for each selected term. The score of non-opinionated sentences is computed as a sum of *Objectivity Score* for each selected term, divided by the number of words in the sentence. Our proposal neither takes into account the detection of relevant terms, nor the objective scores. UNINE also obtained better results than us in the Polarity task; we think that the combination of this proposal with ours could obtain better results. Taking into account that both proposals use Features Extraction we could combine not only Lexical Features but also Semantic Features.

In the Polarity task we could obtain similar results to the first run of UNINE system around 37% of F-measure but with results some distance of the best system that obtained a 51.03% of F-measure. For the relevance task, our proposal obtained a difference of 3.22% as far as F-measure is concerned from the best result of all runs submitted by the National Taiwan University (NTU). So, our proposal could be located around the first places among the three tasks mentioned.

5 Conclusion and further works

In this paper our research was focused on solving a recent problem stemmed from the availability of large volumes of heterogeneous data which provides different kind of information. We have conducted an analysis of how the scientific community confronts the tasks related to Opinion Analysis. One of the most used approaches is to apply Features Extraction and based on this idea, our proposal is to apply Semantic Features Extraction based on Relevant Semantic Trees. With our proposal we are able to associate the polarities presented on the sentences with Concept Semantic Trees. Thus, the Semantic Trees allow the classification of sentences according to their opinionatedness, relevance and polarity, according to MOAT competition. The obtained results were compared with the best results obtained on this competition achieving values very close to the best systems. Several experiments were conducted applying vector normalization and without normalization to know which semantic dimension performed better.

After a comparative analysis with the systems which results were not improved, we propose as further work to include the lexical features extraction in our proposal. We have planned to use Latent Semantic Analysis and other techniques to do this work.

Acknowledgements

This paper has been supported partially by Ministerio de Ciencia e Innovación - Spanish Government (grant no. TIN2009-13391-C04-01), and Conselleria d'Educación - Generalitat Valenciana (grant no. PROMETEO/2009/119, ACOMP/2010/288 and ACOMP/2011/001).

References

Alexandra Balahur, Ester Boldrini, Andrés Montoyo and Patricio Martínez-Barco. 2010. The OpAL System at NTCIR 8 MOAT. *In Proceedings of NTCIR-8 Workshop Meeting*: 241-245. Tokyo, Japan.

Alexandra Balahur and Andrés Montoyo. 2009. A Semantic Relatedness Approach to Classifying Opinion from Web Reviews. *Procesamiento del Lenguaje Natural,* 42:47-54.

Andrea Esuli and Fabrizio Sebastiani. 2006. SentiWordNet: A Publicly Available Lexical Resource for Opinion Mining. *In Fifth international conference on Languaje Resources and Evaluation* 417-422.

Amal Zouaq, Michel Gagnon and Benoit Ozell. 2009. A SUMO-based Semantic Analysis for Knowledge Extraction. *In Proceedings of the 4th Language & Technology Conference.* Poznań, Poland.

Bernardo Magnini and Gabriela Cavaglia. 2000. Integrating Subject Field Codes into WordNet. *In Proceedings of Third International Conference on Language Resources and Evaluation (LREC-2000)*: 1413--1418.

Bernardo Magnini, Carlo Strapparava, Giovanni Pezzulo and Alfio Gliozzo. 2002. Comparing Ontology-Based and Corpus-Based Domain Annotations in WordNet. *In Proceedings of the First International WordNet Conference*: 21-25 Mysore, India.

Bernardo Magnini, Carlo Strapparava, Giovanni Pezzulo and Alfio Gliozzo. 2008. Using Domain Information for Word Sense Disambiguation. *In Proceedings of the First International Conference on Emerging Trends in Engineering and Technology (icetet 2008)*: 1187-1191. Nagpur, India.

Christiane Fellbaum. 1998. WordNet. An Electronic Lexical Database. *The MIT Press.*

Guo-Hau Lai, Jyun-Wei Huang, Chia-Pei Gao and Richard Tzong-Han Tsai. 2010. Enhance Japanese Opinionated Sentence Identification using Linguistic Features: Experiences of the IISR Group at NTCIR-8 MOAT Task. *In Proceedings of NTCIR-8 Workshop Meeting*: 272-275. Tokyo, Japan.

Hatzivassiloglou, Vasileios and Janyce Wiebe. 2000. Effects of Adjective Orientation and Gradability on Sentence Subjectivity. *In International Conference on Computational Linguistics (COLING-2000).*

Ian Niles. 2001. Mapping WordNet to the SUMO Ontology. *Teknowledge Corporation.*

Janyce Wiebe, Theresa Wilson and Claire Cardie. 2005. Annotating Expressions of Opinions and Emotions in Language. *In Kluwer Academic Publishers*: Netherlands.

Luis Villarejo, Lluís Márquez and German Rigau. 2005. Exploring the construction of semantic class classiers for WSD. *In Sociedad Española para el Procesamiento del Lenguaje Natural,* 35: 195-202.

Olena Zubaryeva and Jacques Savoy. 2010. Opinion Detection by Combining Machine Learning & Linguistic Tools *In Proceedings of NTCIR-8 Workshop Meeting*: 221-227. Tokyo, Japan.

Paul Ekman. 1999. Handbook of Cognition and Emotion. *Handbook of Cognition and Emotion*: John Wiley & Sons, Ltd.

Rubén Izquierdo, Armando Suárez and German Rigau. 2007. A Proposal of Automatic Selection of Coarse-grained Semantic Classes for WSD. *Procesamiento del Lenguaje Natural,* 39:189-196.

Rudi L. Cilibrasi and Paul M.B. Vitányi. 2007. The Google Similarity Distance. *IEEE Transactions On Knowledge And Data Engineering,* 19(3).

Soo-Min Kim and Eduard Hovy. 2006. Extracting Opinions, Opinion Holders, and Topics Expressed in Online News Media Text. *In In Proceedings of workshop on sentiment and subjectivity in text at proceedings of the 21st international conference on computational linguistics/the 44th annual meeting of the association for computational linguistics (COLING/ACL 2006)*: 1-8. Sydney, Australia.

Soo-Min Kim and Eduard Hovy. 2005. Identifying Opinion Holders for Question Answering in Opinion Texts. *In Proceedings of AAAI-05 Workshop on Question Answering in Restricted Domains.*

Sonia Vázquez, Andrés Montoyo and German Rigau. 2004. Using Relevant Domains Resource for Word Sense Disambiguation. *In IC-AI'04. Proceedings of the International Conference on Artificial Intelligence*: Ed: CSREA Press. Las Vegas, E.E.U.U.

Yoan Gutiérrez, Antonio Fernández, Andrés Montoyo and Sonia Vázquez. 2010a. UMCC-DLSI: Integrative resource for disambiguation task. *In Proceedings of the 5th International Workshop on Semantic Evaluation*: 427-432. Uppsala, Sweden.

Yoan Gutiérrez, Antonio Fernández, Andrés Montoyo and Sonia Vázquez. 2010b. Integration of semantic resources based on WordNet. *In XXVI Congreso de la Sociedad Española para el Procesamiento del Lenguaje Natural,* 45: 161-168. Universidad Politécnica de Valencia, Valencia, Spain.

On the Difficulty of Clustering Microblog Texts for Online Reputation Management

Fernando Perez-Tellez
SMRG, Institute of Technology
Tallaght Dublin, Ireland
fernandopt@gmail.com

David Pinto
FCC, Benemérita Universidad
Autónoma de Puebla, Mexico
dpinto@cs.buap.mx

John Cardiff
SMRG, Institute of Technology
Tallaght Dublin, Ireland
John.Cardiff@ittdublin.ie

Paolo Rosso
NLE Lab. -ELiRF, Universidad
Politécnica de Valencia, Spain
prosso@dsic.upv.es

Abstract

In recent years microblogs have taken on an important role in the marketing sphere, in which they have been used for sharing opinions and/or experiences about a product or service. Companies and researchers have become interested in analysing the content generated over the most popular of these, the Twitter platform, to harvest information critical for their online reputation management (ORM). Critical to this task is the efficient and accurate identification of tweets which refer to a company distinguishing them from those which do not. The aim of this work is to present and compare two different approaches to achieve this. The obtained results are promising while at the same time highlighting the difficulty of this task.

1 Introduction

Twitter[1] - a microblog of the Web 2.0 genre that allows users to publish brief message updates - has become an important channel through which users can share their experiences or opinions about a product, service or company. In general, companies have taken advantage of this medium for developing marketing strategies.

Online reputation management - the monitoring of media and the detection and analysis of opinions about an entity - is becoming an important area of research as companies need up to the minute information on what is being send on the WWW about them and their products. Being unaware of negative comments regarding a company may affect its reputation and misguide consumers into not buying particular products. On the other hand companies may identify user feedback and use it in order to provide better products and services which could make them more competitive.

A first step in this process is the automatic collection of tweets relating to a company. In this paper we present an approach to the categorisation of tweets which contain a company name, into two clusters corresponding to those which refer to the company and those which do not. Clearly this is not as straightforward as matching keywords due to the potential for ambiguity. Providing a solution to this problem will allow companies to access to the immediate user reaction to their products or services, and thereby manage their reputations more effectively (Milstein et al., 2008).

The rest of this paper is organised as follows. Section 2 describes the problem and the related work. Section 3 presents the data set used in the experiments. Section 4 explains the approaches used in this research work. Section 5 shows the experiments, the obtained results and a discussion of them. Finally, Section 6 presents the conclusions.

2 Problem Description and Related Work

We are interested in discriminating between Twitter entries that correspond to a company from those that do not, in particular where the company name also has a separate meaning in the English language (e.g. *delta*, *palm*, *ford*, *borders*). In this research work, we regard a company name as ambiguous if the word/s that comprise its name can be used in

[1] http://twitter.com

Proceedings of the 2nd Workshop on Computational Approaches to Subjectivity and Sentiment Analysis, ACL-HLT 2011, pages 146–152,
24 June, 2011, Portland, Oregon, USA

different contexts. An example can be seen in Table 1 where the word *borders* is used in the context of a company (row 1 & 3) and as the boundary of a country (row 2). We adapt a clustering approach to solving this problem although the size of tweets presents a considerable challenge. Moreover the small vocabulary size in conjunction with the writing style makes the task more difficult. Tweets are written in an informal style, and may also contain misspellings or be grammatically incorrect. In order to improve the representation of the tweets we have proposed two approaches based on an expansion procedure (enriching semantic similarity hidden behind the lexical structure). In this research

Table 1: Examples of "True" and "False" tweets that contains the *Borders* word

TRUE	excessively tracking the book i ordered from borders.com. kfjgjdfkgjfd.
FALSE	With a severe shortage of manpower, existing threat to our borders, does it make any sense to send troops to Afghanistan? @centerofright
TRUE	33% Off Borders Coupon : http://wp.me/pKHuj-qj

work we demonstrate that a term expansion methodology, as presented in this paper, can improve the representation of the microblogs from a clustering perspective, and as a consequence the performance of the clustering task. In addition, we test the hypothesis that specific company names - names that can not be found in a dictionary - such as *Lennar* or *Warner* may be more easily identified than generic company names such as *Borders*, *Palm* or *Delta*, because of the ambiguity of the latter.

We describe briefly here the work related to the problem of clustering short texts related to companies. In particular those works in the field of categorisation of tweets and clustering of short texts.

In (Sankaranarayanan et al., 2009) an approach is presented for binary classification of tweets (class "breaking news" or other). The class "breaking news" is then clustered in order to find the most similar news tweets, and finally a location of the news for each cluster is provided. Tweets are considered short texts as mentioned in (Sriram et al., 2010) where a proposal for classifying tweets is presented. This work addressed the problem by using a small set of domain-specific features extracted from the author's profile and the tweet text itself. They claim to effectively classify the tweet to a predefined set of generic classes such as News, Events, Opinions, Deals, and Private Messages. Therefore, it is important to analyse some techniques for categorisation of short texts.

The main body of relevant related research emanates from the WePS-3 evaluation campaign in the task 2 called Online Reputation Management (Amigó et al., 2010). In (García-Cumbreras et al., 2010) the authors based their approach on recognising named entities, extracting external information and predefining rules. They use the well-known Name Entity Recogniser (NER) included in GATE[2] for recognising all the entities in their Tweets. They also use the web page of the organisation, Wikipedia and DBpedia[3]. Predefined rules are then applied to determine if a Twitter entry belongs to an organisation or not.

The work presented in (Kalmar, 2010) uses data from the company website. This data is used to create a initial model from which to bootstrap a model from the Tweets, the keywords and description are weighted. The features used are the co-occurring words in each tweet and the relevance of them was calculated according to the Pointwise Mutual Information value. Although it seems to be an interesting approach the results shown are disappointing.

In (Yerva et al., 2010) a support vector machine (SVM) classifier is used with the profiles built a priori. Profiles are constructed for each company which are sets of keywords that are related to the company or sets of keywords unrelated to the company. This system uses external resources such as Wordnet[4], meta-data from the company web page, GoogleSet[5] and user feedback. The research presented in (Yoshida et al., 2010) propose that organisation names can be classified as "organization-line names" or "general-word-like names". The authors have observed that the fact that ratio of positive or negative (if the tweet is related to the organisation or not) has a strong correlation with the types of organisation names i.e., "organization-like names" have high percentages of tweets related to the company

[2]http://gate.ac.uk/

[3]http://dbpedia.org/

[4]http://wordnet.princeton.edu/

[5]http://labs.google.com/sets

and when compared to "general-word-like names" Another approach is described in (Tsagkias and Balog, 2010), in which the authors trained the well-known J48 decision tree classifier using as features the company name, content value such as the presence of URLs, hashtags or is-part-of-a-conversation, content quality such as ratio of punctuation and capital characters and organisational context. This approach is quite interesting but they require a training set.

3 Dataset Description

We base our experiments on the corpus provided for task two of the WePS-3 evaluation campaign[6], related to Online Reputation Management for organisations, or specifically on the problem of organisation (company) name ambiguity.

Table 2: Statistics of company tweets used in the experiments.

Company	T/F	◇	△	○	▽
Bestbuy	24/74	704	14.70	6	22
Borders	25/69	665	12.29	2	20
Delta	39/57	584	12.27	5	20
Ford	62/35	700	12.79	2	22
Leapfrog	70/26	1262	13.14	3	20
Opera	25/73	671	12.32	1	25
Overstock	70/24	613	13.84	3	22
Palm	28/71	762	14.20	4	22
Southwest	39/60	665	13.61	4	21
Sprint	56/38	624	12.10	3	22
Armani	312/103	2325	13.64	2	23
Barclays	286/133	2217	14.10	2	24
Bayer	228/143	2105	13.63	3	22
Blockbuster	306/131	5595	11.75	3	21
Cadillac	271/156	2449	12.19	2	24
Harpers	142/295	2356	12.20	2	23
Lennar	74/25	438	13.37	5	21
Mandalay	322/113	2085	12.42	2	22
Mgm	177/254	1977	13.63	2	24
Warner	23/76	596	13.15	4	20

T/F - No. of true/false Tweets,
◇ - Vocabulary size,
△ - Average words in Tweets,
○ - Minimum number of words in Tweets,
▽ - Maximum number of words in Tweets.

The corpus was obtained from the *trial* and *training* data sets of this evaluation campaign. The *trial* corpus of task 2 contains entries for 17 (English) and 6 (Spanish) organisations; whereas the *training* data set contains 52 (English) organisations. The corpus was labelled by five annotators: the $true$ label means that the tweet is associated to a company, whereas the $false$ one means that the tweet is not related to any company, and the $unknown$ label is used where the annotators were unable to make a decision.

In order to gauge the problem and to establish a baseline for the potential of a clustering approach. We decided to cluster the data sets (trial and training) using the K-means algorithm (MacQueen, 1967) with k equal to three in order to have a clear reference and detect possible drawbacks that the collections may contain. The results were evaluated using the F-measure (van Rijsbergen, 1979) and gave values of 0.52 and 0.53 for the *trial* and *training* data sets respectively. This was expected, as clustering approaches typically work best with long documents and balanced groups (Perez-Tellez et al., 2009). Using this baseline, we then considered how a clustering approach could be improved by applying text enrichment methods. In order to compare only the effect of the enrichment however, we have modified the data set by including only those tweets written in English and for which a $true$ or $false$ label has been established, i.e., in the experiments carried out we do not consider the $unknown$ label.

Furthermore, the subset used in the experiments includes only those 20 companies with a sufficient number of positive and negative samples (true/false), i.e., at least 20 items must be in each category. Finally, each selected company must contain at least 90 labeled tweets, which was the minimum number of tweets associated with a company found in the collection. In Table 2 we present a detailed description of the corpus features such as the number of $true$ and $false$ tweets, the average length of the tweets (average number of words),the minimum and maximum number of words contained in tweets. In the following section we present and compare the different approaches we propose for dealing with this problem.

4 Clustering Company Tweets

The purpose of this research work is to cluster tweets that contain a possible company entity into two

[6]WePS3: searching information about entities in the Web, http://nlp.uned.es/weps/, February 2010

groups, those that refer to the company and those that refer to a different topic. We approach this problem by introducing and, thereafter, evaluating two different methodologies that use term expansion. The term expansion of a set of documents is a process for enriching the semantic similarity hidden behind the lexical structure. Although the idea has been previously studied in literature (Qiu and Frei, 1993; Grefenstette, 1994; Banerjee and Pedersen, 2002; Pinto et al., 2010) we are not aware of any work in which has applied it to microblog texts. In this paper, we evaluate the performance of two different approaches for term enriching in the task of clustering company tweets.

In order to establish the difficulty of clustering company tweets, we split the 20 companies group into two groups that we hypothetically considered easier and harder to be clustered. The first group is composed of 10 companies with generic names, i.e., names that can be ambiguous (i.e., they have another common meaning and appear in a dictionary). The second group contains specific names which are considered to be less ambiguous (words that can be used in limited number of contexts or words that do not appear in a dictionary). We expect the latter group will be easier to be categorised than the former one. In Table 3 we see the distribution of the two groups. We have selected the K-means clustering method (MacQueen, 1967) for the experiments carried out in this paper. The reason is that it is a well-known method, it produces acceptable results and our approaches may be compared with future implementations. The clustering algorithm (including the representation and matrix calculation) is applied after we have improved the representation of tweets in order to show the improvement gained by applying the enriching process.

Table 3: Types of Company names

Generic Company Names			
BestBuy	Borders	Delta	Ford
Leapfrog	Opera	Overstock	Palm
Southwest	Sprint		
Specific Company Names			
Armani	Barclays	Bayer	Blockbuster
Cadillac	Harpers	Mandalay	Mgm
Lennar	Warner		

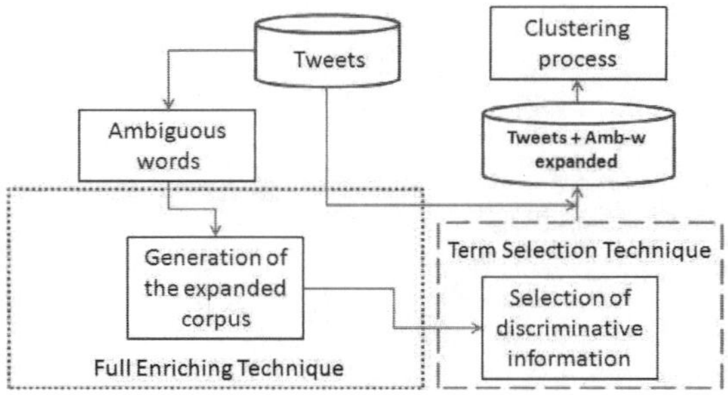

Figure 1: Full Term Expansion Methodology

4.1 Full Term Expansion Methodology (TEM-Full)

In this methodology we expand only the ambiguous word (the company name) with all the words that co-occur alongside it, without restrictions for the level of co-occurrence. Our hypothesis states that the ambiguous words may bring important information from the identification of co-occurrence-relations to the next step of filtering relevant terms. It is important to mention that we have used the Term Selection technique in order to select the most discriminative terms for the categories. The process is shown in Figure 1. Note that this expansion process does not use an external resource. We believe that due to the low term frequency and the shortness of the data, it is better to include all the information that co-occurs in the corpus of a company and provide more information to the enriching process.

The Term Selection Technique helps us to identify the best features for the clustering process. However, it is also useful to reduce the computing time of the clustering algorithms.

4.2 Full Tem Expansion Methodology with a Text Formaliser (TEM-Full+F)

In this approach, we test the hypothesis that we can improve the cluster quality by increasing the level of formality in the document text. Due to the length restriction of 140 characters users tend to write comments using abbreviations. We have used an abbreviation dictionary[7] that contains 5,173 abbreviations commonly used in microblogs, tweets and short messages. After the formalisation step, the expansion is performed but it is only applied to the ambiguous word (the company name) and words

[7] http://noslang.com/dictionary

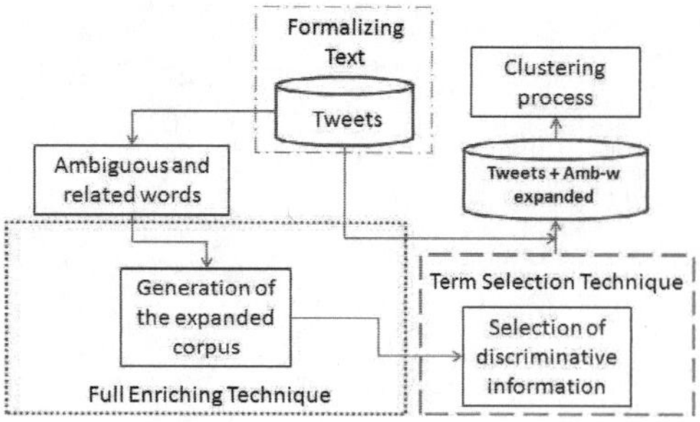

Figure 2: Full Term Expansion Methodology with a Text Formaliser (TEM-Full+F)

which highly co-occur with it. These words were selected as they appear in frequently with the ambiguous word in positive tweets (i.e., those related to the companies). We consider that this kind of word may help us take the correct decision during the clustering process because they are highly related with the company tweets. The words selected to be expanded were closely related to the company such as crew, jet, flight, airlines, airplane for *Delta* company name. In the case of the *Opera* company name the words expanded were software, technology, developers, interface, web, browser. The number of words per company name were between five and ten, showing that even a small number of words that co-occur highly may help in the enriching process. We have used the Term Selection Technique as described in 4.1 and no external resource. The process is shown in Figure 2.

5 Experimental Results

In this section we present the results obtain by the related approaches and also the results obtained by our methodologies proposed.

5.1 Related Approaches

Although the results are not directly comparable with our approaches due to the slightly different dataset used in the experiments (see Section 3), we would like to provide a clear description of the different approaches with the objective of highlight the strengths of the related approaches developed for this purpose.

In Table 4, the best results (F-measure related classes) reported by the approaches presented to the task two of the WePS-3 evaluation campaign (Amigó et al., 2010). It is important to mention that all these systems used the whole collection even if the companies subsets where very imbalanced. In our case, we are interested in proposing approaches that can deal with two different kind of company names such as "generic" and "specific" rather than one methodology for both.

Table 4: Related approaches (F-measure related)

Approaches				
L	S	I	U	K
0.74	0.36	0.51	0.36	0.47

L = LSIR-EPFL, S = SINAI, I = ITC-UT, U = UVA, K = KALMAR

In Table 4 the LSIR-EPFL system (Yerva et al., 2010) showed very good performance even when the subsets are very imbalanced. The SINAI system (García-Cumbreras et al., 2010) took advantage of the entity recognition process and they report that named entities contained in the microblog documents seem to be appropriate for certain company names. ITC-UT (Yoshida et al., 2010) incorporated a classifier and made use of Named Entity Recognition and Part-of-Speech tagger is also good in their performance but as the authors in (Amigó et al., 2010) have mentioned "it is difficult to know what aspect lead the system to get ahead other systems" as each takes advantage of different aspects available such as external resources or tools. UVA (Tsagkias and Balog, 2010) is an interesting contribution but the only problem is training data will not always be available for some domains. Finally, the KALMAR system (Kalmar, 2010) seems to achieve good performance when applied to well-balanced collections. In contrast to these approaches, we would like to emphasize that our approaches are predominantly based on the information to be clustered.

5.2 Results of Our Experiments

In order to present the performance of the different proposed approaches, we have calculated a baseline based on clustering, with K-means, and with no enriching procedure. The obtained results using the two methodologies are compared in Table 5. We have shown in bold text the cases in which the result equalled or improved upon the baseline. We have compared the methodologies presented with the two subsets (generic and specific company names subsets) described previously.

Table 5: A comparison of each methodology with respect to one baseline using the F-measure.

Company	Methodologies		
	TEM-Full	TEM-Full+F	B
Generic Company Names Subset			
Bestbuy	**0.74**	**0.75**	0.62
Borders	**0.73**	**0.72**	0.60
Delta	**0.71**	**0.70**	0.61
Ford	**0.67**	**0.65**	0.64
Leapfrog	**0.71**	0.63	0.63
Opera	**0.73**	**0.74**	0.70
Overstock	**0.66**	**0.72**	0.58
Palm	**0.72**	**0.70**	0.62
Southwest	**0.67**	**0.72**	0.64
Sprint	**0.67**	**0.65**	0.64
Average	0.70	0.69	0.62
Specific Company Names Subset			
Armani	**0.73**	**0.70**	0.62
Barclays	**0.72**	**0.72**	0.55
Bayer	**0.71**	**0.70**	0.63
Blockbuster	**0.71**	**0.71**	0.66
Cadillac	**0.69**	**0.69**	0.61
Harpers	**0.68**	**0.68**	0.63
Mandalay	**0.74**	**0.84**	0.64
Mgm	0.54	**0.75**	0.69
Lennar	0.72	**0.97**	0.96
Warner	0.54	0.67	0.67
Average	0.67	0.74	0.66
OA	0.68	0.72	0.64

B - Baseline, OA - Overall Average

We consider that there still some limitations on obtaining improved results due to the particular writing style of tweets. The corpus exhibits a poor grammatical structure and many out-of-vocabulary words, a fact that makes the task of clustering tweets very difficult. There is, however, a clear improvement in most cases in comparison with the baseline. This indicates that the enriching procedure yields benefits for the clustering process.

The TEM-Full methodology has demonstrated good performance with the corpus of generic company names with 0.70 average (F-measure value) 8 points over the average baseline. In this case, we have expanded only the ambiguous word (the name of the company), whereas the TEM-Full+F methodologies performed well (0.74 F-measure) with the corpus of specific company names. We have observed that, regardless of whether or not we are using an external resource in TEM-Full and TEM-Full+F approaches, we may improve the representation of company tweets for the clustering task. It is important to mention that the good results presented in companies such as *Bestbuy* or *Lennar* were obtained because the low overlapping vocabulary between the two categories (positive and negative) and, therefore, the clustering process could find well-delimited groups. We also would like to note that sometimes the methodologies have produced only minor performance improvement. This we believe is largely due to the length of the tweets, as it has been demonstrated in other experiments that better results can bc achieved with longer documents (Perez-Tellez et al., 2009; Pinto et al., 2010).

The best result has been achieved with the TEM-Full+F methodology which achieved an overall average F-measure value 0.72, it is 8 points more than the overall average of the baseline. This methodology has not disimproved on the baseline in any instance and it produces good results in most cases. Although the term expansion procedure has been shown to be effective for improving the task of clustering company tweets, we believe that there is still room for improving the obtained F-Measure values by detecting and filtering stronger relations that may help in the identification of the positive company tweets. This fact may lead us to consider that regardless of the resource used (internal or external), the clustering company tweets is a very difficult task.

6 Conclusions

Clustering short text corpora is a difficult task. Since tweets are by definition short texts (having a maximum of 140 characters), the clustering of tweets is also a challenging problem as stronger results typically achieved with longer text documents. Furthermore, due to the nature of writing style of these kinds of texts - typically they exhibits an informal writing style, with poor grammatical structure and many out of vocabulary words - this kind of data typically causes most clustering methods to obtain poor performance.

The main contribution of this paper has been to propose and compare two different approaches for representing tweets on the basis term expansion and their impact on the problem of clustering company tweets. In particular, we introduced two methodologies for enriching term representation of tweets. We expected that these different representations would lead classical clustering methods, such as K-means, to obtain a better performance than when clustering the same data set and the enriching methodology is not applied.

We consider that TEM-Full performed well on the former data set and, another methodology obtained the best results on the latter data set TEM-Full+F. However, the TEM-Full+F methodology appears suitable for both kinds of corpora, and does not require any external resource. TEM-Full and TEM-Full+F are completely unsupervised approaches which construct a thesaurus from the same data set to be clustered and, thereafter, uses this resource for enriching the terms. On the basis of the results presented, we can say that using this particular data, the unsupervised methodology TEM-Full+F has shown improved results.

This paper has reported on our efforts to apply clustering and term enrichment to the important problem of company identification in microblogs. We expect to do further work in proposing highly scalable methods that may be able to deal with the huge amounts of information published every day in Twitter.

Acknowledgments

This work was carried out in the framework of the MICINN Text-Enterprise TIN2009-13391-C04-03 research project and the Microcluster VLC/Campus (International Campus of Excellence) on Multimodal Intelligent Systems, PROMEP #103.5/09/4213 and CONACYT #106625, as well as a grant provided by the Mexican Council of Science and Technology (CONACYT).

References

E. Amigó, J. Artiles, J. Gonzalo, D. Spina, B. Liu, and A. Corujo. 2010. WePS-3 evaluation campaign: Overview of the online reputation management task. In *CLEF 2010 (Notebook Papers/LABs/Workshops)*.

S. Banerjee and T. Pedersen. 2002. An adapted lesk algorithm for word sense disambiguation using wordnet. In *Proc. of the CICLing 2002 Conf.*, pages 136–145. LNCS Springer-Verlag.

M. A. García-Cumbreras, M. García Vega, F. Martínez Santiago, and J. M. Perea-Ortega. 2010. Sinai at weps-3: Online reputation management. In *CLEF 2010 (Notebook Papers/LABs/Workshops)*.

G. Grefenstette. 1994. *Explorations in Automatic Thesaurus Discovery*. Kluwer Ac.

P. Kalmar. 2010. Bootstrapping websites for classification of organization names on twitter. In *CLEF 2010 (Notebook Papers/LABs/Workshops)*.

J.B. MacQueen. 1967. Some methods for classification and analysis of multivariate observations. In *Proc. of the 5th Berkeley Symposium on Mathematical Statistics and Probability*, pages 281–297. University of California Press.

S. Milstein, A. Chowdhury, G. Hochmuth, B. Lorica, and R. Magoulas. 2008. *Twitter and the micro-messaging revolution: Communication, connections, and immediacy-140 characters at a time*. O'Really Report.

F. Perez-Tellez, D. Pinto, Cardiff J., and P. Rosso. 2009. Improving the clustering of blogosphere with a self-term enriching technique. In *Proc. of the 12th Int. Conf. on Text, Speech and Dialogue*, pages 40–49. LNAI.

D. Pinto, P. Rosso, and H. Jimenez. 2010. A self-enriching methodology for clustering narrow domain short texts. *The Computer Journal*, doi:10.1093/comjnl/bxq069.

Y. Qiu and H.P. Frei. 1993. Concept based query expansion. In *Proc. of the 16th Annual Int. ACM SIGIR Conf. on Research and Development in Information Retrieval*, pages 160–169. ACM.

J. Sankaranarayanan, H. Samet, B.E. Teitler, M.D. Lieberman, and J. Sperling. 2009. Twitterstand: news in tweets. In *Proc. of the 17th ACM SIGSPATIAL Int. Conf. on Advances in Geographic Information Systems*, pages 42–51. ACM.

B. Sriram, D. Fuhry, E. Demir, and H. Ferhatosmanoglu. 2010. Short text classification in twitter to improve information filtering. In *The 33rd ACM SIGIR'10 Conf.*, pages 42–51. ACM.

M. Tsagkias and K. Balog. 2010. The university of amsterdam at weps3. In *CLEF 2010 (Notebook Papers/LABs/Workshops)*.

C.J. van Rijsbergen. 1979. *Information Retrieval*. Butterworths, London.

S. R. Yerva, Z. Miklós, and K. Aberer. 2010. It was easy, when apples and blackberries were only fruits. In *CLEF 2010 (Notebook Papers/LABs/Workshops)*.

M. Yoshida, S. Matsushima, S. Ono, I. Sato, and H. Nakagawa. 2010. Itc-ut: Tweet categorization by query categorization for on-line reputation management. In *CLEF (Notebook Papers/LABs/Workshops)*.

EMOCause: An Easy-adaptable Approach to Emotion Cause Contexts

Irene Russo **Tommaso Caselli** **Francesco Rubino**
ILC "A.Zampolli" – CNR
Via G. Moruzzi, 1- 56124 Pisa
{irene.russo}{tommaso.caselli}{francesco.rubino}@ilc.cnr.it
Ester Boldrini **Patricio Martínez-Barco**
DSLI – University of Alicante
Ap. de Correos, 99 – 03080 Alicante
{eboldrini}{patricio}@dlsi.ua.es

Abstract

In this paper we present a method to automatically identify linguistic contexts which contain possible causes of emotions or emotional states from Italian newspaper articles (La Repubblica Corpus). Our methodology is based on the interplay between relevant linguistic patterns and an incremental repository of common sense knowledge on emotional states and emotion eliciting situations. Our approach has been evaluated with respect to manually annotated data. The results obtained so far are satisfying and support the validity of the methodology proposed.

1 Introduction

As it has been demonstrated in Balahur et al. (2010), mining the web to discriminate between objective and subjective content and extract the relevant opinions about a specific target is today a crucial as well as a challenging task due to the growing amount of available information.
Opinions are just a part of the subjective content, which is expressed in texts. Emotions and emotional states are a further set of subjective data. Natural Language is commonly used to express emotions, attribute them and, most importantly, to indicate their cause(s).
Due to the importance of linking the emotion to its cause, a recent subtask of Sentiment Analysis (SA) consists in the detection of the *emotion cause event* (ECE, Lee et al., 2010; Chen et al., 2010) and focuses on the identification of the phrase (if present, as in 1 in bold) mentioning the event that is related to the emotional state (in italics):

(1) Non poteva mancare un accenno alla ***strage* di Bologna**, che costringe l' animo *a infinita vergogna.*
[*There was a mention of Bologna massacre,*
that forces us to feel ashamed.]

This kind of information is extremely interesting, since it can provide pragmatic knowledge about content words and their emotional/subjective polarity and consequently it can be employed for building up useful applications with practical purposes.
The paper focuses on the development of a method for the identification of Italian sentences which contain an emotion cause phrase. Our approach is based on the interplay between linguistic patterns which allow the retrieval of emotion – emotion cause phrase couples and on the exploitation of an associated incremental repository of commonsense knowledge about events which elicit emotions or emotional states. The methodology is only partially language dependent and this approach can be easily extended to other languages such as Spanish. The repository is one of the main results of this work. It allows the discovery of pragmatic knowledge associated with various content

Proceedings of the 2nd Workshop on Computational Approaches to Subjectivity and Sentiment Analysis, ACL-HLT 2011, pages 153–160,
24 June, 2011, Portland, Oregon, USA ©2011 Association for Computational Linguistics

words and can assign them a polarity value which can be further exploited in more complex SA and Opinion Mining tasks.

The present paper is structured as follows. Section 2 shortly describes related work and state of the art on this task. Section 3 focuses on the description of the methodology. Section 4 describes the annotation scheme and the corpus used for the creation of the test set. Section 5 reports on the experiments and their results. Conclusions and future works are described in Section 6.

1 Related Works

Emotional states are often triggered by the perception of external events (pre-events) (Wierzbicka, 1999). In addition to this, emotional states can also be the cause of events (post-events; Chun-Ren, 2010). This suggests to consider emotional states as a pivot and structure the relations between emotional states and related events as a tri-tuple of two pairs:

(2) <<pre-events, emotional state>
<emotional state, post-event>>

This study focuses on the relationship between the first pair of the tri-tuple, namely pre-events (or ECE), and emotional states.

Previous works on this task have been carried out for Chinese (Lee et al., 2009, Chen et al., 2009, Lee et al., 2010). ECE can be explicitly expressed as arguments, events, propositions, nominalizations and nominals. Lee et al (2010) restrict the definition of ECE as the immediate cause of the emotional state which does not necessarily correspond to the actual emotional state trigger or what leads to the emotional state. Their work considers all possible linguistic realization of EKs (nouns, verbs, adjectives, prepositional phrases) and ECEs. On the basis of an annotated corpus, correlations between emotional states and ECEs have been studied in terms of different linguistic cues (e.g. position of the cause events, presence of epistemic markers...) thus identifying seven groups of cues. After that, they have been implemented in a rule-based system, which is able to identify: i.) the EK; ii.) the ECE and its position (same sentence as the EK, previous sentence with respect to the EK, following sentence with respect to the EK) and (iii.) the experiencer of the emotional state(s).The system evaluation has been performed on the annotated corpus in two phases: firstly, identifying those sentences containing a co-occurrence of EK and ECE; secondly, for those contexts where an EK and ECE co-occurs, identifying the correct ECE. Standard Precision, Recall and F-measure have been used. The baseline is computed by assuming that the first verb on the left of the EK is the ECE. The system outperforms the baseline f-score by 0.19. Although the results are not very high, the system accuracy for the detection of ECEs is reported to be three times more accurate than the baseline.

2 Emotional states between linguistic patterns and commonsense knowledge

The work of Lee et al. (2010) represents the starting point for the development of our method. We depart from their approach in the following points: i.) use of data mining techniques (clustering plus a classifier) to automatically induce the rules for sentential contexts in which an event cause phrase is expressed; and ii.) exploitation of a commonsense repository of EK - eliciting ECE noun couples for the identification of the correct ECE noun. The remaining of this section will describe in details the creation of the repository and the methodology we have adopted.

2.1 A source for commonsense knowledge of EKs and ECEs in Italian

Recently crowdsourcing techniques that exploit the functionalities of the Web 2.0 have been used in AI and NLP for reducing the efforts, costs and time for the creation of Language Resources. We have exploited the data from an on-line initiative launched in December 2010 by the Italian newspaper "*Il Corriere della Sera*" which asked its readers to describe the year 2010 with 10 words. 2,378 people participated in the data collection for a total of 22,469 words. We exploited these data to identify preliminary couples of emotional states and cause events, and thus create a repository of affective commonsense knowledge, by extracting all bigrams realized by nouns for a total of 18,240 couples *noun1-noun2*. After this operation, an adapted Italian version of WN-Affect (Strapparava – Valitutti, 2004) obtained by means of mapping procedures through MultiWordNet (MWN) has been applied to each item of the bigrams. By means of a simple query, we have extracted all bigrams where at least one item has an associated sense corresponding to the "*emotion*" category in WN-Affect. We have applied WN-Affect again to these results and extracted only those bigrams where the unclassified item corresponded to the WN-Affect label of *"emotion eliciting situation*". Finally, two lists of keywords have been obtained: one denoting EKs (133 lemmas) and the other denoting possible ECEs associated with a specific EK. The possible ECEs have been extended by exploiting MWN synsets and lexical relations of `similar-to`, `pertains-to`, `attribute` and `is-value-of`. We have filtered the set of ECE keywords by selecting only those nouns whose top nodes uniquely belongs to the following ontological classes, namely: *event*, *state*, *phenomenon*, and *act*. After this operation we have 161 nominal lemmas of possible ECEs.

2.2 Exploiting the repository for pattern induction

The preliminary version of the repository of EK - ECE couples has been exploited in order to identify relevant syntagmatic patterns for the detection of nominal ECEs. The pattern induction phase has been performed on a parsed version of a large corpus of Italian, the La Repubblica Corpus (Baroni et al., 2004).

We have implemented a pattern extractor that takes as input the couples of the seed words from the commonsense repository and extracted all combinations of EKs and its/their associated ECEs occurring in the same sentence, with a distance ranging from 1 to 8 possible intervening parts-of-speech. We have thus obtained 1,339 possible patterns. This set has been cleaned both on the basis of pattern frequencies and with manual exploration. In total 47 patterns were selected and were settled among the features for the clustering and classifier ensemble which will be exploited for the identification of the sentential contexts which may contain an emotion cause phrase (see Section 5 for details).

3 Developing a gold standard and related annotation scheme

With the purpose of evaluating the validity and reliability of our approach, a reference annotated corpus (*gold standard*) has been created.

The data collection has been performed in a semi-automatic way. In particular, we have extracted from an Italian lexicon, SIMPLE/CLIPS (Ruimy et al., 2003), all nouns marked with semantic type "*Sentiment*" to avoid biases for the evaluation and measure the coverage of the commonsense repository. The keywords have been used to query the La Repubblica Corpus and thus creating the corpus collection. We have restricted the length of the documents to be annotated to a maximum of three sentences, namely the sentence containing the emotion keyword, the one preceding it and the sentence immediately following. As a justification for this choice, we have assumed that causes are a local focus discourse phenomenon and should not be found at a long distance with respect to their effects (i.e. the emotion keyword). Finally, the corpus is composed by 6,000 text snippets for a total of 738,558 tokens.

The corresponding annotation scheme, It-EmoCause, is based on recommendations and previous experience in event annotation (*ISO-TimeML*), emotion event annotation (Lee et al., 2009, Chen et al., 2010), emotion and affective computing annotation (*EARL*[1], the HUMAINE Emotion Annotation and Representation Language, *EmotiBlog*, Boldrini et al, 2010). The scheme applies at two levels: phrase level and token level and it allows nested tags. Figure 1 reports the BNF description of the scheme.

Text consuming markables are `<emotionWord>`, `<causePhrase>` and `<causeEmotion>` tags, which are responsible, respectively, for marking the emotion keyword, the phrase expressing the cause emotion event and the token expressing the cause emotion. The values of the attribute `emotionClass` is derived from Ekman

[1] http://emotion-research.net/earl

(1972)'s classification and extended with the value UNDERSPECIFIED. This value is used as a cover term for all other types of emotion reducing disagreement and allowing further classifications on the basis of more detailed and different lists of emotions that each user can specify. Finally, the non-text consuming <EmLink> link puts in relation the cause emotion event or phrase with the emotion keyword.

```
entry ::= <emotionWord> <causePhrase>+
<ELink>*

<emotionWord>      ::=      ewid      lemma
emotionClass          appraisalDimension,
emotionHolder polarity comment
ewid ::= ew<digit>
lemma ::= CDATA
emotionClass  ::= HAPPINESS  | ANGER  |
FEAR | SURPRISE| SADNESS| DISGUST |
 UNDERSPECIFIED
appraisalDimension ::= CDATA
emotionHolder ::= CDATA
polarity ::= POSITIVE | NEGATIVE
comment ::= CDATA

<causePhrase> ::= epid <causeEmotion>+
epid ::= ep<digit>
<causeEmotion> ::= eid lemma
eid ::= e<digit>
lemma ::= CDATA

<EmLink>       ::=       elid       linkType
emotionInstanceID   causeEventInstanceID
causePhraseID comment
elid ::= el<digit>
linkType ::= POSITIVE | NEGATIVE
relatedToEmotion ::= IDREF
{relatedToEmotion ::= ewid}
causeEventID ::= IDREF
{causeEventID ::= eid}
causePhraseID  ::= IDREF
{causePhraseID ::= epid}
comment ::= CDATA
```

Figure 1 – BNF description of the EmoContext Scheme

The annotation has been performed by two expert linguists and validated by a judge. The tool used for the annotation is the Brandeis Annotation Tool (BAT)[2]. The corpus is currently under annotation and we concentrated mainly on the development of a test set. Not all markables and attributes have been annotated in this phase.

[2] http://www.batcaves.org/bat/tool/

The inter-annotator agreement (IAA)[3] on the detection of the cause event and the cause phrase are not satisfactory. To have reliable data, we have adopted a correction strategy by asking the annotators to assign a common value to disagreements. This has increased the IAA on cause emotion to K=0.45, and P&R= 0.46. A revision procedure of the annotation guidelines is necessary and annotation specifications must be developed so that the disagreement can be further reduced. Table 1 reports the figures about the annotated data so far.

It-EmoContext Corpus	
# of tokens	32,525
# of emotion keyword	356
# of cause emotion	84
# of causePhrase emotion	104
# emotion – cause emotion couples	95
# of emotion – cause phrase couples	121
Agreement on emotion keyword detection	K = 0.91 P&R = 0.91
Agreement on cause emotion detection	K = 0.34 P&R = 0.33
Agreement on causePhrase detection	K = 0.21 P&R = 0.26

Table 1 - It-EmoContext Corpus Figures

4 Emotion cause detection: experiments and results

In order to find out a set of rules for the detection of emotion cause phrase contexts, we experimented a combination of Machine Learning techniques, namely clustering and rule induction classifier algorithms. In particular, we want to exploit the output of a clustering algorithm as input to a rule learner classifier both available in the Weka platform (Witten and Frank, 2005).

The clustering algorithm is the Expectation-Maximization algorithm (EM; Hofmann and Puzicha, 1998). The EM is an unsupervised algorithm, commonly used for model-based

[3] Cohen's Kappa, Precision and Recall have been used for computing the IAA.

clustering and also applied in SA tasks (Takamura et al. 2006). In this work, we equipped the EM clustering model with syntagmatic, lexical and contextual features. The clustering algorithm has been trained on 2,000 corpus instances of the potential EK - ECE couples of the repository from the La Repubblica corpus along with a three sentence context (i.e the sentence immediately preceding and that immediately following the sentence containing the EK).

Four groups of features have been identified: the first set of features corresponds to a re-adaptation of the rules implemented in Lee et al. (2010); the second set of features implements the 47 syntagmatic patterns that specifically codify the relation between the EK and the ECE (see Section 3.2); the last two set of features are composed, respectively, by a list of intra-sentential bigrams, trigrams and fourgrams for a total of 364 different part-of-speech sequences with the EK as the first element and by a list of 6 relevant collocational patterns which express cause-effect relationship between the ECE and the EK, manually identified on the basis of the authors' intuitions. In Table 2 some examples of each group of features are reported[4].

Group of feature	Instance
Re-adaptation of Lee et al., 2010's rules	Presence of an ECE after the EK in the same sentence
Syntagmatic patterns manually identified	S E S | S E RI S | S V RI A S ...
Bigrams, trigrams and fourgrams POS sequences	S EA | S EA AP | S EA AP S
Relevant collocational patterns	S A per RD/RI S ...

Table 2 – Features for the EM cluster.

We expected two data clusters, one which includes cause emotion sentential contexts where the EK and the emotion cause co-occurs in the same sentence and another where either the emotion cause it is not present or it occurs in a different sentence (i.e. the one before the EK or in the one following it).

In order to evaluate the goodness of the cluster configuration created by the Weka version of the EM algorithm, we have run different clustering experiments. The results of each clustering analysis have been passed to the Weka PART rule-induction classifier. The best results were those which confirmed our working hypothesis, i.e. two clusters. The first cluster contains 869 items while the second 1,131 items.

The PART classifier provided a total of 49 detection rules for the detection of EK – ECE contexts. The classifier identifies the occurrence of a cause phrase in the same sentence but is not able to identify the noun which corresponds to the ECE.

The evaluation of the classifier has been performed on the 121 couples of EK – cause phrase of the test set. As we are aiming at spotting nominal causes of EKs, we have computed the baseline by considering as the correct phrase containing the ECE the first noun phrase occurring at the right of the emotion keyword and in the same sentence since this kind of ECEs tends to occur mostly at this position. In this way the baseline has an accuracy of 0.14 (only 33 NPs were correct over a total of 227 NPs at the right of the EKs). By applying the rules of the PART classifier, we have obtained an overall accuracy of 0.71, outperforming the baseline. As for the identification of the EK - cause phrase couples occurring in the same sentence, we computed standard Precision, Recall and F-measure. The results are reported in Table 3. The system tends to have a high precision (0.70) and a low recall (0.58).

	Total	Correct	P	R	F
EK – cause phrase couple	121	85	0.70	0.58	0.63

Table 3 – Evaluation of the classifier in detecting EF – cause phrase couples.

After this, we tried to identify the correct nominal ECE in the cause phrase. Provided the reduced dimensions of the annotated corpus, no training set was available to train a further

[4] The tags S, EA, RI and similar reported for the last three groups of features are abbreviations for the POS used by the parser. The complete list can be found at http://medialab.di.unipi.it/wiki/Tanl_POS_Tagset

classifier. Thus, to perform this task we decided to exploit the commonsense repository. However, the first version of the repository is too small to obtain any relevant results. We enlarged it by applying two set of features (the syntagmatic patterns manually identified and the collocational patterns used for the clustering analysis).

4.1 Incrementing the repository and discovering EK – ECE couples

Our hypothesis is that the identification of the ECE(s) in context could be performed by looking for a plausible set of nouns which are associated with a specific EK and assumed to be its cause. This type of information is exactly the one contained in the repository described in Section 3.1.

In order to work with a larger data set of ECE entries per emotion keyword, we have applied the syntagmatic patterns manually identified and the collocational patterns on two corpora: i.) La Repubblica and ii.) ItWaC[5] (Baroni et al., 2009). For each EK - ECE couple identified we have kept track of the co-occurrence frequencies and computed the Mutual Information (MI). Frequency and MI are extremely relevant because they provide a reliability threshold for each couple of EK and ECE. In Table 4 we report some co-occurrences of the EK *"ansia"* [anxiety] and ECEs.

ECE	Frequency (La Repubblica Corpus)	Mutual Information
crisi [crisis]	119	5,514
angoscia [anguish]	80	8.762
guerra [war]	185	6.609
pianificazione [planning]	1	4.117
ricostruzione [reconstruction]	19	5.630

Table 4- ECEs co-occurrences with EK *"ansia"*[anxiety].

Each ECE has been associated to a probability measure of eventivity derived from MWN top ontological classes, obtained from the ratio between 1 and the sum of all top ontological classes associated to the ECE lemma. The top nodes *"event"*, *"state"*, *"phenomenon"*, and *"act"* have been considered as a unique top class by applying the TimeML definition of event[6]. This measure is useful in case more than one ECEs is occurring in the context in analysis as a disambiguation strategy. In fact, if more than one ECEs is present, that with the higher frequency, MI and eventivity score should be preferred.

Furthermore, to make the repository more effective and also to associate an emotional polarity to the ECEs (i.e. whether they have positive, negative or neutral values) we have further extended the set of information by exploiting WN-Affect 1.1. In particular we have associated each EK to its emotional category (e.g. despondency, resentment, joy) and its emotional superclass (e.g. positive-emotion, negative-emotion, ambiguous-emotion).

This extended version of the repository has been applied to identify the correct ECE noun for the 95 couples of EK – ECE in the test set. We have splitted the whole set of EK – ECE couples into two subgroups: i.) EK – ECE couples occurring in the same sentence (82/95); and ii.) EK – ECE couples occurring in different sentences (13/95). By applying the repository to the first group, we were able to correctly identify 50% (41/82) of the ECE nouns for each specific EK when occurring in the same sentence. Moreover, we applied the repository also to the EK – ECE couples of the second group: a rough 30.76% (4/13) of the ECE occurring in sentences other that the one containing the EK can be correctly retrieved without increasing the number of false positives. This is possible thanks to the probability score computed by means of MWN top ontological classes, even if the number of annotated examples is too small to justify strong conclusions.

5 http://wacky.sslmit.unibo.it

6 To clarify, the ECE *"guerra"* [war] has four senses in MWN. Three of them belong to the top ontological class of *"event"* and one to *"state"*. This possible ECE has 1 top ontological node, and its eventivity mesure is 1.

5 Conclusions and future works

In this paper we describe a methodology based on the interplay between relevant linguistic patterns and an incremental repository of common sense knowledge of EK – ECE couples, which can be integrated into more complex systems for SA and Opinion Mining.

The experimental results show that clustering techniques (EM clustering model) and a rule learner classifier (the PART classifier) can be efficiently combined to select and induce relevant linguistic patterns for the discovery of EK – ECE couples in the same sentence. The information thus collected has been organized into the repository of commonsense knowledge about emotions and their possible causes. The repository has been extended by using corpora of varying dimensions (la Repubblica and ItWaC) and effectively used to identify ECEs of specific emotion keywords.

One interesting aspect of this approach is represented by the reduced manual effort both for the identification of linguistic patterns for the extraction of reliable information and for the maintenance and extension of specific language resources which can be applied also to domains other than SA. In addition to this, the method can be extended and applied to identify ECE realized by other POS, such as verbs and adjectives.

As future works, we aim to extend the repository by extracting data from the Web and connecting it to SentiWordNet and WN-Affect. In particular, the connection to the existing language resources could be used to spot possible misclassifications and polarity values.

Acknowledgments

The authors want to thank the RSC Media Group. This work has been partially founded by the projects TEXTMESS 2.0 (TIN2009-13391-C04-01), Prometeo (PROMETEO/2009/199), the Generalitat valenciana (ACOMP/2011/001) and the EU FP7 project METANET (grant agreement n° 249119)

References

Baccianella S., A. Esuli and F. Sebastiani. (2010) . SentiWordNet 3.0: An Enhanced Lexical Resource for Sentiment Analysis and Opinion Mining. In: Proceedings of the 7th conference on International Language Resources and Evaluation (LREC 2010), Malta, May 2010

Balahur A., R. Steinberger, M.A. Kabadjov, V. Zavarella, E. van der Goot, M. Halkia, B. Pouliquen, J. Belyaeva. (2010). Sentiment Analysis in the News. In: Proceedings of the 7th International Conference on Language Resources and Evaluation (LREC 2010), Malta, May 2010.

Baroni, M., Bernardini, S., Comastri, F., Piccioni, L., Volpi, A., Aston, G.,Mazzoleni, M. (2004). Introducing the "la Repubblica" corpus: A large, annotated, TEI(XML)-compliant corpus of newspaper italian. In: Proceedings of the 4th International conference on Language Resources and Evaluation (LREC-04), Lisbon, May 2004.

Boldrini E, A. Balahur, P. Martìnez-Barco and A. Montoyo. (2010). EmotiBlog: a finer-grained and more precise learning of subjectivity expression models. In: Proceedings of the Fourth Linguistic Annotation Workshop (LAW IV '10). Association for Computational Linguistics.

Chen Y., S.Y.M. Lee, S. Li, and C. Huang. (2010) Emotion Cause Detection with Linguistic Constructions. In: Proceeding of the 23rd International Conference on Computational Linguistics (COLING 2010).

Ekman, P. (1972). Universals And Cultural Differences In Facial Expressions Of Emotions.In: J. Cole (ed.), Nebraska Symposium on Motivation, 1971. Lincoln, Neb.: University of Nebraska Press, 1972. pp. 207- 283.3.

Huang, C. (2010). Emotions as Events (and Cause as Pre-Events). Communication at the Chinese Temporal/discourse annotation workshop, Los Angeles, June 2010,.

Lee S.Y.M., Y. Chen, C. Huang. (2010). A Text-driven Rule-based System for Emotion Cause Detection. In: Proceedings of the NAACL HLT 2010 Workshop on Computational Approaches to Analysis and Generation of Emotion in Text.

Pianta, E., Bentivogli, L., Girardi, C. (2002). Multiwordnet: Developing and aligned multilingual database. In: Proceedings of the First International Conference on Global WordNet, Mysore, India, January 2002.

Pustejovsky, J., Castao, J., Saur`ı, R., Ingria, R., Gaizauskas, R., Setzer, A., Katz, G. (2003). TimeML: Robust specification of event and temporal expressions in text. In: Proceedings of the 5th International Workshop on Computational Semantics (IWCS-5).

Ruimy, N., Monachini, M., Gola, E., Calzolari, N., Fiorentino, M.D., Ulivieri, M., Rossi, S. (2003). A computational semantic lexicon of italian: SIMPLE. In: Linguistica Computazionale XVIII-XIX, Pisa, pp. 821–64

Schroeder M., H. Pirker and M. Lamolle. (2006). First Suggestion for an Emotion Annotation and Representation Language. In: Proceedings of the 5th International Conference on Language Resources and Evaluation (LREC 2006), Genoa, May 2006.

Strapparava C. and A. Valitutti. (2004) WordNet-Affect: an affective extension ofWordNet". In: Proceedings of the 4th International Conference on Language Resources and Evaluation (LREC 2004), Lisbon, May 2004.

Takamura H., I. Takashi, M. Okumura. (2006). Latent Variables Models for Semantic Orientation of Phrases. In: Proceedings of 11th Conference of the European Chapter of the Association for Computational Linguistics (EACL 2006).

Wierzbicka, A. (1999) Emotion Across Languages and Cultures Diversity and Universals. Cambidge.CUP.

A Cross-corpus Study of Unsupervised Subjectivity Identification based on Calibrated EM

Dong Wang Yang Liu
The University of Texas at Dallas
{dongwang,yangl}@hlt.utdallas.edu

Abstract

In this study we investigate using an unsupervised generative learning method for subjectivity detection in text across different domains. We create an initial training set using simple lexicon information, and then evaluate a calibrated EM (expectation-maximization) method to learn from unannotated data. We evaluate this unsupervised learning approach on three different domains: movie data, news resource, and meeting dialogues. We also perform a thorough analysis to examine impacting factors on unsupervised learning, such as the size and self-labeling accuracy of the initial training set. Our experiments and analysis show inherent differences across domains and performance gain from calibration in EM.

1 Introduction

Subjectivity identification is to identify whether an expression contains opinion or sentiment. Automatic subjectivity identification can benefit many natural language processing (NLP) tasks. For example, information retrieval systems can provide affective or informative articles separately (Pang and Lee, 2008). Summarization systems may want to summarize factual and opinionated content differently (Murray and Carenini, 2008). In this paper, we perform subjectivity detection at sentence level, which is more appropriate for some subsequent processing such as opinion summarization.

Previous work has shown that when enough labeled data is available, supervised classification methods can achieve high accuracy for subjectivity detection in some domains. However, it is often expensive to create such training data. On the other hand, a lot of unannotated data is readily available in various domains. Therefore an interesting and important problem is to develop semi-supervised or unsupervised learning methods that can learn from an unannotated corpus. In this study, we use an unsupervised learning approach where we first use a knowledge-based method to create an initial training set, and then apply a calibrated EM method to learn from an unannotated corpus. Our experiments show significant differences among the three domains: movie, news article, and meeting dialog. This can be explained by the inherent difference of the data, especially the task difficulty and classifier's performance for a domain. We demonstrate that for some domains (e.g., movie data) the unsupervised learning methods can rival the supervised approach.

2 Related Work

In the early age, knowledge-based methods were widely used for subjectivity detection. They used a lexicon or patterns and rules to predict whether a target is subjective or not. These methods tended to yield a high precision and low recall, or low precision and high recall (Kim and Hovy, 2005). Recently, machine learning approaches have been adopted more often (Ng et al., 2006). There are limitations in both methods. In knowledge-based approaches, a predefined subjectivity lexicon may not adapt well to different domains. While in machine learning approach, human labeling efforts are required to create a large training set.

To overcome the above drawbacks, unsupervised or semi-supervised methods have been explored in sentiment analysis. For polarity classification, some previous work used spectral techniques (Dasgupta and Ng, 2009) or co-training (Li et al., 2010) to mine the reviews in a semi-supervised manner. For subjectivity identification, Wiebe and Riloff (Wiebe and Riloff, 2005) applied a rule-based method to create a training set first and then used it to train a naive Bayes classifier. Melville et al. (Melville et al., 2009) used a pooling multinomial method to combine lexicon derived probability and statistical probability.

Our work is similar to the study in (Wiebe and Riloff, 2005) in that we both use a rule-based method to create an initial training set and learn from

Proceedings of the 2nd Workshop on Computational Approaches to Subjectivity and Sentiment Analysis, ACL-HLT 2011, pages 161–167, 24 June, 2011, Portland, Oregon, USA

unannotated corpus. However, there are two key differences. First, unlike the self-training method they used, we use a calibrated EM iterative learning approach. Second, we compare the results on three different corpora in order to evaluate the domain/genre effect of the unsupervised method. Our cross-corpus study shows how the unsupervised learning approach performs in different domains and helps us understand what are the factors impacting the learning methods.

3 Data

We use three data sets from different domains: movie, news resource, and meeting conversations. The first two are from written text domain and have been widely used in many previous studies for sentiment analysis (Pang and Lee, 2004; Raaijmakers and Kraaij, 2008). The third one is from speech transcripts. It has been used in a few recent studies (Raaijmakers et al., 2008; Murray and Carenini, 2009), but not as much as those text data. The following provides more details of the data.

- The first corpus is movie data (Pang and Lee, 2004). It contains 5,000 subjective sentences collected from movie reviews and 5,000 objective sentences collected from movie plot summaries. The sentences in each collection are randomly ordered.
- The second one is extracted from MPQA corpus (version 2.0) (Wilson and Wiebe, 2003), which is collected from news articles. This data has been annotated with subjective information at phrase level. We adopted the same rules as in (Riloff and Wiebe, 2003) to create the sentence level label: if a sentence has at least one private state of strength medium or higher, then the sentence is labeled SUBJECTIVE, otherwise it is labeled OBJECTIVE. We randomly extracted 5,000 subjective and 5,000 objective sentences from this corpus to make it comparable with the movie data.
- The third data set is from AMI meeting corpus. It has been annotated using the scheme described in (Wilson, 2008). There are 3 main categories of annotations regarding sentiments: subjective utterances, subjective questions, and objective polar utterances. We consider the union of subjective utterance and subjective question as subjective and the rest as objective. The subjectivity classification task is done at the dialog act (DA) levels. We label each DA using the label of the utterance that has overlap with it. We create a balanced data set using this corpus, containing 9,892 DAs in total. This number is slightly less than those for movie and MPQA data because of the available data size in this corpus. The data is also randomly ordered without considering the role of the speaker and which meeting it belongs to.

Table 1 summarizes statistics for the three data sets. We can see that sentences in meeting dialogs (AMI data) are generally shorter than the other domains, and that sentences in news domain (MPQA) are longer, and also have a larger variance. In addition, the inter-annotator agreement on AMI data is quite low, which shows it is even difficult for human to determine whether an utterance contains sentiment in meeting conversations.

		Movie	MPQA	AMI
sent length	**min**	3	1	3
	max	100	246	67
	mean	20.37	22.38	8.78
	variance	75.26	147.18	34.26
vocabulary size		15,847	13,414	3,337
Inter-annotator agreement		N/A	0.77	0.56

Table 1: Statistics for the three data sets: movie, MPQA, and AMI data. The inter-annotator agreement on movie data is not available because it is not annotated by human.

4 Unsupervised Subjectivity Detection

In this section, we describe our unsupervised learning process that uses a knowledge-based method to create an initial training set, and then uses a calibrated EM approach to incorporate unannotated data into the learning process. We use a naive Bayes classifier as the base supervised classifier with a bag-of-words model.

4.1 Create Initial Training Set

A lexicon-based method is used to create an initial training set, since it can often achieve high precision rate (though low recall) for subjectivity detection. We use a subjectivity lexicon (Wilson et al., 2005) to calculate the subjectivity score for each sentence.

This lexicon contains 8,221 entries that are categorized into strong and weak subjective clues.

For each word w, we assign a subjectivity score $sub(w)$: 1 to strong subjective clues, 0.5 to weak clues, and 0 for any other word. Then the subjectivity score of a sentence is the sum of the values of all the words in the sentence, normalized by the sentence length. We noticed that for sentences labeled as SUBJECTIVE in the three corpora, the subjective clues appear more frequently in movie data than the other two corpora. Thus we perform different normalization for the three data sets to obtain the subjectivity score for each sentence, $sub(s)$: Equation 1 for the movie data, and Equation 2 for MPQA and AMI data.

$$sub(s) = \sum_{w \in s} sub(w)/sent\_length \tag{1}$$

$$sub(s) = \sum_{w \in s} sub(w)/log(sent\_length) \tag{2}$$

We label the top m sentences with the highest subjective scores as SUBJECTIVE, and label m sentences with the lowest scores as OBJECTIVE. These $2m$ sentences form the initial training set for the iterative learning methods.

4.2 Calibrated EM Naive Bayes

Expectation-Maximization (EM) naive Bayes method is a semi-supervised algorithm proposed in (Nigam et al., 2000) for learning from both labeled and unlabeled data. In the implementation of EM, we iterate the E-step and M-step until model parameters converge or a predefined iteration number is reached. In E-step, we use naive Bayes classifier to estimate the posterior probabilities of each sentence s_i belonging to each class c_j (SUBJECTIVE and OBJECTIVE), $P(c_j|s_i)$:

$$P(c_j|s_i) = \frac{P(c_j)\prod_{k=1}^{|s_i|} P(w_k|c_j)}{\sum_{c_l \in C} P(c_l)\prod_{k=1}^{|s_i|} P(w_k|c_l)} \tag{3}$$

The M-step uses the probabilistic results from the E-step to recalculate the parameters in the naive Bayes classifier, the probability of word w_t in class c_j and the prior probability of class c_j:

$$P(w_t|c_j) = \frac{0.1 + \sum_{s_i \in S} N(w_t, s_i) P(c_j|s_i)}{0.1 \times |V| + \sum_{k=1}^{|V|}\sum_{s_i \in S} N(w_k, s_i) P(c_j|s_i)} \tag{4}$$

$$P(c_j) = \frac{0.1 + \sum_{s_i \in S} P(c_j|s_i)}{0.1 \times |C| + |S|} \tag{5}$$

S is the set of sentences. $N(w_t, s_i)$ is the count of word w_t in a sentence s_i. We use additive smoothing with $\alpha = 0.1$ for probability parameter estimation. $|C|$ is the number of classes, which is 2 in our case, and $|V|$ is the vocabulary size, obtained from the entire data set.

In the first iteration, we assign $P(c_j|s_i)$ using the pseudo training data generated based on lexicon information. If a sentence is labeled SUBJECTIVE, then $P(sub|s_i)$ is 1 and $P(obj|s_i)$ is 0; for the sentences with OBJECTIVE labels, $P(sub|s_i)$ is 0 and $P(obj|s_i)$ is 1.

In our work, we use a variant of standard EM: calibrated EM, introduced by (Tsuruoka and Tsujii, 2003). The basic idea of this approach is to shift the probability values of unlabeled data to the extent such that the class distribution of unlabeled data is identical to the distribution in labeled data (balanced class in our case). In our approach, before model training ("M-step") in each iteration, we adjust the posterior probability of each sentence in the following steps:

- Transform the posterior probabilities through the inverse function of the sigmoid function. The outputs are real values.
- Sort them and use the median of all the values as the border value. This is because our data is balanced.
- Subtract this border value from the transformed values.
- Transform the new values back into probability values using a sigmoid function.

Note that there is a caveat here. We are assuming we know the class distribution, based on labeled training data or human knowledge. This is often a reasonable assumption. In addition, we are assuming that this class distribution is the same for the unlabeled data. If this is not true, then the distribution adjustment performed in calibrated EM may hurt system performance.

5 Empirical Evaluation

In this section, we evaluate our unsupervised learning method and analyze various impacting factors.

In preprocessing, we removed the punctuation and numbers from the data and performed word stemming. To measure performance, we use classification accuracy.

5.1 Unsupervised Learning Results

In experiments of unsupervised learning, we perform 5-fold cross validation. We divide the corpus into 5 parts with equal size (each with balanced class distribution). In each run we reserve one part as the test set. From the remaining data, we use the lexicon-based method to create the initial training data, containing 1,000 SUBJECTIVE and 1,000 OBJECTIVE sentences. The rest is used as unlabeled data to perform iterative learning. The final model is then applied to the reserved test set. Figure 1 shows the learning curves of calibrated EM on movie, MPQA and AMI data respectively.

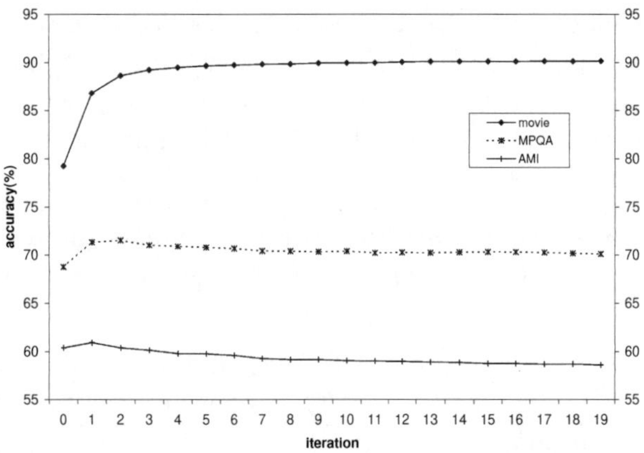

Figure 1: Calibrated EM results using unsupervised setting (2,000 self-labeled initial samples) on movie, MPQA, and AMI data.

On movie data, calibrated EM improves the performance significantly ($p<0.005$), compared to that based on the initial training set (iteration 0). It takes only a few iterations for the EM method to converge and at the end of the iteration, it achieves 90.15% accuracy, which rivals the fully supervised learning performance (91.31% when using all the 8,000 labeled sentences for training). On MPQA data, this method yields some improvement ($p<0.1$) compared to the initial point. But there is a peak accuracy in the first couple of iterations, and then performance starts dropping thereafter. On AMI data, the performance degrades after the first iteration.

5.2 Analysis and Discussion

5.2.1 Effect of initial set

For unsupervised learning, our first question is how the accuracy and size of the initial training set affect performance. We calculate the self-labeling accuracy for the initial set using the lexicon based method. Table 2 shows the labeling accuracy when using different initial size, measured for SUBJECTIVE and OBJECTIVE class separately. In addition, we present the classification performance on the test set when using the naive Bayes classifier trained from the initial set. Each size in the table represents the total number of sentences in the initial set.

Table 2 shows that when the size is 2,000 (as we used in previous experiments), the accuracy for both classes on MPQA are even better than on movies, even though we have seen that iterative learning methods perform much better on movies, suggesting that the initial data set accuracy is not the reason for the worse performance on MPQA than movies. It also shows that on movie data, as the initial size increases, the accuracy of the pseudo training set decreases, which is as expected (the top ranked self-labeled samples are more confident and accurate). However, this is not the case on MPQA and AMI data. There is no obvious drop of accuracy, rather in many cases accuracy even increases when the initial size increases. It shows that on these two corpora, our lexicon-based method does not perform very well because the most highly ranked sentences according to the subjective lexicon are not those most subjective sentences.

size		100	200	1000	2000	3000
movie	sub	95.20	92.20	82.48	79.24	77.13
	obj	82.20	82.00	80.88	79.04	77.31
	Acc_Test	59.93	71.63	77.62	79.24	79.64
MPQA	sub	83.20	85.60	85.76	85.18	82.53
	obj	87.60	86.60	87.64	87.46	85.92
	Acc_Test	60.45	63.83	66.98	68.75	70.05
AMI	sub	49.60	53.40	65.96	66.98	67.05
	obj	71.60	71.00	68.56	69.04	69.89
	Acc_Test	50.51	53.81	60.53	60.39	60.46

Table 2: Initial pseudo training accuracy for SUBJECTIVE (sub) and OBJECTIVE (obj) class, and performance on the test using this initial training set (Acc_Test). Results (all in %) are shown for different initial data size.

From the results on the test set, we find that when

the size is smaller, such as containing 100 or 200 samples, the accuracy on test set is lower than using a bigger initial set. This is mainly because there is not sufficient data for model training. For AMI data, this is also due to the low accuracy in the training set. When the initial size is large enough, the improvement from a larger training set is not as substantial, for example, using 1,000, 2,000, or 3,000 sentences. On AMI data, there is almost no difference among the three sets. There is a tradeoff between the two factors, self-labeling accuracy and the data size. Often an improvement in one aspect causes degradation of the other. A reasonable starting point needs to be chosen considering both factors. Overall, it shows that the performance on test set can benefit more from using a larger initial training set, though it may be noisy.

In order to further investigate the impact of self-labeled initial data set, we perform standard semi-supervised learning using reference labels in the initial data set. The learning curve of this semi-supervised setting is shown in Figure 2.

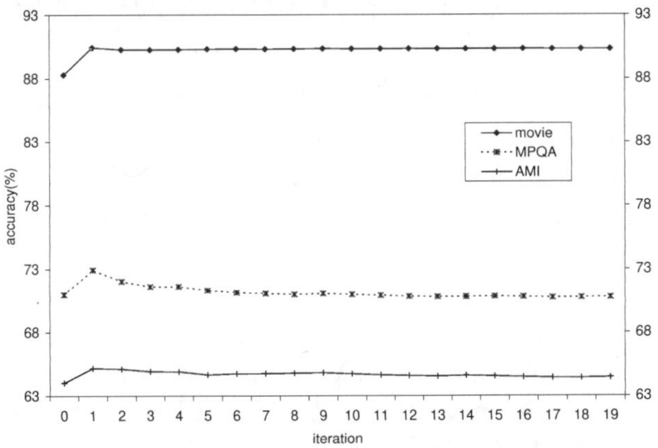

Figure 2: Calibrated EM results using semi-supervised learning (2,000 labeled seed) on movie, MPQA, and AMI data.

On movie data, calibrated EM yields better performance over that based on the initial training data (iteration 0). We can see that calibrated EM converges very fast and achieves very high performance in the first iteration. On MPQA and AMI data, calibrated EM increases the accuracy at the first iteration but then degrades thereafter. This shows that incorporating unlabeled data in training is helpful, however, more EM iterations do not yield further gain.

We noticed that on AMI data, even when the initial set has 100% accuracy (i.e., semi-supervised setting), it still fails to yield any performance gain on AMI data. It shows that the low accuracy of initial training set does not explain the poor performance of unsupervised learning method. Therefore, we conducted another set of experiments which use the same semi-supervised setting but start from different initial training sizes. We observed that on MPQA and AMI data, calibrated EM is able to increase the accuracy only when the initial training set is small (less than 100 instances) and the performance at the start point is poor. We believe this is related to the data property and the assumptions used in EM. Similar patterns have been found in some previous studies (Chapelle et al., 2006). They attribute this to the incorrect model assumption, i.e., when the modeling assumptions for a particular classifier do not match the characteristics of the distribution of the data, unlabeled data may degrade the performance of classifiers.

5.2.2 Effect of calibration

Figure 3 compares calibrated EM with standard EM using unsupervised learning on the three domains. We can see that calibrated EM outperforms standard EM, with a larger improvement on MPQA and AMI data. When using standard EM, we find that there is a larger difference between the number of instances in the two classes based on the model's prediction on MPQA and AMI data than movie data. For example, in one run using EM, in the first iteration the ratio of the two classes is 2.21, 1.88, and 1.23 for MPQA, AMI, and movie data respectively. Calibrated EM is more effective on the two domains because it adjusts the posterior probability of each sample according to the class distribution in the data, making it more accurate in training the model in the next iteration.

5.2.3 Error analysis

There are two points worth discussing based on our error analysis.

A. Domain difference.

Much of the difference we have observed can be attributed to the genre difference. In movie reviews, often a person expresses his/her favor (or not) of the movie explicitly, making the task relatively easy for automatic subjectivity classification. MPQA data is collected from news resource, where subjectivity mostly means an attitude or a judgment. Take

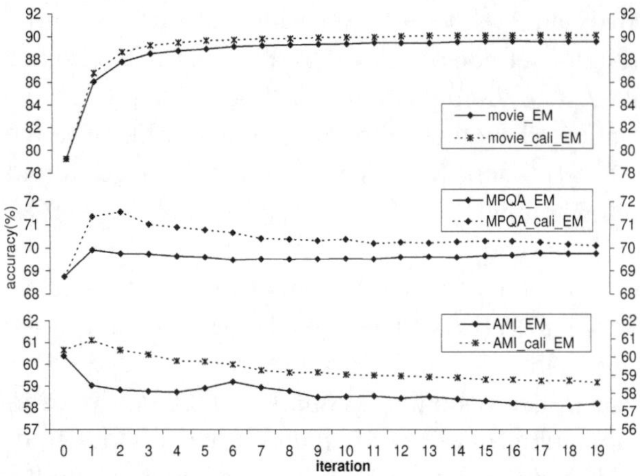

Figure 3: Comparison of standard EM and calibrated EM.

the following sentence as an example: "The United States is prepared to fight terrorism alone". It is labeled as SUBJECTIVE because it expresses a determination. However, it may also be interpreted as an objective statement.

The AMI corpus consists of meeting conversations. The free-style dialogues are very different from the style in review and news articles. There are many incomplete sentences and disfluencies. More importantly, the meaning of a sentence is often context dependent. In the examples shown below, the two sentences look very similar, however, the first sentence is labeled as "OBJECTIVE", and the second one as "SUBJECTIVE". This is because of the different context and speaker information – the second sentence expresses agreement, but the first example is just a sequence of discourse marker words.

- Alright yeah okay
- Yeah okay, true, true.

We notice that many of the classification errors in AMI occur in very short sentences, like in the example shown above. These short sentences are very ambiguous for subjectivity classification.

B. Limitation of the bag-of-word model.

Our analysis also showed that some sentences are difficult to classify if simply using surface words. In the following, we show some examples of system errors.

False negatives: subjective sentences recognized as objective

- Johnson has, in his first film, set himself a task he is not nearly up to. (movie data)
- The news from Israel is almost earth-shattering. (MPQA)
- We can stick with what we already get. (AMI)

False positives: objective sentences recognized as subjective

- Cathy (Julianne Moore) is the **perfect** 50s housewife, living the **perfect** 50s life: **healthy** kids, **successful** husband, social **prominence**. (movie data)
- The committee Wednesday opened a formal debate on human rights questions, including alternative approaches for **improving** the **effective** enjoyment of human rights and **fundamental freedoms**. (MPQA)
- um uh you know apple been really **successful** with this surgical white kind of business or this **sleek** kind of (AMI)

In the first three examples, there are no explicit subjective clues, resulting in false negative errors. The subjective word "earth-shattering" is not included in subjective lexicon and rarely used in the corpus. The last three examples contain several subjective words, and are therefore labeled as subjective. These are the problems with the current word based approaches.

6 Conclusion and Future Work

This paper investigates an unsupervised learning procedure for subjectivity identification at sentence level. We use a lexicon-based method to create initial training data and then apply a calibrated EM to utilize unlabeled corpus. We evaluate this method across three different data sets and observe significant difference. It yields good performance on movie data but does not achieve much performance gain on MPQA corpus, while on AMI corpus it fails to yield improvement. Our analysis showed that performance of the base classifier has a substantial impact on iterative learning methods. In addition, we found that calibrated EM outperforms the standard EM method when the class distribution based on classifier's hypotheses does not match the real one.

Our iterative learning approach uses a naive Bayes classifier that may not have accurate posterior probabilities. Therefore in our future work, we will evaluate using other base models. Our cross-corpus analysis shows poor performance of subjectivity detection in AMI data. We plan to explore more information from multiparty dialogs to help improve performance for that domain.

7 Acknowledgment

The authors thank Theresa Wilson for sharing annotation for the AMI corpus and helping with data processing for that data. Part of this work is supported by an NSF award CNS-1059226.

References

O. Chapelle, B. Schölkopf, and A. Zien, editors. 2006. Semi-supervised learning. MIT Press.

Sajib Dasgupta and Vincent Ng. 2009. *Mine the easy, classify the hard: a semi-supervised approach to automatic sentiment classification*. In *Proceedings of ACL-IJCNLP*, pages 701–709.

Soo-Min Kim and Eduard Hovy. 2005. *Automatic detection of opinion bearing words and sentences*. In *Proceedings of ACL*.

Shoushan Li, Chu-Ren Huang, Guodong Zhou, and Sophia Yat Mei Lee. 2010. *Employing personal/impersonal views in supervised and semi-supervised sentiment classification*. In *Proceedings of ACL*, pages 414–423.

Prem Melville, Wojciech Gryc, and Richard D. Lawrence. 2009. *Sentiment analysis of blogs by combining lexical knowledge with text classification*. In *Proceedings of ACM SIGKDD*, pages 1275–1284.

Gabriel Murray and Giuseppe Carenini. 2008. *Summarizing spoken and written conversations*. In *Proceedings of EMNLP*, pages 773–782.

Gabriel Murray and Giuseppe Carenini. 2009. *Detecting subjectivity in multiparty speech*. In *Proceedings of Interspeech*.

Vincent Ng, Sajib Dasgupta, and S. M. Niaz Arifin. 2006. *Examining the role of linguistic knowledge sources in the automatic identification and classification of reviews*. In *Proceedings of COLING/ACL*, pages 611–618.

Kamal Nigam, Andrew Kachites McCallum, Sebastian Thrun, and Tom Mitchell. 2000. *Text classification from labeled and unlabeled documents using EM*. *Machine Learning*, 39:103–134.

Bo Pang and Lilian Lee. 2004. *A sentimental education: sentiment analysis using subjectivity summarization based on minimum cuts*. In *Proceedings of ACL*, pages 271–278.

Bo Pang and Lillian Lee. 2008. *Using very simple statistics for review search: An exploration*. In *Proceedings of COLING*, pages 73–76.

Stephan Raaijmakers and Wessel Kraaij. 2008. *A Shallow approach to subjectivity classification*. In *Proceedings of ICWSM*.

Stephan Raaijmakers, Khiet Truong, and Theresa Wilson. 2008. *Multimodal subjectivity analysis of multiparty conversation*. In *Proceedings of EMNLP*, pages 466–474.

Ellen Riloff and Janyce Wiebe. 2003. *Learning extraction patterns for subjective expressions*. In *Proceedings of EMNLP*, pages 105–112.

Yoshimasa Tsuruoka and Jun'ichi Tsujii. 2003. *Training a naive bayes classifier via the EM algorithm with a class distribution constraint*. In *Proceedings of NAACL*, pages 127–134.

Janyce Wiebe and Ellen Riloff. 2005. *Creating subjective and objective sentence classifiers from unannotated texts*. In *Proceedings of CICLing*, pages 486–497.

Theresa Wilson and Janyce Wiebe. 2003. *Annotating opinions in the world press*. In *Proceedings of SIGdial*, pages 13–22.

Theresa Wilson, Janyce Wiebe, and Paul Hoffmann. 2005. *Recognizing contextual polarity in phrase-level sentiment analysis*. In *Proceedings of HLT-EMNLP*, pages 347–354.

Theresa Wilson. 2008. *Annotating subjective content in meetings*. In *Proceedings of LREC*.

Towards a Unified Approach for Opinion Question Answering and Summarization

Elena Lloret and **Alexandra Balahur** and **Manuel Palomar** and **Andrés Montoyo**
Department of Software and Computing Systems
University of Alicante
Alicante 03690, Spain
{elloret,abalahur, mpalomar, montoyo}@dlsi.ua.es

Abstract

The aim of this paper is to present an approach to tackle the task of opinion question answering and text summarization. Following the guidelines TAC 2008 Opinion Summarization Pilot task, we propose new methods for each of the major components of the process. In particular, for the information retrieval, opinion mining and summarization stages. The performance obtained improves with respect to the state of the art by approximately 12.50%, thus concluding that the suggested approaches for these three components are adequate.

1 Introduction

Since the birth of the Social Web, users play a crucial role in the content appearing on the Internet. With this type of content increasing at an exponential rate, the field of Opinion Mining (OM) becomes essential for analyzing and classifying the sentiment found in texts.

Nevertheless, real-world applications of OM often require more than an opinion mining component. On the one hand, an application should allow a user to query about opinions in natural language. Therefore, Question Answering (QA) techniques must be applied in order to determine the information required by the user and subsequently retrieve and analyze it. On the other hand, opinion mining offers mechanisms to automatically detect and classify sentiments in texts, overcoming the issue given by the high volume of such information present on the Internet. However, in many cases, even the result of the opinion processing by an automatic system still contains large quantities of information, which are still difficult to deal with manually. For example, for questions such as "Why do people like George Clooney?" we can find thousands of answers on the Web. Therefore, finding the relevant opinions expressed on George Clooney, classifying them and filtering only the positive opinions is not helpful enough for the user. He/she will still have to sift through thousands of texts snippets, containing relevant, but also much redundant information. For that, we need to use Text Summarization (TS) techniques. TS provides a condensed version of one or several documents (i.e., a summary) which can be used as a substitute of the original ones (Spärck Jones, 2007). In this paper, we will concentrate on proposing adequate solutions to tackle the issue of opinion question answering and summarization. Specifically, we will propose methods to improve the task of question answering and summarization over opinionated data, as defined in the TAC 2008 "Opinion Summarization pilot"[1]. Given the performance improvements obtained, we conclude that the approaches we proposed for these three components are adequate.

2 Related Work

Research focused on building factoid QA systems has a long tradition, however, it is only recently that studies have started to focus on the creation and development of opinion QA systems. Example of this can be (Stoyanov et al., 2004) who took advantage of opinion summarization to support Multi-Perspective QA system, aiming at extracting opinion-oriented information of a question. (Yu and Hatzivassiloglou, 2003) separated opinions from facts and summarized them as answer to opinion questions. Apart from these studies, specialized competitions for systems dealing with opinion retrieval and QA have been organized in the past few years. The TAC 2008 Opinion Summarization Pilot track proposed a mixed setting of factoid and opinion questions.

[1] http://www.nist.gov/tac/2008/summarization/

Proceedings of the 2nd Workshop on Computational Approaches to Subjectivity and Sentiment Analysis, ACL-HLT 2011, pages 168–174,
24 June, 2011, Portland, Oregon, USA ©2011 Association for Computational Linguistics

It is interesting to note that most of the participating systems only adapted their factual QA systems to overcome the newly introduced difficulties related to opinion mining and polarity classification. Other relevant competition focused on the treatment of subjective data is the NTCIR MOAT (Multilingual Opinion Analysis Test Collection). The approaches taken by the participants in this task are relevant to the process of opinion retrieval, which is the first step performed by an opinion mining question answering system. For example, (Taras Zabibalov, 2008) used an almost unsupervised approach applied to two of the sub-tasks: opinionated sentence and topic relevance detection.(Qu et al., 2008) applied a sequential tagging approach at the token level and used the learned token labels in the sentence level classification task and their formal run submission was is trained on MPQA (Wiebe et al., 2005).

3 Text Analysis Conferences

In 2008, the *Opinion Summarization Pilot* task at the Text Analysis Conferences[2] (TAC) consisted in generating summaries from blogs, according to specific opinion questions provided by the TAC organizers. Given a set of blogs from the Blog06 collection[3] and a list of questions, participants had to produce a summary that answered these questions. The questions generally required determining opinion expressed on a target, each of which dealt with a single topic (e.g. George Clooney). Additionally, a set of text snippets were also provided, which contained the answers to the questions. Table 1 depicts an example of target, question, and optional snippet.

Target:	George Clooney
Questions:	Why do people like George Clooney? Why do people dislike George Clooney?
Snippets:	1050 BLOG06-20060209-006-0013539097 he's a great actor.

Table 1: Example of target, question, and snippet.

Following the results obtained in the evaluation at TAC 2008 (Balahur et al., 2008), we propose an opinion question answering and summarization (OQA&S) approach, which is described in detail in the following sections.

[2]www.nist.gov/tac/

[3]http://ir.dcs.gla.ac.uk/test_collections/access_to_data.html

4 An Opinion Question Answering and Summarization Approach

In order to improve the results of the OQA&S system presented at TAC, we propose new methods for each of the major components of the system: information retrieval, opinion mining and text summarization.

4.1 Opinion Question Answering and Summarization Components

- **Information Retrieval**

  JAVA Information Retrieval system (JIRS) is a IR system especially suited for QA tasks (Gómez, 2007). Its purpose is to find fragments of text (passages) with more probability of containing the answer to a user question made in natural language instead of finding relevant documents for a query. To that end, JIRS uses the own question structure and tries to find an equal or similar expression in the documents. The more similar the structure between the question and the passage is, the higher the passage relevance.

  JIRS is able to find question structures in a large document collection quickly and efficiently using different n-gram models. Subsequently, each passage is assessed depending on the extracted n-grams, the weight of these n-grams, and the relative distance between them. Finally, it is worth noting that the number of passages in JIRS is configurable, and in this research we are going to experiment with passages of length 1 and 3.

- **Opinion Mining**

  The first step we took in our approach was to determine the opinionated sentences, assign each of them a polarity (positive or negative) and a numerical value corresponding to the polarity strength (the higher the negative score, the more negative the sentence and vice versa). In our first approximation (OMaprox1), we employed a simple, yet efficient method, presented in Balahur et al. (Balahur et al., 2009). As lexicons for affect detection, we used WordNet Affect (Strapparava and Valitutti, 2004), SentiWordNet (Esuli and Sebastiani, 2006), and MicroWNOp (Cerini et al., 2007). Each of the resources we employed were mapped to four categories, which were given different scores: positive (1), negative (-1), high positive (4) and high negative (-4). First, the score of each of the blog posts was computed as the sum of the values of the words that were identified. Subsequently, we performed sentence splitting[4] and classified the sentences we thus obtained according to their polarity, by adding the individual scores of the affective words identified.

In the second approach (OMaprox2), we first filter out the sentences that are associated to the topic discussed, using LSA. Further on, we score the sentences identified as relating to the topic of the blog post, in the same manner as in the previous approach. The aim of this approach is to select for further processing only the sentences which contain opinions on the post topic. In order to filter these sentences in, we first create a small corpus of blog posts on each of the topics included in our collection[5]. For each of the corpora obtained, we apply LSA, using the Infomap NLP Software[6]. Subsequently, we compute the 100 most associated words with two of the terms that are most associated with each of the topics and the 100 most associated words with the topic word. The approach was proven to be successful in (Balahur et al., 2010).

- **Text Summarization**

  The text summarization approach used in this paper was presented in (Lloret and Palomar, 2009). In order to generate a summary, the suggested approach first carries out a basic preprocessing stage comprising HTML parsing, sentence segmentation, tokenization, and stemming. Once the input document or documents have been pre-processed, a relevance detection stage, which is the core part of the approach, is applied. The objective of this step is to identify potential relevant sentences in the document by means of three techniques: textual entailment, term frequency and the code quantity principle (Givón, 1990). Then, each potential relevant sentence is given a score which is computed on the basis of the aforementioned techniques. Finally, all sentences are ordered according to their scores, and the highest ranked ones (which mean those sentences contain more important information) are selected and extracted up to the desired length, thus building the final summary. It is worth stressing upon the fact that in an attempt to maintain the coherence of the original documents, sentences are shown in the same order they appear in the original documents.

[4]http://alias-i.com/lingpipe/

[5]These small corpora (30 posts for each of the topics) are gathered using the search on topic words on http://www.blogniscient.com/ and crawling the resulting pages.

[6]http://infomap-nlp.sourceforge.net/

4.2 Experimental Framework

The objective of this section is to describe the corpus used and the experiments performed with the data provided in TAC 2008 *Opinion Summarization Pilot*[7] task. The approaches analyzed comprise:

- **OQA&S:** The three components explained in the previous section (information retrieval, opinion mining and summarization) were bound together in order to produce summaries that include the answer to opinionated questions. First, the most relevant passages of length 1 and 3 are retrieved by the IR module, as in the aforementioned approach, and then the subjective information is found and classified within them using the OM approaches described in the previous section. Further on, we incorporate the TS module, to select and extract the most relevant opinionated facts from the pool of subjective information identified by the OM module. We generate opinion-oriented summaries of compression rates ranging from 10% to 50%. In the end, four different approaches result from the integration of the three components: ***IRp1-OMaprox1-TS***; ***IRp1-OMaprox2-TS***; ***IRp3-OMaprox1-TS***; and ***IRp3-OMaprox2-TS***.

Moreover, apart from these approaches, two baselines were also defined. On the one hand, we sug-

[7]http://www.nist.gov/tac/data/past-blog06/2008/OpSummQA08.html#OpSumm

gest a baseline using the list of snippets provided by the TAC organization (**QA-snippets**). This baseline produces a summary by joining all the answers in the snippets that related to the same topic On the other hand, we took as a second baseline the approach from our participation in TAC 2008 (**DLSIUAES**), without not taking into account any information retrieval or question answering system to retrieve the fragments of information which may be relevant to the query. In contrast, this was performed by computing the cosine similarity[8] between each sentence in the blog and the query. After all the potential relevant sentences for the query were identified, they were classified in terms of subjectivity and polarity, and the most relevant ones were selected for the final summary.

4.3 Evaluation Methodology

Since we used the corpus provided at the *Opinion Summarization Pilot* task, and we followed similar guidelines, we should evaluate our OQA&S approach in the same way as participant systems were assessed. However, the evaluation methodology proposed differs slightly from the one carried out in the competition. The reason why we took such decision was due to the fact that the evaluation carried out in TAC had some limitations, and therefore was not suitable for our purposes. In this manner, our evaluation is also based on the gold-standard nuggets provided by TAC, but in addition we proposed an extended version of them, by adding other pieces of information that are also relevant to the topics.

In this section, all the issues concerning the evaluation are explained. These comprise the original evaluation method used in the Opinion Summarization Pilot task at TAC (Section 4.3.1) , its drawbacks (Section 4.3.2), and the extended version for the evaluation method we propose (Section 4.3.3). Further on, the results obtained together with a wide discussion, as well as its comparison with the baselines and the TAC participants is provided in Section 4.4.

4.3.1 Nugget-based Evaluation at TAC

Within the *Opinion Summarization Pilot* task, each summary was evaluated according to its content using the Pyramid method (Nenkova et al., 2007). A list of nuggets was provided and the assessors used such list of nuggets to count the number of nuggets a summary contained. Depending on the number of nuggets the summary included and the importance of each one given by their weight, the values for recall, precision and F-measure were obtained. An example of several nuggets corresponding to different topics can be seen in Table 2, where the weight for each one is also shown in brackets.

Topic	Nugget (weight)
Carmax	CARMAX prices are firm, the price is the price (0.9)
Jiffy Lube	They should have torque wrenches (0.2)
Talk show hosts	Funny (0.78)

Table 2: Example of evaluation nuggets and associated weights.

4.3.2 Limitations of the Nugget Evaluation

The evaluation method suggested at TAC requires a lot of human effort when it comes to identify the relevant fragments of information (nuggets) and compute how many of them a summary contains, resulting in a very costly and time-consuming task. This is a general problem associated to the evaluation of summaries, which makes the task of summarization evaluation especially hard and difficult.

But, apart from this, when an exhaustive examination of the nuggets used in TAC is done, some other problems arised which are worth mentioning. The average number of nuggets for each topic is 27, and this would mean, that longer summaries will be highly penalized, because it will contain more useless information according to the nuggets. After analyzing in detail all the provided nuggets, we mainly classified the possible problems into six groups, which are:

1. **Some of the nuggets were expressed differently from how they appeared in the original blogs.** Since most of the summarization systems are extractive, this fact forced that humans had to evaluate the summaries, otherwise it would be very difficult to account for the presence of such nugget in the summary, if they are not using the same vocabulary as the original blogs.

2. **Some nuggets for the same topic express the**

[8]http://www.d.umn.edu/ tpederse/text-similarity.html

same idea, despite not being identical. In these cases, we are counting a single piece of information in the summary twice, if the idea that nuggets expressed is included.

3. Moreover, **the meaning of one nugget can be deduced from another's**, which is also related to the problem stated before.

4. **Some of the nuggets are not very clear in meaning** (e.g. *"hot"*, *"fun"*). This would mean that a summary might include such terms in a different context, thus, obtaining incorrectly that it is revelant when might be out of context.

5. **A sentence in the original blog can be covered by several nuggets**. For instance, both nuggets *"it is an honest book"* and *"it is a great book"* correspond to the same sentence *"It was such a great book-honest and hard to read (content not language difficulty)"*. In this case, it is not clear how to proceed with the evaluation; whether to count both nuggets or just one of them.

6. **Some information which is also relevant for the topic is not present in any nugget**. For instance: *"I go to Starbucks because they generally provide me better service"*. Although it is relevant with respect to the topic and it appears in a number of summaries, it would be not counted because it has not been chosen as a nugget.

4.3.3 Extended Nugget-based Evaluation

Since we are interested in testing a wide range of approaches involving IR, OM and TS, sticking to the rules to the original TAC evaluation would mean that a lot of time as well as human effort will be required, as well as not accounting for important information that summaries may contain in addition to the one expressed by the nuggets. Therefore, taking as a basis the nuggets provided at TAC, we set out a modified version of them.

The underlying idea behind this is to create an extended set of nuggets that serve as a reference for assessing the content of the summaries. In this manner, we will map each original nugget with the set of sentences in the original blogs that are most similar to it, thus generating a gold-standard summary for each topic. For creating this extended gold-standard nuggets we compute the cosine similarity[9] between every nugget and all the sentences in the blog related to the same topic. We empirically established a similarity threshold of 0.5, meaning that if a sentence was equal or above such similarity value, it will be considered also relevant. One main disadvantage of such a lower threshold value is that we can consider relevant sentences that share the same vocabulary but in fact they are not relevant to the summary. In order to avoid this, once we had identified all the most similar sentences to each nugget, we carried out a manual analysis to discard cases like this. Having created the extended set of nuggets, we grouped all of them pertaining to the same topic, and considered it a gold-standard summary. Now, the average number of nuggets per topic is 53, which we have increased by twice the number of original nuggets provided at TAC.

Further on, our summaries are compared against this new gold-standard using ROUGE (Lin, 2004). This tool computes the number of different kinds of overlap n-grams between an automatic summary and a human-made summary. For our evaluation, we compute ROUGE-1 (unigrams), ROUGE-2 (bigrams), ROUGE-SU4 (it measures the overlap of skip-bigrams between a candidate summary and a set of reference summaries with a maximum skip distance of 4), and ROUGE-L (Longest Common Subsequence between two texts). The results and discussion are next provided.

4.4 Results and Discussion

This section contains the results obtained for our OQA&S approach and all the sub-approaches tested. IRp*N* refers to the length of the passage employed in the information retrieval approach, whereas OMaprox*N* indicates the approach used for the opinion mining component. Firstly, we show and analyze the results of our different approaches, and then we compared the best performing one with the baselines and the average *Opinion Summarization Pilot* task participants results in TAC.

Table 3 shows the precision (Pre), recall (Rec) and F-measure results of ROUGE-1 (R-1) for all the approaches we experimented with.

Generally speaking, the results obtained show better figures for precision than for recall, and there-

[9] The cosine similarity was computed using Pedersen's Text Similarity Package: http://www.d.umn.edu/ tpederse/text-similarity.html

Approach		Summary length				
Name	**R-1**	**10%**	**20%**	**30%**	**40%**	**50%**
	Pre	24.29	26.17	29.73	30.82	32.54
IRp1	Rec	14.45	18.58	22.32	23.63	26.32
-OMaprox1-TS	$F_{\beta=1}$	16.53	20.65	24.58	25.75	28.12
	Pre	24.29	26.17	29.73	30.82	32.54
IRp1	Rec	16.90	20.02	23.36	24.15	26.77
-OMaprox2-TS	$F_{\beta=1}$	19.45	22.13	25.36	25.94	28.40
	Pre	27.27	30.18	30.91	30.05	30.19
IRp3	Rec	20.56	24.76	28.25	31.67	34.47
-OMaprox1-TS	$F_{\beta=1}$	22.65	26.23	27.98	29.18	29.74
	Pre	30.16	32.11	32.35	32.41	32.11
IRp3	Rec	20.64	24.03	27.25	29.78	32.68
-OMaprox2-TS	$F_{\beta=1}$	23.28	25.64	27.42	28.44	29.21

Table 3: Results of our OQA&S approaches

Approach		Performance (ROUGE)			
Name	**%**	**R-1**	**R-2**	**R-L**	**R-SU4**
	Pre	32.11	7.34	29.00	11.37
IRp3-OMaprox2	Rec	32.68	8.31	33.24	12.76
-TS (50%)	$F_{\beta=1}$	29.21	7.22	28.60	11.13
	Pre	17.97	8.76	17.65	9.98
QA-snippets	Rec	71.24	31.30	70.10	37.44
	$F_{\beta=1}$	24.73	11.58	24.29	13.45
	Pre	20.54	7.00	19.46	9.29
DLSIUAES	Rec	57.66	18.98	54.61	25.77
	$F_{\beta=1}$	27.04	9.10	25.59	12.22
	Pre	23.74	8.35	22.72	10.81
Average TAC	Rec	56.65	19.37	54.56	25.40
participants	$F_{\beta=1}$	27.45	9.64	26.33	12.46
	Pre	20.42	6.06	19.55	8.62
Average TAC	Rec	56.45	17.3	54.40	24.11
participants'	$F_{\beta=1}$	24.31	7.25	23.31	10.29

Table 4: Comparison with other systems

fore the F-measure value, which combines both values, will be affected. Good precision values means that the information our approaches select is the correct one, despite not including all the relevant information.

Our best performing approach in general is the one which uses a length passage of 3 and, as far as OM is concerned, when topic-sentiment analysis is carried out (*IRp3-OMaprox2-TS*). This shows that the approach dealing with topic-sentiment analysis in opinion mining is more suitable than the one which does not consider topic relevance. Taking a look at some individual results, we next try to elucidate the reasons why our approach performs better at some approaches and not so good at others. Concerning the IR module, it is important to mention that a passage length of 1 always obtains poorer results that when it is increased to 3, meaning that the longer the passage, the better.

Regarding the best summary length, we observed that in general terms, the more content we allow for the summary, the better. In other words, compression rates of 50% get higher results than 20% or 10%. However, there are cases in which shorter summaries (10% and 20%) obtains better results than longer ones (e.g. *IRp3-OMaprox2-TS* vs. *IRp3-OMaprox1-TS*).

Although the results theirselves are not very high (around 30%), they are in line with the state-of-the-art, as can be seen in Table 4, where our best performing approach is compared with respect to other approaches.

Although the compression rate which obtains best results is not very high (50%), indeed the final summaries have an average length of 2,333 non-white space characters. This is really low compared to the length that TAC organization allowed for the Opinion Summarization Pilot task, which was 7,000 non-white space characters per question, and most of the times there were two questions for each topic. Whereas the results of TAC participants are much better for the recall value than ours, if we take a look at the precision, our approach outperforms them according to this value in all of the cases. The longer a summary is, the more chances it has to contain information related to the topic. However, not all this information may be relevant, as it is shown in the results for the precision values, which decrease considerably compared to the recall ones. In contrast, due to the fact that our approach is missing some relevant information because we use a rather short passage length (3 sentences), we do not obtain such high values for the recall, but we obtain good precision results, which indicate that the information that we keep is important.

Moreover, comparing those results with the ones obtained by our approach, it is worth mentioning that *IRp3-OMaprox2-TS* outperforms the F-measure value for all the ROUGE metrics with respect to *Average TAC participants'*. More in detail, when the ROUGE scores are averaged, *IRp3-OMaprox2-TS* improves by 12.50% the *Average TAC participants'* for the F-measure value.

5 Conclusion and Future Work

In this paper, we tackled the process of OQA&S. In particular, we analyzed specific methods within each component of this process, i.e., information retrieval, opinion mining and text summarization. These components are crucial in this task, since our final goal was to provide users with the correct information containing the answer of a question. However, contrary to most research work in question answering, we focus on opinionated questions rather than factual, increasing the difficulty of the task.

Our analysis comprises different configurations and approaches: i) varying the length for retrieving the passages of the documents in the retrieval information stage; ii) studying a method that take into consideration topic-sentiment analysis for detecting and classifying opinions in the retrieved passages and comparing it to another that does not; and iii) generating summaries of different compression rates (10% to 50%). The results obtained showed that the proposed methods are appropriate to tackle the OQA&S task, improving state of the art approaches by 12.50% approximately.

In the future, we plan to continue investigating suitable approaches for each of the proposed components. Our final goal is to build an integrated and complete approach.

Acknowledgments

This research work has been funded by the Spanish Government through the research program FPI (BES-2007-16268) associated to the project TEXT-MESS (TIN2006-1526-C06-01). Moreover, it has been also partially funded by projects TEXT-MESS 2.0 (TIN2009-13391-C04), and PROMETEO (PROMETEO/2009/199) from the Spanish and the Valencian Government, respectively.

References

A. Balahur, E. Lloret, O. Ferrández, A. Montoyo, M. Palomar, and R. Muñoz. 2008. The DLSIUAES team's participation in the tac 2008 tracks. In *Proceedings of the Text Analysis Conference*.

Alexandra Balahur, Ralf Steinberger, Erik van der Goot, Bruno Pouliquen, and Mijai Kabadjov. 2009. Opinion mining from newspaper quotations. In *Proceedings of the Workshop on Intelligent Analysis and Processing of Web News Content*.

A. Balahur, M. Kabadjov, and J. Steinberger. 2010. Exploiting higher-level semantic information for the opinion-oriented summarization of blogs. In *Proceedings of CICLing'2010*.

S. Cerini, V. Compagnoni, A. Demontis, M. Formentelli, and G. Gandini. 2007. Micro-WNOp: A gold standard for the evaluation of automatically compiled lexical resources for opinion mining. In *Language resources and linguistic theory: Typology, second language acquisition, English linguistics*.

A. Esuli and F. Sebastiani. 2006. SentiWordNet: A publicly available resource for opinion mining. In *Proceedings of LREC*.

Talmy Givón, 1990. *Syntax: A functional-typological introduction, II*. John Benjamins.

José M. Gómez. 2007. *Recuperación de Pasajes Multilingüe para la Búsqueda de Respuestas*. Ph.D. thesis.

Chin-Yew Lin. 2004. ROUGE: a Package for Automatic Evaluation of Summaries. In *Proceedings of ACL Text Summarization Workshop*, pages 74–81.

Elena Lloret and Manuel Palomar. 2009. A gradual combination of features for building automatic summarisation systems. In *Proceedings of TSD*, pages 16–23.

Ani Nenkova, Rebecca Passonneau, and Kathleen McKeown. 2007. The pyramid method: Incorporating human content selection variation in summarization evaluation. *ACM Transactions on Speech and Language Processing*, 4(2):4.

Lizhen Qu, Cigdem Toprak, Niklas jakob, and iryna Gurevych. 2008. Sentence level subjectivity and sentiment analysis experiments in ntcir-7 moat challenge. In *Proceedings of NTCIR-7 Workshop meeting*.

Karen Spärck Jones. 2007. Automatic summarising: The State of the Art. *Information Processing & Management*, 43(6):1449–1481.

V. Stoyanov, C. Cardie, D. Litman, and J. Wiebe. 2004. Evaluating an opinion annotation scheme using a new multi-perspective question and answer corpus. In *AAAI Spring Symposium on Exploring Attitude and Affect in Text: Theories and Applications*.

C. Strapparava and A. Valitutti. 2004. WordNet-Affect: an affective extension of wordnet. In *Proceedings of the 4th International Conference on Language Resources and Evaluation*, pages 1083–1086.

John Carroll Taras Zabibalov. 2008. Almost-unsupervised cross-language opinion analysis at ntcis-7. In *Proceedings of NTCIR-7 Workshop meeting*.

J. Wiebe, T. Wilson, and C. Cardie. 2005. Annotating expressions of opinions and emotions in language. In *Language Resources and Evaluation*, volume 39.

D. Yu and V. Hatzivassiloglou. 2003. Towards answering opinion questions: Separating facts from opinions and identifying the polarity of opinion sentences. In *Proceedings of EMNLP*.

Corporate News Classification and Valence Prediction: A Supervised Approach

Syed Aqueel Haider
Dept. of Computer Science & Engineering

MIT, Manipal University
KA-576104, India.
Aqueel.h.rizvi@gmail.com

Rishabh Mehrotra
Computer Science & Information Systems Group
BITS,Pilani
Rajasthan,India.
erishabh@gmail.com

Abstract

News articles have always been a prominent force in the formation of a company's financial image in the minds of the general public, especially the investors. Given the large amount of news being generated these days through various websites, it is possible to mine the general sentiment of a particular company being portrayed by media agencies over a period of time, which can be utilized to gauge the long term impact on the investment potential of the company. However, given such a vast amount of news data, we need to first separate corporate news from other kinds namely, sports, entertainment, science & technology, etc. We propose a system which takes news as, checks whether it is of corporate nature, and then identifies the polarity of the sentiment expressed in the news. The system is also capable of distinguishing the company/organization which is the subject of the news from other organizations which find mention, and this is used to pair the sentiment polarity with the identified company.

Introduction

With the rapid advancements in the field of information technology, the amount of information available has increased tremendously. News articles constitute the largest available portion of factual information about events happening in the world. Corporate news constitutes a major chunk of these news articles.

Sentiment Mining applied to the corporate domain would help in various ways like Automatic Recommendation Systems, to help organizations evaluate their market strategies help them frame their advertisement campaigns. Our system tries to address these issues by automating the entire process of news collection, organization/product detection and sentiment mining.

This paper is divided into two main parts. The first part describes a way of identifying corporate news from a collection of news articles and then pairing the news with the organization/company which is being talked about in the article. The second part of our paper works on the output of the first part (corporate news) and detects the valence of the identified corporate news articles. It calculates an overall score and identifies valence a s positive, negative or neutral based on this score. The system is immune to addition/mergers of companies, with regards to their identification, as it does not use any name lists.

The model uses a machine learning approach to do this task. We extract a set of features from the news and use them to train a set of classifiers. The best model is then used to classify the test data. One advantage of our approach described below is that it only requires a very small amount of annotated training data. We trained the model on the NewsCorp dataset consisting of 860 annotated news articles. The system has shown promising

Proceedings of the 2nd Workshop on Computational Approaches to Subjectivity and Sentiment Analysis, ACL-HLT 2011, pages 175–181,
24 June, 2011, Portland, Oregon, USA ©2011 Association for Computational Linguistics

results on test data with classification accuracy being 92.05% and a f-measure of 92.00. The final average valence detection accuracy measured was 79.93%.

Related Work

Much work has been done on text classification.(Barak, 2009; Sebastiani,2002) There have been earlier attempts (Research on Sports Game News Information Extraction, Yonggui YANG,et al) However, they had focused mainly on information extraction and not classification.

Earlier attempts on web news classification(Krishnlal et al, 2010) concentrated mainly on classification according to the domain of the news articles. Not much work has been done in the field of corporate news-company pairing. This paper tries to address a more general problem of detecting the main organization being talked about in the articles.

Sentiment analysis in computational linguistics has focused on examining what textual features contribute to affective content of text and automatically detecting these features to derive a sentiment metric for a word, sentence or whole text. Niederhoffer (1971) after classifying New York Times headlines into 19 categories evaluated how the markets react to good and bad news.

Davis et al (2006) investigate the effects of optimistic or pessimistic language used in financial press releases on future firm performance. Sumbaly et al(2009) used k gram models to detect sentiment in large news datasets. Devitt(2007) improves upon and Melville(2009) have done work on sentiment analysis of web blogs

PART I : News Classification

Steps involved in news classification

3.1 News Pre-processing

The preprocessor merges all the files into one but defines start/end delimiters for each file in the merged file, to enable bulk processing. The merged news file is acted upon by a log-linear part of speech tagger we obtained from the Stanford NLP webpage(Manning,2000).

3.2 Organization detection

We follow a two step approach to organization detection:

Step 1: We extract the NNP/NNPS[1] clusters in the POS-tagged file using reguar expressions. For example, the pos-tagged version of “General Electric Co”, is “ General_NNP Electric_NNP Co_NNP” which is detected as a likely candidate for an organization.

Step 2: We use a Named Entity Recognizer[2] to obtain organization names. They are sorted in order of their frequencies and top three organizations are stored for later use. This ensures that even if some names have crept in as organizations due to misclassification by NER tagger, they end up at the bottom of the list and are discarded.

Multiple Organization Focus: Let f1,f2 be the frequencies of top 2 organizations. Now if f2>f1/2 then the news article is paired with organizations corresponding to both f1 and f2.

Baseline: Using just the frequency of top 3 organizations as features, we get an accuracy of 48.89% which is very low. Therefore, we add additional features which are described below.

3.3 Keyword Detection

The system matches each news article for occurrence of a set of keywords like “company”, “share”, “asset”, etc. which have been derived from statistical observation of corporate news. We have used POS tags to differentiate between the contexts in which the keywords have been used. For example, “share” (verb) is not a keyword but “share” (noun) is a keyword. We calculate the net keyword occurrence frequency as $N(key)=\sum_{i=0} n(k_i)$ where N(key) is the total keyword frequency and $n(k_i)$ is the frequency of each keyword.

3.4 Headline Preprocessing

We process the headline and detect likely candidates for organization names and then cross check with the top 3 organization names detected in the step 2.2. We introduce a new feature h_value described as follows:

---

[1] Please refer Appendix A for details of the POS Tags.

$$h\_value = \begin{cases} \text{no. of matches in headline; if N(key) >5} \\ \text{0 , otherwise} \end{cases}$$

3.5 Detection of Products

The system detects likely candidates for products using three empirical rules:

- 1. _NNP followed by _POS followed by _NNP cluster. Ex: Google's ***Wave***
- 2.The followed by _NNP cluster. Example: The new ***POWER7*** processors from IBM
- 3._PRP$ followed by _NNP cluster. Example: Apple announced that its ***iPhone 3G*** will not be launched in India.

3.6 Executives Detection

We follow a similar POS based approach to detect executives, and store their frequency.

3.7 Feature Generation

We use a total of 9 features to train the SVM classifier. They are described below:
1-3: frequency of top 3 organizations
4: frequency of Executives in the news article
5-7: frequencies of top 3 products discussed in the news.
8. The N(key) value defined above in section 3.3
9. h_value defined above in section 3.2.

4 Classification and training

We tested our method with several classifiers.

First we used Support Vector Machines using LibSVM[**]. The results obtained were satisfactory. However, we experimented with other models to see model variation can lead to some improvement.

We tried **Logistic Regression** which is a class for building and using a multinomial logistic regression model with a ridge estimator. We trained our model with ridge parameter 1.0E-8.

We compared our classification results with **Naives Bayes** classifier which uses estimator classes for making the model. Numeric estimator precision values are chosen based on analysis of the training data.

We also tested our dataset with **AdaBoost** (Adaptive Boosting) classifier. AdaBoost calls a weak classifier repeatedly in a series of rounds to correctly identify the weights of the parameters.

The detailed results of the classification algorithms are discussed in the Experiments and Results section.

PART II : Headline Sentiment tagging

We describe a lexical features based approach to detect the sentiment polarity in a news article.

5.1 Preprocessing

One of the features of the news headlines extracted from the Internet was that many had all words capitalized. The system detects the improperly capitalized words and de-capitalizes their common words. This task is accomplished by using the following rule on the output given initially by the POS Tagger in Part I of our framework.

Rule: Only the words with POS tags as NNP or NNPS retain their capitalization, all others are decapitalized. Headline processing helps the POS Tagger to tag the words correctly and hence the dependencies will now be correct.

5.2 Stemming

Words which might carry opinions may be present in inflected forms which requires stemming of the words before any rules can be applied on them. Words that are identified to have the same root form are grouped in a finite number of clusters with the identified root word as cluster center. We have used the Porter Stemmer(Porter 1980)for this purpose.

5.3 Noise Reduction

The news article contains many parts of speech which are irrelevant to sentiment detection in our case, for example, prepositions, conjunctions, etc.

We give a list of Penn Treebank tags which we eliminate:

CC , CD, DT, EX, IN, PRP, PRP$, TO . Please refer to the Appendix A for the meaning of each POS-tag.

5.4 Polarity Estimation

We used the SentiWordNet (Sebastiani,2006) in order to calculate the sentiment polarity(valence) of all the words in the headline and the body.

We use WordNet to find sentiment polarity value(**SPV**) of each word. In WordNet, nouns, verbs, adjectives and adverbs are grouped into synonym sets (synsets). Synsets represent terms or concepts. For example, following is a synset from WordNet:

stadium, bowl, arena, sports stadium – (a large structure for open-air sports or entertainments)

The synsets are related to other synsets higher or lower in the hierarchy by different types of relationships e.g.

□ Hyponym/Hypernym (Is-A relationships)

□ Meronym/Holonym (Part-Of relationships)

□ Nine noun and several verb Is-A hierarchies

Using WordNet's word hierarchy we boosted sentiment polarities of a word (synset in WordNet), depending on whether a noun/verb, having a particular sentiment polarity is a hyponym of the given synset. The candidate synsets for polarity detection were extracted using a bootstrapping approach starting with some positive and negative seed words.

Parent synset	Boosted Polarity
poor	negative
good	positive
rise	positive
down	negative
decrease	negative
growth	positive
loss	negative

Table 1: Examples of hypernyms boosting sentiment polarity

5.5 Overall Valence Classification

After valences for each word have been detected, we proceed to find out the overall valence of the news article. We follow 2 rules for this task:

1. Since each word can have several meanings, to calculate the SPV of a word, we assumed that the these values were the average of all its possible meanings.

2. The SPV of words occurring in the headline are given higher weightage, as compared to those in the body. After several experimental trials, we concluded that a weight ratio of 4:1 was optimal.(4 for words in headline).

The second rule is a direct consequence of the fact that news writers always try to provide the overall sentiment of the news in the headline itself so as to ease the understanding of the reader.

Now the overall valence score(OVS) is calculated using the simple expression OVS=

where SP is the Sentiment polarity value of each word in the news article.

Final decision:

OVS > +k,	positive polarity
OVS < -k,	negative polarity
$-k \leq OVS \leq k$,	neutral polarity

We experimented with different values of k and found out that a value of k=3 was most suitable for our task. Also, we could have normalized k according to the length of the news article to account for larger number of polar words in lengthier articles. However, we avoid doing so, because the probability of occurrence of positive polar words is the same as that of negative polar words, hence, neutralizing the effect of each other. Finally, the OVS value provides a metric for the strength of the valence of news article. Higher magnitudes of OVS correspond to more strongly expressed sentiments.

6 Experiments and Results

In this section we discuss the dataset used in our experiments, the evaluation settings and the classification results obtained with our model.

6.1 The NewsCorp Dataset

We obtained 860 news samples from different news sites including:

1.ABC news
2. Reuters
3. MSNBC
4. CBC News Online, etc.

Our research team read these 860 news articles and created files for each of the news articles which contained details whether the article is corporate or non-corporate and if it is corporate then other details like main Organization being talked about in the article, different products and/or executives related to the organization mentioned in the article. We used these metadata files to evaluate our results regarding Organization, product and executive detection.

This dataset is then used to train the model for classification and also for sentiment mining task.

Sample metadata file:


```
<article>
        <headline>Apple Sells Three Million iPads in 80
Days</headline>
        <organization>
                <OrgName>Apple</OrgName>
                <product>iPad</product>
                <product>iPhone</product>
                <executive>Steve Jobs</executive>
        </organization>
        <sentiment>positive</sentiment>
</article>
```


6.2 Evaluation Methodology

We evaluate our method via 10-fold cross-validation, where we have sub-sampled the training folds in order to (a) keep the computational burden as low as possible and (b) show that we can learn sensible parameterizations based upon relatively low requirements in terms of the preferences seen on previous users. We evaluate the system in stages so that the contribution of each stage in the overall result becomes clear. We tested 860 news samples for corporate news detection. There were 261 true negative, 39 false positive, 83 false negative and 477 true positive articles. Precision, Recall and F-score are computed as:

Recall= TP / (TP+FN) Precision= TP / (TP+FP)

F-Score=(2.Precision.Recall)/(Precision+Recall)

We evaluated our results in three different stages. We first used basic Organization detection using NER tagger output as our baseline. Next we incorporated headline processing and keyword frequency detection in the second stage. Finally the third stage included the Product and Executive detection feature for result evaluation.

6.3 Classification Results

In order to classify the news article as corporate and non-corporate we used 4 different classification algorithms and compared their results. The four algorithms are:

1. Support Vector Machines
2. Logistic Regression
3. Naives Bayes
4. AdaBoost

Algorithm	Precision	Recall	F-Val	ROC Area
Naives Bayes	88.3	88.4	88.3	0.94
Support Vector Machine	85.81	92.44	85.17	0.94
Logistic Regression	90.4	89.9	90.0	0.95
AdaBoost	92.0	92.1	92.0	0.937

Table 2 (Classification Results)

Support Vector Machine gave us a third stage F Value of 88.66% while Naives Bayes gave a F Value of 88.3%.

Logistic Regression showed an improvement factor of 1.7% over Naives Bayes by giving F Value of 90.0%.

AdaBoost technique gave us the best classification result of 92& as the F value.

The different Precision, Recall, ROC Area and F Measure of the four algorithms are tabulated in Table 2 and Fig.2.

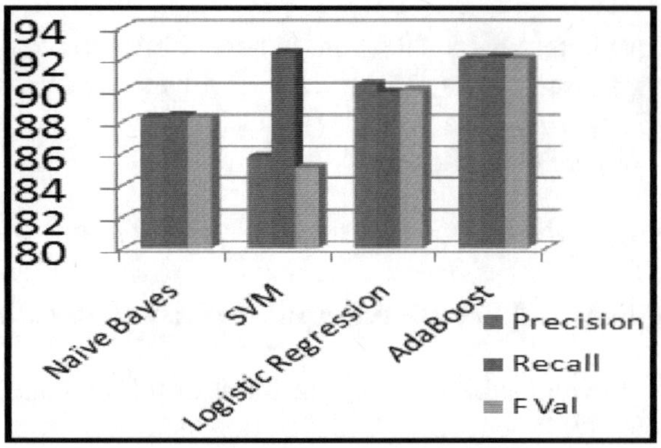

Fig. 1: Classification Results

6.4 Valence detection experimental results

The proposed system was tested with 608 articles since out of 860, 608 were identified to be of corporate type. The classification was 3 way, namely POS, NEG and NEUT (representing +ve, -ve and neutral respectively). The results are shown in Figure 1 in the form of a confusion matrix. Out of a total 608 financial news articles, 264 were tagged with positive sentiment, 162 with negative sentiment and 182 were found to be neutral.

		Predicted		
		POS	NEG	NEUT
Actual	POS	224	06	34
	NEG	04	148	10
	NEUT	50	18	114

Fig 2. Confusion Matrix for Valence Detection

However, our proposed approach yields an accuracy of 84.84, 91.35 and 62.35 for positive , negative and neutral news sentiments respectively . A possible reason for a low accuracy in case of neutral news articles could be because of the presence of some stray polar words in the body of the news, which might have added to a sum of more than 'k' in magnitude(as defined in Section 5.5), thereby leading to the development of an unwanted polarity.

Also, we observe a higher accuracy in predicting negative articles, the reason for which could not be identified. However, as proposed by a colleague, it could possibly be attributed to the fact that negative sentiment is more strongly expressed by Journalists in news articles, as compared to positive sentiment, which might have aided in better detection of words with negative polarity. Finally, we calculated the overall prediction accuracy by taking the average of accuracies for all three sentiments, which comes out to be 79.93%(Table 4).

	Precision	Recall	Accuracy
POS	80.58	84.85	84.84
NEG	86.05	91.46	91.35
NEUT	72.15	66.27	62.35

Table 3:Scores for Valence Detection

7 Conclusion and Future Work

A framework for valence identification and news classification has been proposed. News articles mined from the web by a crawler are fed to the system to filter the financial news from other kinds of news(sports, entertainment etc). Next, the organization which is the subject of this news is identified. Finally, we determine the sentiment polarity of the news by utilizing several lexical features and semantic relationships from WordNet.

We experiment with the system using our own manually tagged corpus of 860 news articles to fine tune various parameters like weights and threshold values. The resulting system performs well with identification of financial news as well as detection of valence in those articles. The system gives good result for positive and negative sentiments but satisfactory results for neutral sentiments. An overall accuracy of 79.93 % is obtained.

In the near future, we intend to apply anaphora resolution and use anaphoric distance to rank polar words according to relevance. This will help us to identify and give more weight to words which describe the sentiment of the author, from other "stray" words which are external references, not determining the overall sentiment of the news.

References

A New Text Mining Approach Based on HMM-SVM for Web News ClassificationLewis, D. D.: Reuters-21578 Document Corpus V1.0

Angela K. Davis, Jeremy M. Piger, and Lisa M. Sedor. 2006.Beyond the numbers: An analysis of optimistic and pessimistic language in earnings press releases. Technical report, Federal Reserve Bank of St Louis.

B. E. Boser, I. Guyon, and V. Vapnik. A training algorithm for optimal margin classiers. In Proceedings of the Fifth Annual Workshop on Computational Learning Theory, pages 144{152. ACM Press, 1992.

Barak and Dagan.2009. Text Categorization from Category Name via Lexical Reference. Proceedings of NAACL HLT 2009.

Chih-Chung Chang and Chih-Jen Lin, LIBSVM : a library for support vector machines, 2001. Software available at http://www.csie.ntu.edu.tw/~cjlin/libsvm http://acl.ldc.upenn.edu/J/J93/J93-2004.pdf

Devitt et al,(2007) Sentiment Polarity Identification in Financial News: A Cohesion-based Approach

George A. Miller (1995). WordNet: A Lexical Database for English.Communications of the ACM Vol. 38, No. 11: 39-41.

Jenny Rose Finkel, Trond Grenager, and Christopher Manning. 2005. Incorporating Non-local Information into Information Extraction Systems by Gibbs Sampling. Proceedings of the 43nd Annual Meeting of the Association for Computational Linguistics (ACL 2005), pp. 363-370.

Kristina Toutanova and Christopher D. Manning. 2000. Enriching the Knowledge Sources Used in a Maximum Entropy Part-of-Speech Tagger. In Proceedings of the Joint SIGDAT Conference on Empirical Methods in Natural Language Processing and Very Large Corpora (EMNLP/VLC-2000), pp. 63-70.

Melville et al.(2009) Sentiment Analysis of Blogs by Combining. Lexical Knowledge with Text Classification.

Ozgur, A.: Supervised and Unsupervised Machine Learning Techniques for Text Document Categorization. Master‘s Thesis (2004), Bogazici University, Turkey.

Porter, M.F. (1980) An Algorithm for Suffix Stripping, Program, 14(3): 130–137

Sebastiani, F.: Machine Learning in Automated Text Categorization. ACM Computing Surveys 34 no. 5 (2002)

Sentiment Mining in Large News Datasets. Roshan Sumbaly, Shakti Sinha, May 10, 2009.

UPAR7: A knowledge-based system for headline sentiment tagging. François-Régis Chaumartin Lattice/Talana – Université Paris 7

U. Hahn and M. Romacker Content Management in the SynDiKATe system — How t
documents are automatically transformed to text knowledge bases. Data & Knowledge E
ing, 35, 2000, pages 137-159.

Victor Niederhoffer. 1971. The analysis of world events and stock prices. Journal of Business, 44(2):193–219.

Appendix A. POS Tags

The POS tags used in Part I of the paper are described as follows:

NN = Noun
NNS = Plural Noun
NNP = Proper Noun
PRP = Personal Pronoun
PRP$ = Possessive Pronoun
JJ = Adjective
TO = *'to'*
CD = Cardinal Number
DT = Determiner
CC = Coordinating conjunction
EX = Existential *there*
IN = Preposition or subordinating conjunction

Instance Level Transfer Learning for Cross Lingual Opinion Analysis

Ruifeng Xu, Jun Xu and Xiaolong Wang
Key Laboratory of Network Oriented Intelligent Computation
Department of Computer Science and Technology
Shenzhen Graduate School, Harbin Institute of Technology, Shenzhen, China
{xuruifeng,xujun}@hitsz.edu.cn, wangxl@insun.hit.edu.cn

Abstract

This paper presents two instance-level transfer learning based algorithms for cross lingual opinion analysis by transferring useful translated opinion examples from other languages as the supplementary training data for improving the opinion classifier in target language. Starting from the union of small training data in target language and large translated examples in other languages, the Transfer AdaBoost algorithm is applied to iteratively reduce the influence of low quality translated examples. Alternatively, starting only from the training data in target language, the Transfer Self-training algorithm is designed to iteratively select high quality translated examples to enrich the training data set. These two algorithms are applied to sentence- and document-level cross lingual opinion analysis tasks, respectively. The evaluations show that these algorithms effectively improve the opinion analysis by exploiting small target language training data and large cross lingual training data.

1 Introduction

In recent years, with the popularity of Web 2.0, massive amount of personal opinions including comments, reviews and recommendations in different languages have been shared on the Internet. Accordingly, automated opinion analysis has attracted growing attentions. Opinion analysis, also known as sentiment analysis, sentiment classification, and opinion mining, aims to identify opinions in text and classify their sentiment polarity (Pang and Lee, 2008).

Many sentiment resources such as sentiment lexicons (e.g., SentiWordNet (Esuli and Sebastiani, 2006))and opinion corpora (e.g., MPQA (Blitzer et al., 2007)) have been developed on different languages in which most of them are for English. The lack of reliably sentiment resources is one of the core issues in opinion analysis for other languages. Meanwhile, the manually annotation is costly, thus the amount of available annotated opinion corpora are still insufficient for supporting supervised learning, even for English. These facts motivate to "borrow" the opinion resources in one language (source language, SL) to another language (target language, TL) for improving the opinion analysis on the target language.

Cross lingual opinion analysis (CLOA) techniques are investigated to improve opinion analysis in TL through leveraging the opinion-related resources, such as dictionaries and annotated corpus in SL. Some CLOA works used bilingual dictionaries (Mihalcea et al., 2007), or aligned corpus (Kim and Hovy, 2006) to align the expressions between source and target languages. These works are puzzled by the limited aligned opinion resources. Alternatively, some works used machine translation system to do the opinion expression alignment. Banea et al. (2008) proposed several approaches for cross lingual subjectivity analysis by directly applying the translations of opinion corpus in source language to train the opinion classifier on target language. Wan (2009) combined the annotated English reviews, unannotated Chinese reviews and their translations to co-train two separate classifiers for each language, respectively.

Proceedings of the 2nd Workshop on Computational Approaches to Subjectivity and Sentiment Analysis, ACL-HLT 2011, pages 182–188,
24 June, 2011, Portland, Oregon, USA ©2011 Association for Computational Linguistics

These works directly used all of the translation of annotated corpus in source language as the training data for target language without considering the following two problems: (1) the machine translation errors propagate to following CLOA procedure; (2) The annotated corpora from different languages are collected from different domains and different writing styles which lead the training and testing data having different feature spaces and distributions. Therefore, the performances of these supervised learning algorithms are affected.

To address these problems, we propose two instance level transfer learning based algorithms to estimate the confidence of translated SL examples and to transfer the promising ones as the supplementary TL training data. We firstly apply Transfer AdaBoost (TrAdaBoost) (Dai et al., 2007) to improve the overall performance with the union of target and translated source language training corpus. A boosting-like strategy is used to down-weight the wrongly classified translated examples during iterative training procedure. This method aims to reduce the negative affection of low quality translated examples. Secondly, we propose a new Transfer Self-training algorithm (TrStr). This algorithm trains the classifier by using only the target language training data at the beginning. By automatically labeling and selecting the translated examples which is correct classified with higher confidence, the classifier is iteratively trained by appending new selected training examples. The training procedure is terminated until no new promising examples can be selected. Different from TrAdaBoost, TrStr aims to select high quality translated examples for classifier training. These algorithms are evaluated on sentence- and document-level CLOA tasks, respectively. The evaluations on simplified Chinese (SC) opinion analysis by using small SC training data and large traditional Chinese (TC) and English (EN) training data, respectively, show that the proposed transfer learning based algorithms effectively improve the CLOA. Noted that, these algorithms are applicable to different language pairs.

The rest of this paper is organized as follows. Section 2 describes the transfer learning based approaches for opinion analysis. Evaluations and discussions are presented in Section 3. Finally, Section 4 gives the conclusions and future work.

2 CLOA via Transfer Learning

Given a large translated SL opinion training data, the objective of this study is to transfer more high quality training examples for improving the TL opinion analysis rather than use the whole translated training data. Here, we propose to investigate the instance level transfer learning based approaches.

In the case of transfer learning, the set of translated training SL examples is denoted by $T_s = \{(x_i, y_i)\}_{i=1}^{n}$, and the TL training data is denoted by T_t=$\{(x_i, y_i)\}_{i=n+1}^{n+m}$, while the size of T_t is much smaller than that of T_s, i.e., $|m| \ll |n|$. The idea of transfer learning is to use T_t as the indicator to estimate the quality of translated examples. By appending selected high quality translated examples as supplement training data, the performance of opinion analysis on TL is expected to be enhanced.

2.1 The TrAdaBoost Approach

TrAdaBoost is an extension of the AdaBoost algorithm (Freund and Schapir, 1996). It uses boosting technique to adjust the sample weight automatically (Dai et al., 2007). TrAdaBoost joins both the source and target language training data during learning phase with different re-weighting strategy. The base classifier is trained on the union of the weighted source and target examples, while the training error rate is measured on the TL training data only. In each iteration, for a SL training example, if it is wrongly classified by prior base classifier, it tends to be a useless examples or conflict with the TL training data. Thus, the corresponding weight will be reduced to decrease its negative impact. On the contrary, if a TL training example is wrongly classified, the corresponding weight will be increased to boost it. The ensemble classifier is obtained after several iterations.

In this study, we apply TrAdaBoost algorithm with small revision to fit the CLOA task, as described in **Algorithm 1**. Noted that, our revised algorithm can handle multi-category problem which is different with original TrAdaBoost algorithm for binary classification problem only. More details and theoretical analysis of TrAdaBoost are given in Dai et al.'s work (Dai et al., 2007).

Algorithm 1 CLOA with TrAdaBoost.

Input: T_s, translated opinion training data in SL, $n = |T_s|$; T_t, training data in TL , $m = |T_t|$; L, base classifier; K, iteration number.

1: Initialize the distribution of training samples: $D_1(i) = 1/(n+m)$.
2: **for** each $k \in [1, K]$ **do**
3: Get a hypothesis h_k by training L with the combined training set $T_s \cup T_t$ using distribution D_k: $h_k = L(T_s \cup T_t, D_k)$.
4: Calculate the training error of h_k on T_t: $\epsilon_t = \sum_{i=n+1}^{n+m} \frac{D_k(i) \cdot I[h_k(x_i) \neq y_i]}{\sum_{i=n+1}^{n+m} D_k(i)}$.
5: **if** $\epsilon_t = 0$ or $\epsilon_k \geq 1/2$ **then**
6: $K = k - 1$, break.
7: **end if**
8: Set $\beta_k = \epsilon_k/(1-\epsilon_k)$, $\beta = 1/(1+\sqrt{\frac{2\ln n}{K}})$.
9: **if** $h_k(x_i) \neq y_i$ **then**
10: Update the distribution:
$$D_{k+1}(i) = \begin{cases} \frac{D_k(i)\beta}{Z_k} & 1 \leq i \leq n \\ \frac{D_k(i)/\beta_k}{Z_k} & n+1 \leq i \leq n+m \end{cases}, \text{ where}$$
Z_k is a normalization constant and $\sum_{i=1}^{n+m} D_{k+1}(i) = 1$.
11: **end if**
12: **end for**

Output: $\arg\max_y \sum_{\lceil K/2 \rceil}^{K} I[h_k(x) = y] \log(1/\beta_k)$
/* $I[\cdot]$ *is an indicator function, which equals* 1 *if the inner expression is* $true$ *and* 0 *otherwise.**/

Algorithm 2 CLOA with Transfer Self-training.

Input: T_s, translated opinion training data in SL, $n = |T_s|$; T_t, training data in TL , $m = |T_t|$; L, base classifier; K, iteration number.

1: $T_0 = T_t$, $k = 1$.
2: Get a hypothesis h_k by training a base classifier L with the training set T_{k-1}.
3: **for** each instance $(x_i, y_i) \in T_s$ **do**
4: Use h_k to label (x_i, y_i) .
5: **if** $h_t(x_i) = y_i$ **then**
6: Add $(x_i, y_i)$to T'
7: **end if**
8: **end for**
9: Choose p instances per class with top confidence from T' and denote the set as T_p.
10: $T_k = T_{k-1} \bigcup T_p$, $T_s = T_s - T_p$.
11: $k = k + 1$.
12: Iterate K times over steps 2 to 11 or repeat until $T_p = \emptyset$.

Output: Final classifier by using the enriched training set T_k.

2.2 The Transfer Self-training Approach

Different from TrAdaBoost which focuses on the filtering of low quality translated examples, we propose a new Transfer Self-training algorithm (TrStr) to iteratively train the classifier through transferring high quality translated SL training data to enrich the TL training data. The flow of this algorithm is given in **Algorithm 2**.

The algorithm starts from training a classifier on T_t. This classifier is then applied to T_s, the translated SL training data. For each category in T_s (subjective/objective or positive/negative in our different experiments), top p correctly classified translated examples are selected. These translated examples are regarded as high quality ones and thus they are appended in the TL training data. Next, the classifier is re-trained on the enriched training data. The updated classifier is applied to SL examples again to select more high quality examples. Such procedure terminates until the increments are less than a specified threshold or the maximum number of iterations is exceeded. The final classifier is obtained by training on the union of target data and selected high quality translated SL training data.

3 Evaluation and Discussion

The proposed approaches are evaluated on sentence- and document-level opinion analysis tasks in the bi-lingual case, respectively. In our experiments, the TL is simplified Chinese (SC) and the SL for the two experiments are English (EN)/traditional Chinese (TC) and EN, respectively.

3.1 Experimental Setup

3.1.1 Datasets

In the sentence-level opinionated sentence recognition experiment , the dataset is from the NTCIR-7 Multilingual Opinion Analysis Tasks (MOAT) (Seki et al., 2008) corpora. The information of this dataset is given in Table 1. Two experiments are performed. The first one is denoted by $SenOR : TC \rightarrow SC$, which uses TC_s as source language training dataset, while the second one is $SenOR: EN \rightarrow SC$, which uses EN_s[1]. SC_s is shrunk to different scale as the target language training corpus by random. The opinion analysis results are evaluated with simplified Chinese testing dataset SC_t under lenient and strict evaluation standard [2], respectively, as described in (Seki et al., 2008).

Note	Lang.	Data	Total	subjective/objective	
				Lenient	Strict
SC_s	SC	Training	424	130/294	\
SC_t		Test	4877	1869/3008	898/2022
TC_s	TC	Training	1365	740/625	\
EN_s	EN	Training	1694	648/1046	\

Table 1: The NTCIR-7 MOAT Corpora(unit:sentence).

In the document-level review polarity classification experiment,, we used the dataset adopted in (Wan, 2009). Its English subset is collected by Blitzer et al. (2007), which contains a collection of 8,000 product reviews about four types of products: books, DVDs, electronics and kitchen appliances. For each type of products, there are 1,000 positive reviews and 1,000 negative ones, respectively. The Chinese subset has 451 positive reviews and 435 negative reviews of electronics products such as mp3 players, mobile phones etc. In our experiments, the Chinese subset is further split into two parts randomly: TL training dataset and test set. The cross lingual review polarity classification task is then denoted by $DocSC$: $EN \rightarrow SC$.

In this study, Google Translate[3] is choose for providing machine translation results.

3.1.2 Base Classifier and Baseline Methods

This study focus on the approaches improving the opinion analysis by using cross lingual examples, while the classifier improving on target language is not our major target. Therefore, in the experiments, a Support Vector Machines (SVM) with linear kernel is used as the base classifier. We use the open source SVM package –LIBSVM(Chang and Lin, 2001) with all default parameters. In the opinionated sentence recognition experiment, we use the presences of following linguistic features to represent each sentence example including opinion word, opinion operator, opinion indicator, the unigram and bigram of Chinese words. It is developed with the reference of (Xu et al., 2008). In the review polarity classification experiment, we use unigram, bigram of Chinese words as features which is suggested by (Wan, 2009). Here, document frequency is used for feature selection. Meanwhile, term frequency weighting is chosen for document representation.

In order to investigate the effectiveness of the two proposed transfer learning approaches, they are compared with following baseline methods: (1) NoTr(T), which applies SVM with only TL training data; (2) NoTr(S),which applies SVM classifier with only the translated SL training data; (3) NoTr(S&T), which applies SVM with the union of TL and SL training data.

3.1.3 Evaluation Criteria

Accuracy (Acc), precision (P), recall (R) and F-measure (F1) are used as evaluation metrics. All the performances are the average of 10 experiments.

3.2 Experimental Results and Discussion

Here, the number of iterations in TrAdaBoost is set to 10 in order to avoid over-discarding SL examples.

3.2.1 Sentence Level CLOA Results

The achieved performance of the opinionated sentence recognition task under lenient and strict evaluation are given in Table 2 respectively, in which only 1/16 target train data is used as T_t. It is shown that NoTr(T) achieves a acceptable accuracy, but the recall and F1 for "subjective" category are obviously low. For the two sub-tasks, i.e. $SenOR: TC \rightarrow SC$ and $SenOR: EN \rightarrow SC$ tasks, the accuracies achieved by NoTr(S&T) are always between that of NoTr(T) and NoTr(S). The reason is that some translated examples from source language may likely conflict with the target language training data. It is shown that the direct use of all of the translated training data is infeasible. It is also shown that our approaches achieve better

[1]There are only 248 sentences in NTCIR-7 MOAT English training data set. It is too small to use for CLOA. We split some samples from the test set to build a new English dataset for training, which contains all sentences from topics: N01,N02,T01,N02,N03,N04,N05,N06 and N07.

[2]All sentences are annotated by 3 assessors, strict standard means all 3 assessors have the same annotation and lenient means any 2 of them have the same annotation.

[3]http://translate.google.com/

Method	Sub-task	Lenient Evaluation							Strict Evaluation						
		Acc	subjective			objective			Acc	subjective			objective		
			P	R	F1	P	R	F1		P	R	F1	P	R	F1
NoTr(T)		.6254	.534	.3468	.355	.6824	.7985	.7115	.6922	.5259	.3900	.3791	.7725	.8264	.7776
NoTr(S)	TC→SC	.6059	.4911	.7828	.6035	.7861	.4960	.6082	.6448	.4576	.8352	.5912	.8845	.5603	.6860
NoTr(S&T)	TC→SC	.6101	.4943	.7495	.5957	.7711	.5236	.6235	.6531	.4632	.8051	.588	.8714	.5856	.7004
TrAdaBoost	TC→SC	.6533	.5335	.7751	.6314	.8063	.5777	.6720	.7184	.5273	.8473	.6494	.9077	.6611	.7643
TrStr	TC→SC	**.6625**	.5448	.7309	.6238	.7884	.6199	.6934	**.7304**	.5414	.8182	.6511	.896	.6914	.7801
NoTr(S)	EN→SC	.6590	.5707	.4446	.4998	.6966	.7922	.7413	.7390	.5872	.5100	.5459	.7944	.8408	.8169
NoTr(S&T)	EN→SC	.6411	.5292	.5759	.5515	.7212	.6817	.7009	.7105	.5254	.608	.5637	.8129	.7560	.7834
TrAdaBoost	EN→SC	**.6723**	.5988	.4371	.5018	.7019	.8184	.7549	**.7630**	.6485	.5019	.5614	.8002	.8789	.8371
TrStr	EN→SC	.6686	.5691	.5746	.5678	.7360	.7271	.7292	.7484	.589	.6276	.6026	.8315	.8021	.8147

Table 2: The Performance of Opinionated Sentence Recognition Task.

performance on both tasks while few TL training data is used. In which, TrStr performances the best on $SenOR{:}TC \rightarrow SC$ task while TrAdaBoost outperforms other methods on $SenOR{:}EN \rightarrow SC$ task. The proposed transfer learning approaches enhanced the accuracies achieved by NoTr(S&T) for 4.2-8.6% under lenient evaluation and 5.3-11.8% under strict evaluation, respectively.

3.2.2 Document Level CLOA Results

Method	Acc	positive			negative		
		P	R	F1	P	R	F1
NoTr(T)	.7542	.7447	.8272	.7747	.8001	.6799	.7235
NoTr(S)	.7122	.6788	.8248	.7447	.7663	.5954	.6701
NoTr(S&T)	.7531	.714	.8613	.7801	.8187	.6415	.7179
TrAdaBoost	.7704	.8423	.6594	.7376	.7285	.8781	.7954
TrStr	**.7998**	.8411	.7338	.7818	.7727	.8638	.8144

Table 3: The Results of Chinese Review Polarity Classification Task (Features:Unigrams; m=20).

Method	Acc	positive			negative		
		P	R	F1	P	R	F1
NoTr(T)	.7518	.7399	.8294	.7741	.7983	.6726	.7185
NoTr(S)	.7415	.7143	.8204	.7637	.7799	.6598	.7148
NoTr(S&T)	.7840	.7507	.8674	.8035	.8385	.6982	.7592
TrAdaBoost	.7984	.8416	.7297	.7792	.7707	.8652	.8138
TrStr	**.8022**	.8423	.7393	.7843	.7778	.8634	.8164

Table 4: The Results of Chinese Review Polarity Classification Task (Features:Unigrams+Bigrams; m=20).

Table 3 and Table 4 give the achieved results of different methods on the task $DocSC{:}\ EN \rightarrow SC$ by using 20 Chinese annotated reviews as T_t. It is shown that transfer learning approaches outperform other methods, in which TrStr performs better than TrAdaBoost when unigram+bigram features are used. Compared to NoTr(T&S), the accuracies are increased about 1.8-6.2% relatively. Overall, the transfer learning approaches are shown are beneficial to TL polarity classification.

3.2.3 Influences of Target Training Corpus Size

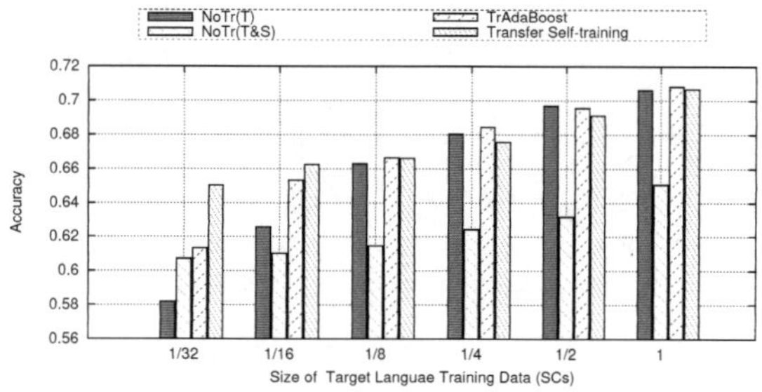

(a) $SenOR: TC \rightarrow SC$

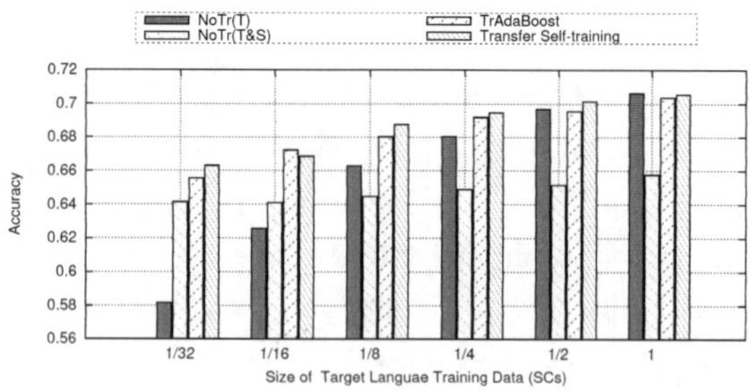

(b) $SenOR: EN \rightarrow SC$

Figure 1: Performances with Different Size of SC_s on Opinionated Sentence Recognition Task under Lenient Evaluation

In order to estimate the influence of different size of TL training data, we conduct a set of experiments on both tasks. Fig 1 and Fig 2 show the influence

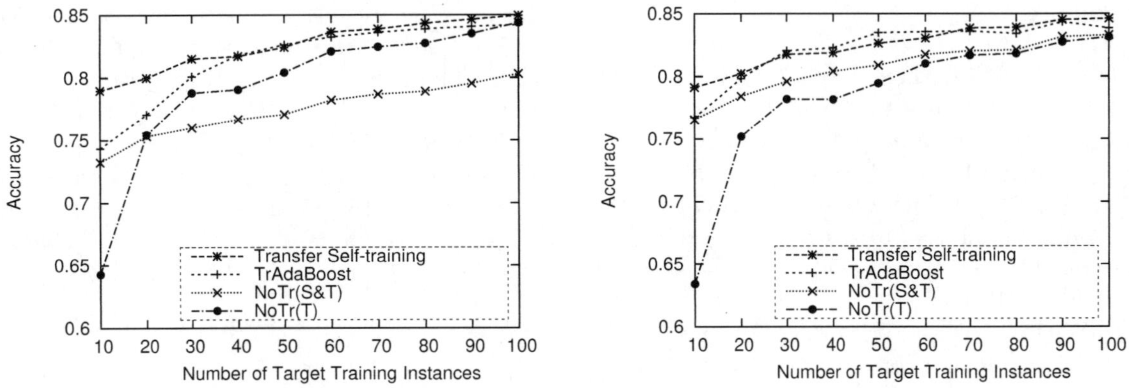

(a) Unigrams

(b) Unigrams+Bigrams

Figure 3: Performances with Different Number of TL Training Instances on Task of $DocSC$: $EN \rightarrow SC$

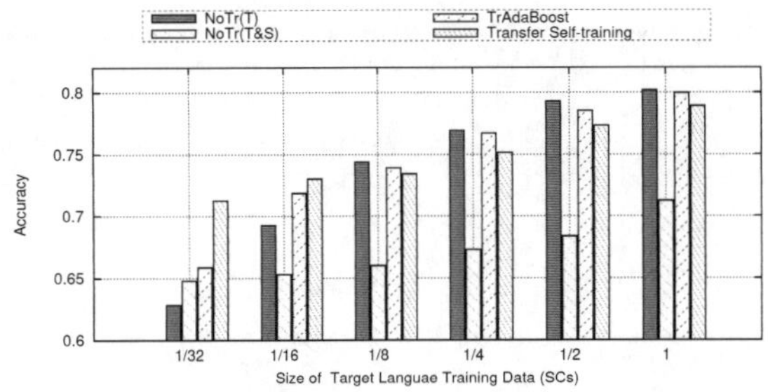

(a) $SenOR : TC \rightarrow SC$

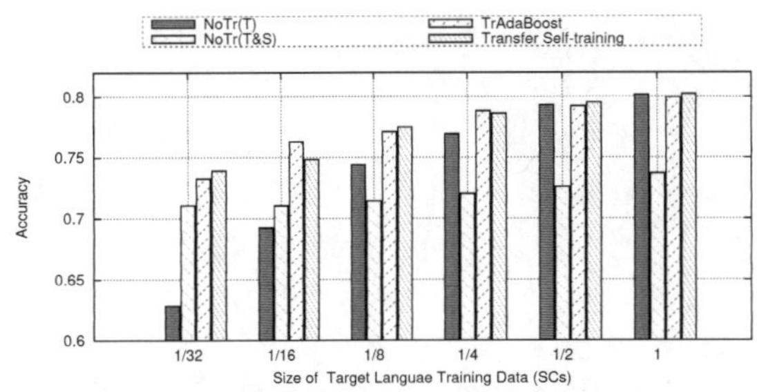

(b) $SenOR : EN \rightarrow SC$

Figure 2: Performances with Different Size of SC_s on Opinionated Sentence Recognition Task under Strict E-valuation

on the opinionated sentence recognition task under lenient and strict evaluation respectively. Fig 3 shows the influence on task $DocSC: EN \rightarrow SC$. Fig 3(a) shows the results use unigram features and Fig 3(b) uses both unigrams and bigrams. It is observed that TrAdaBoost and TrStr achieve better performances than the baseline NoTr(S&T) in most cases. More specifically, TrStr performs the best when few TL training data is used. When more TL training data is used, the performance improvements by transfer learning approaches become small. The reason is that less target training data is helpful to transfer useful knowledge in translated examples. If too much TL training data is used, the weights of SL instances may decrease exponentially after several iterations, and thus more source training data is not obviously helpful.

4 Conclusions and Future Work

To address the problems in CLOA caused by inaccurate translations and different domain/category distributions between training data in different languages, two transfer learning based algorithms are investigated to transfer promising translated SL training data for improving the TL opinion analysis. In this study, Transfer AdaBoost and Transfer Self-Training algorithms are investigated to reduce the influences of low quality translated examples and to select high quality translated examples, respectively. The evaluations on sentence- and document-level opinion analysis tasks show that the proposed algorithms improve opinion analysis by using the union of few TL training data and selected cross lingual training data.

One of our future directions is to develop other transfer leaning algorithms for CLOA task. Another future direction is to employ other moderate weighting scheme on source training dataset to reduce the over-discarding of training examples from source language.

References

Bo Pang and Lillian Lee. 2008. Opinion mining and sentiment analysis. *Foundations and Trends in Information Retrieval*, 2(1–2):1–135.

Andrea Esuli and Fabrizio Sebastiani. 2006. SENTI-WORDNET: A publicly available lexical resource for opinion mining. *Proceedings of the 5th International Conference on Language Resources and Evaluation*, 417–422.

Janyce Wiebe, Theresa Wilson, and Claire Cardie. 2005. Annotating expressions of opinions and e-motions in language. *Language Resources and E-valuation*, 39(2–3):165–210.

Rada Mihalcea, Carmen Banea, and Janyce Wiebe. 2007. Learning multilingual subjective language via cross-lingual projections. *Proceedings of the 45th Annual Meeting of the Association of Computational Linguistics*, Prague, Czech Republic.

Soo-Min Kim and Eduard Hovy. 2006. Identifying and analyzing judgment opinions. *Proceedings of HLT/NAACL-2006*, 200–207.

Carmen Banea, Rada Mihalcea, Janyce Wiebe and Samer Hassan. 2008. Multilingual subjectivity analysis using machine translation. *Proceedings of the 2008 Conference on Empirical Methods in Natural Language Processing*, Honolulu, Hawaii, 127–135.

Xiaojun Wan. 2009. Co-training for cross-lingual sentiment classification. *Proceedings of the 47th Annual Meeting of the ACL and the 4th IJCNLP of the AFNLP*, Suntec, Singapore, 235–243.

Wenyuan Dai ,Qiang Yang, GuiRong Xue and Yong Yu. 2007. Boosting for transfer learning. *Proceedings of the 24th International Conference on Machine Learning*, 193–200.

John Blitzer, Mark Dredze, and Fernando Pereira. 2007. Biographies, bollywood, boom-boxes and blenders: domain adaptation for sentiment classification. *Proceedings of the 45th Annual Meeting of the Association of Computational Linguistics*, 440–447.

Xiaojun Wan. 2008. Using bilingual knowledge and ensemble techniques for unsupervised chinese sentiment analysis. *Proceedings of EMNLP 2008*,553–561.

Yoav Freund and Robert E. Schapire. 1996. Experiments with a new boosting algorithm. *Proceedings of the 13th International Conference on Machine Learning*, 148–156.

Yohei Seki, David K. Evans, Lun-Wei Ku, Le Sun, Hsin-Hsi Chen, and Noriko Kand. 2008. Overview of multilingual opinion analysis task at NTCIR-7. *Proceeding of NTCIR-7*, NII, Tokyo, 185–203.

Ruifeng Xu, Kam-Fai Wong, Qin Lu, and Yunqing Xia 2008. Learning Multilinguistic Knowledge for Opinion Analysis. D. S. Huang et al., editors:*Proceedings of ICIC 2008*, volume 5226 of L-NCS, 993–1000, Springer-Verlag.

Chih-Chung Chang and Chih-Jen Lin. 2001. LIBSVM: a library for support vector machines. *Software available at http://www.csie.ntu.edu.tw/ cjlin/libsvm.*

Sentimatrix – Multilingual Sentiment Analysis Service

Alexandru-Lucian Gînscă[1], Emanuela Boroș[1], Adrian Iftene[1], Diana Trandabăț[1], Mihai Toader[2], Marius Corîci[2], Cenel-Augusto Perez[1], Dan Cristea[1, 3]
[1]"Al. I. Cuza" University, Faculty of Computer Science, Iasi, Romania
[2]Intelligentics, Cluj-Napoca, Romania
[3]Institute of Computer Science, Romanian Academy, Iasi, Romania
{lucian.ginsca, emanuela.boros, adiftene, dtrandabat, augusto.perez, dcristea}@info.uaic.ro, {mtoader, marius}@intelligentics.ro

Abstract

This paper describes the preliminary results of a system for extracting sentiments opinioned with regard with named entities. It also combines rule-based classification, statistics and machine learning in a new method. The accuracy and speed of extraction and classification are crucial. The service oriented architecture permits the end-user to work with a flexible interface in order to produce applications that range from aggregating consumer feedback on commercial products to measuring public opinion on political issues from blog and forums. The experiment has two versions available for testing, one with concrete extraction results and sentiment calculus and the other with internal metrics validation results.

1 Motivation

Nowadays, big companies and organizations spend time and money in order to find users' opinions about their products, the impact of their marketing decisions, or the overall feeling about their support and maintenance services. This analysis helps in the process of establishing new trends and policies and determines in which areas investments must be made. One of the focuses of our work is helping companies build such analysis in the context of users' sentiment identification. Therefore, the corpus we work on consists of articles of newspapers, blogs, various entries of forums, and posts in social networks.

Sentiment analysis, i.e. the analysis and classification of the opinion expressed by a text on its subject matter, is a form of information extraction from text, which recently focused a lot of research and growing commercial interest.

This paper describes Sentimatrix, a sentiment analysis service, doing sentiment extraction and associating these analyses with named entities, in different languages. We seek to explore how sentiment analysis methods perform across languages, especially Romanian. The main applications that this system experiments with are monitoring the Internet before, during and after a campaign/message release and obtaining consumer feedback on different topics/products.

In Section 2 we briefly discuss a state of the art in sentiment analysis, the system's architecture is described in Section 3 and in Section 4 we focus on identifying opinions on Romanian. Subsequently, we present the experiment results, analysis and discussion in Sections 5 and 6. Future work and conclusions are briefly described in Section 7.

2 Sentimatrix compared with state-of-the-art

A comprehensive state of the art in the field of sentiment analysis, together with potential applications of such opinion identification tools, is presented in (Pang and Lee, 2008).

Starting from the early 1990s, the research on sentiment-analysis and point of views generally assumed the existence of sub-systems for rather sophisticated NLP tasks, ranging from parsing to the resolution of pragmatic ambiguities (Hearst, 1992; Wiebe 1990 and 1994). In Sentimatrix, in order to identify the sentiment a user expresses about a specific product or company, the company name must be first identified in the text. Named

Proceedings of the 2nd Workshop on Computational Approaches to Subjectivity and Sentiment Analysis, ACL-HLT 2011, pages 189–195,
24 June, 2011, Portland, Oregon, USA ©2011 Association for Computational Linguistics

entity recognition (NER) systems typically use linguistic grammar-based techniques or statistical models (an overview is presented in (Nadeau and Satoshi Sekine. 2007)). Hand-crafted grammar-based systems typically obtain better precision, but at the cost of lower recall and months of work by experienced computational linguists. Besides, the task is hard to adapt to new domains. Various sentiment types and levels have been considered, starting from the "universal" six level of emotions considered in (Ovesdotter Alm, 2005; Liu et al., 2003; Subasic and Huettner, 2001): anger, disgust, fear, happiness, sadness, and surprise. For Sentimatrix, we adapted this approach to five levels of sentiments: strong positive, positive, neutral, negative and strong negative.

The first known systems relied on relatively shallow analysis based on manually built discriminative word lexicons (Tong 2001), used to classify a text unit by trigger terms or phrases contained in a lexicon. The lack of sufficient amounts of sentiment annotated corpora led the researchers to incorporate learning components into their sentiment analysis tools, usually supervised classification modules, (e.g., categorization according to affect), as initiated in (Wiebe and Bruce 1995).

Much of the literature on sentiment analysis has focused on text written in English. Sentimatrix is designed to be, as much as possible, language independent, the resources used being easily adaptable for any language.

Some of the most known tools available nowadays for NER and Opinion Mining are: Clarabridge (www.clarabridge.com), RavenPack (ravenpack.com), Lexalytics (www.lexalytics.com) OpenAmplify (openamplify.com), Radian6 (www.radian6.com), Limbix (lymbix.com), but companies like Google, Microsoft, Oracle, SAS, are also deeply involved in this task.

3 System components

In Figure 1, the architecture and the main modules of our system are presented: preprocessing, named entity extraction and opinion identification (sentiment extraction per fragment).

The final production system is based on service oriented architecture in order to allow users flexible customization and to enable an easier way for marketing technology. Each module of the system (Segmenter, Tokenizer, Language Detector, Entity Extractor, and Sentiment Extractor) can be exposed in a user-friendly interface.

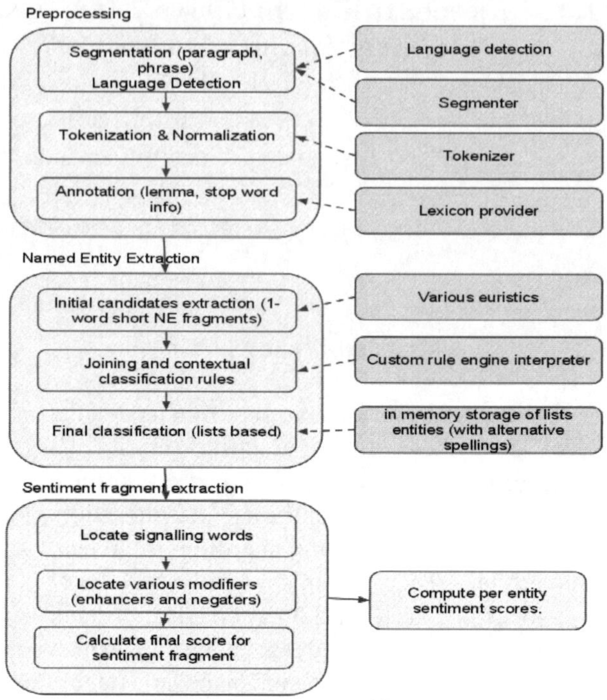

Figure 1. System architecture

3.1 Preprocessing

The preprocessing phase is made out of a text segmentator and a tokenizer. Given a text, we divide it into paragraphs, every paragraph is split into sentences, and every phrase is tokenized. Each token is annotated with two pieces of information: its lemma (for Romanian it is obtained from our resource with 76,760 word lemmas corresponding to 633,444 derived forms) and the normalized form (translated into the proper diacritics[1]).

3.2 Language Detection

Language detection is a preprocessing step problem of classifying a sample of characters based on its features (language-specific models). Currently, the system supports English, Romanian and Romanian without Diacritics. This step is needed in order to correctly identify a sentiment or a sentiment modifier, as the named entity detection depends on this. We combined three methods for

[1] In Romanian online texts, two diacritics are commonly used, but only one is accepted by the official grammar.

identifying the language: *N-grams detection*, strictly *3-grams detection* and *lemma correction*.

The 3-grams classification method uses corpus from Apache Tika for several languages. The Romanian 3-gram profile for this method was developed from scratch, using our articles archive. The language detection in this case performs simple distance measurement between every language profile that we have and the test document profile. The N-grams classification method implies, along with computing frequencies, a posterior Naive Bayes implementation. The third method solves the problematic issue of short phrases language detection and it implies looking through the lemmas of several words to obtain the specificity of the test document.

3.3 Named Entity Recognition

The Named Entity Recognition component for Romanian language is created using linguistic grammar-based techniques and a set of resources. Our component is based on two modules, the named entity identification module and the named entity classification module. After the named entity candidates are marked for each input text, each candidate is classified into one of the considered categories, such as Person, Organization, Place, Country, etc.

Named Entity Extraction: After the pre-processing step, every token written with a capital letter is considered to be a named entity candidate. For tokens with capital letters which are the first tokens in phrases, we consider two situations:

1. *this first token of a phrase is in our stop word list* (in this case we eliminate it from the named entities candidate list),
2. *the first token of a phrase is in our common word list*. In the second situation there are considered two cases:
   a. *this common word is followed by lowercase words* (then we check if the common word can be found in the list of trigger words, like *university*, *city*, *doctor*, etc.),
   b. *this common word is followed by uppercase words* (in this case the first word of the sentence is kept in the NEs candidate list, and in a further step it will be decided if it will be combined with the following word in order to create a composed named entity).

Named Entities Classification: In the classification process we use some of rules utilized in the unification of NEs candidates along with the resource of NEs and several rules specifically tailored for classification. Thus, after all NEs in the input text are identified and, if possible, compound NEs have been created, we apply the following classification rules: *contextual rules* (using contextual information, we are able to classify candidate NEs in one of the categories Organization, Company, Person, City and Country by considering a mix between regular expressions and trigger words) and *resource-based rules* (if no triggers were found to indicate what type of entity we have, we start searching our databases for the candidate entity).

Evaluation: The system's Upper Bound and its performance in real context are evaluated for each of the two modules (identification and classification) and for each named entity type. The first part of the evaluation shows an upper bound of 95.76% for F-measure at named entity extraction and 95.71% for named entity classification. In real context the evaluation shows a value of 90.72% for F-measure at named entity extraction and a value of 66.73% for named entity classification. The results are very promising, and they are being comparable with the existing systems for Romanian, and even better for Person recognition.

4 Identify users opinions on Romanian

4.1 Resources

In such a task as sentiment identification, linguistic resources play a very important role. The core resource is a manually built list of words and groups of words that semantically signal a positive or a negative sentiment. From now on, we will refer to such a word or group of words as "sentiment trigger". Certain weights have been assigned to these words after multiple revisions. The weights vary from -3, meaning strong negative to +3, which translates to a strong positive. There are a total of 3,741 sentiment triggers distributed to weight groups as can be observed in Figure 2. The triggers are lemmas, so the real number of words that can be identified as having a sentiment value is much higher.

This list is not closed and it suffers modifications, especially by adding new triggers, but in certain cases, if a bad behavior is observed, the weights may also be altered.

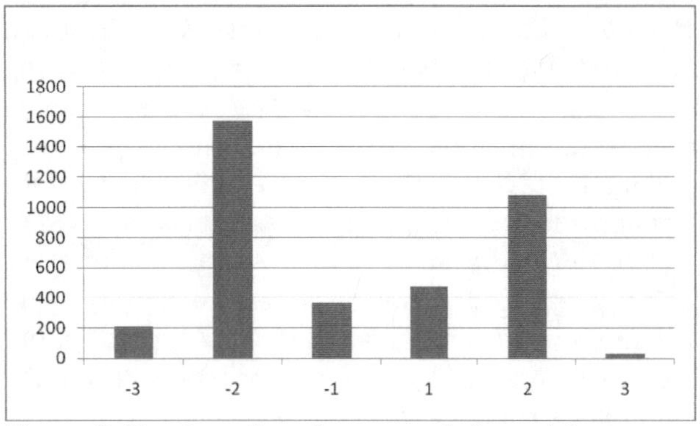

Figure 2. Number of sentiment words by weight groups

We define a modifier as a word or a group of words that can increase or diminish the intensity of a sentiment trigger. We have a manually built list of modifiers. We consider negation words a special case of modifiers that usually have a greater impact on sentiment triggers. So, we also built a small list of negation words.

4.2 Formalism

General definitions: We define a sentiment segment as follows:

$$s_{SG} = ([negation], [modifier], sentimentTrigger)$$

s_{SG} is a tuple in which the first two elements are optional.

Let N_L be the set of negation words that we use, M_L the set of modifiers and T_L the set of sentiment triggers. We define two partially ordered sets:

$$P_+ = (S_+, \leq_+), \quad where\ S_+ \subseteq N_L\ X\ M_L\ X\ T_L \text{ and}$$
$$P_- = (S_-, \leq_-), \quad where\ S_- \subseteq N_L\ X\ M_L\ X\ T_L$$

We consider $\leq_+$ and $\leq_-$ are two binary relations that order sentiment segments based on their weights. The weights give a numeric representation of how strong or weak is the sentiment expressed by the sentiment segment. For instance, if we have s_{SG1}, s_{SG2}, s_{SG3} with the weights 1, 2, 3 and s_{SG4}, s_{SG5}, s_{SG6} with the weights 4, 5, 6, then $s_{SG1} \leq_+ s_{SG2} \leq_+ s_{SG3}$ and $s_{SG4} \leq_- s_{SG5} \leq_- s_{SG6}$.

We define a weight function, *weightS*: $S \rightarrow R$, over the set of sentiment segments that returns a real number representing the global weight that takes into consideration the effect of the negation words and modifiers on the sentiment trigger.

Global sentiment computation: In this section, we will describe how the cumulative value of a sentiment segment, expressed by the *weightS,* is computed.

At the base of a sentiment segment stands the given weight of the sentiment trigger that is part of the general segment. Besides that, modifiers and negation words have a big impact. For example, consider the following three sentences.

1. *John is a good person.*
2. *John is a very good person.*
3. *John is the best.*

In the first one, a positive sentiment is expressed towards *John*. In the second one, we also have a positive sentiment, but it has a bigger power and in the third one the sentiment has the strongest intensity.

We distinguish two separate cases in which negation appears. The first one is when the negation word is associated with a sentiment trigger and it changes a positive one into a negative trigger and vice versa; and the second one refers to the case in which the negation affects a trigger accompanied by a modifier. We illustrate these situations in the following examples.

A1. *John is a good person.*
A2. *John is not a good person.*
B1. *John is the best.*
B2. *John is not the best.*

If we assign the weight +2 to *good* in the A1 sentence, it is safe to say that in A2, *not good* will have the weight -2. From a semantic perspective, we have the antonym relation: *good* $\neq$ $\urcorner$ *good* and the synonym relation $\urcorner$ *good* = *bad).*

On the other hand, in the B2 example, *not the best* is not the same as *the worst*, the antonym of *the best*. In this case, we consider *not the best* to be somewhere between *good* and *the best*. We give a more detailed description of this kind of ordering in the formalisms section.

Entity sentiment computation: Let *E* denote a named entity and *Sent* a sentence. We define the sentiment value, *sv,* of an entity *E* in a sentence

Sent as the general sentiment expressed towards *E* in *Sent*. This value is a real number and is the cumulative effect of all the sentiment segment's weights in that sentence.

Let S_{Sent} be the set of all sentiment segments in the sentence *Sent* and *distance(E,* s_{SG}*)* the number of tokens between *E* and s_{SG}. The expression for computing the sentiment value of an entity in a sentence is given below:

$$\mathrm{sv(E, Sent)} = \frac{\sum_{s_{SG} \in S_{Sent}} \frac{\mathrm{weightS}(s_{SG})}{\ln\,[1 + \mathrm{distance}(E, s_{SG})]}}{|S_{Sent}|}$$

The *sv* for an entity *E* in a larger text will be the sum of the sentiment values for *E* in every sentence of the text.

4.3 Evaluation

For testing our system, we were interested in two aspects: how well does it recognize sentiment segments and how accurate is the semantic meaning given by the system compared to the one attributed by a person. More than that, we dissected the sentiment segment and analyzed the system's performance on finding sentiment triggers and modifiers.

Evaluation resources: Finding or developing clean resources is the most difficult part of the evaluation task. We used 100 complex sentences selected from news articles that were manually annotated as a gold standard. Despite the small number of sentences, they were specially thought to capture a large number of situations.

Evaluation methods: We used precision, a widely known information retrieval metric and other measures that we developed for this task, such as a relaxed precision and deviation mean. We provide below a more detailed description of these metrics.

We computed the precision for sentiment segments, sentiment triggers and modifiers as follows:

$$P_{entity} = \frac{\#\, correct\, found\, entities}{\#\, total\, found\, entities},$$
$$where\ entity \in \{\, sentiment\ segment,\ sentiment\ trigger, modifier\,\}$$

For the weight associated with the sentiment segment, we use two types of precision: an exact match precision, P_{weight} in which we considered a found weight to be correct if it is equal to the weight given in the gold corpus and a relaxed precision, RP_{weight}. We computed these metrics only on the correctly identified segments. Let CS be the set of correctly identified segments, w_F the weight of the sentiment segment returned by our system and w_G the weight of the sentiment segment from the gold corpus.

$$RP_{weight} = \frac{\sum_{s_{SG} \in CS} partialMatch(s_{SG})}{|CS|},$$

$$where\ partialMatch(s_{SG}) = \begin{cases} 1, & |w_F - w_G| < 1.5 \\ 0, & otherwise \end{cases}$$

The RP_{weight} measure is important because the weights given to a sentiment segment can differ from one person to another and, by using this metric, we allow our system to make small mistakes.

Besides the sentiment segments, we also tested the sentiment values of entities. For this task, we used four metrics. The first one is a relaxed precision measure for the sentiment values computed for the entities. Let S_{SV} be the set of the sentiment values returned by the system, sv_F the sentiment value found by the system and sv_G the sentiment value specified in the gold corpus.

$$RP_{sv} = \frac{\sum_{sv_F \in S_{sv}} partialMatch(sv_F)}{|S_{sv}|},$$

$$where\ partialMatch(sv_F) = \begin{cases} 1, & |sv_F - sv_G| \le 0.5 \\ 0, & otherwise \end{cases}$$

The last three metrics address the problem of how far the sentiment values are returned by the system from those considered correct by a human annotator. We called these measures *sv positive deviation,* D_{sv+}, which takes into account only positive sentiment values, *sv negative deviation,* D_{sv-}, which takes into account only negative sentiment values and *sv general deviation,* D_{sv+-}, an average of the first two.

$$D_{sv+} = \frac{\sum_{sv_F \in S_{sv+}} |sv_F - sv_G|}{|S_{sv+}|}$$

S_{SV+} is the set of positive sentiment values found by the system. D_{sv-} is calculated in a similar manner as D_{sv+}.

5 Results

The results were obtained using the manually annotated sentences presented in the Evaluation resources section. Out of those sentences, 58% contain entities and 42% contain only sentiment segments. The entity-related metrics could be applied only on the first type of sentences. The results can be observed in Figure 3.

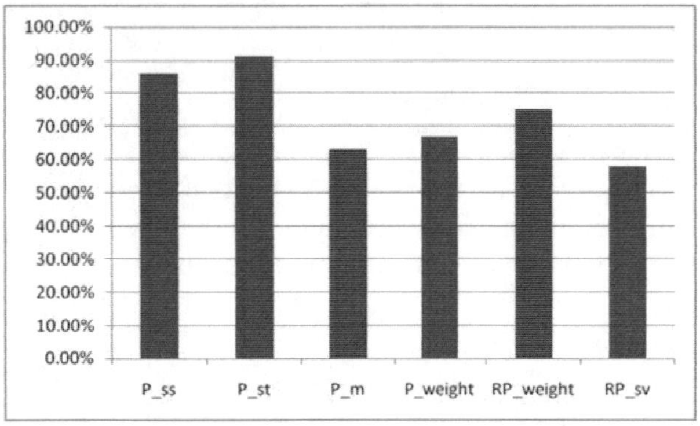

Figure 3. Precision metrics results

In Figure 3, $P\_ss = P_{sentiment\ segment}$, $P\_st = P_{sentiment\ trigger}$, $P\_m = P_{modifier}$ and the rest of the metrics have the same meaning as defined in the evaluation methods section.

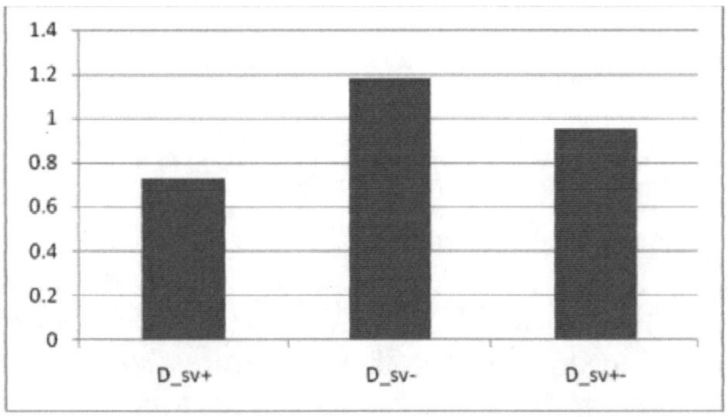

Figure 4. Deviation metrics results

In Figure 4, we show the results of the metrics that follow the sentiment value deviation.

6 Discussion

The main problem encountered is the contexts in which the opinions that we identify appear. It is possible that the same trigger has a positive meaning in a context, and in another context to be negative. For example, "scade TVA" (En: "reduce VAT") which is positive, compared to "scad salariile" (En: "reduce salaries") which is negative. In these cases the trigger "scade" (En: reduce) can lead to opposing opinions. As for "inchide fabrica" (En: "close the plant"), that has a negative context compared to "inchide infractorul" (En: "close the offender") which is positive.

Another problem in quantifying the sentiments and opinions is related to numerical values that we identify in the text. For example "15 profesori protesteaza" (En: "15 teachers protest") compared to "2.000.000 de profesori protesteaza" (En: "2,000,000 teachers protest"). In both cases we have negative sentiments, but it is clear that the second case has even a stronger sense due to the large number of people who participate in the protest. If in the first case it seems to be a local issue, at the school, in the second case, it seems to be a general problem that is seen nationwide.

7 Conclusion and Future Work

This paper introduces the Sentimatrix system. The main components of the system are dedicated to identifying named entities, opinions and sentiments. Preliminary evaluation show promising results.

Future work includes completing the resources lists with entities, sentiment triggers and modifiers. As we have seen in the tests, rapid improvements can be achieved by taking into consideration modifiers such as "daca", "posibil", "ar putea" (En: "if", "possible", "could") which have the effect of lowering the intensity of opinions and sentiments. Also, we intend to build a bigger gold corpus to evaluate sentiments by using a semi-automatic approach (at first the system generates annotation, which is later to be validates and completed by a human annotator).

Acknowledgments

The research presented in this paper is partially funded by the Sectoral Operational Program for Human Resources Development through the project "Development of the innovation capacity and increasing of the research impact through post-doctoral programs" POSDRU/89/1.5/S/49944.

References

Bo Pang, Lillian Lee. 2008. *Opinion Mining and Sentiment Analysis*, Found. Trends Inf. Retr., Vol. 2, No. 1–2. (January 2008), pp. 1-135

Cecilia Ovesdotter Alm, Dan Roth, and Richard Sproat. 2005. Emotions from text: machine learning for text-based emotion prediction. In *Proceedings of the Human Language Technology Conference and the Conference on Empirical Methods in Natural Language Processing (HLT/EMNLP).*

David Nadeau and Satoshi Sekine. 2007. *A survey of named entity recognition and classification*, Linguisticae Investigationes 30, no. 1, 3{26, Publisher: John Benjamin's Publishing Company

David Nadeau. 2007. *Semi-supervised named entity recognition: Learning to recognize 100 entity types with little supervision*, PhD Thesis.

Ellen Riloff, Janyce Wiebe, and William Phillips. 2005. Exploiting subjectivity classification to improve information extraction. In *Proceedings of AAAI*, pages 1106–1111.

Hugo Liu, Henry Lieberman, and Ted Selker. 2003.A model of textual affect sensing using real-world knowledge. In *Proceedings of Intelligent User Interfaces (IUI)*, pages 125–132.

Iadh Ounis, Maarten de Rijke, Craig Macdonald, Gilad Mishne, and Ian Soboroff. 2006. Overview of the TREC-2006 Blog Track. In *Proceedings of the 15th Text REtrieval Conference (TREC 2006).*

Janyce M. Wiebe 1990. Identifying subjective characters in narrative. In *Proceedings of the International Conference on Computational Linguistics (COLING)*, pages 401–408.

Janyce M. Wiebe. 1994. Tracking point of view in narrative. *Computational Linguistics*, 20(2):233–287.

Janyce Wiebe and Rebecca Bruce. 1995. Probabilistic classifiers for tracking point of view. In *Proceedings of the AAAI Spring Symposium on Empirical Methods in Discourse Interpretation and Generation*, pages 181–187.

Marti Hearst. 1992. Direction-based text interpretation as an information access refinement. In Paul Jacobs, editor, *Text-Based Intelligent Systems*, pages 257–274. Lawrence Erlbaum Associates.

Namrata Godbole, Manjunath Srinivasaiah, and Steven Skiena. 2007. Large-scale sentiment analysis for news and blogs. In *Proceedings of the International Conference on Weblogs and Social Media (ICWSM).*

Pero Subasic and Alison Huettner. 2001. Affect analysis of text using fuzzy semantic typing. *IEEE Transactions on Fuzzy Systems*, 9(4):483–496.

Richard M. Tong. 2001. An operational system for detecting and tracking opinions in on-line discussion. In *Proceedings of the Workshop on Operational Text Classification (OTC).*

Scurtu V., Stepanov E., Mehdad, Y. 2009. *Italian named entity recognizer participation in NER task@evalita 09*, 2009.

Author Index

Association for Computational Linguistics
209 N. Eighth Street
Stroudsburg, Pennsylvania 18360